14th Conference of the Association for Machine Translation in the Americas (AMTA 2020)

Volume 2: MT User Track

Online
6 – 9 October 2020

Editors:

Janice Campbell
Dmitriy Genzel

Ben Huyck
Patricia O'Neill-Brown

ISBN: 978-1-7138-1983-7

The 14th Conference of The Association for Machine Translation in the Americas

www.amtaweb.org

PROCEEDINGS

Vol. 2: MT User Track

Editors:

Janice Campbell & Dmitriy Genzel (Commercial Users)
Ben Huyck & Patricia O'Neill-Brown (Government Users)

Welcome to the 14th Biennial Conference of the Association for Machine Translation in the Americas

— AMTA 2020 Virtual!

AMTA conferences traditionally provide a unique opportunity for academic and commercial researchers to share their results with colleagues as well as to understand real-world user requirements. Business and government participants benefit from updates on leading-edge R&D in MT and have a chance to present and discuss their use cases. At the same time, students who attend gain a broad perspective and understanding of the fascinating field of MT.

This year's conference, however, is significant in at least two aspects. The first is that neural machine translation (NMT) has become a de facto standard in research and industry. At our last conference in March of 2018, generic NMT systems had just begun to be widely used during the preceding year, but it was later in 2018 that customizable NMT systems became widely available, enabling many companies, governments, and other organizations to benefit from an even higher level of MT quality for their specific applications. Since then, NMT customization and usage across the spectrum from individual translators to large corporations has continued to snowball.

The second aspect has been more of a difficulty than an advantage. The COVID-19 pandemic has resulted in transforming AMTA 2020 from an in-person event at a spectacular venue in Orlando, Florida to a completely online conference. While this transformation has presented many unique challenges, we now see some silver linings in this cloud. Without the need to travel and its associated costs, our attendance numbers have doubled from previous years, and participation has come from around the globe. We have been fortunate to receive tremendous support from our many sponsors, for which we are most grateful. Notably, Microsoft has provided their Teams platform to support the virtual conference sessions.

I wish to offer my sincerest thanks to our conference organizing committee, without whom this virtual conference would not have taken place. They have worked long hours to organize and prepare for this unique format, navigating uncharted waters and overcoming various roadblocks. I trust that all who attend will benefit from the results of their diligent efforts.

Steve Richardson
AMTA President

Introduction

Commercial Track

The Commercial MT Users and Translators Track at AMTA 2020 features twenty-two presentations from enterprises and individuals who supply or implement machine translation. These include technology and language service providers, as well as a host of commercial entities seeking to leverage the benefits of machine translation for better customer engagement.

A common theme that runs through many of the presentations this year is the use of metrics, such as MTPE and Quality Estimation, and setting acceptability thresholds therefor. The goals are to continually improve and interactively adapt models, and predict quality in order to increase language and content coverage, enhance linguists' productivity, ensure end-user trust, or even forego post editing, in some cases. Presentations explore novel applications of MT such as in building multilingual datasets; creating input for select NLP tasks; and translation memory alignment.

On the business side are presentations that explore the challenges an enterprise might face in adopting machine translation and in using technology and metrics to find the best engines or brands to meet their use cases. A unique approach to measuring the Return on Investment for adopting MT is detailed. Students put to the test various NMT claims to determine if valid or hype.

Whether a buyer or supplier, more organizations are building their own engines, thanks to a multitude of toolkits and available training data. Domain customization is the norm. Presentations discuss how to use metadata in source to fine tune customization and they detail strategies for handling tags and placeholders to achieve better output results.

On the practical side, there are presentations on scaling up MT specifically for software and continuous localization scenarios in order to reduce or delay human intervention and still achieve maximum customer impact.

Finally, what bodes for the very near future? Presenters offer that it is identifying and resolving societal biases encoded in machine learning systems, or simultaneously translating speech.

The Commercial Track Co-Chairs

Janice Campbell
Dmitriy Genzel

Government Track

The AMTA 2020 Government and Military MT Stakeholders Track brings together machine translation users, developers, and researchers in government, military and public service worldwide. The proceedings include eight presentations covering a broad range of topics. Two of these presentations include papers that provide in-depth detail and context to the presentations.

Several submissions describe how to effectively use MT in government, as well as how to augment human translation efforts, including the use of complementary NLP tools such as Speech-to-Text (STT) technologies. Others describe the practical application, insertion and measurement of MT into government space. One discusses video to text MT for sign language. Another presentation describes a custom MT engine trained using US Government data to assist with the COVID-19 crisis.

This track is made possible by the hard work and contributions of many individuals. We would like to thank Steve Richardson and all members of the conference committee for their organizational support, Jennifer Doyon and the rest of the organizing committee for guidance on the government track, and all of the AMTA 2020 authors and reviewers.

The Government Track Co-Chairs

Benjamin Huyck
Patricia O'Neill-Brown

Contents

Commercial Track

Government Track

RWS Moravia
Operationalizing
Machine Translation
Quality Estimation (QE)

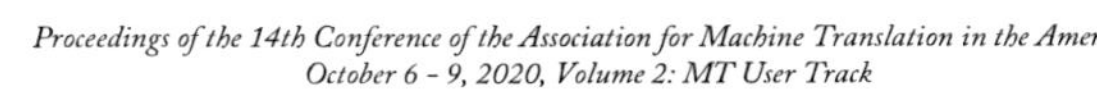

Miklós Urbán,
Senior Solutions Architect

Maribel Rodríguez,
Language Technology Deployment
Manager

www.rws.com/moravia

Proceedings of the 14th Conference of the Association for Machine Translation in the Americas
October 6 – 9, 2020, Volume 2: MT User Track

Agenda

> Introduction

> Methodology

> Potential Business Cases

> Technical Setup

> Conclusions

Proceedings of the 14th Conference of the Association for Machine Translation in the Americas
October 6 - 9, 2020, Volume 2: MT User Track

ebay

Quality estimation is a method used to automatically provide a quality indication for machine translation output without depending on human reference translations. In more simple terms, it's a way to find out how good or bad the translations are that are produced by an MT system without human intervention.

Forbes

Yet in the machine translation space, there's evidence to show that good quality estimation eases the burden on human editors. With an automated system that highlights mistakes before the human process even begins, the editors can zero in on the areas of a piece of content that most likely need attention.

https://www.forbes.com/sites/forbestechcouncil/2019/01/24/why-quality-estimation-is-the-missing-link-for-machine-translation-adoption
https://tech.ebayinc.com/engineering/machine-translation-the-basics-of-quality-estimation/

RWS
Moravia

Proceedings of the 14th Conference of the Association for Machine Translation in the Americas
October 6 – 9, 2020, Volume 2: MT User Track

The Challenge

With so many different approaches to QE out there and so many variables, **how can we**:

> Evaluate QE performance for different QE options, customers, content types, languages, etc.?

> Identify the business cases that could bring value to RWS Moravia and our clients?

> Figure out when is the right time to implement QE in a specific workflow?

> Continue to monitor the performance of QE after it has been implemented?

Proceedings of the 14th Conference of the Association for Machine Translation in the Americas
October 6 – 9, 2020, Volume 2: MT User Track

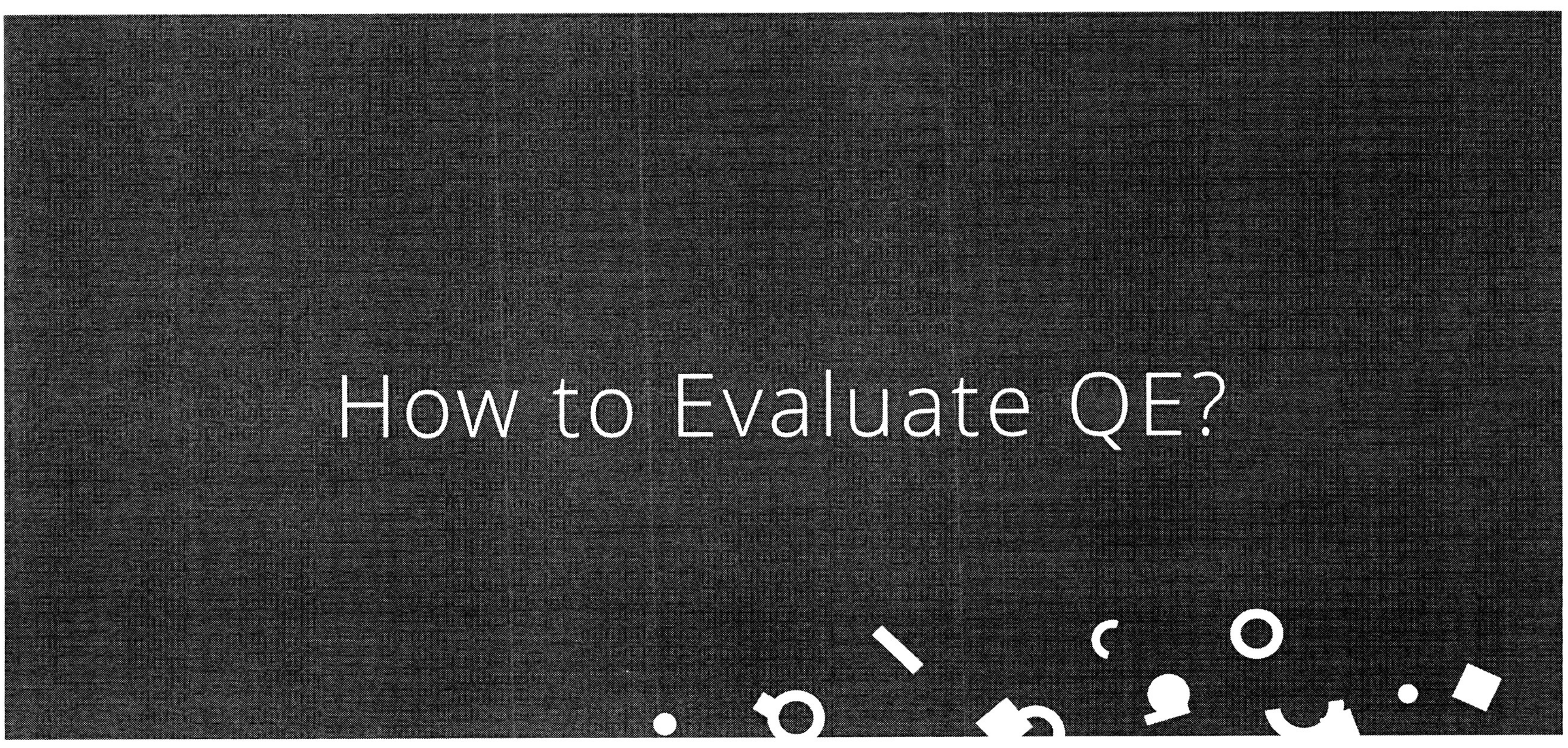

How to Evaluate QE?
RWS
Moravia

Common Methodology

 Pre-translate the content using MT

Obtain both pre-production MT QE and post-production TER scores

Compare QE score with actual TER score

Analyze the results

Considerations:

> Post-editors are not exposed to QE

> QE initially runs in the background

> Production may apply different workflows

> Translation is not analyzed for over-editing or under-editing

Input Metric | Quality Estimation

> Quality estimation is available from multiple sources

> QE is based on machine learning algorithms

> To make results comparable, we convert QE results to a 4-choice numeric score system

> **100%** means QE predicts good raw MT quality
> **67%** means QE predicts some editing is needed
> **33%** means QE predicts more editing is needed
> **0%** means QE predicts poor raw MT quality

RWS
Moravia

Proceedings of the 14th Conference of the Association for Machine Translation in the Americas
October 6 – 9, 2020, Volume 2: MT User Track

Input Metric | Translation Edit Rate (TER)

- Suited to quantify the post-editing effort
- RWS Moravia has been using TER in production for over a decade
  - Number of edits needed to modify raw MT to produce a final translation
  - TER = edits / reference word count
    - where edits = insertions, deletions, substitutions and shifts
  - The closer the score is to 0, the less post-editing effort is assumed
- We round TER scores to multiples of 10%

Proceedings of the 14th Conference of the Association for Machine Translation in the Americas
October 6 – 9, 2020, Volume 2: MT User Track

How to Use the Data?

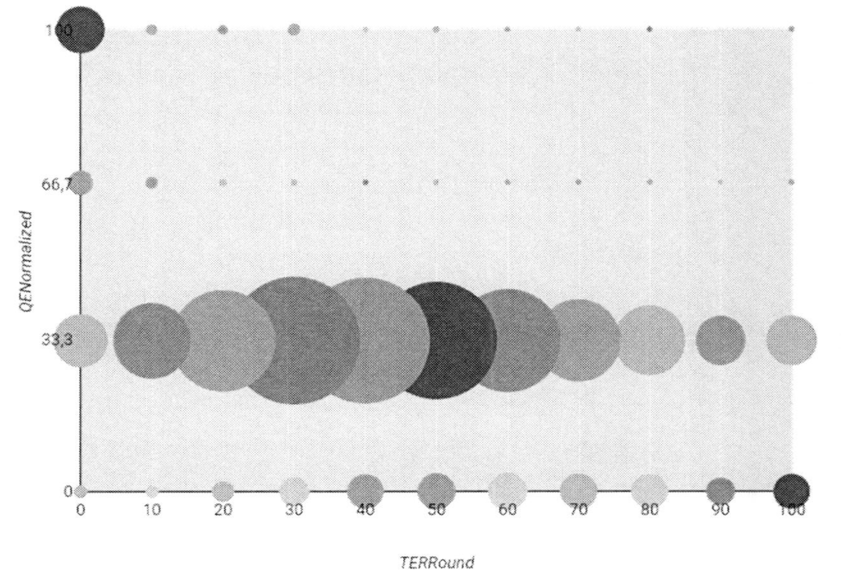

Each segment can be plotted on a chart

We created a bubble chart with:

> Y-axis: QE score
> X-axis: TER score
> Size of bubble: number of segments

Interpreting the Bubble Chart

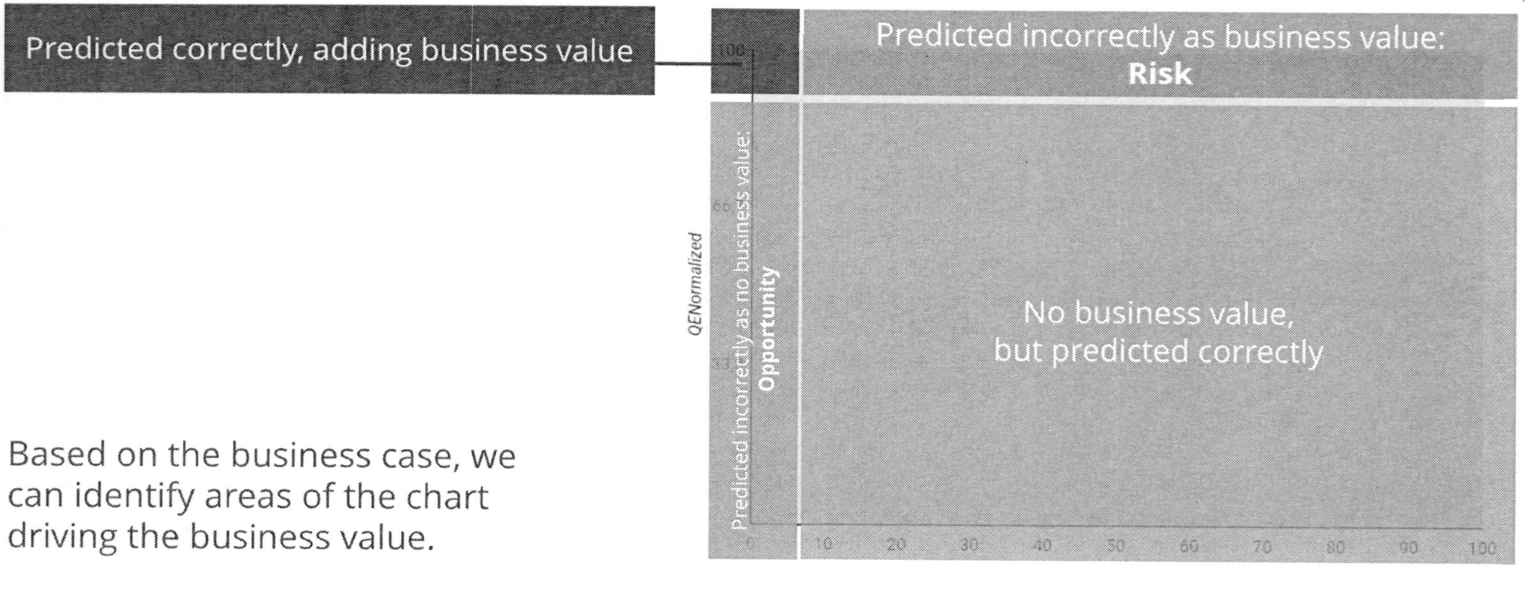

Based on the business case, we can identify areas of the chart driving the business value.

Proceedings of the 14th Conference of the Association for Machine Translation in the Americas
October 6 – 9, 2020, Volume 2: MT User Track

Output Metrics

$$\text{Accuracy} = \frac{\text{True Positive} + \text{True Negative}}{\text{Total}}$$

$$\text{Precision} = \frac{\text{True Positive}}{\text{True Positive} + \text{False Positive}}$$

$$\text{Recall} = \frac{\text{True Positive}}{\text{True Positive} + \text{False Negative}}$$

$$\text{F1} = \frac{2 \times \text{Precision} \times \text{Recall}}{\text{Precision} + \text{Recall}}$$

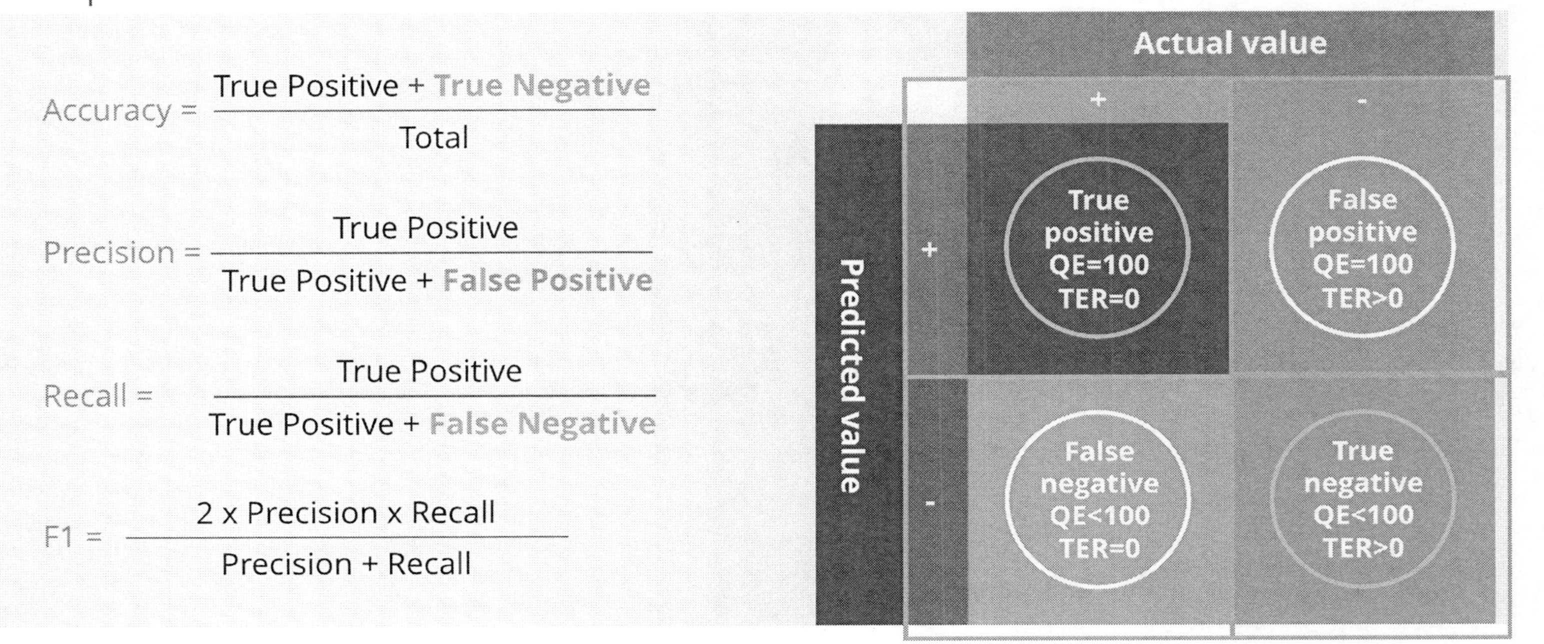

Proceedings of the 14th Conference of the Association for Machine Translation in the Americas
October 6 - 9, 2020, Volume 2: MT User Track

Proceedings of the 14th Conference of the Association for Machine Translation in the Americas
October 6 - 9, 2020, Volume 2: MT User Track

Take Advantage of Good MT Segments

> Eliminate post-editing or apply a light post-editing workflow for good raw MT segments (up to 30% of segments)

> Quality risk for false positives

> We expect a high proportion of non-edited segments to be identified, keeping the quality risk close to zero

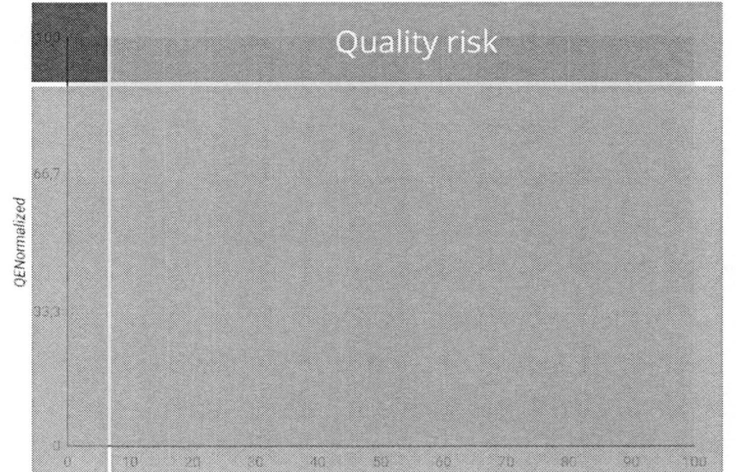

Proceedings of the 14th Conference of the Association for Machine Translation in the Americas
October 6 – 9, 2020, Volume 2: MT User Track

Remove Burden of Reading Poor MT

> Does it really increase productivity?

> Risk of deleting good MT

> We expect a high proportion of poor-quality raw MT to be discarded with minimal loss of good MT

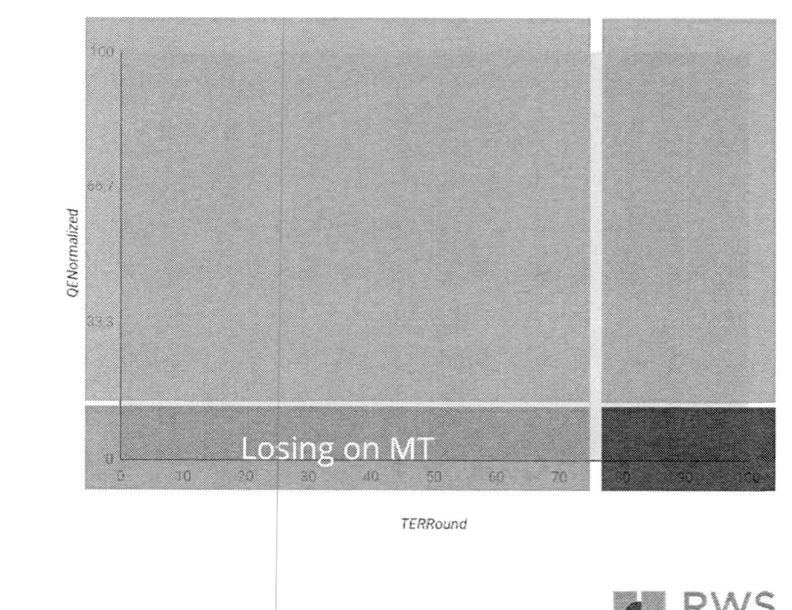

RWS
Moravia

Proceedings of the 14th Conference of the Association for Machine Translation in the Americas
October 6 - 9, 2020, Volume 2: MT User Track

Assessing MT Quality and Applying Fair, Pre-production Pricing

> A good accuracy could allow MT quality measurement without human reference

> High accuracy (95+%) could allow pricing to be based on QE

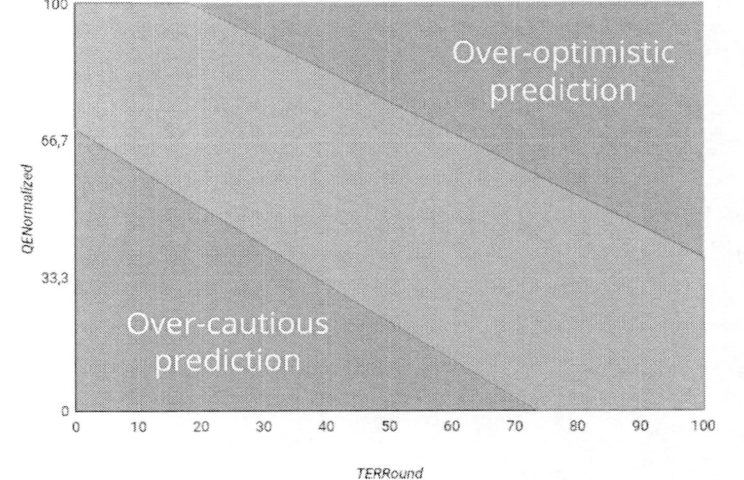

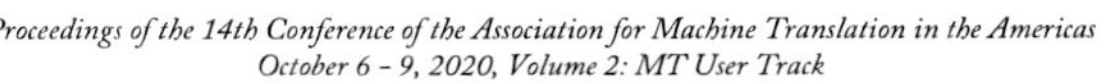

Proceedings of the 14th Conference of the Association for Machine Translation in the Americas
October 6 – 9, 2020, Volume 2: MT User Track

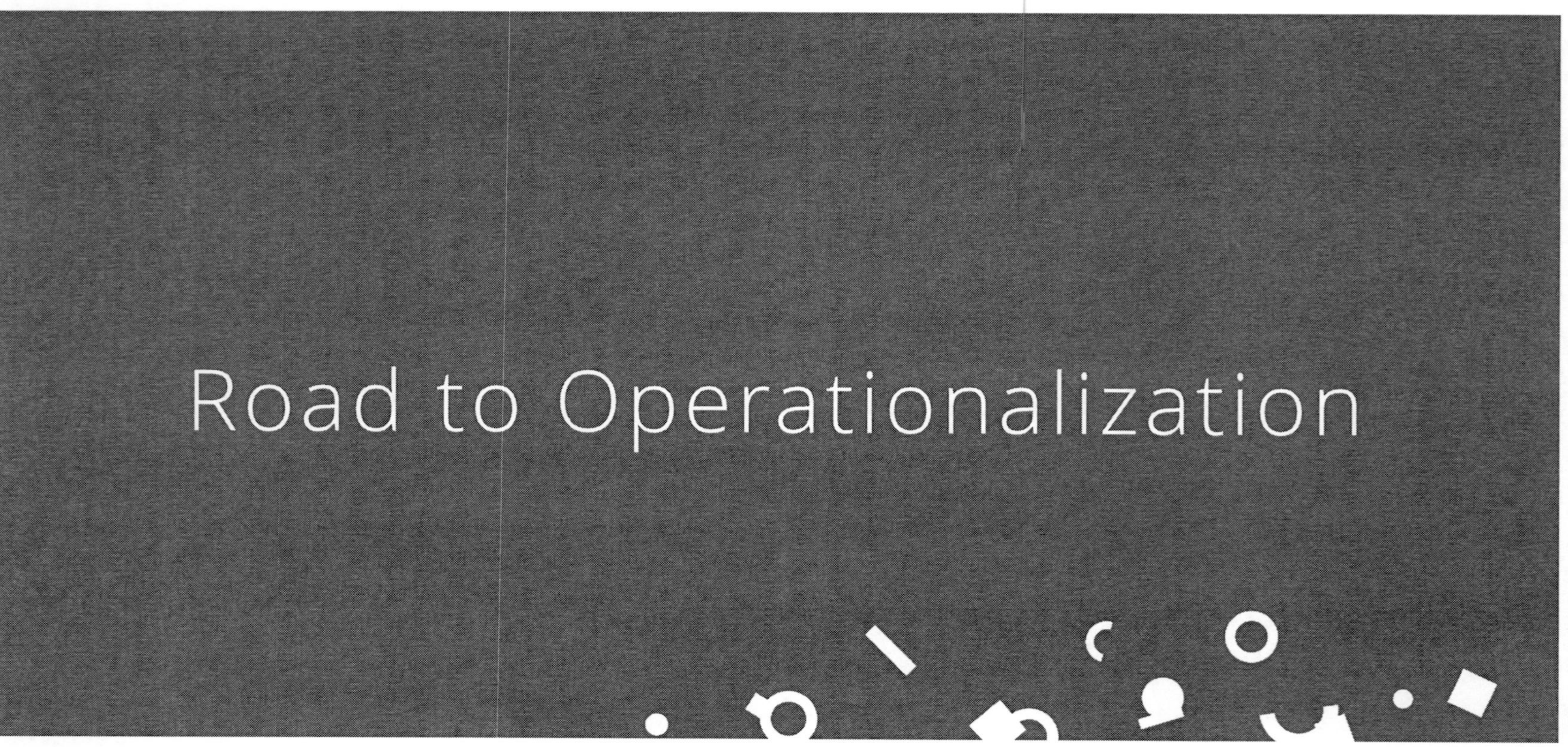

Proceedings of the 14th Conference of the Association for Machine Translation in the Americas
October 6 - 9, 2020, Volume 2: MT User Track

Considerations

- Multiple QE sources
  - Choose the best option that fits our purposes
- QE performance may depend on multiple factors
  - Language pair
  - Client
  - Content type
- We need to establish reproducible metrics that can be measured over a large sample

Proceedings of the 14th Conference of the Association for Machine Translation in the Americas
October 6 - 9, 2020, Volume 2: MT User Track

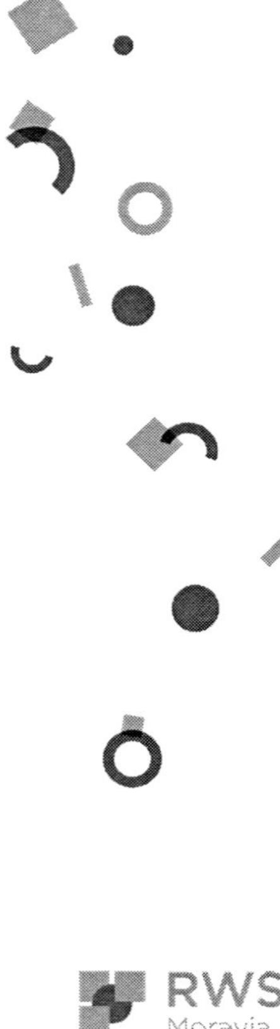

Pilot

> No. of customers: **1**
> Content types: **2**
> Language pairs: **17**
> Experiment duration: **8 months**

RWS
Moravia

Proceedings of the 14th Conference of the Association for Machine Translation in the Americas
October 6 - 9, 2020, Volume 2: MT User Track

Pilot Results

- Methodology enabling:
  - Consistent evaluation of QE technology and tracking its progress
  - Monitoring results against preset thresholds before going live
- Automated dataflow solution
  - Evaluation of usability of different QE systems
  - Data insights through dashboards
- Findings
  - Dependency of QE performance across languages and content types
  - Technology still evolves and shows improved performance over time

RWS
Moravia

Proceedings of the 14th Conference of the Association for Machine Translation in the Americas
October 6 - 9, 2020, Volume 2: MT User Track

Technical Setup

After populating raw MT into
the CAT tool, the QE prediction
was run and scores were stored

Technical Setup

Post-editors completed
the task in the translation tool
without being exposed to QE

Proceedings of the 14th Conference of the Association for Machine Translation in the Americas
October 6 - 9, 2020, Volume 2: MT User Track

Technical Setup

We created a streaming data solution that:

> Takes segment data from the production environment

> Runs the segment through the TER score evaluation in our proprietary software, LTGear

> Matches the QE data stored earlier for the segment

> Streams this data into the bigdata infrastructure of Google Cloud

Proceedings of the 14th Conference of the Association for Machine Translation in the Americas
October 6 – 9, 2020, Volume 2: MT User Track

Technical Setup

> For each segment, we store its coordinates, timestamp, language pair, client and domain metadata and the MT QE and TER results in BigQuery

> Google Data Studio dashboards help us track and analyze the results

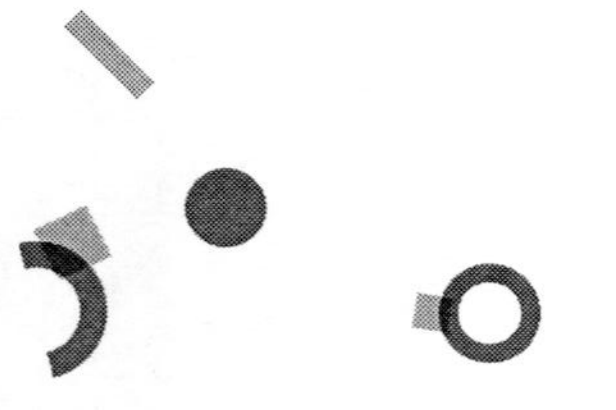

Proceedings of the 14th Conference of the Association for Machine Translation in the Americas
October 6 - 9, 2020, Volume 2: MT User Track

Sample Dashboard

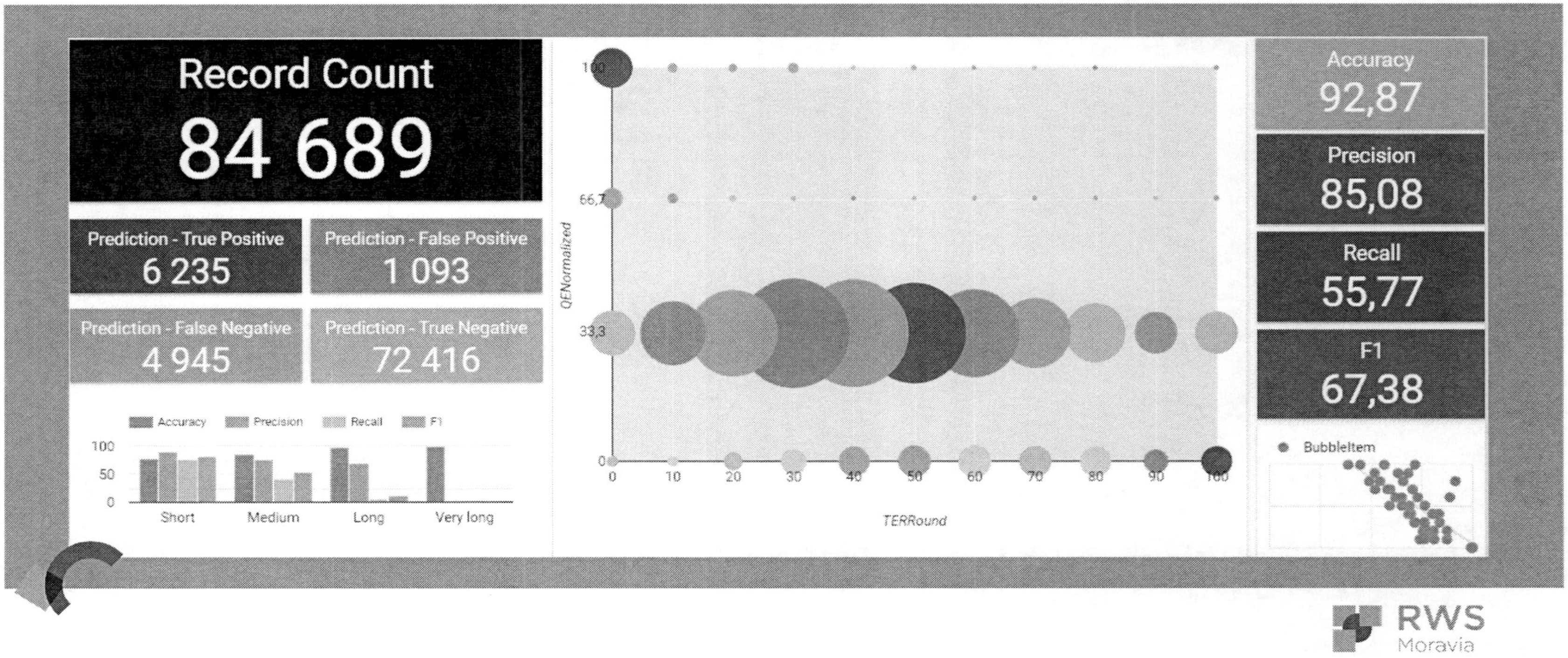

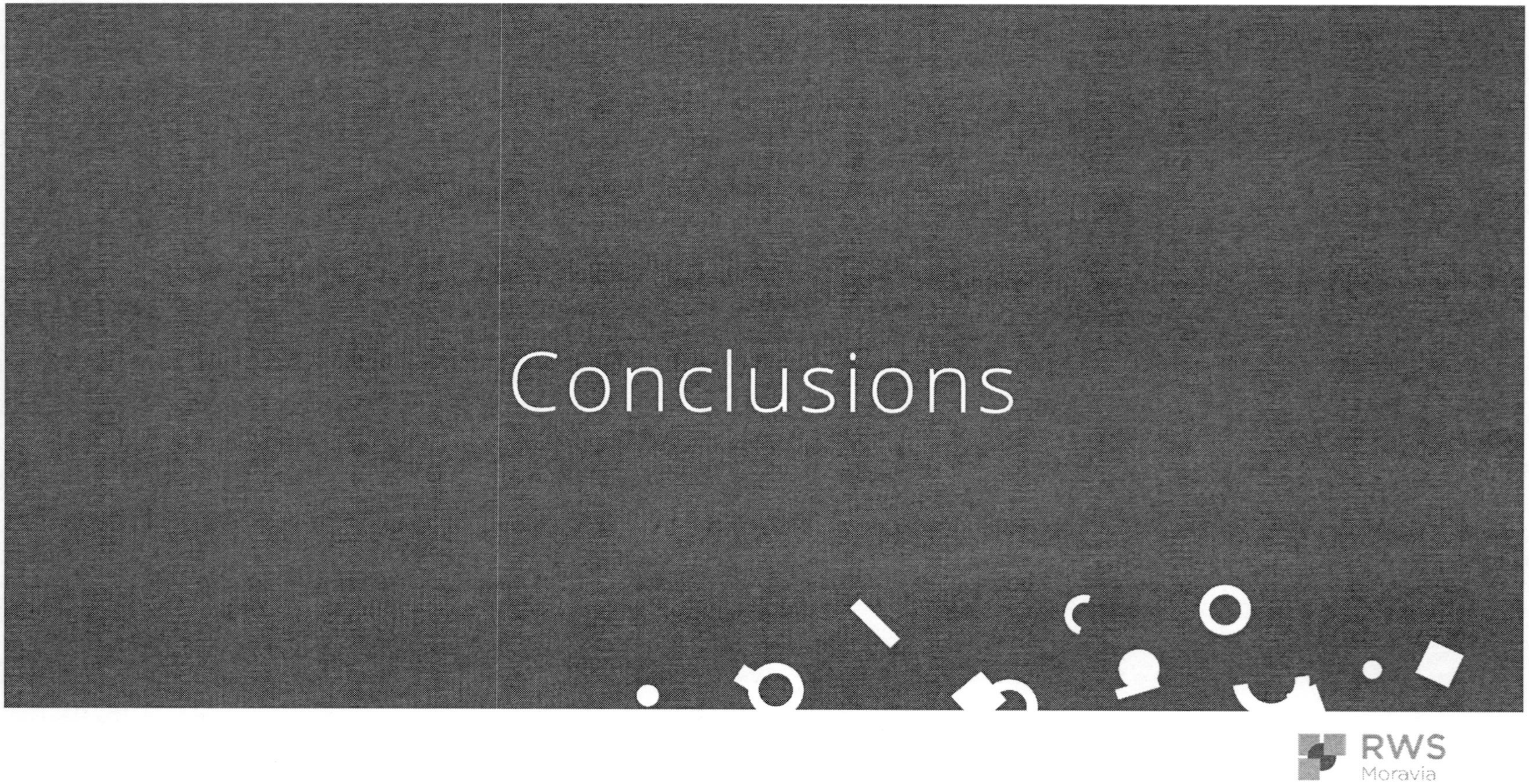

Conclusions
RWS
Moravia

Conclusions

- QE shows improvement over time and is approaching production readiness in a large LSP setting
- QE performance is highly dependent on language pair and content type
- Robust solution to track performance of QE predictions against post-production metrics is needed
- Thanks to the framework we have put in place, we now have the means to easily monitor the aggregated data in a continuous stream and compare the performance of multiple QE sources

Proceedings of the 14th Conference of the Association for Machine Translation in the Americas
October 6 - 9, 2020, Volume 2: MT User Track

Some Questions We Are Really Eager to Answer

> Does it make sense to include segment length beside QE to refine the precision of predictions?

> Is quality retained for high-ranking QE segments that will likely get less attention?

> Do post-editors start from scratch for low-ranking QE segments?

> Is productivity enhanced compared to a workflow without QE?

Proceedings of the 14th Conference of the Association for Machine Translation in the Americas
October 6 – 9, 2020, Volume 2: MT User Track

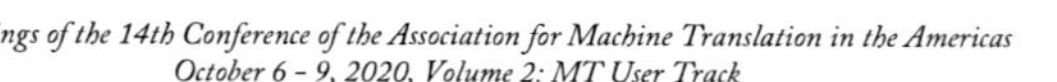

Acknowledgement to All the Team Members that Participated in This Research

Tomáš Burkert
Solutions Architect

Tomáš Fulajtár
MT Researcher

Miklós Urbán
Senior Solutions Architect

Maribel Rodríguez
Language Technology
Deployment Manager

Q&A

Proceedings of the 14th Conference of the Association for Machine Translation in the Americas
October 6 – 9, 2020, Volume 2: MT User Track

Thank you

Proceedings of the 14th Conference of the Association for Machine Translation in the Americas
October 6 – 9, 2020, Volume 2: MT User Track

In search of an acceptability/ unacceptability threshold in machine translation post-editing automated metrics

Lucía Guerrero

Machine Translation Specialist, CPSL

AMTA, October 2020

Proceedings of the 14th Conference of the Association for Machine Translation in the Americas
October 6 – 9, 2020, Volume 2: MT User Track

Why MT?

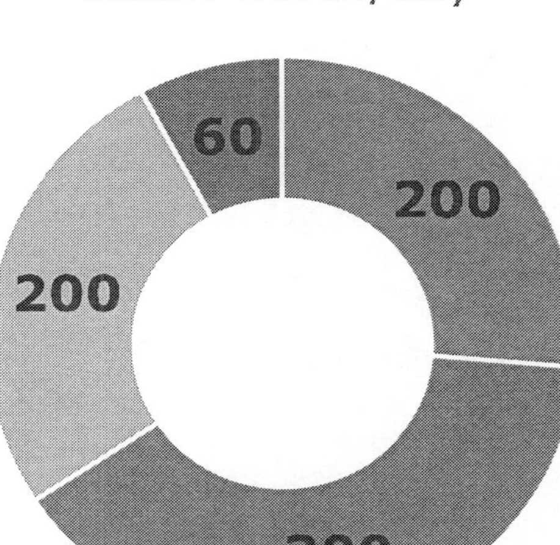

Proceedings of the 14th Conference of the Association for Machine Translation in the Americas
October 6 – 9, 2020, Volume 2: MT User Track

MT main use cases and drivers

Translation for understanding:
raw MT / light postediting

E-commerce platforms
Forums and user reviews
Support pages
Communication apps

To cut costs and/or improve deadlines:
light / full post-editing

Proceedings of the 14th Conference of the Association for Machine Translation in the Americas
October 6 – 9, 2020, Volume 2: MT User Track

MT at CPSL

SMT: Moses, ModernMT
NMT: Marian, 3rd-party platforms
RBMT: Apertium

Generic systems
and
Domain-based systems:

- Life sciences
- Medical devices
- Automotive
- Technical

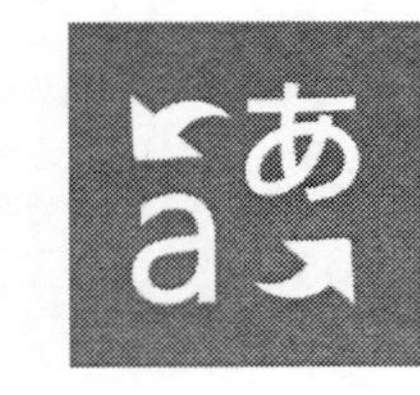

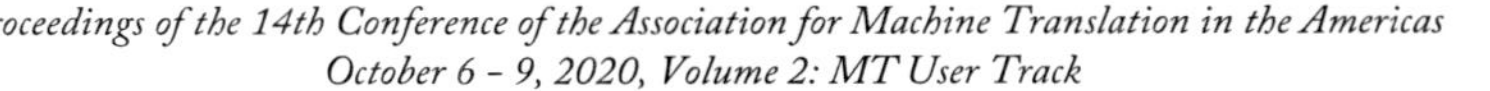

Proceedings of the 14th Conference of the Association for Machine Translation in the Americas
October 6 – 9, 2020, Volume 2: MT User Track

Translator-centered MT workflow

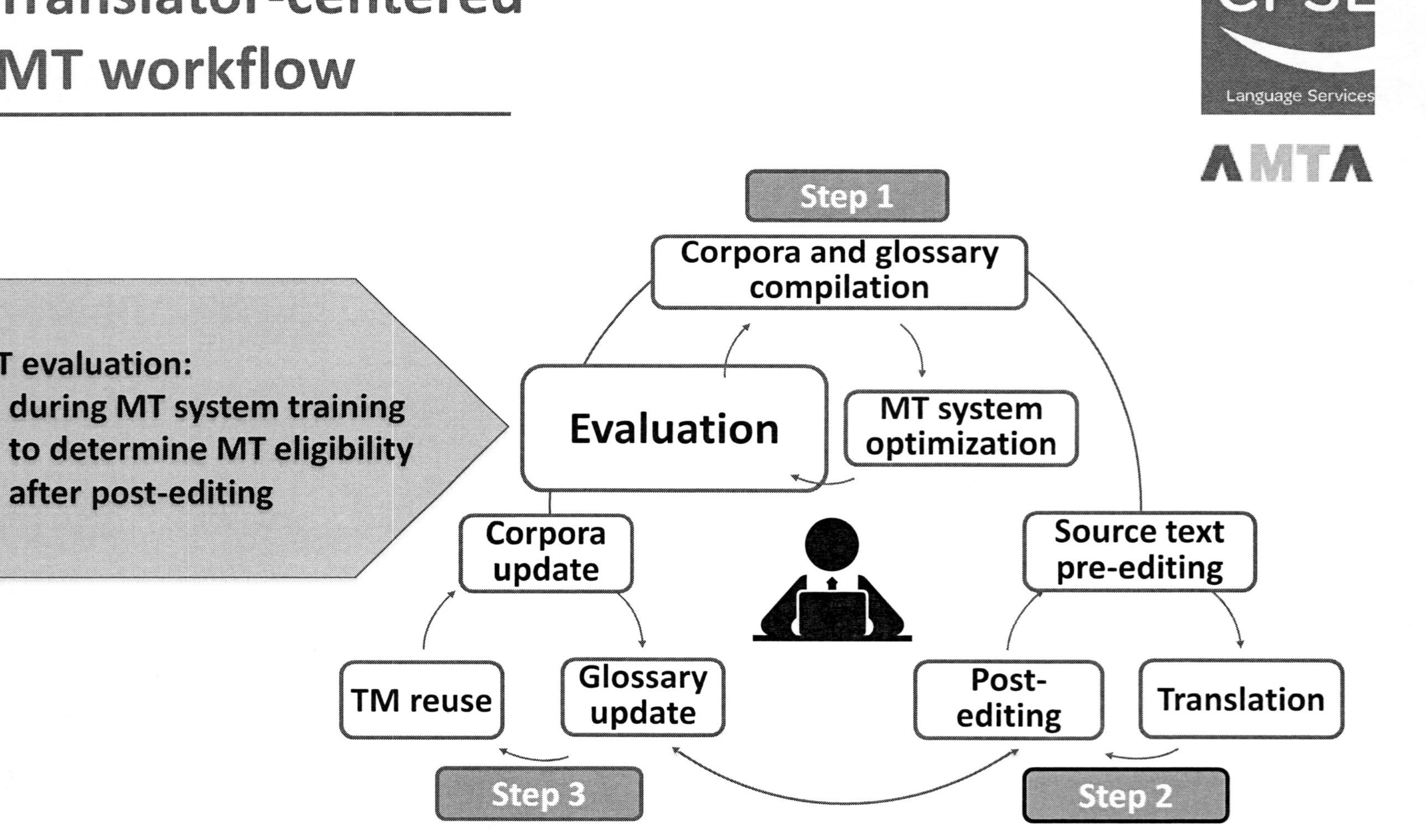

Rico, Celia. 2017. La formación de traductores en traducción automática. *Revista Tradumàtica. Tecnologies de la traducció*, 15, pages 75-96

MT evaluation

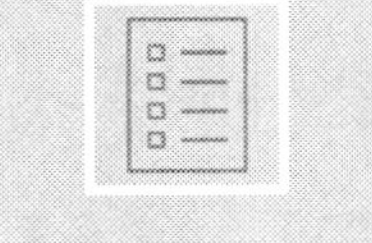
Holistic (adequacy/fluency) scoring
Perceived PE effort scoring

Reference-based metrics
(BLEU, edit distance, (H)TER...)

Productivity tests: post-editing time

Analytical: all/main errors, categorized

Proceedings of the 14th Conference of the Association for Machine Translation in the Americas
October 6 - 9, 2020, Volume 2: MT User Track

MT feedback template

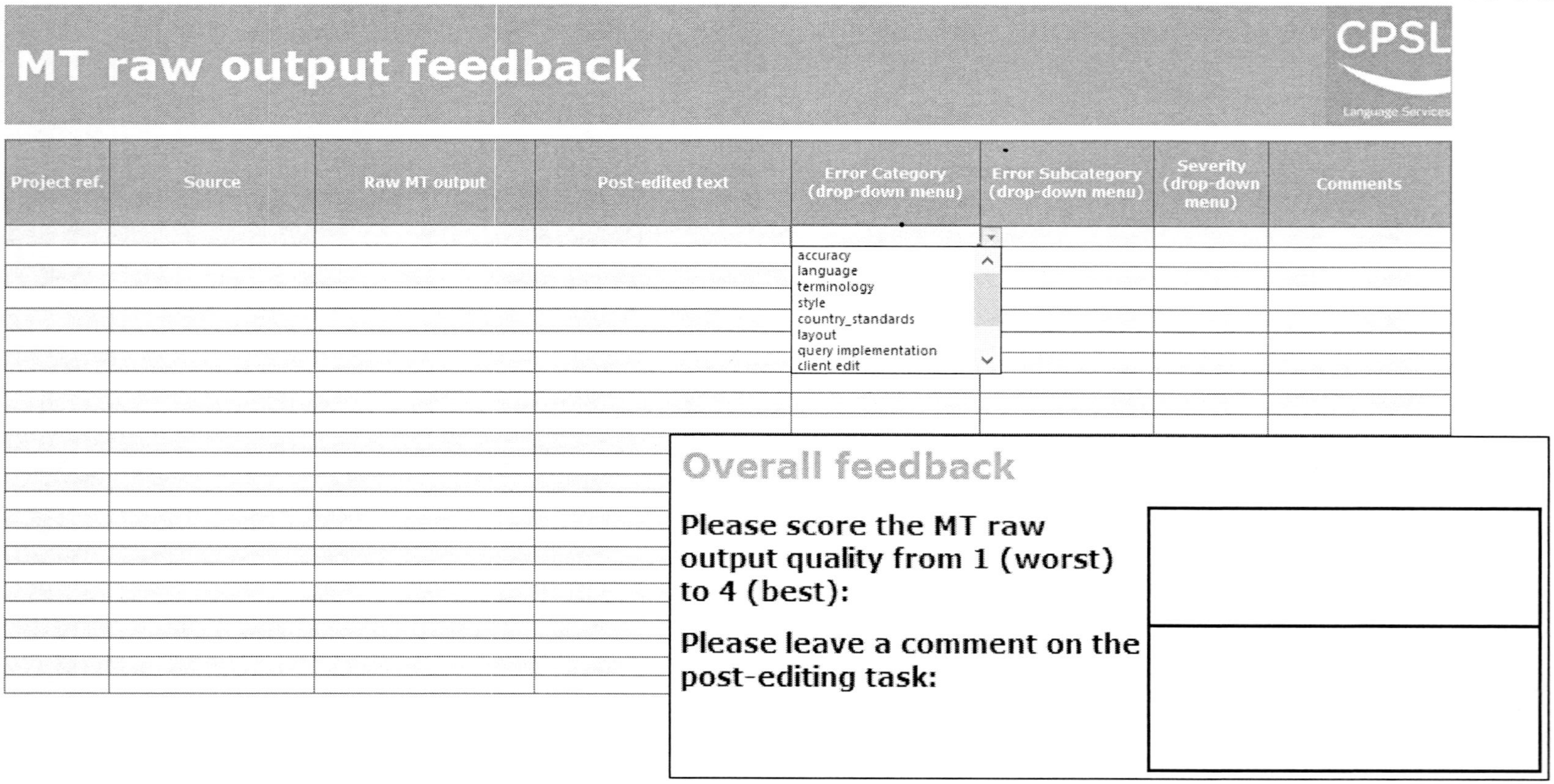

MT raw output feedback

Project ref.	Source	Raw MT output	Post-edited text	Error Category (drop-down menu)	Error Subcategory (drop-down menu)	Severity (drop-down menu)	Comments
				accuracy			
				language			
				terminology			
				style			
				country_standards			
				layout			
				query implementation			
				client edit			

Overall feedback

Please score the MT raw output quality from 1 (worst) to 4 (best):

Please leave a comment on the post-editing task:

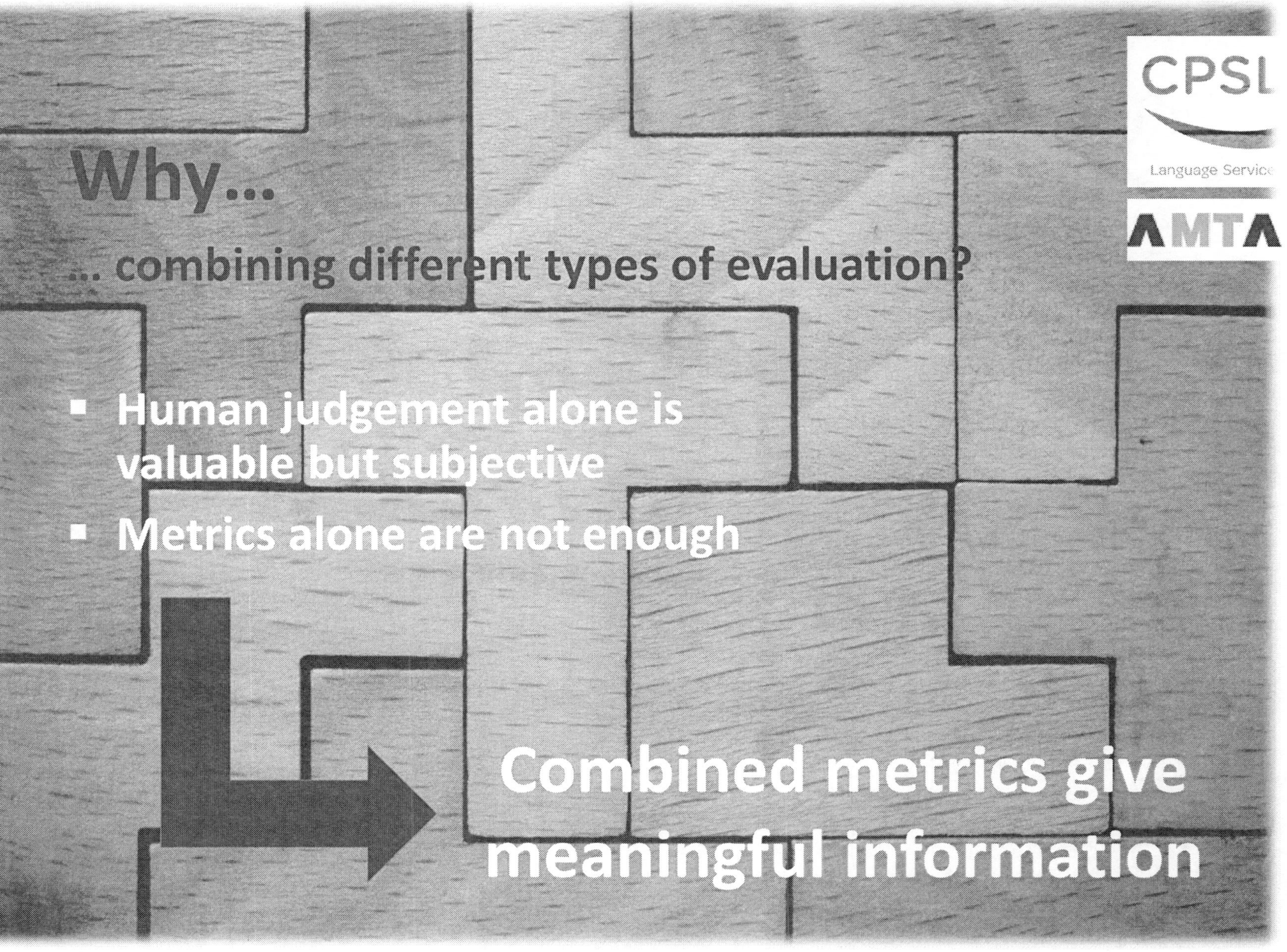

CPSL
Language Service
AMTA
Why...
... combining different types of evaluation?
Human judgement alone is valuable but subjective
Metrics alone are not enough
Combined metrics give meaningful information

Why...

... searching for an acceptability threshold?

- Define goals when training systems
- Know when to retrain a system
- Cherry-picking projects for MT
- Avoid discussions on remuneration

What % of edit distance is acceptable/unacceptable for post-editing?

Proceedings of the 14th Conference of the Association for Machine Translation in the Americas
October 6 – 9, 2020, Volume 2: MT User Track

Previous studies

On acceptability:

- Castilho, S. (2016): "Measuring Acceptability of Machine Translated Enterprise Content". Dublin City University, Dublin, Ireland.

On correlation between automated metrics and human judgement:

- Fomicheva, M.; Specia, L. (2019); "Taking MT Evaluation Metrics to Extremes: Beyond Correlation with Human Judgments". On *Computational Linguistics*, Association for Computational Linguistics, Stroudsburg, USA.
- Scarton, C.; Forcada, M.; Esplà-Gomis, M.; Specia, L. (2019): "Estimating post-editing effort: a study on human judgements, task-based and reference-based metrics of MT quality". Proceedings of IWSLT 2019, Hong Kong, China.

Hypothesis:

Description of study

- 29 evaluations
  - Automated metrics: edit distance (Levenshtein algorithm from nltk.metrics)
  - Human evaluation after post-editing: PE effort perceived (1-4 Likert scale)
- 3 MT systems: Marian, Google Translate Basic and GT Advanced
- Evaluators' profile: professional post-editors
- 10 language combinations and 6 subject areas

- Limitations:
  - Usually only 1 post-editor (and evaluator) per project
  - Likert scores are subjective
  - Metrics result from comparing with the final version (sometimes there is an extra review)
  - Too few evaluations

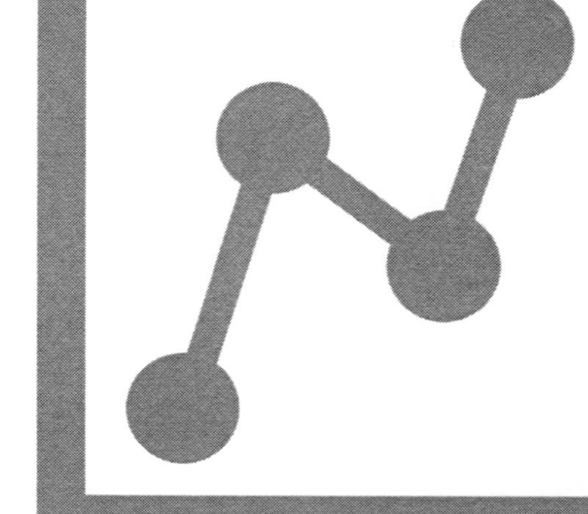

Proceedings of the 14th Conference of the Association for Machine Translation in the Americas
October 6 – 9, 2020, Volume 2: MT User Track

Correlation table

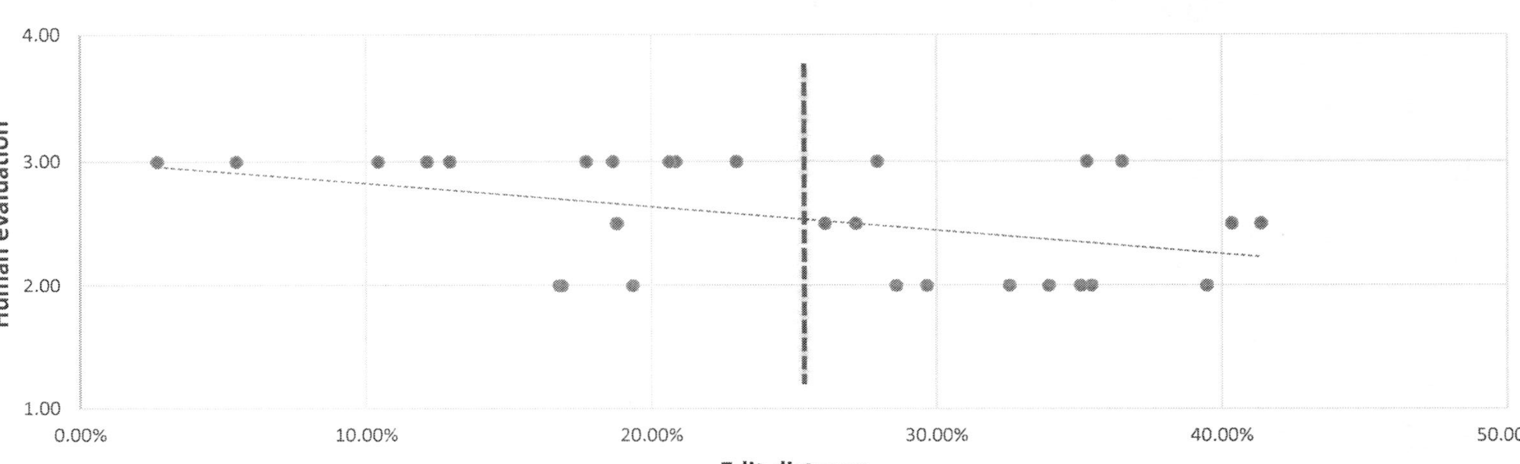

Proceedings of the 14th Conference of the Association for Machine Translation in the Americas
October 6 – 9, 2020, Volume 2: MT User Track

Interpretation

- Raw MT output scores: 2-3

- Most edit distances: 15%-45%

- Correlation? A high edit distance usually has a low score, and the other way around (but note the exceptions)

- According to the specific comments, 3 is usually related to good quality, whereas 2 seems to be closer to unacceptability

Possible interpretation: with an edit distance > 30%, post-editors expect an improvement of the raw MT output in the next job

Ideas for further study

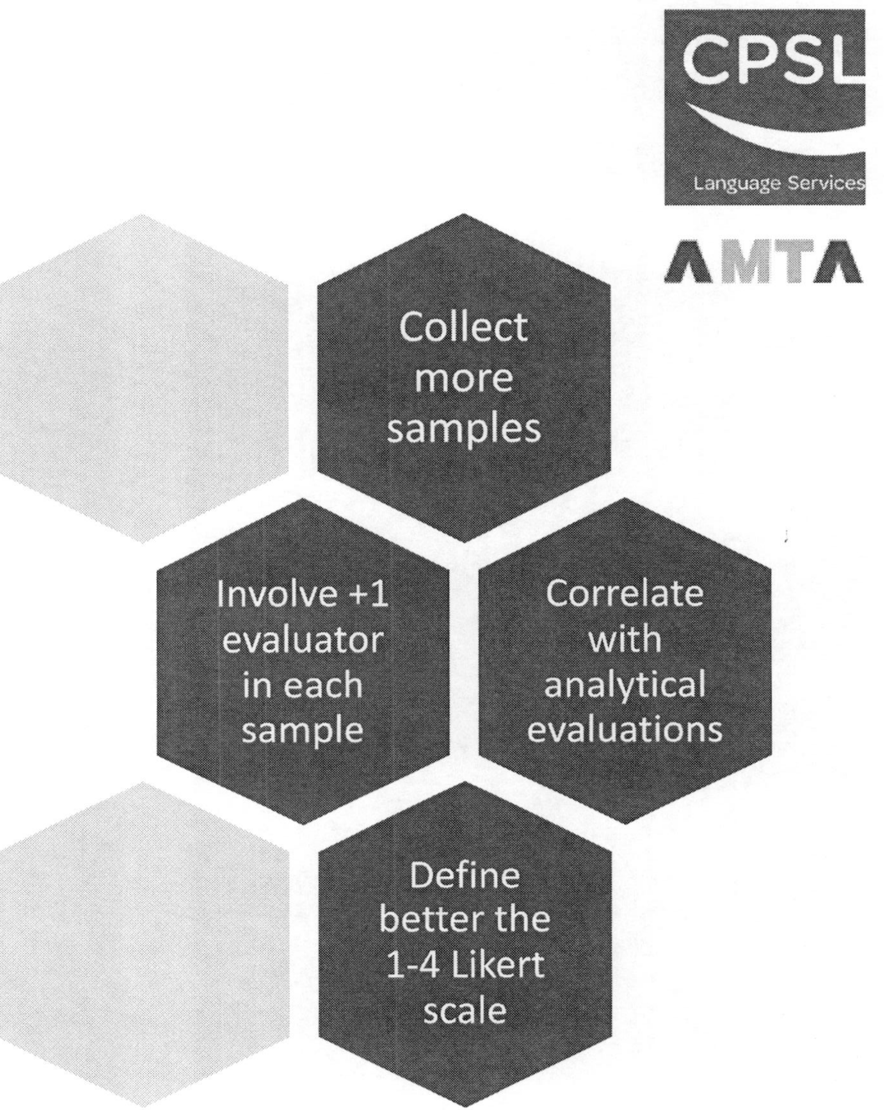

Questions?
Thank you!

A Survey of Qualitative Error Analysis for Neural Machine Translation Systems

Denise Diaz

Joint work with Vishrav Chaudhary, James Cross, Ahmed El-Kishky, Philipp Koehn

What prompts this study?

- Internet and social media are proliferating rapidly
- Communication and information need to be available to a wide audience in many different languages
- MT has become widely adopted

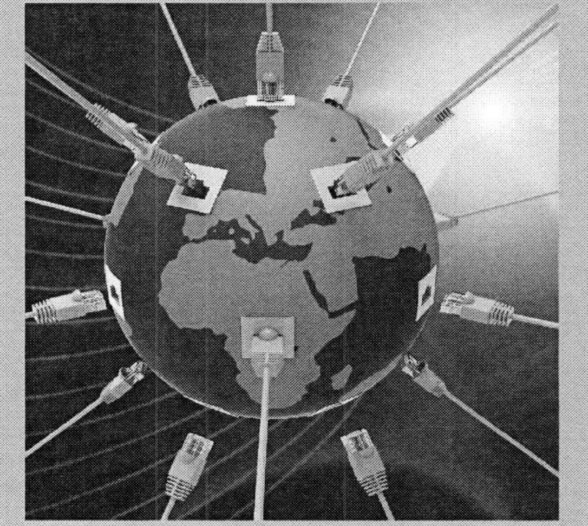

End-user trust is the goal

With this wide adoption, it has become important to understand where MT models excel and where they struggle in order to improve MT models and ensure end-user trust (Lommel, 2018).

2020 MT Challenges - **Problematic translations**

Problematic translations are those that are **misleading** and may:

- Carry health, safety, political, legal or financial implications

or

- Introduce toxic language not present in source

Proceedings of the 14th Conference of the Association for Machine Translation in the Americas
October 6 – 9, 2020, Volume 2: MT User Track

Qualitative analytic evaluation

- Specific common errors found in neural machine translations (NMT) on the FB platform

- Problematic errors since these are the riskiest of the bunch

Proceedings of the 14th Conference of the Association for Machine Translation in the Americas
October 6 – 9, 2020, Volume 2: MT User Track

Why a qualitative analysis is important

While automatic metrics such as BLEU capture the average case for how well a MT model translates sentences, they don't give insight into _which linguistic aspects_ MT models struggle with.

In this qualitative analysis, we investigated MT samples with native speakers so we could review the _linguistic aspects_ of MT errors.

Categorizing errors and making a challenging test set is the first step in benchmarking and improving MT performance in linguistic aspects.

Proceedings of the 14th Conference of the Association for Machine Translation in the Americas
October 6 – 9, 2020, Volume 2: MT User Track

10 Language families, 33 languages

Proceedings of the 14th Conference of the Association for Machine Translation in the Americas
October 6 – 9, 2020, Volume 2: MT User Track

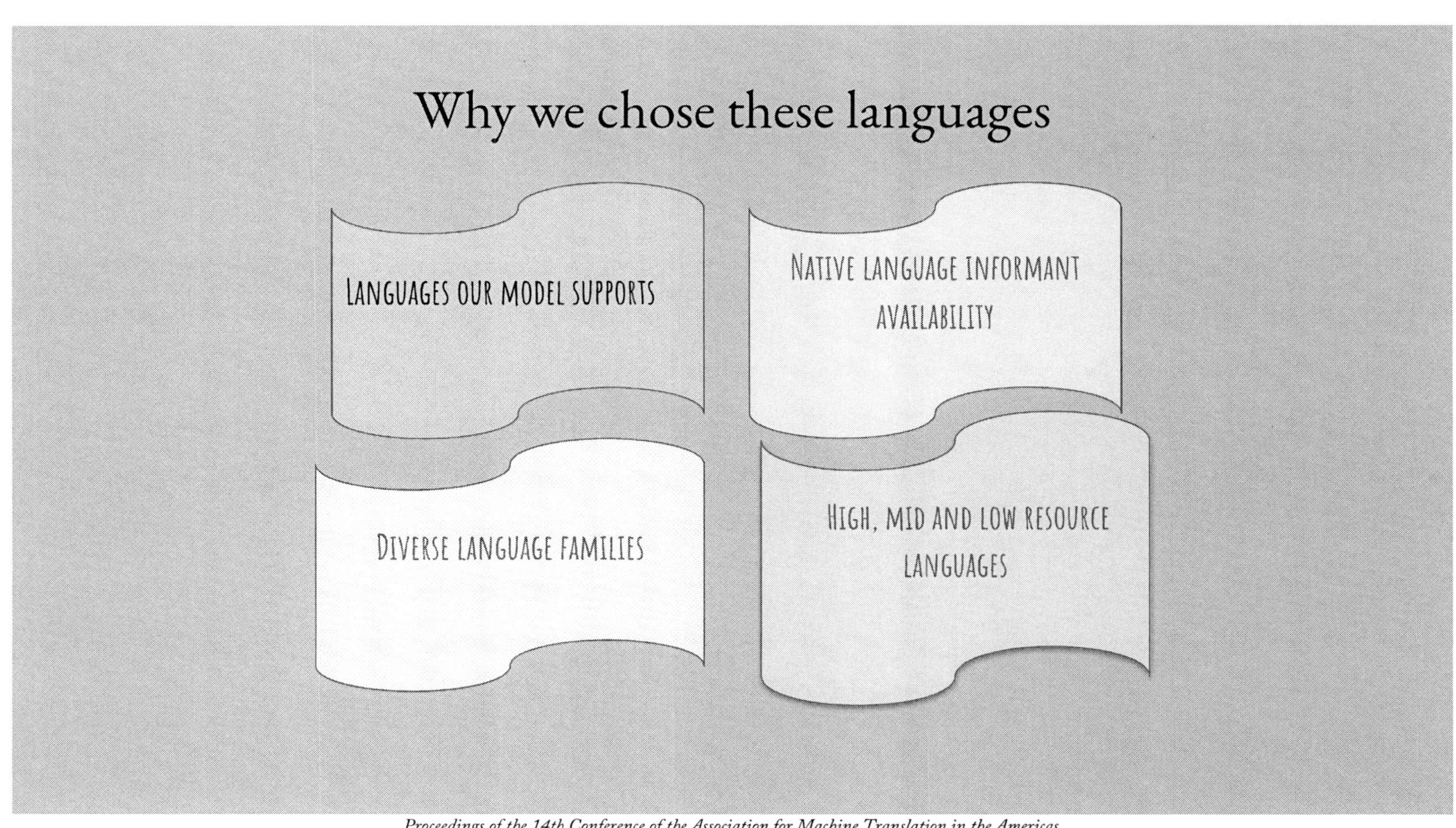

Proceedings of the 14th Conference of the Association for Machine Translation in the Americas
October 6 – 9, 2020, Volume 2: MT User Track

Error categories

1. Lexical-semantic
2. Named entity issues
3. Morphology
4. Syntax
5. Omission or addition of text
6. Punctuation
7. Capitalization
8. Pathological

★ synthetic samples for illustration

★ no user data is displayed for privacy reasons

Proceedings of the 14th Conference of the Association for Machine Translation in the Americas
October 6 – 9, 2020, Volume 2: MT User Track

Error category average percentages - all languages

Lexical semantic
  Word ambiguity
  Noisy source
  Unknown words
  Code-switching
  Dialectal variants
	30.00%

Named entity issues	4.00%
Omission or addition of text	7.00%
Pathological translations	3.00%
Syntax	3.00%
Morphology	2.00%
Capitalization	1.00%
Punctuation	0.01%

Proceedings of the 14th Conference of the Association for Machine Translation in the Americas
October 6 – 9, 2020, Volume 2: MT User Track

Lexical semantic

Broad triggers for inappropriate lexical choices in MT include:

- **Word ambiguity**
- **Idiomatic expressions**
- **Phrasal verbs**
- **Noisy source**
  - Misspellings / typos
  - Reduplicated letters
  - Typographical substitution
- **Unknown words**
  - Abbreviations
  - Neologisms or archaic words
  - Vernacular
- **Code switching**
- **Dialectal variants of lexical items**

THIS WAS THE MOST PREVALENT ERROR CATEGORY ACROSS ALL 33 LANGUAGES WITH AN AVERAGE OF 30%. IN THESE INSTANCES THE MODEL WAS UNABLE TO OUTPUT AN APPROPRIATE LEXICAL CHOICE TO MATCH THE SOURCE, THUS DERAILING THE MEANING OF TRANSLATIONS.

Proceedings of the 14th Conference of the Association for Machine Translation in the Americas
October 6 – 9, 2020, Volume 2: MT User Track

Word ambiguity

"Learning how to disambiguate ambiguous words is one of the most difficult and most important challenges in MT." (Popovic, 2018)

Source Portuguese	Target English	Desired English output
Morro de São Paulo	I die of São Paulo	Morro de São Paulo

Source Portuguese	Target English
Vou para o Morro de São Paulo	I'm going to São Paulo hill

Idiomatic expressions

Source English	Target Italian	Desired Italian output
Twist my arm!	Girami il braccio!	Non devi convincermi!

Phrasal verbs

The model sometimes does not recognize phrasal verbs, verbs that are accompanied by a particle or more.

The particles flanking the verb tend to nuance or even change the original meaning of the verb within the phrase, confusing the model.

Source English	Target Spanish	Expected Spanish output
Could you break down those dance moves?	Podrías romper esos movimientos de baile?	Podrías mostrar esos movimientos de baile?

Proceedings of the 14th Conference of the Association for Machine Translation in the Americas
October 6 – 9, 2020, Volume 2: MT User Track

Noisy source: typos

Source French	Target English	Desired English output
Occupez vous de vis enfants	English: Take care of kids screws	Take care of your kids

Proceedings of the 14th Conference of the Association for Machine Translation in the Americas
October 6 – 9, 2020, Volume 2: MT User Track

Unknown words: vernacular, neologisms, abbreviations

Source English	Decoded	Target Spanish
steezy	Style with ease	Steezy
TMI	Too much information	tmi tmi

Proceedings of the 14th Conference of the Association for Machine Translation in the Americas
October 6 – 9, 2020, Volume 2: MT User Track

Dialectal differences

- Phonetic:

English term	IPA transcription with stressed back vowel /ɑ/	IPA transcription with stressed front vowel, /æ/
pajamas	pə ˈdʒɑː ˌməz	pə ˈdʒæː ˌməz

- Semantic:

Source: British English vernacular	(equivalent Standard American English)	French output:
Dying for a fag!	Dying for a smoke!	Je meurs d'envie d'une tapette

Proceedings of the 14th Conference of the Association for Machine Translation in the Americas
October 6 – 9, 2020, Volume 2: MT User Track

2. Named entity issues

"Named entities have proven to be some of the most difficult lexical items for the model to tackle." (Ugawa et al., 2018)

Arabic: أم كلثوم

English: *The mother of Kalthoum*

Desired output: *Oum Kalthoum*

3. Morphology

English: *Cool down the brake system, cool it!*

Portuguese: *Esfrie o sistema de freio, esfrie!*

Desired output: *Esfrie o sistema de freio, esfrie-o!*

4. Syntax

Source Spanish	Target English	Desired English output
disponibles relojes originales en cali	Original Cali watches available	Original watches available in Cali

3% average across all languages

5. Omission or addition of text

Source Spanish	English output	Desired English output
Dr. Núñez	Dr.	Dr. Núñez

Proceedings of the 14th Conference of the Association for Machine Translation in the Americas
October 6 – 9, 2020, Volume 2: MT User Track

6. Punctuation

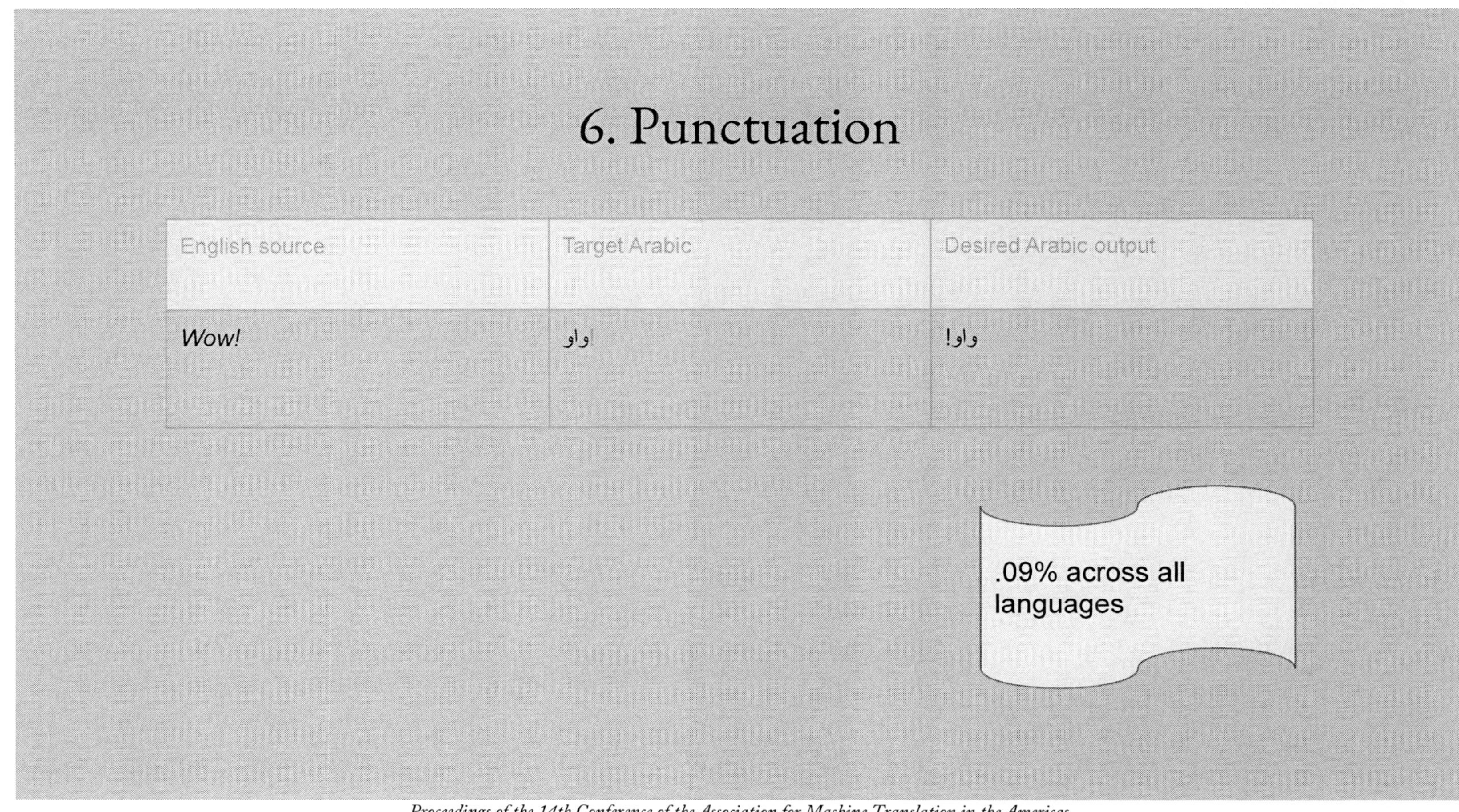

7. Capitalization

Source English	Target Italian	Desired Italian output
Vivaldi's Four Seasons!	Le quattro stagioni di Vivaldi!	Le Quattro Stagioni di Vivaldi!

Proceedings of the 14th Conference of the Association for Machine Translation in the Americas
October 6 – 9, 2020, Volume 2: MT User Track

8. Pathological errors

- Nonsensical or ludicrous
- Problematic, introducing language that is confusing or even potentially dangerous

- Stuttering
- Toxic language not present in source
- A reversal in polarity or sentiment
- Health or safety risks due to misinformation
- Mistranslated named entities
- Changed units/time/date/numbers

"With pathological errors the model renders an aberrant output, untethered from source, displaying what are known in industry as hallucinating errors." (Koehn and Knowles, 2017; Stahlberg, 2020).

Pathological translation samples

Source Italian	Target English	Desired English output
Congratulazioni!	I'm sorry!	Congratulations
È deceduto Antonio	F..k Antonio	Antonio passed away

Source English	Target Italian	Backtranslation	Desired output Italian
J. Hill I think	Ciao. Ciao. Hill, credo	Hi. Hi. Hill, think	J. Hill credo

Proceedings of the 14th Conference of the Association for Machine Translation in the Americas
October 6 – 9, 2020, Volume 2: MT User Track

Machine translation is continuously improving!

- Source phrases sampled last year no longer display many of the original errors from 2018-2019!

- MT models continue to improve with more training data

but

- They need to keep improving in order to ensure optimal end-user trust!

Proceedings of the 14th Conference of the Association for Machine Translation in the Americas
October 6 - 9, 2020, Volume 2: MT User Track

What is next?

1. Developing techniques to improve translations for named entities

2. Developing techniques for profanity aware translation (false positives)

3. Developing techniques for translating into morphologically-rich languages.

   a. Small changes in morphology can mean important changes in meaning

4. Curating a new dataset that includes a variety of errors described today

   a. In addition to BLEU, evaluate MT performance on these error types

Proceedings of the 14th Conference of the Association for Machine Translation in the Americas
October 6 – 9, 2020, Volume 2: MT User Track

Q & A

Contact information:

denisediaz@fb.com

Proceedings of the 14th Conference of the Association for Machine Translation in the Americas
October 6 – 9, 2020, Volume 2: MT User Track

References

Koehn, P. and Knowles, R. (2017). Six challenges for neural machine translation.

Lommel, A. (2018). Metrics for translation quality assessment: a case for standardising error typologies.
In Translation Quality Assessment, pages 109–127. Springer.

Popovic, M. (2018). Error classification and analysis for machine translation quality assessment.
In Translation Quality Assessment, pages 129–158. Springer.

Stahlberg, F. (2020).
The Roles of Language Models and Hierarchical Models in Neural Sequence-to-Sequence Prediction.
PhD thesis, University of Cambridge.

Ugawa, A., Tamura, A., Ninomiya, T., Takamura, H., and Okumura, M. (2018). Neural MT incorporating named entity.
In Proceedings of the 27th International Conference on Computational
Linguistics, pages 3240–3250, S

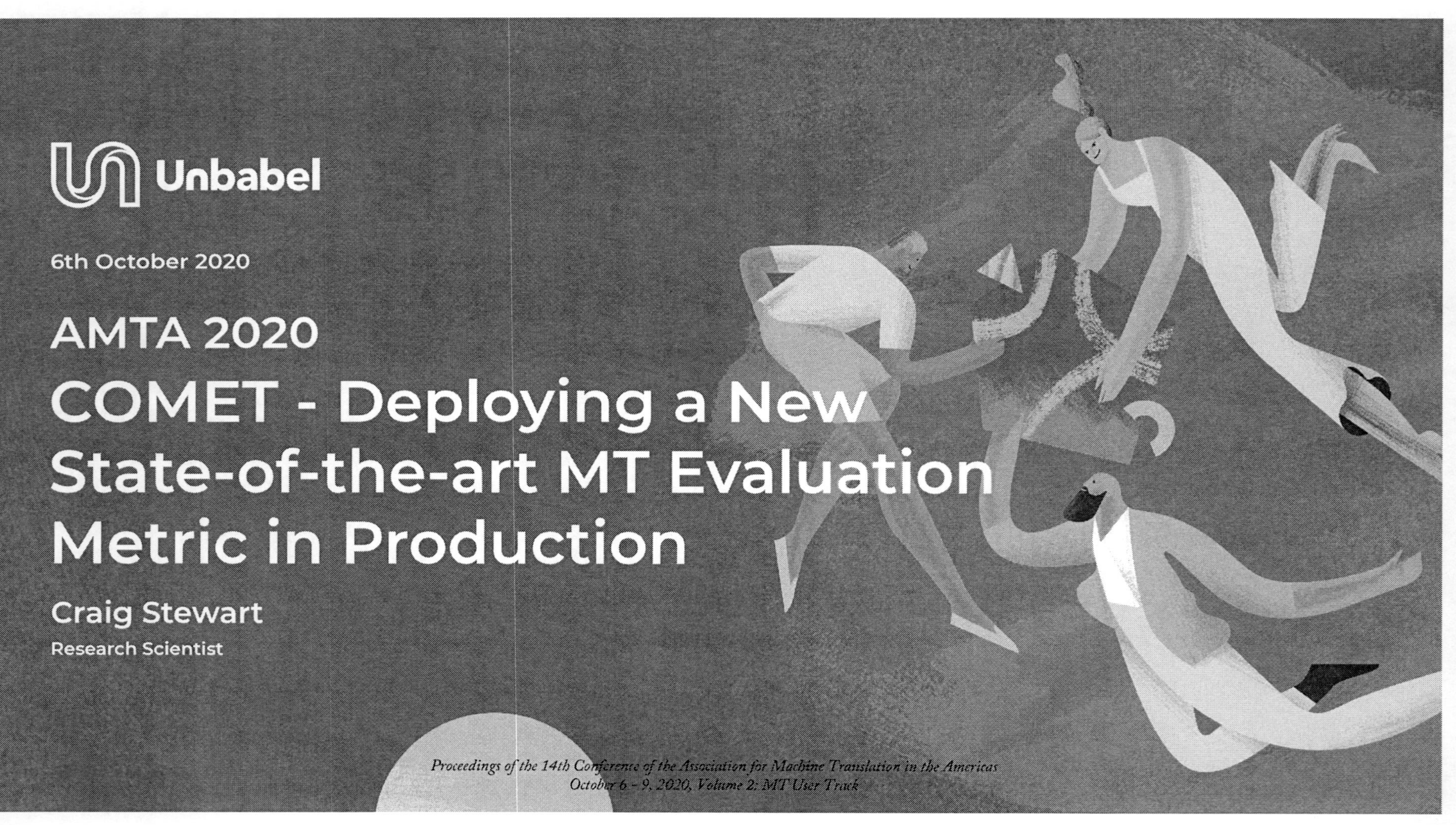

Proceedings of the 14th Conference of the Association for Machine Translation in the Americas
October 6 - 9, 2020, Volume 2: MT User Track

Unbabel AI Metrics

Craig Stewart

Research Scientist

craig,stewart@unbabel.com

Ricardo Rei

Research Engineer

ricardo.rei@unbabel.com

Catarina Farinha

Research Engineer

catarina.farinha@unbabel.com

Alon Lavie

VP of Language Technologies

alon.lavie@unbabel.com

6 October 2020

Proceedings of the 14th Conference of the Association for Machine Translation in the Americas
October 6 – 9, 2020, Volume 2: MT User Track

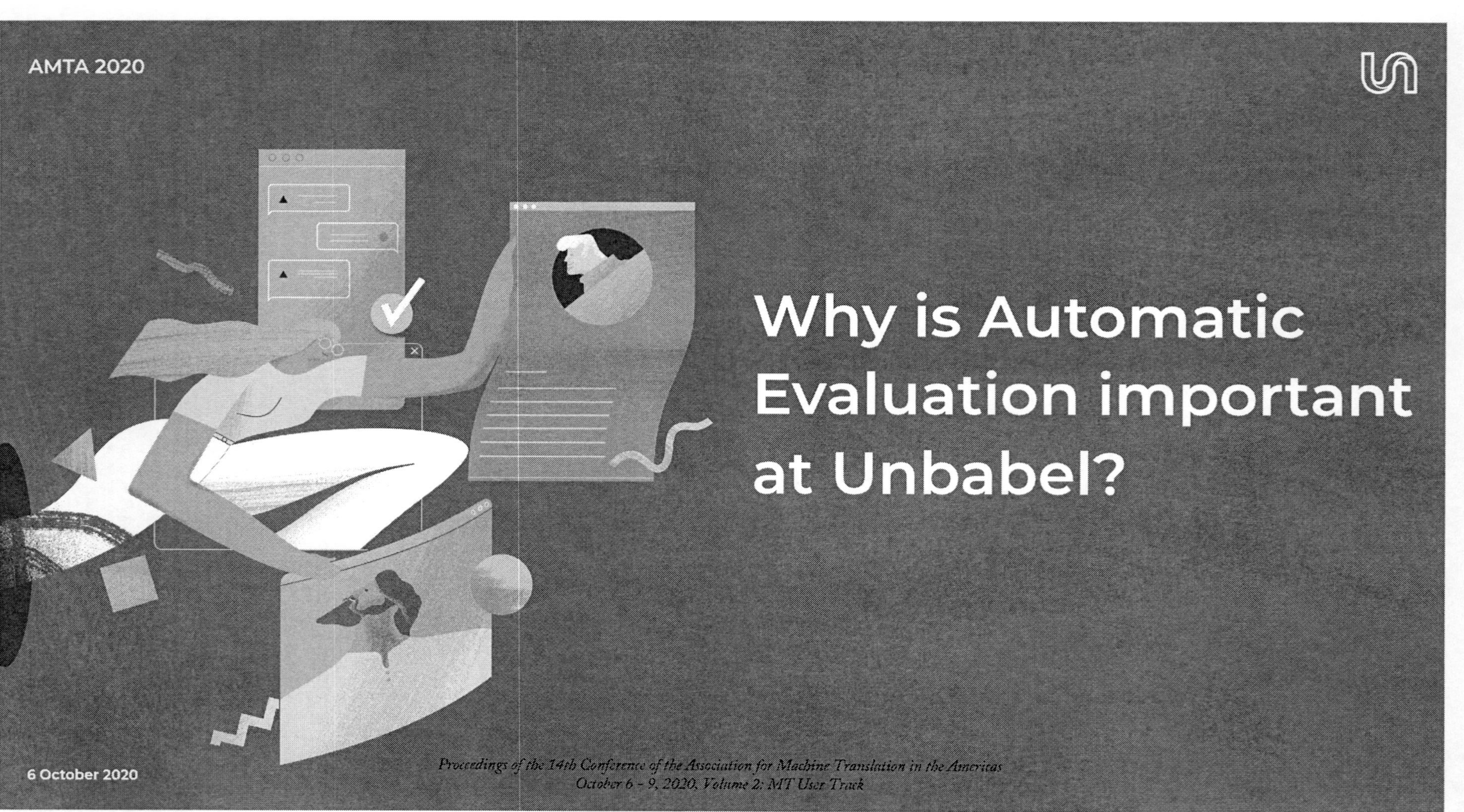
AMTA 2020
Why is Automatic
Evaluation important
at Unbabel?
6 October 2020
Proceedings of the 14th Conference of the Association for Machine Translation in the Americas
October 6 - 9, 2020, Volume 2: MT User Track

Unbabel's Translation Pipeline

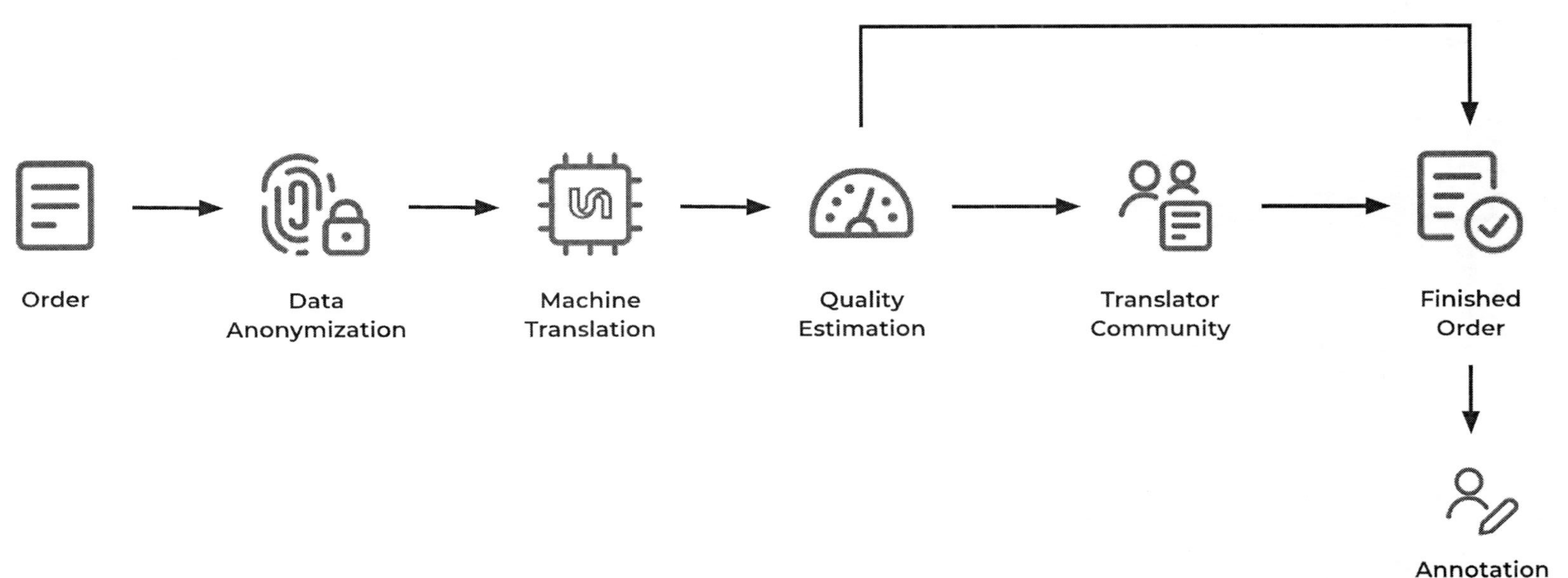

Proceedings of the 14th Conference of the Association for Machine Translation in the Americas
October 6 - 9, 2020, Volume 2: MT User Track

Unbabel's Translation Pipeline

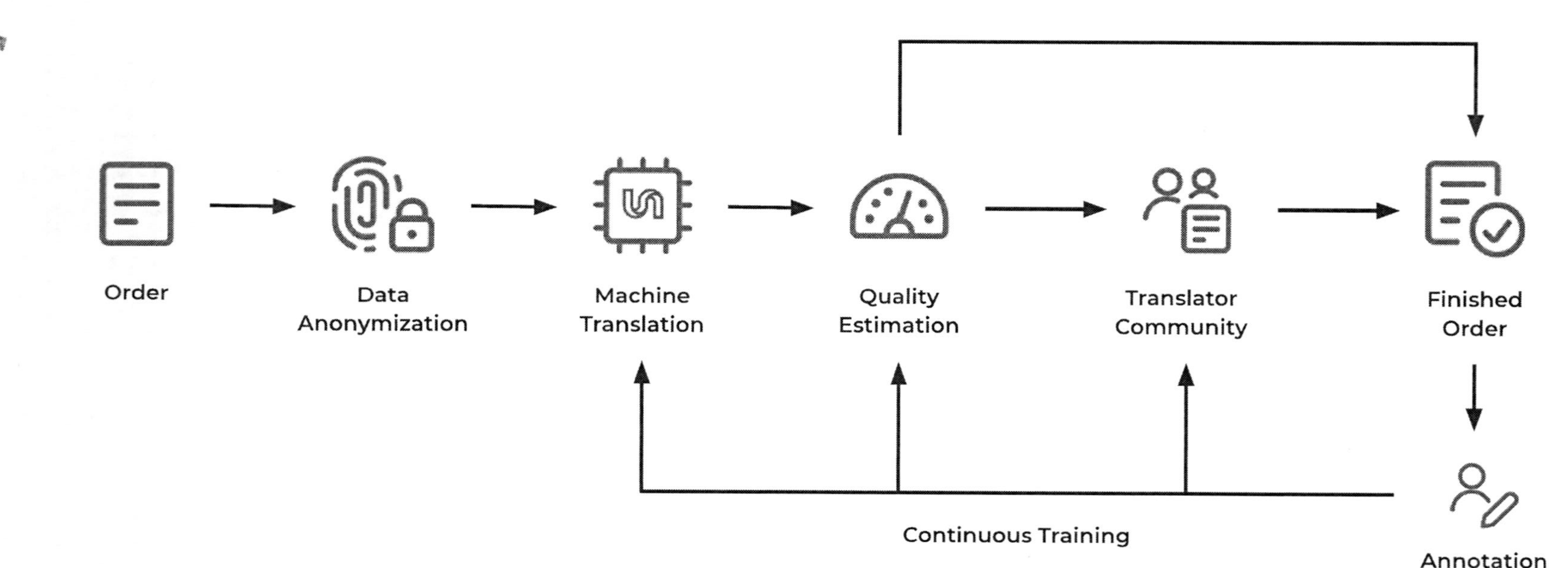

6 October 2020

Proceedings of the 14th Conference of the Association for Machine Translation in the Americas
October 6 – 9, 2020, Volume 2: MT User Track

Evaluation at Unbabel

We process high volumes of translations using highly specialized models for customer service solutions in a wide range of domains.

Our MT engines are continually retrained to ensure that we maintain the highest quality of translation and robustness to new content.

How do we know that MT Engine A is better than MT Engine B?

- Our engineers and scientists rely on existing metrics such as BLEU and METEOR to make initial modelling decisions
- We leverage our community of linguists to provide human evaluation using MQM

Proceedings of the 14th Conference of the Association for Machine Translation in the Americas
October 6 – 9, 2020, Volume 2: MT User Track

Multidimensional Quality Metrics (MQM)

Our primary method of evaluating MT quality involves sending batches of translations to our community for annotation.

We ask annotators to highlight errors according to an internal error typology (for things like 'style', 'content and 'accuracy') and rank the error as either **minor, major** or **critical.**

We then calculate a segment-level score as a function of the **number** and **severity** of errors in the translation. Post-edition by our community of editors provides us with a 'gold-standard'.

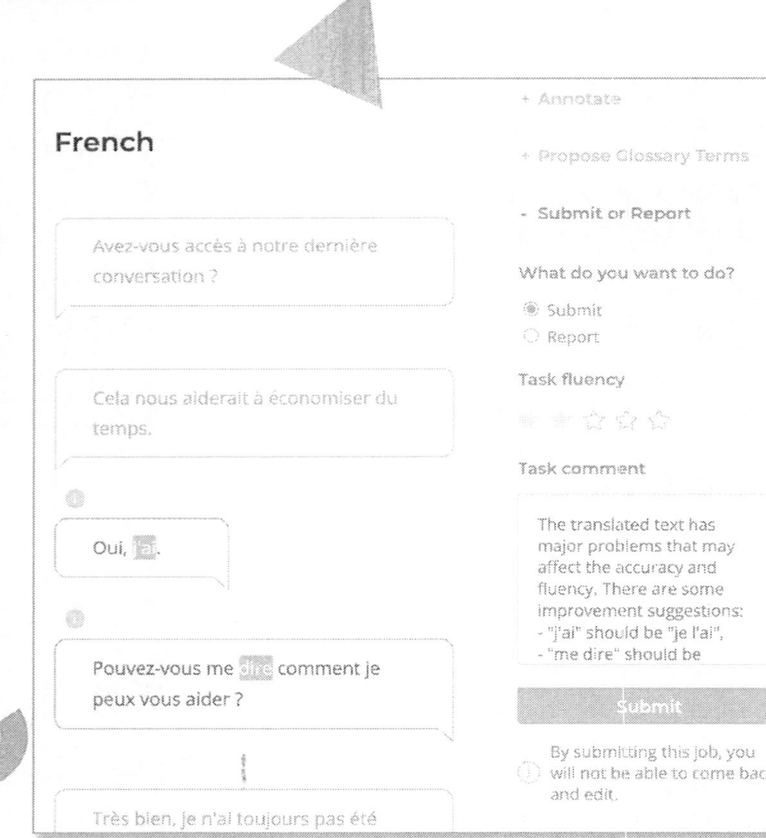

AMTA 2020
What's wrong with using existing metrics like BLEU?
6 October 2020

Automatic VS Human evaluation of MT

Automatic (BLEU)

PRO: Allows our scientists and engineers to iterate quickly over MT models

CON: Less reliable and not sensitive to granular error

Human (MQM)

PRO: More reliable and sensitive to nuanced error

CON: Slow and expensive

Proceedings of the 14th Conference of the Association for Machine Translation in the Americas
October 6 – 9, 2020, Volume 2: MT User Track

Inability to differentiate high-performing systems

Much of the time in developing or retraining MT engines we are comparing two systems or versions of the same system that already perform very well. The gap in performance of the two iterations might be very small.

One of the key findings of the WMT 2019 Metrics Shared Task was that **even modern metrics struggle to successfully rank high-performing systems**.

Proceedings of the 14th Conference of the Association for Machine Translation in the Americas
October 6 – 9, 2020, Volume 2: MT User Track

Correlation with Human Judgement

In general, metrics such as BLEU and METEOR (based on n-gram matches with a reference translation) correlate poorly with human judgement.

What does this mean for us and our customers?

- Modelling decisions are poorly informed and often don't align with human opinion
- Cost of verifying and rectifying modelling decisions is huge
- Degradation of performance downstream results in unhappy customers

Proceedings of the 14th Conference of the Association for Machine Translation in the Americas
October 6 – 9, 2020, Volume 2: MT User Track

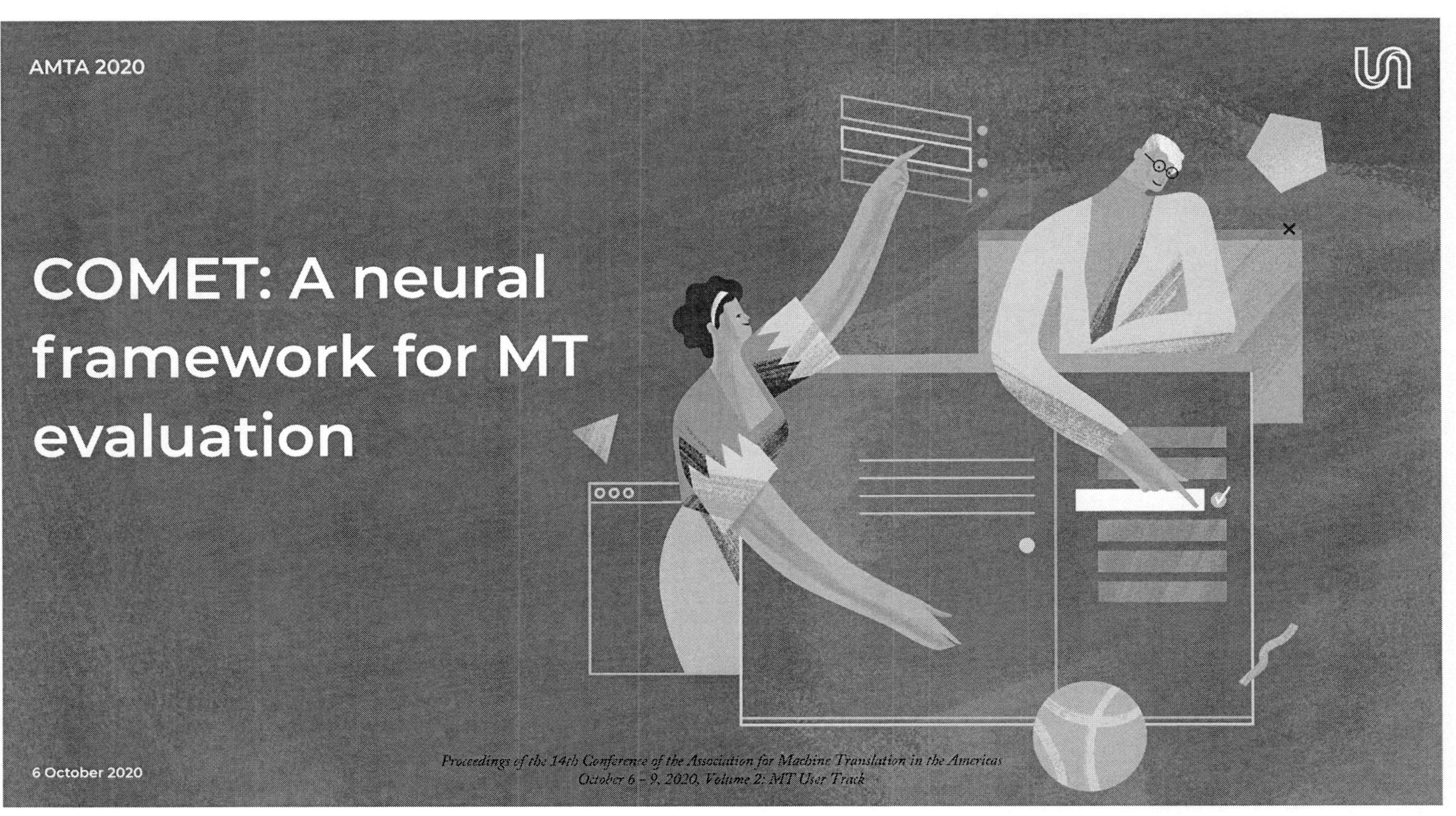

AMTA 2020
COMET: A neural framework for MT evaluation
6 October 2020
Proceedings of the 14th Conference of the Association for Machine Translation in the Americas
October 6 – 9, 2020, Volume 2: MT User Track

COMET: Basic Modelling Approach

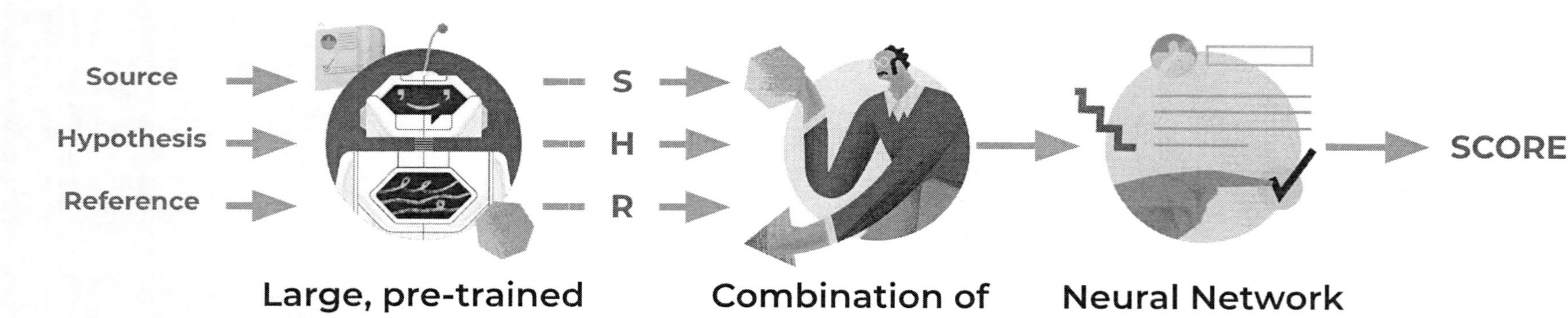

Proceedings of the 14th Conference of the Association for Machine Translation in the Americas
October 6 – 9, 2020, Volume 2: MT User Track

COMET: Performance

Kendall's Tau on segment level WMT 19 Metrics Shared Task

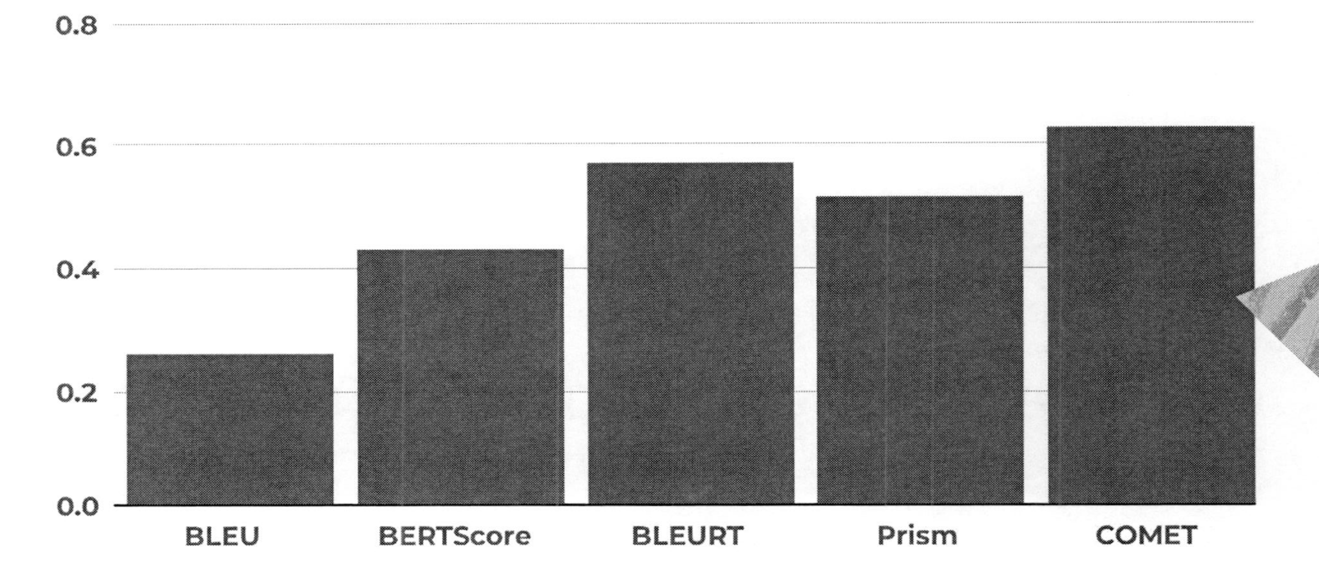

Proceedings of the 14th Conference of the Association for Machine Translation in the Americas
October 6 – 9, 2020, Volume 2: MT User Track

COMET: Strengths and weaknesses

EN-PT_BR

SRC: "Is there anything else I can help with?"
REF: "Existe mais alguma coisa com a qual eu possa ajudar?"
MT: "Posso ajudar com mais alguma coisa?"

MQM	100
BLEU	0.5696
COMET	0.9689

COMET can capture semantic similarities even where there is lexical disparity.

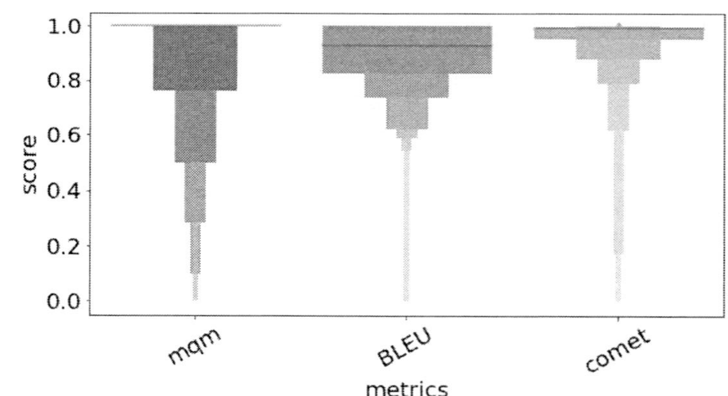

COMET has a tendency to overestimate which presents a challenge for interpretation

92

COMET: The Importance of Good References

EN-DE

Reference*	Adequacy	r (1-ref)	r (2-refl)
WMT	85.3	**0.523**	-
AR	86.7	0.539	**0.555**
WMTp	81.8	0.470	**0.529**
ARp	80.8	0.476	**0.537**

More references doesn't, necessarily, mean a higher correlation.

DE-EN

Reference	r (1-ref)	r (2-refl)
WMT	**0.42**	-
ALT	0.34	**0.40**

Using more references can even hurt the correlation!

* *Data from Freitag et al (2020)* - https://arxiv.org/pdf/2004.06063.pdf

Proceedings of the 14th Conference of the Association for Machine Translation in the Americas
October 6 – 9, 2020, Volume 2: MT User Track

Proceedings of the 14th Conference of the Association for Machine Translation in the Americas
October 6 – 9, 2020, Volume 2: MT User Track

How do we know that COMET is good enough?

We started by assessing the different use cases for COMET internally and realized that these fall into two fairly distinct categories:

- **Single model evaluation** - we just want a score to tell us how well our model is doing
- **Dual model comparison** - particularly in retrainings, we have two systems (usually very close in performance) and we want to know which is better

Proceedings of the 14th Conference of the Association for Machine Translation in the Americas
October 6 – 9, 2020, Volume 2: MT User Track

What do we want out of COMET?

High Quality Assurance

If our ultimate goal is high quality translation, we want to ensure that our engineers have the best tools to make well-informed modelling decisions. Fundamentally we want a metric that performs better than BLEU.

Low Risk Cost Reduction

Having humans verify our engine deployment with MQM annotation is not cost effective or scaleable. We want a metric that aligns well enough with human judgement that we can make deployment decisions based on COMET alone.

Proceedings of the 14th Conference of the Association for Machine Translation in the Americas
October 6 – 9, 2020, Volume 2: MT User Track

Tiered Evaluation

In light of the above we defined a tiered system of evaluation whereby we calculate a Pearson's r correlation score on internal test sets to assess how closely the metric aligns with MQM. We start by figuring out what we think is an **acceptable risk margin** which we set at **+/-0.1 Pearson**

TIER 1 (near enough to human parity)

- Internal analysis revealed that human annotators correlate with each other at around 0.6-0.7 Pearson
- **Does COMET achieve a Pearson of >0.5** (i.e. is it within our risk margin of human agreement)?

TIER 2 (better than BLEU)

- **Does COMET perform better than BLEU** at a level exceeding our risk margin?

Proceedings of the 14th Conference of the Association for Machine Translation in the Americas
October 6 – 9, 2020, Volume 2: MT User Track

Tiered LPs for out of English

Ticket Products

Proceedings of the 14th Conference of the Association for Machine Translation in the Americas
October 6 – 9, 2020, Volume 2: MT User Track

No Language left behind

The ideal scenario for COMET is that it puts us in a postition where all of our products can rely on COMET scores without the need for human annotation (i.e. that all LPs land in Tier 1).

For LPs in Tier 2:

• We are actively seeking opportunities to improve COMET performance on these LPs. This involves both general model improvement and augmentation of our datasets.

For other LPs:

• Where we don't have data for existing LPs we rely on our editors to generate more data for testing and training.

Proceedings of the 14th Conference of the Association for Machine Translation in the Americas
October 6 – 9, 2020, Volume 2: MT User Track

Evaluation Process

Identify products and
language pairs across the
business and collect data
sufficient to give a
reasonably reliable
Pearson's r score

Evaluate iterations of
COMET across settings and
compare results with
human assessments

Based on our tiered
evaluation scheme, assess
reliability of COMET in each
use case and iterate until
we are satisfied of the
impact of the model

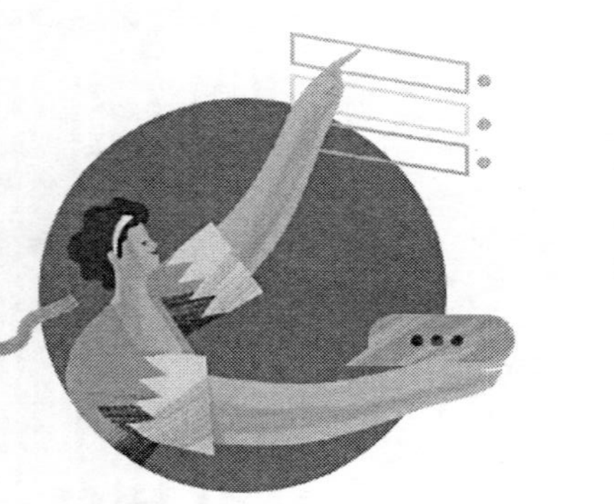

Deploy the best model and
provide clear information
to our engineers about
how and where to use
COMET

Proceedings of the 14th Conference of the Association for Machine Translation in the Americas
October 6 – 9, 2020, Volume 2: MT User Track

COMET in deployment

To provide an extra layer of certainty and trust in COMET for our engineers, we are implementing **statistical significance testing** in our retrainings evaluation.

In deciding whether to deploy a retrained system we apply a bootstrapped t-test for significance to determine, with a 95% confidence interval, that the new system is better than the old.

We also complement our COMET evaluation with a range of other metrics to ensure that our engineers have a full toolkit when making modelling decisions.

Proceedings of the 14th Conference of the Association for Machine Translation in the Americas
October 6 – 9, 2020, Volume 2: MT User Track

What to do when metrics disagree?

It is important to note that even where metrics like BLEU don't correlate well with human judgement, their input is still valuable, if only because metrics based on lexical similarity tell us something unique from metrics such as COMET which are more grounded in semantics.

As such we encourage our engineers to look at a variety of metrics including BLEU, METEOR, TER, BERTScore and COMET to get a fuller picture of what our models are doing.

Where all metrics agree the decision to deploy is black and white. Where it isn't:

- **COMET and other semantic metrics (e.g. BERTScore) agreeing? Good chance that MT is semantically accurate**
- **COMET disagrees with everyone? Check the magnitude of the difference before discarding and consider the statistical significance of the improvement**

6 October 2020

*Proceedings of the 14th Conference of the Association for Machine Translation in the Americas
October 6 – 9, 2020, Volume 2: MT User Track*

AMTA 2020
Keeping tabs on
COMET over time
6 October 2020
Proceedings of the 14th Conference of the Association for Machine Translation in the Americas
October 6 - 9, 2020, Volume 2: MT User Track
26

How do we continue to adapt COMET?

As the range of products and languages at Unbabel grows, we need to ensure that COMET is keeping up.

With COMET in production, we are developing a procedure to re-evaluate COMET on a rolling basis by sampling retrainings for annotation with MQM.

We are also coordinating with product managers to anticipate future product and language demand and perform evaluations and adaptation on new data.

Outside of Unbabel

We we plan to release an open source version of the COMET framework to benefit the wider MT community, and we are hopeful that development will continue over the next year.

The code will be available at:

https://github.com/Unbabel/COMET

Key takeaways

Metrics in a commercial setting:

- Automatic metrics like BLEU are of limited use

- Adaptive evaluation frameworks trained to correlate well provide an attractive solution

- Our COMET framework is publicly available

Evaluating Metrics:

- Metrics can have different use cases and applications

- A tiered evaluation method can help to align expectations

- Considering the statistical significance of modelling decisions can be insightful

Proceedings of the 14th Conference of the Association for Machine Translation in the Americas
October 6 – 9, 2020, Volume 2: MT User Track

Proceedings of the 14th Conference of the Association for Machine Translation in the Americas
October 6 – 9, 2020, Volume 2: MT User Track

Thank you

Craig Stewart
Research Scientist, Unbabel
craig.stewart@unbabel.com

Unbabel

Proceedings of the 14th Conference of the Association for Machine Translation in the Americas
October 6 – 9, 2020, Volume 2: MT User Track

Unbabel

Proceedings of the 14th Conference of the Association for Machine Translation in the Americas
October 6 – 9, 2020, Volume 2: MT User Track

Scaling up automatic translation for software: reduction of post-editing volume with well-defined customer impact

Dag Schmidtke, Senior Program Manager

Microsoft E&D Global, Dublin

dags@microsoft.com

AMTA 2020

Microsoft

Proceedings of the 14th Conference of the Association for Machine Translation in the Americas
October 6 - 9, 2020, Volume 2: MT User Track

Automatic Translation for software (AT4SW)

Challenge
- Publish more MT for software without human review, with minimal customer impact
- MT quality is highly variable, both within and across languages

Approach
- Safe velocity: sw workflow with configurable constraints and quality gates
- Quality Estimation (QE) enables us to predict MT translation quality
- Workflow tuned to limit low quality MT to 10% of translation volume

Outcomes
- MT now used for 9% of published software translation volumes across 37 languages
- No notable negative impact on customer sat

Proceedings of the 14th Conference of the Association for Machine Translation in the Americas
October 6 - 9, 2020, Volume 2: MT User Track

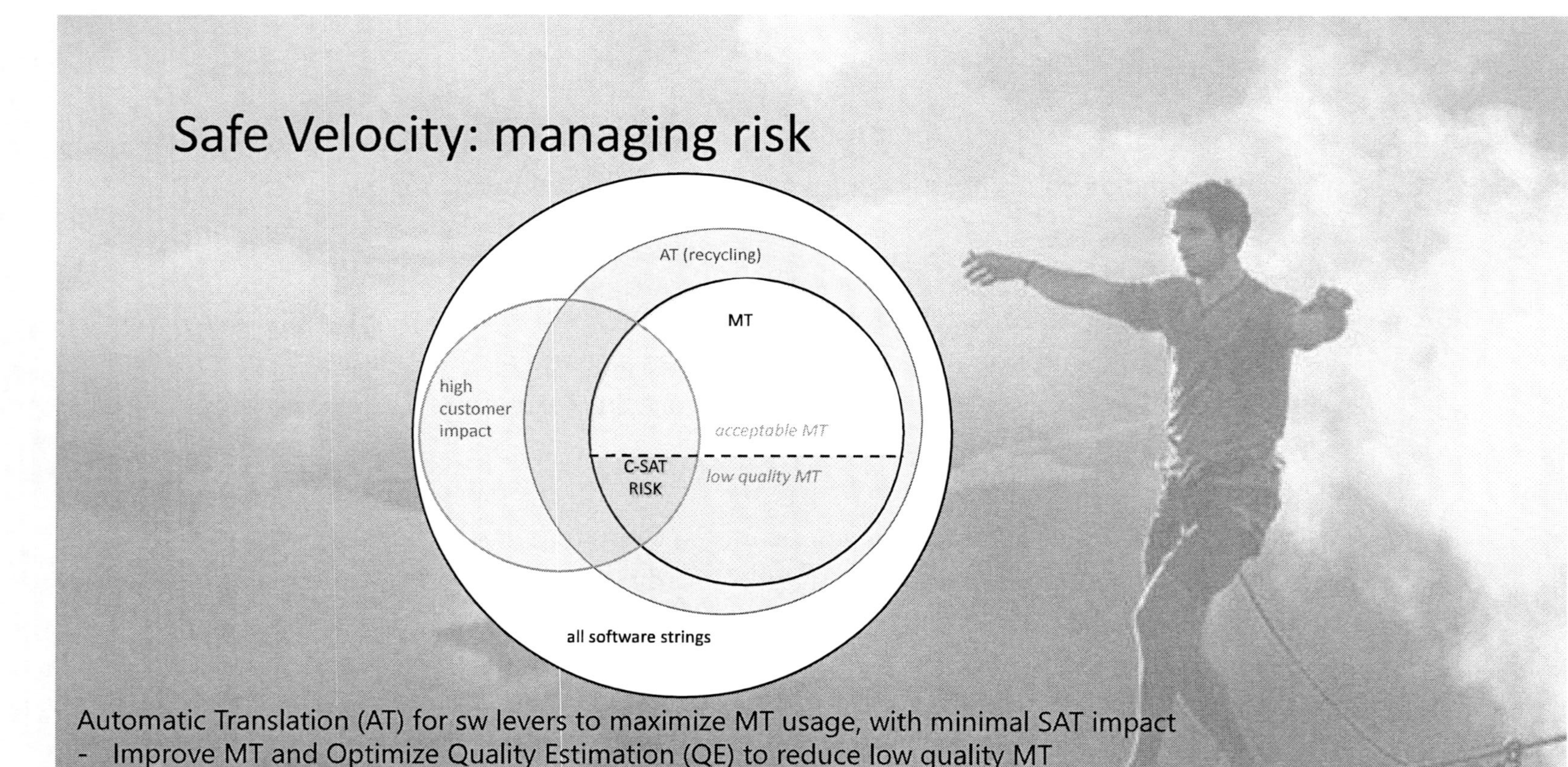

Automatic Translation (AT) for sw levers to maximize MT usage, with minimal SAT impact
- Improve MT and Optimize Quality Estimation (QE) to reduce low quality MT
- Protect high customer impact strings: exclusion, length thresholding
- Listen and respond to customer feedback

Proceedings of the 14th Conference of the Association for Machine Translation in the Americas
October 6 - 9, 2020, Volume 2: MT User Track

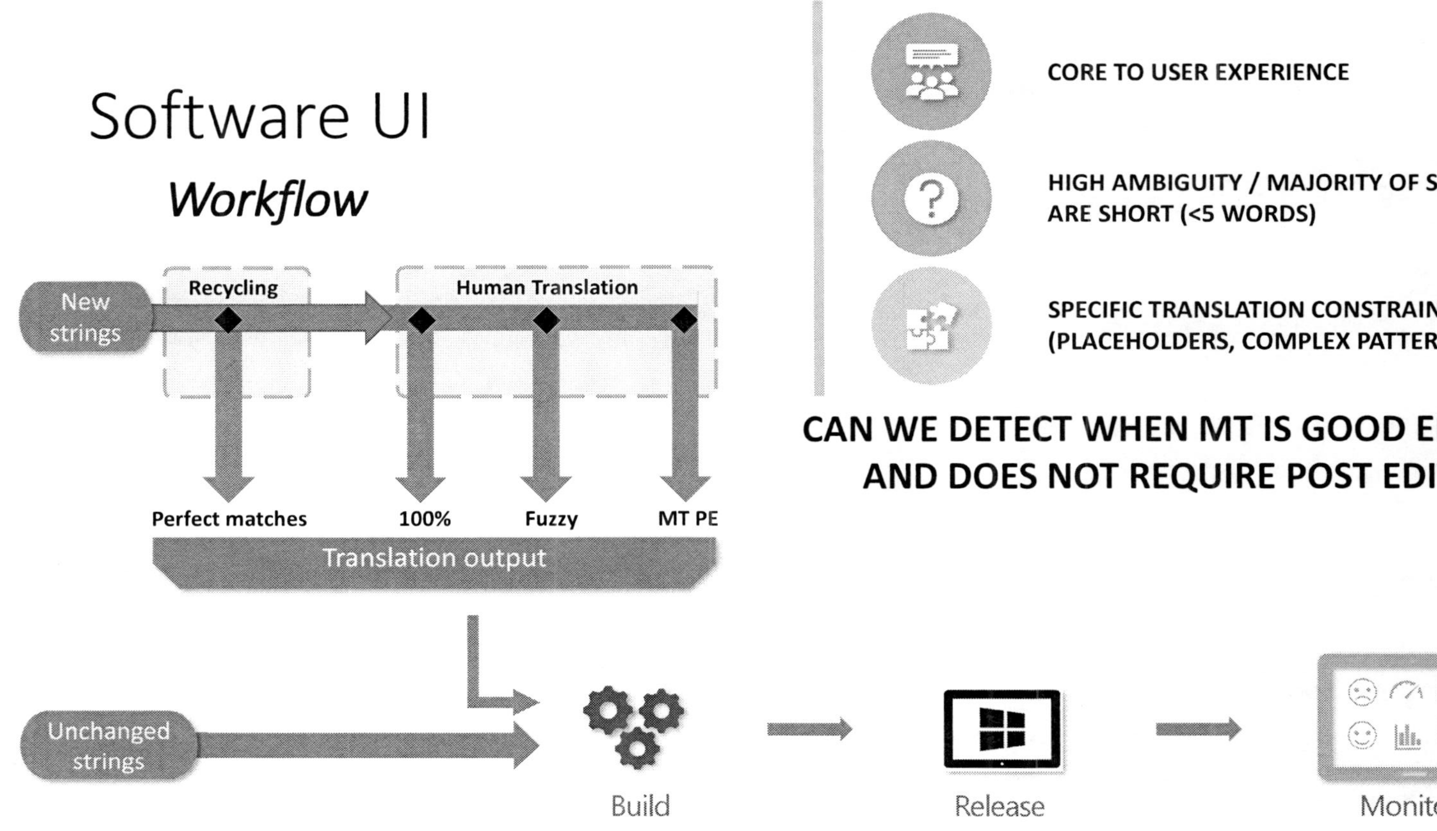

Software UI
Workflow
New strings
Recycling
Human Translation
Perfect matches
100%
Fuzzy
MT PE
Translation output
Unchanged strings
Build
Release
Monitor
CORE TO USER EXPERIENCE
HIGH AMBIGUITY / MAJORITY OF SEGMENTS ARE SHORT (<5 WORDS)
SPECIFIC TRANSLATION CONSTRAINTS (PLACEHOLDERS, COMPLEX PATTERNS...)
CAN WE DETECT WHEN MT IS GOOD ENOUGH AND DOES NOT REQUIRE POST EDITING?

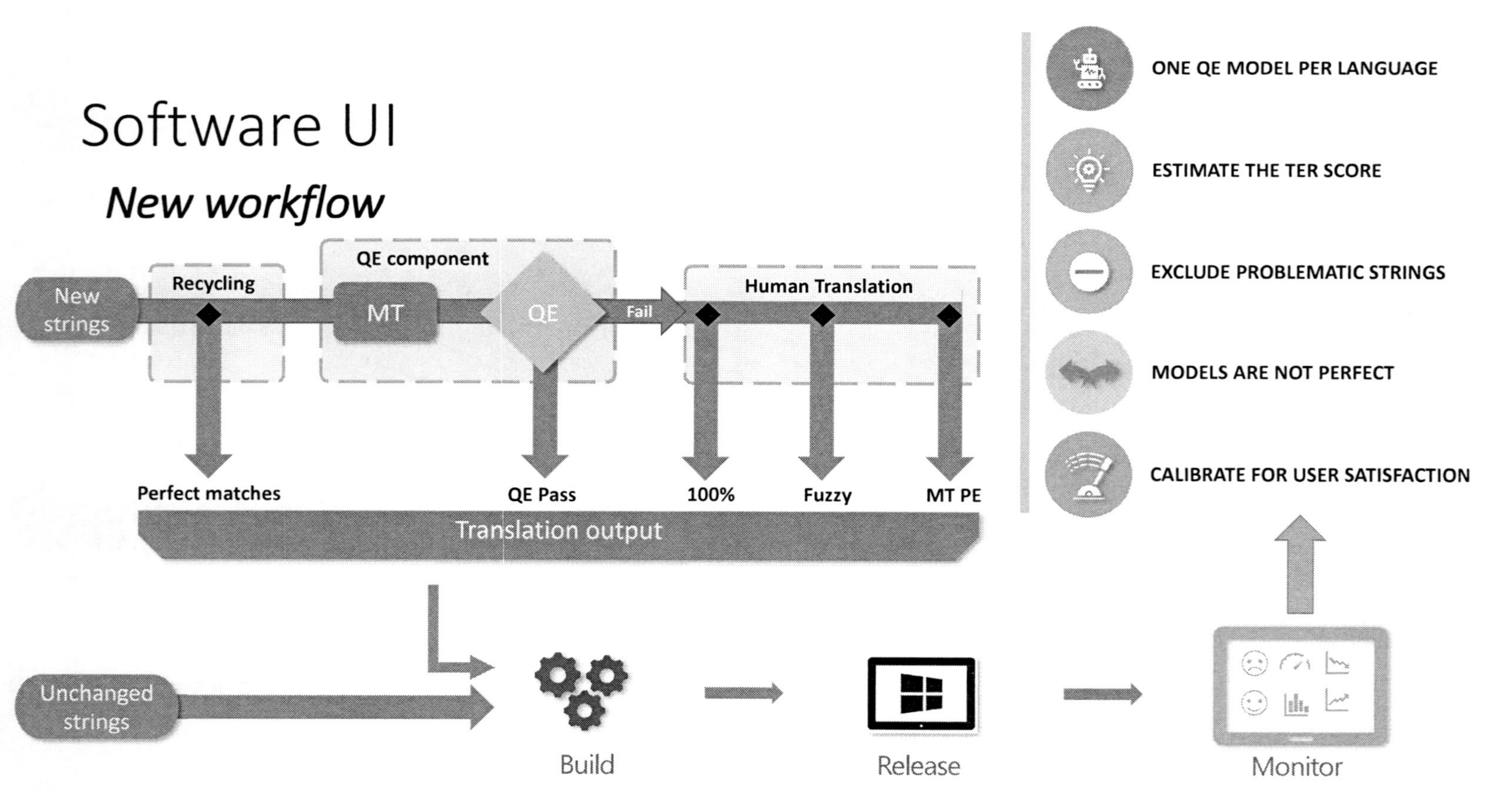

Proceedings of the 14th Conference of the Association for Machine Translation in the Americas
October 6 - 9, 2020, Volume 2: MT User Track

Exclusion for High Customer Impact

Why a need for exclusion?
- MT output quality can vary between string type/context & languages
- Some UI strings need get Human Review, as the risk of customer impact is high

Marketing	What's New	Legal
Welcome to Office Your place to create, communicate, collaborate, and get great work done.	**"Starting from scratch is hard.** QuickStarter automatically creates an outline for your topic of choice with suggested talking points and designs that **make your presentation pop"**	"By checking this box and entering your name below, you represent that you have read and understand above agreement, have authority to bind Customer, and that Customer agrees to be bound by the Agreement terms and the websites therein."

Mechanisms for exclusion
- By resource: targeting specific words and phrases in strings, resource names, or developer comments
- By feature: not suitable or ready for MT, such as 'What's New', or resource groups with complex formatting

Initial target for exclusion: up to 20% of new words per month

Proceedings of the 14th Conference of the Association for Machine Translation in the Americas
October 6 – 9, 2020, Volume 2: MT User Track

Quality and customer impact: Error rate

We manage MT quality based on error rate: % of predicted low quality MT

- Based on volume of new words per product and month
- Assumption is users will tolerate a certain ratio of low-quality translations, without significant impact on customer satisfaction
- Historical human translation Linguistic Quality Assurance fail rate is 5%, by string
- MT error rate threshold, per product, language and month, is set to 10%, by word count – this is the amount of low-quality MT we tolerate

We use Quality Estimation (QE) to estimate the error rate

- Feature based ML model based on Quest++, trained on 100k+ segments /language
- MT low quality strings are those with a TER score >0.3, as predicted by QE
- QE threshold is calibrated per language, taking precision and throughput into account, against the 10% error rate

Proceedings of the 14th Conference of the Association for Machine Translation in the Americas
October 6 - 9, 2020, Volume 2: MT User Track

Calibration and MT error rate

Maximize AT volume against a MT error rate

- Recycle rate for contextual (perfect match) recycling
- High customer impact exclusion (AT exclusion)
- Length threshold for MT – we exclude short strings, <8 words
- QE precision and throughput per language
- This allows us to intentionally publish some low-quality MT

Example: QE threshold set to not exceed the error rate

- We select the QE threshold for the right balance of throughput and precision, to hit the target error rate given volume in scope
- In the example, 36% of volume is in scope for MT. A QE threshold of 0.42 results in throughput of 58% and precision of 62%, and an 8% error rate

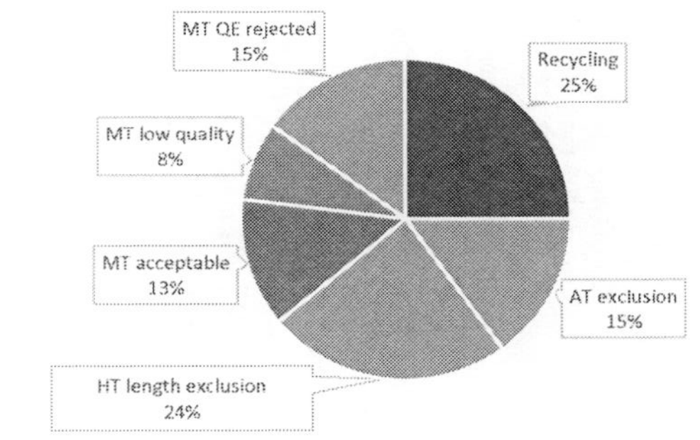

Scaling out AT4SW to a wider range of products

Goal for FY20: (Jul-19 to June-20) – expand AT4SW from Office to Windows products

Key Question: Would existing QE models provide sufficient accuracy, or need retraining?

- QE initially trained on Office product range, 2+ years worth of Post-edit data

Outcome: QE precision for Windows products sufficient to maintain MT volume level similar to Office products

- Good indication that our QE models are robust

- Office and Windows products are of a similar/overlapping domain

Proceedings of the 14th Conference of the Association for Machine Translation in the Americas
October 6 - 9, 2020, Volume 2: MT User Track

MT model training, evaluation, bug-fixing

- AT4SW makes use of Microsoft Translator custom models
- Automation and analytics in place to train and evaluate models for 90+ languages, for multiple domains

- Custom MT pre and post-processing in place for tag protection
- Custom training cleanup tools, aligned with pre-processing tools, to ensure we train on the same format text we process at runtime

- Monitoring of quality, analysis of post-editing, and collaboration with Translator team on bug-fixing

Proceedings of the 14th Conference of the Association for Machine Translation in the Americas
October 6 – 9, 2020, Volume 2: MT User Track

Development and optimization

- MT audit rate: measuring error rate in production
  - QE score assigned to all MTd strings, including those that get post-edited
  - Actual TER scores used to calculate Audit Rate: in production edit rate
  - Preliminary results indicate QE predicted scores and error rate is achieved in production

- AT4SW optimization to increase volume against error rate
  - Word count threshold reduction from 10 to 8 words in scope for MT QE

- Reduction of validation failures for MT by integrating upstream string information (dev comments) on placeholders

Proceedings of the 14th Conference of the Association for Machine Translation in the Americas
October 6 – 9, 2020, Volume 2: MT User Track

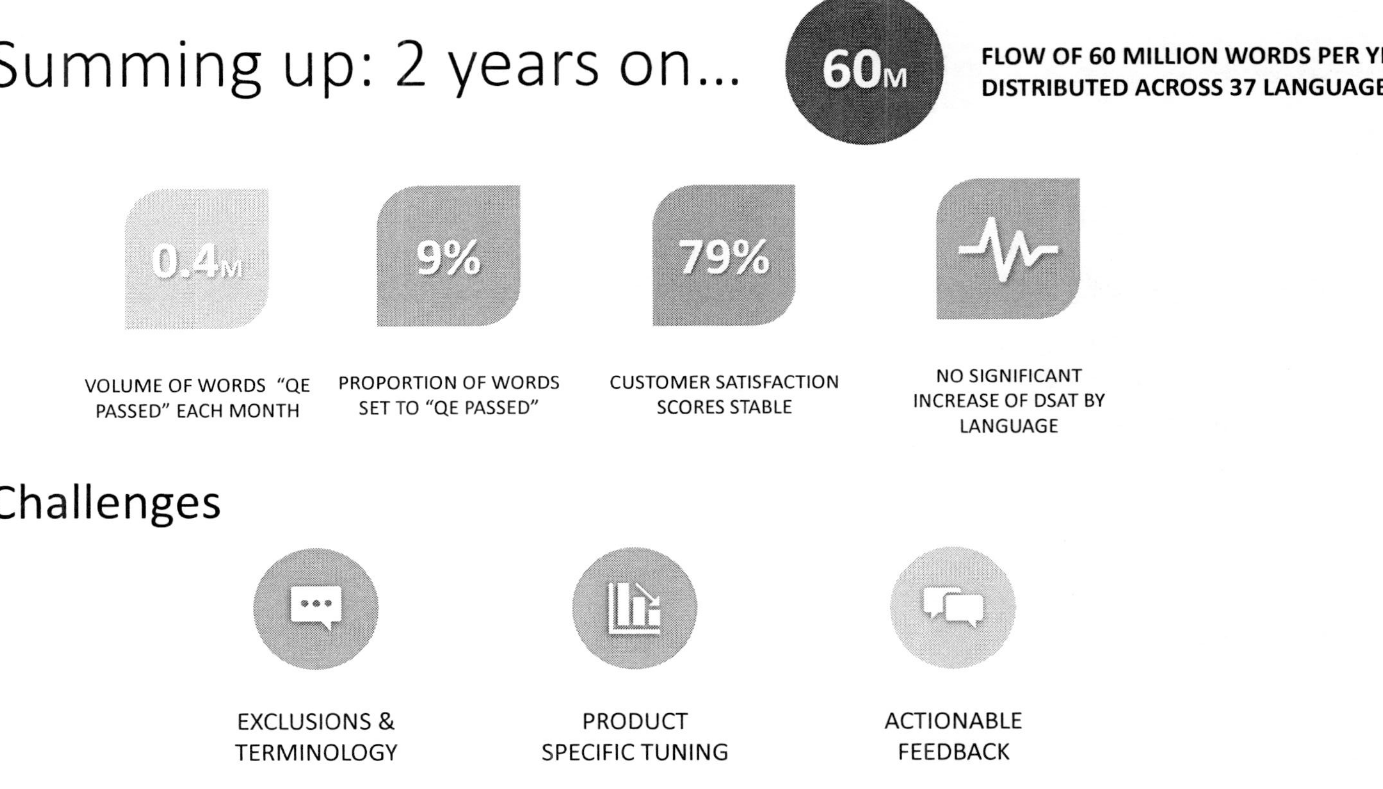

Summing up: 2 years on...
60M
FLOW OF 60 MILLION WORDS PER YEAR DISTRIBUTED ACROSS 37 LANGUAGES
0.4M
VOLUME OF WORDS "QE PASSED" EACH MONTH
9%
PROPORTION OF WORDS SET TO "QE PASSED"
79%
CUSTOMER SATISFACTION SCORES STABLE
NO SIGNIFICANT INCREASE OF DSAT BY LANGUAGE
Challenges
EXCLUSIONS & TERMINOLOGY
PRODUCT SPECIFIC TUNING
ACTIONABLE FEEDBACK

References

- Glen Poor. 2018. Use more Machine Translation and Keep Your Customers Happy. Commercial Keynote at AMTA 2018, Boston

- Dag Schmidtke. 2016. MT Tresholding: Achieving a defined quality bar with a mix of human and machine translation. Paper presented at AMTA 2016 Users Track, Austin

- Dag Schmidtke, Declan Groves. 2020. Automatic Translation for Software with Safe Velocity, in proceedings of Proceedings of Machine Translation Summit XVII

- Lucia Specia, Gustavo Paetzold, and Carolina Scarton. 2015. Multi-level Translation Quality Prediction with QuEst++. In Proc. ACL, pages 115–120. Beijing, China

Proceedings of the 14th Conference of the Association for Machine Translation in the Americas
October 6 - 9, 2020, Volume 2: MT User Track

Q & A

Proceedings of the 14th Conference of the Association for Machine Translation in the Americas
October 6 – 9, 2020, Volume 2: MT User Track

Agenda

01 Program overview

02 Data collection and model training

03 Perfect MT scenario

04 Inference acceleration

05 Future works

vmware

Proceedings of the 14th Conference of the Association for Machine Translation in the Americas
October 6 - 9, 2020, Volume 2: MT User Track

Program overview

Why prediction is needed

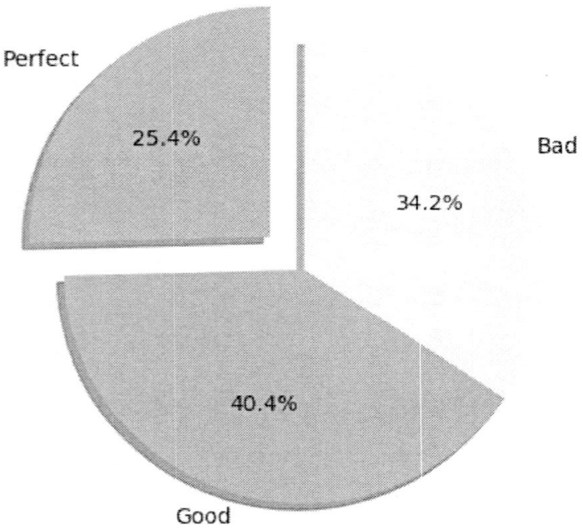

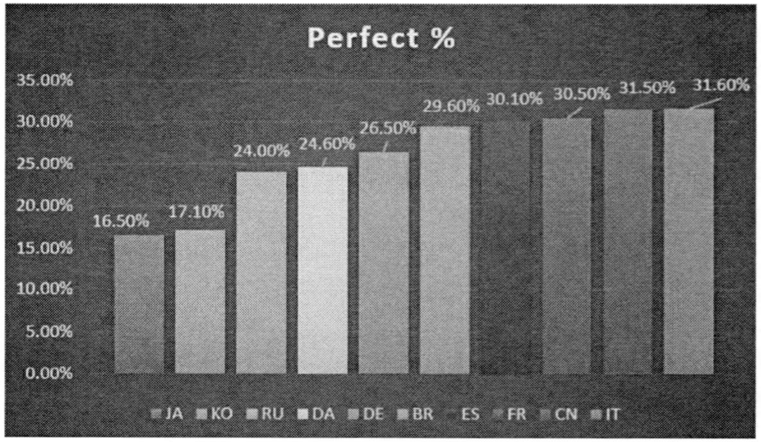

vmware·

Proceedings of the 14th Conference of the Association for Machine Translation in the Americas
October 6 – 9, 2020, Volume 2: MT User Track

Program overview

POC	Model fine-tune	Deploy to Stag.	Deploy to Prod.	Scenarios
• Data collection • Data washing • Conceptual design • Result analyze • Prove of concept	• Added source English as feature(English + MT as input, PE as the label) • Added regression to get linear output • Generated training data from fuzzy/ICE • Validation framework (correlation scatter diagram with actual PE etc.) • Trained models	• Model validation by real data • Load balancing by using multiple instances • Model performance against 25,000 new words project (5-10 in average) • Quality index invented and patent applied	• Model size reduction • Further validate the model by running pilot projects • Deploy trained models in DECC (CPU only, with load balancer) • OpenVINO inference accelerator (CPU) • Tensor RT ML inference accelerator validation (GPU) • Exclusion rules • Integration with TMS	• Perfect MT scenario • RAW MT quality auto scoring scenario • Engine quality auto evaluation scenario

vmware·

Proceedings of the 14th Conference of the Association for Machine Translation in the Americas
October 6 - 9, 2020, Volume 2: MT User Track

Data collection and model training

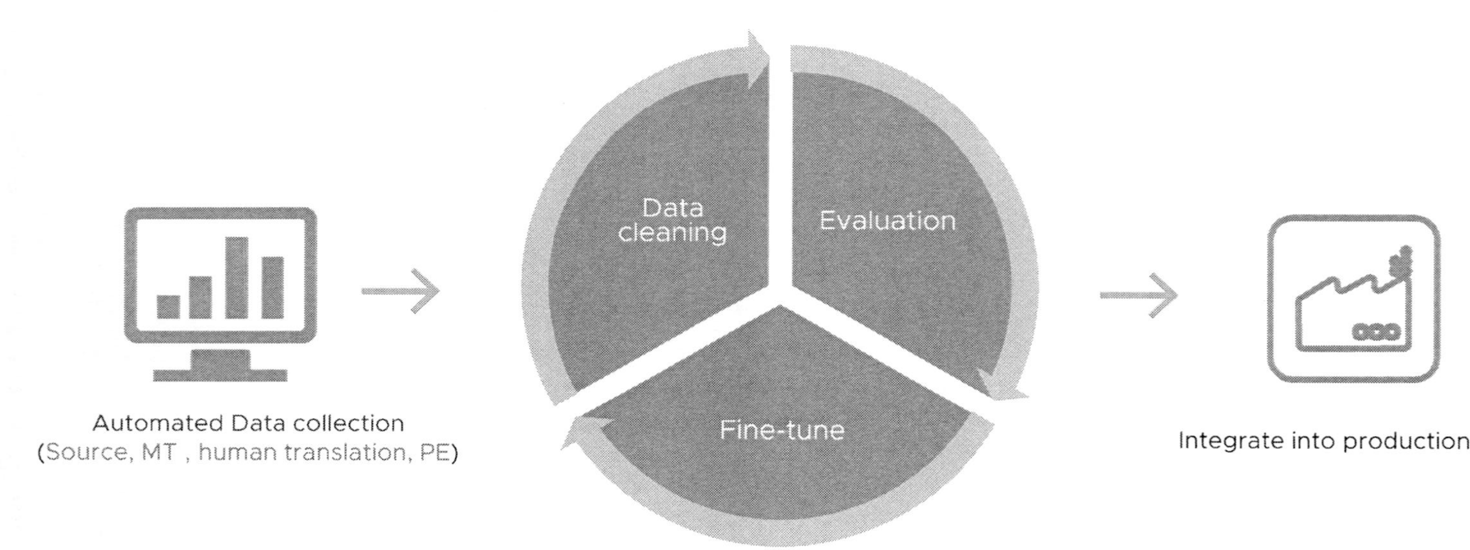

Proceedings of the 14th Conference of the Association for Machine Translation in the Americas
October 6 - 9, 2020, Volume 2: MT User Track

Data collection and model training

Algorithm – Transformer

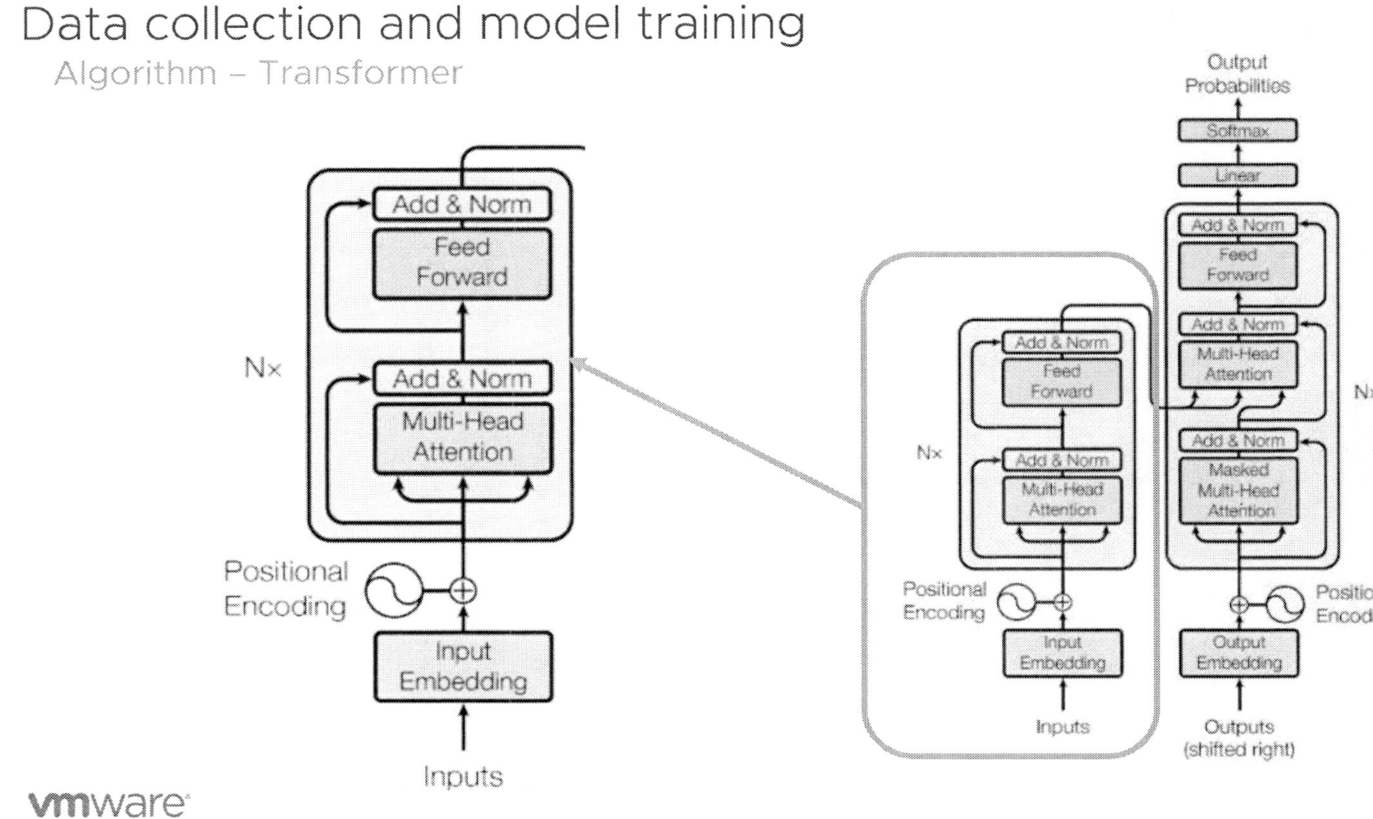

vmware

129

Perfect MT scenario

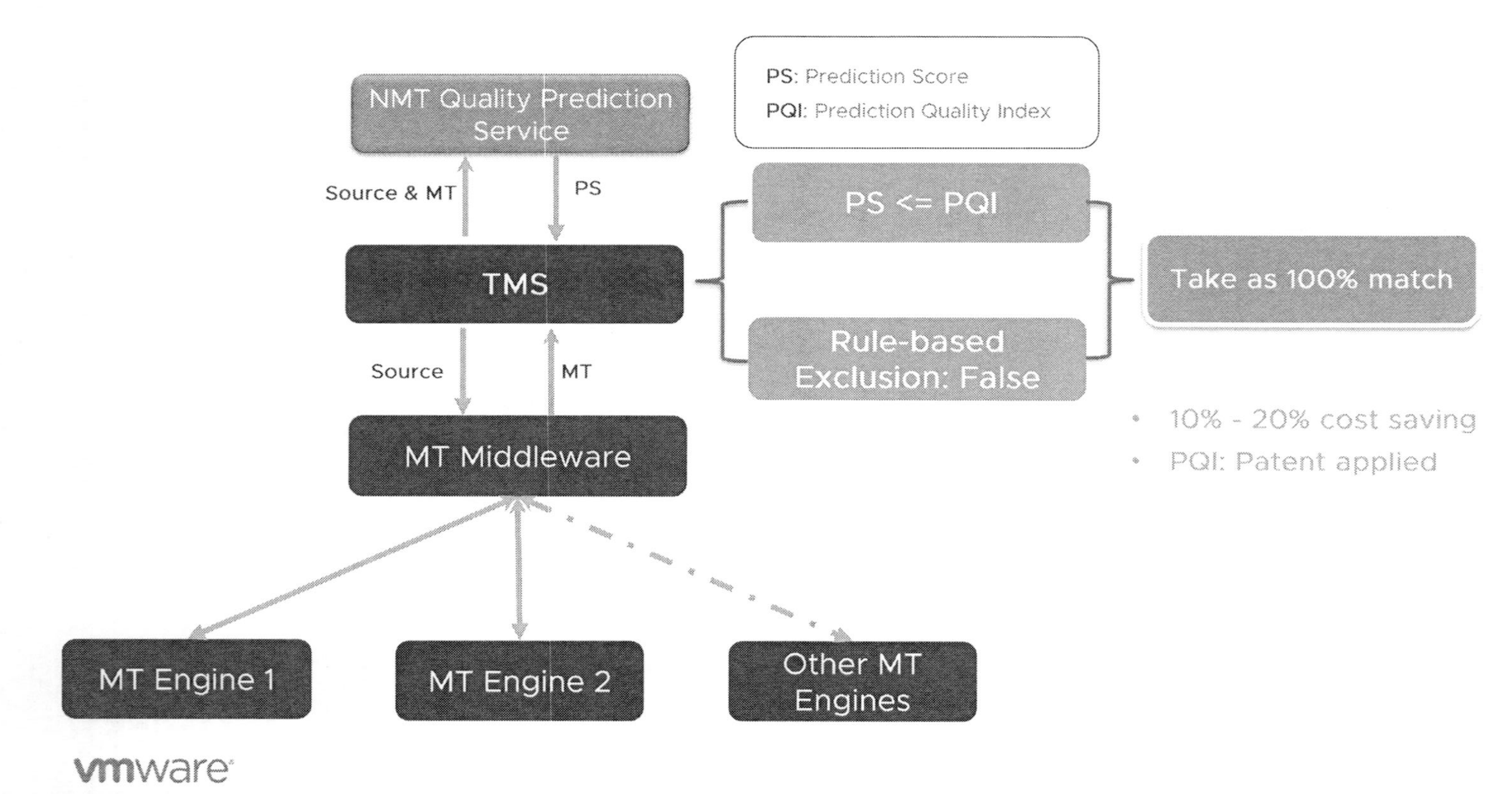

Proceedings of the 14th Conference of the Association for Machine Translation in the Americas
October 6 – 9, 2020, Volume 2: MT User Track

Perfect MT Scenario

Overall accuracy

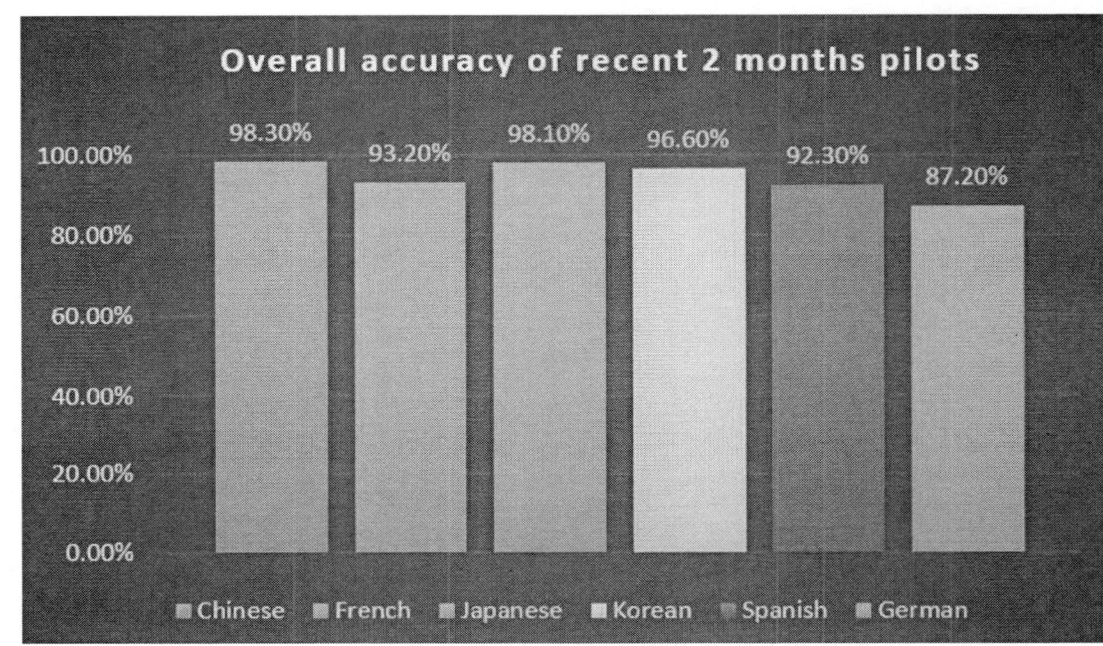

vmware

Proceedings of the 14th Conference of the Association for Machine Translation in the Americas
October 6 - 9, 2020, Volume 2: MT User Track

Perfect MT Scenario

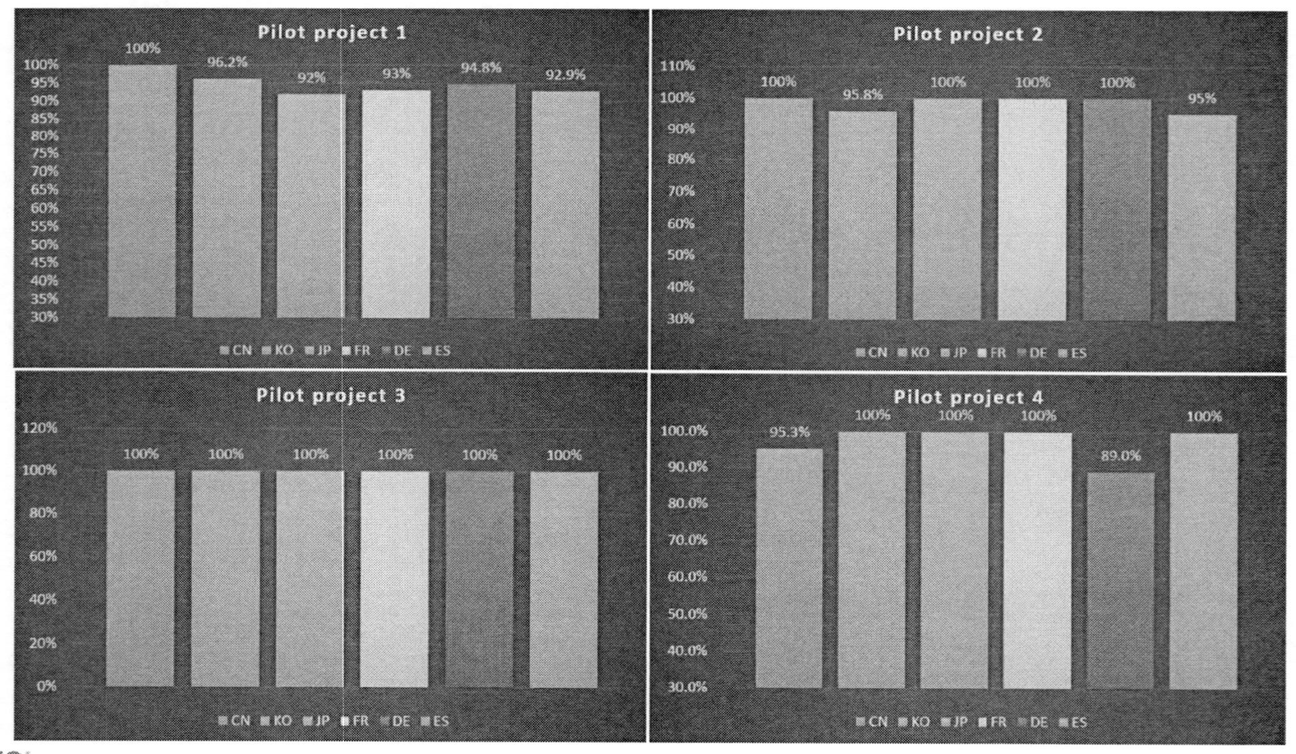

vmware

Perfect MT Scenario

Typical prediction failure example

DE golden MT that human linguist marked as "bad":

Source:

Directory sync is handled by the connector component of the service and can only be enabled on one connector instance at a time.

MT:

Die Verzeichnissynchronisierung wird von der Konnektorkomponente des -Diensts durchgeführt und kann jeweils nur auf einer Konnektorinstanz aktiviert werden.

Human MTPE:

Die Verzeichnissynchronisierung wird von der Connector-Komponente des Diensts durchgeführt und kann jeweils nur auf einer Connector-Instanz aktiviert werden.

vmware

Proceedings of the 14th Conference of the Association for Machine Translation in the Americas
October 6 - 9, 2020, Volume 2: MT User Track

Prediction PE vs. Actual PE

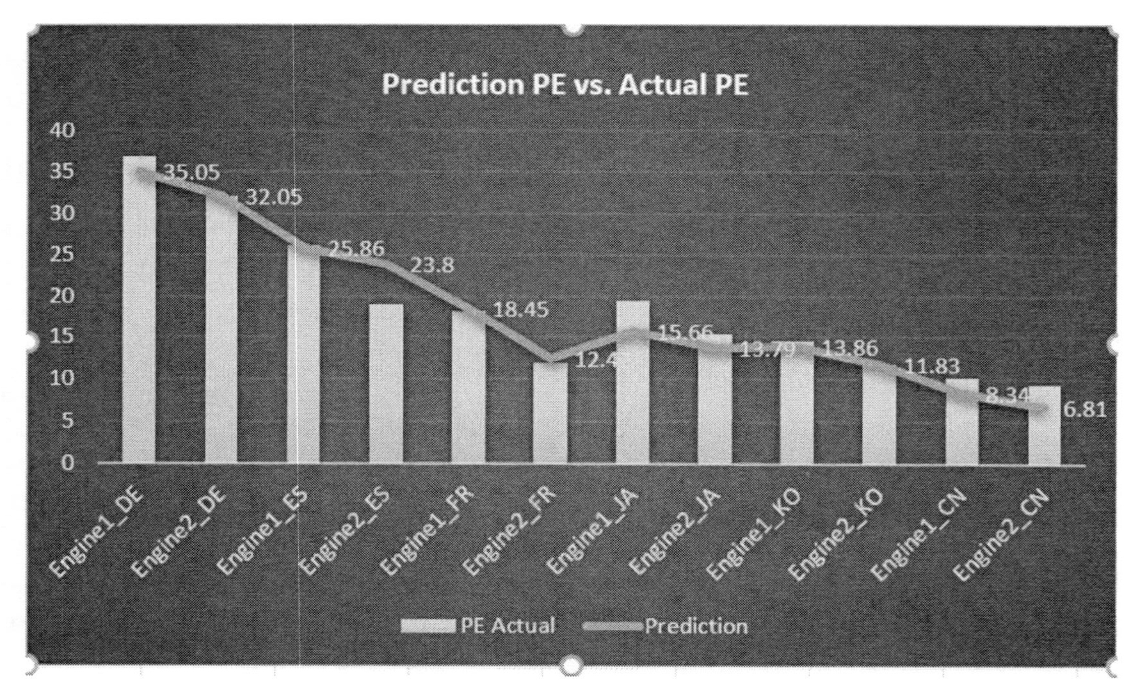

Proceedings of the 14th Conference of the Association for Machine Translation in the Americas
October 6 - 9, 2020, Volume 2: MT User Track

ML Model Inference Acceleration Solutions

Inference time comparison

CPU without acceleration:

400 ms/string

CPU + OpenVINO

130 ms/string, 3 x

GPU + TensorRT:

2.8 ms/string, 140 x

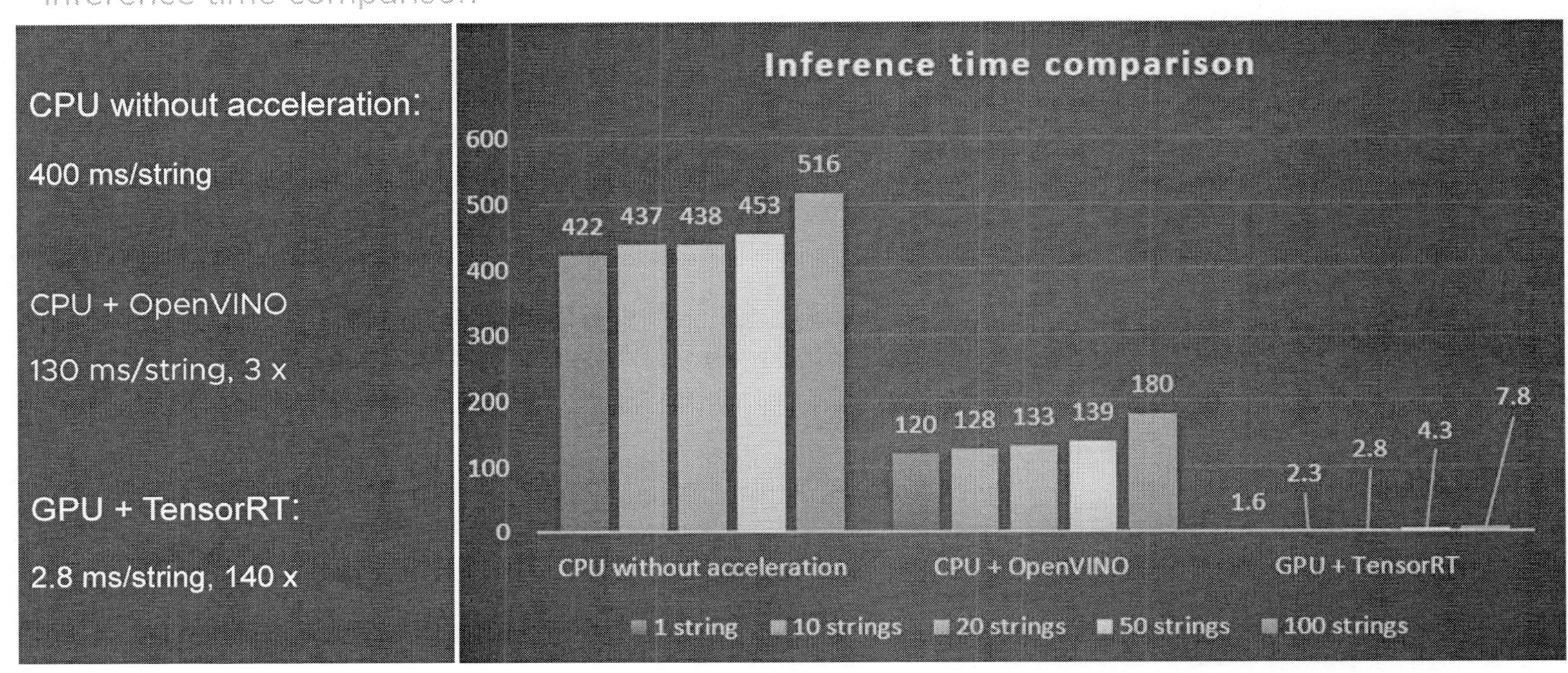

vmware

Proceedings of the 14th Conference of the Association for Machine Translation in the Americas
October 6 – 9, 2020, Volume 2: MT User Track

What's next: APE (Automatic Post Editing)

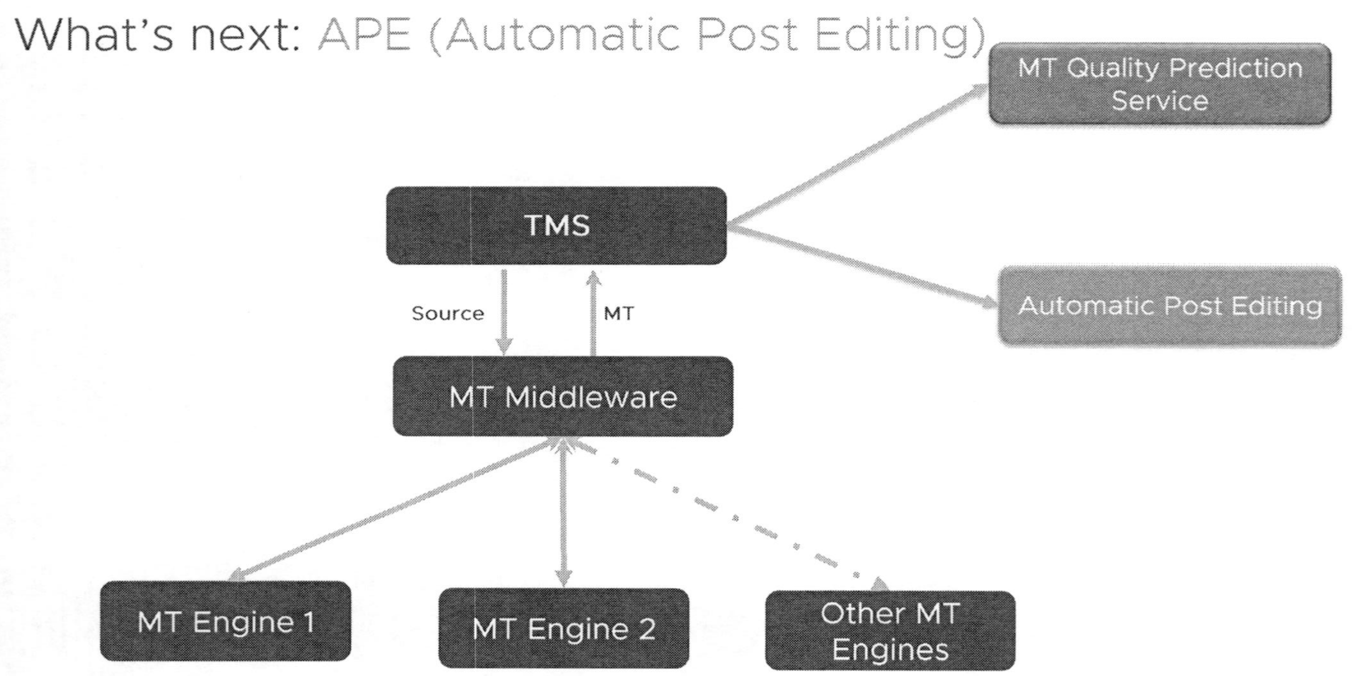

vmware

Proceedings of the 14th Conference of the Association for Machine Translation in the Americas
October 6 - 9, 2020, Volume 2: MT User Track

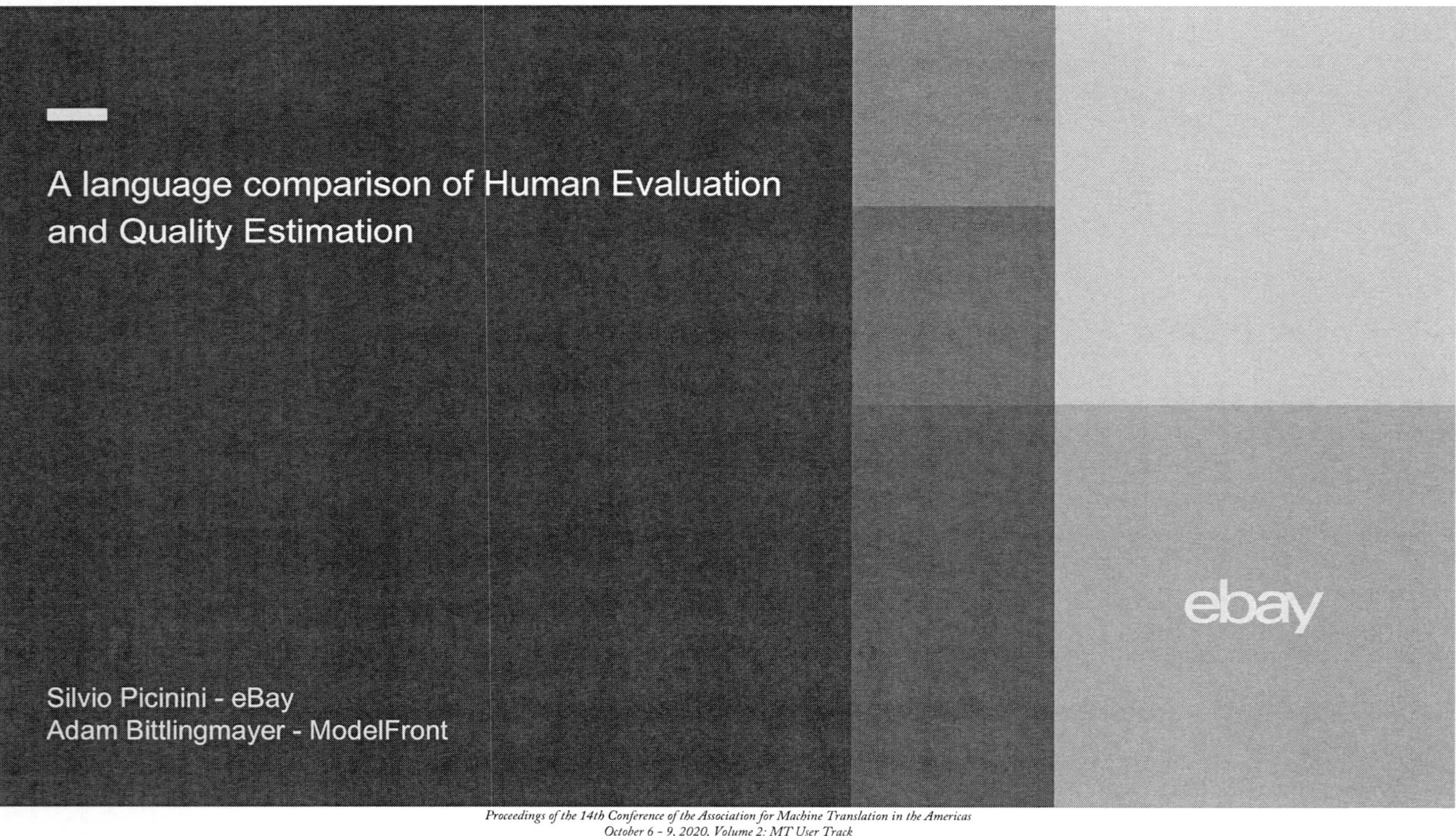

Proceedings of the 14th Conference of the Association for Machine Translation in the Americas
October 6 – 9, 2020, Volume 2: MT User Track

MT Quality

Human Evaluation	Quality Estimation
Quality scores by human linguists	Quality scores by machine
	No reference translation used
	Also called "confidence score" and "risk prediction"
	Aggregated for automatic quality *evaluation*

Proceedings of the 14th Conference of the Association for Machine Translation in the Americas
October 6 - 9, 2020, Volume 2: MT User Track

Goals

"How does machine QE correlate with human evaluation?"

- Compare line-level and aggregate numbers

"What causes differences between QE and human evaluation?"

- Analyse QE line-level issues

  - Get insights for QE

Proceedings of the 14th Conference of the Association for Machine Translation in the Americas
October 6 - 9, 2020, Volume 2: MT User Track

Human Evaluation

The content:

- 200 segments
  - Various lengths
  - With and without placeholders/tags
- 4 MT outputs per language - one customized
- 2 languages - pt-BR and es-CO

Three expert evaluators per language - reliable results

Scores range from 1 to 4 stars - normalized to 0-100

Quality Estimation

Generic production system - no custom data, no locales, no context, used for many use cases

Originally a Risk Prediction (0% good, 100% bad), which includes *source-side ambiguity*

Risk is reversed to become QE score (0 bad, 100 good)

Very convenient, but challenging for the QE system to match humans operating with many more inputs.

Proceedings of the 14th Conference of the Association for Machine Translation in the Americas
October 6 - 9, 2020, Volume 2: MT User Track

Numbers

Proceedings of the 14th Conference of the Association for Machine Translation in the Americas
October 6 - 9, 2020, Volume 2: MT User Track

Comparison for the set

QE for pt-BR was closer to the HE, es-CO was a little further

QE was close to the best HE and further away for the worse

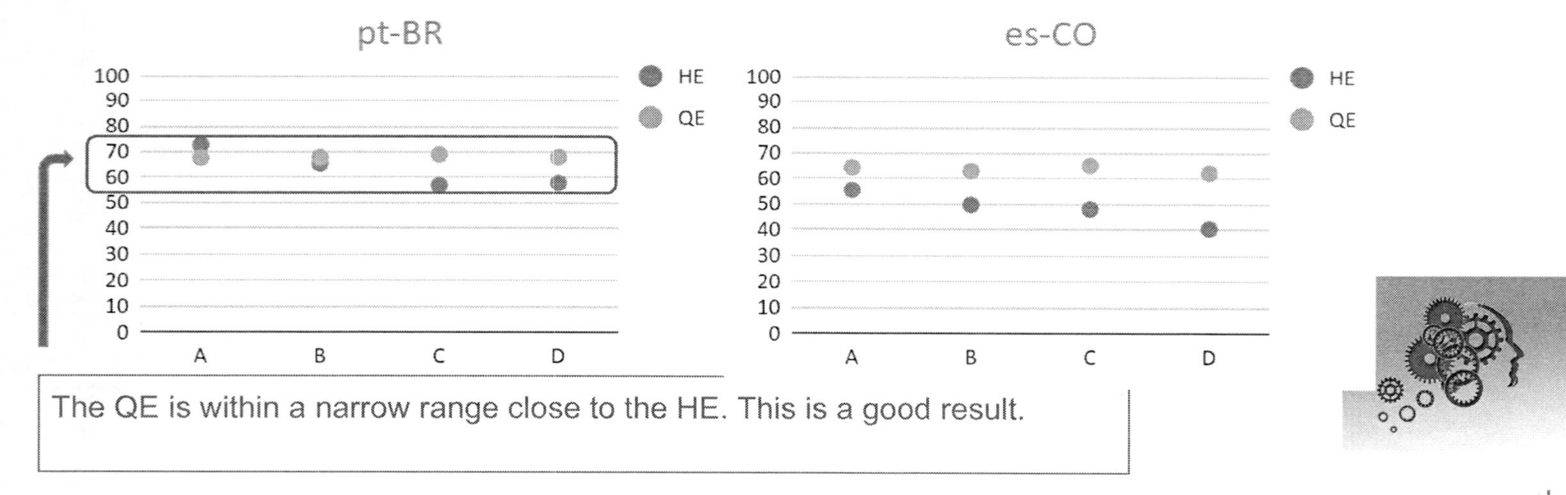

Proceedings of the 14th Conference of the Association for Machine Translation in the Americas
October 6 – 9, 2020, Volume 2: MT User Track

Comparison QE HE histograms - pt-BR

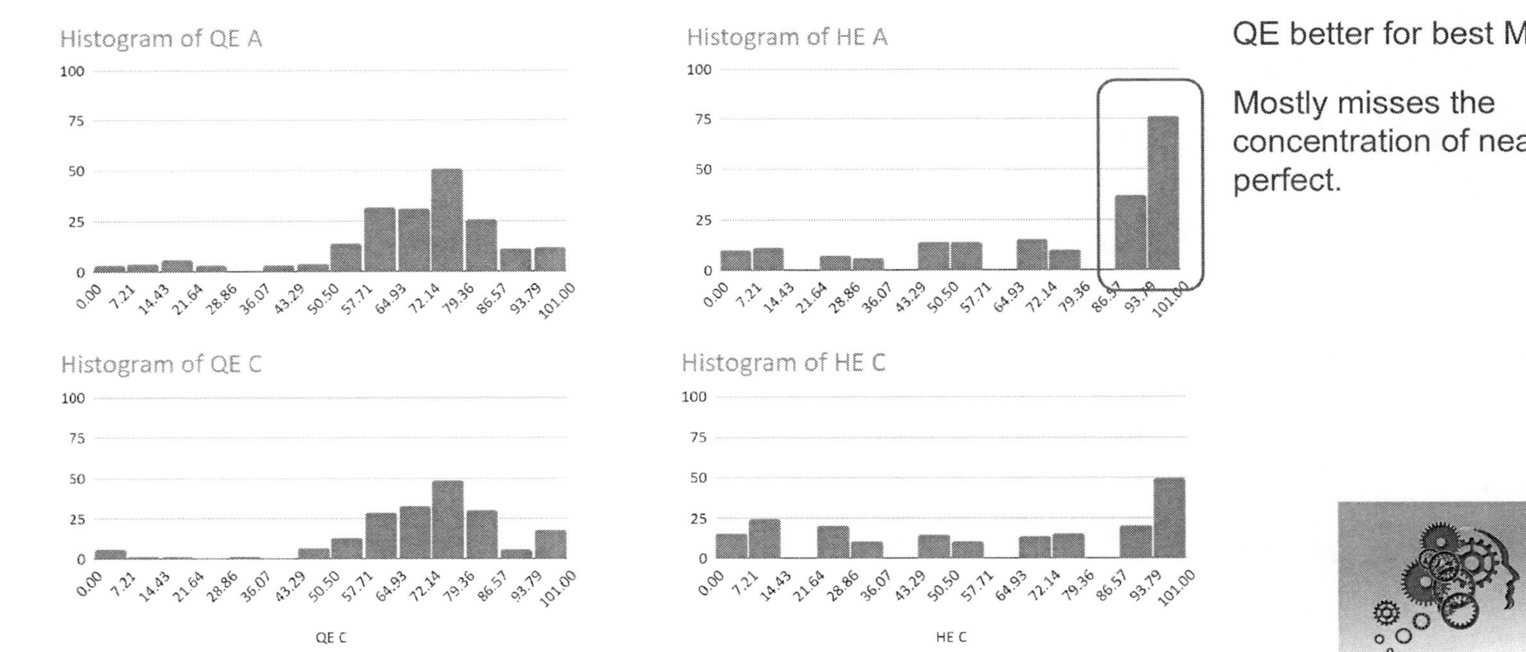

Proceedings of the 14th Conference of the Association for Machine Translation in the Americas
October 6 – 9, 2020, Volume 2: MT User Track

Comparison for Placeholders

HE had lower scores for segments with placeholders - in { } format

QE had higher results with placeholders

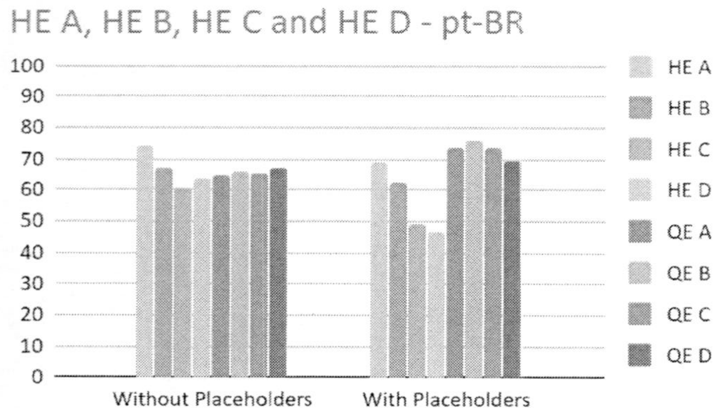

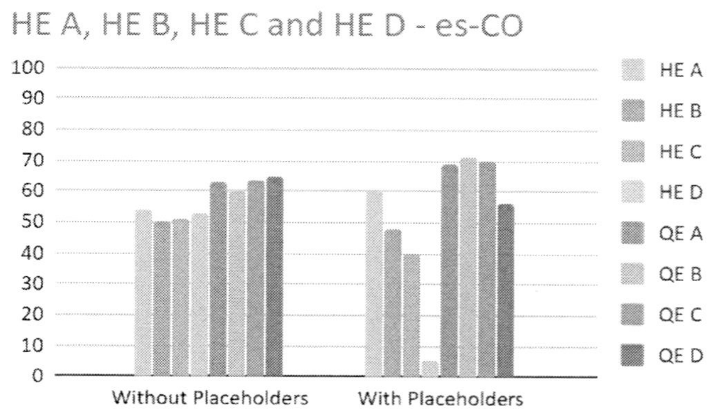

ebay

Comparison for differences HE - QE

QE in general overestimates the quality (most differences are negative)

The worst the HE, the greater the difference to the QE

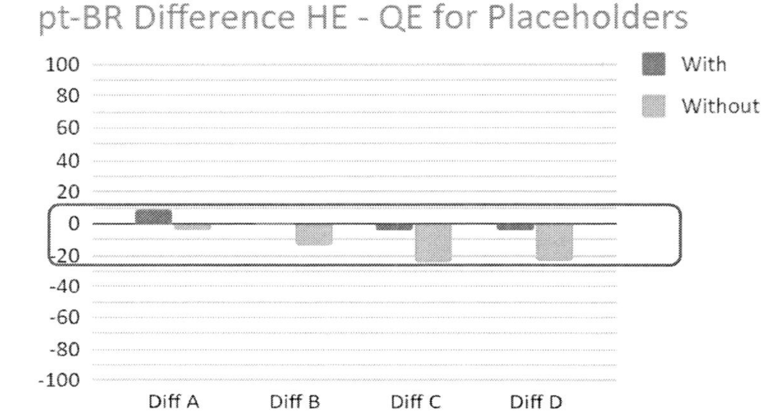

ebay

Proceedings of the 14th Conference of the Association for Machine Translation in the Americas
October 6 – 9, 2020, Volume 2: MT User Track

Comparison for Length

HE clearly scored Long < Med < Short

QE did not differentiate, but results for Short are close

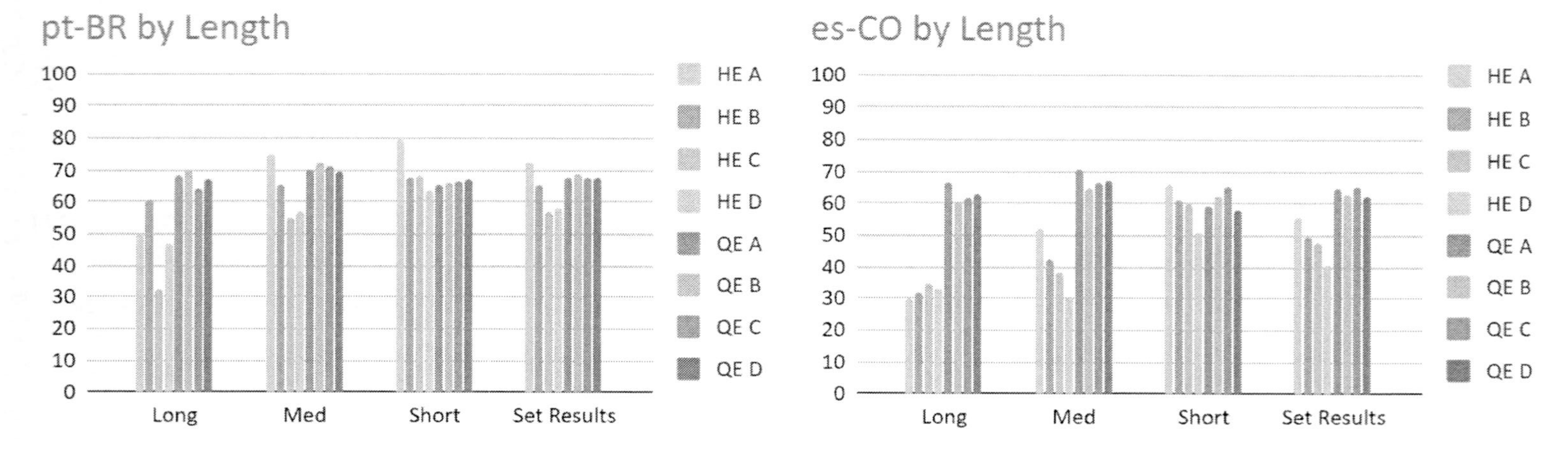

Language Issues

Proceedings of the 14th Conference of the Association for Machine Translation in the Americas
October 6 - 9, 2020, Volume 2: MT User Track

Language Issues

Where we looked:

- HE is much higher than QE - QE **underestimates** quality

- HE is much lower than QE - QE **overestimates** quality

- HE has a wide range of values among the 4 MT outputs (shows **varied translations**, from good to bad)

Examples

If we don't hear back, this request will be closed on {1} and the hold on this transaction will be removed.	Si no recibimos una respuesta, esta solicitud se cerrará el {1} y se borrará la cuenta de esta transacción.

Mistranslation: the meaning changed from "the hold on the transaction will be removed" (positive) to "the account will be erased" (negative).

HE:11
QE:89

The HE noticed that but the QE did not.

If we don't hear back, this request will be closed on {1} and the hold on this transaction will be removed.	Si no recibimos respuesta, esta solicitud se cerrará el {1} y se eliminará la retención de esta transacción.

Proceedings of the 14th Conference of the Association for Machine Translation in the Americas
October 6 – 9, 2020, Volume 2: MT User Track

Examples

Click to learn about Top Rated Sellers	Clique para saber mais sobre vendedores nível Top

Glossary SRC	Glossary TGT
Top Rated Seller	Vendedor nível Top

Terminology: eBay has a specific terminology for "Top Rated Seller", which includes the use of an "untranslated" word Top.

HE:92
QE:8

The QE may see this as a possible defect and rate the translation low. HE is aware that in our context the translation is perfect.

Examples

Silver shooting star for feedback score from 1,000,000 or more	Estrela de tiro de prata para a pontuação de feedback de 1 milhão ou mais

Idioms and figurative meaning:

The expression "shooting star" was translated as "a star of the activity of shooting a gun".

HE:11
QE:66

Basketball? Also a shooting star.

Proceedings of the 14th Conference of the Association for Machine Translation in the Americas
October 6 – 9, 2020, Volume 2: MT User Track

Examples

| {1}Not a registered user{2} | {1} Não é um utilizador registado {2} |

Locale: One MT is more influenced by data from European Portuguese. The MT above contains two examples of that.

HE:0
QE:81

| {1}Not a registered user{2} | {1}Não é um usuário cadastrado{2} |

Proceedings of the 14th Conference of the Association for Machine Translation in the Americas
October 6 – 9, 2020, Volume 2: MT User Track

Examples

A decision has been made about the dispute that was filed by {1}.	Uma decisão foi feita sobre A disputa que foi registrada em {1}.

Placeholders: they introduced an ambiguity for the MT, which was clear for HE. The source says "filed by {1}" and it means "filed by a person". The MT and the QE thought that it meant "filed by this date".

HE:0
QE:97

A decision has been made about the dispute that was filed by {1}.	Foi tomada uma decisão sobre a disputa que foi apresentada por {1}.

Examples

PostePay	Envío postal
PostePay	PostePay

Untranslatable:

The name of a service was translated as "Postal shipping".

The HE noticed that, the QE somewhat.

HE:0
QE:24

Proceedings of the 14th Conference of the Association for Machine Translation in the Americas
October 6 - 9, 2020, Volume 2: MT User Track

Examples

We're aware of this issue and are working to fix it as soon as possible.	Este problema y estamos tratando de solucionar el problema lo antes posible.

Omission:

The translation just says "This issue", omitting "We're aware of".

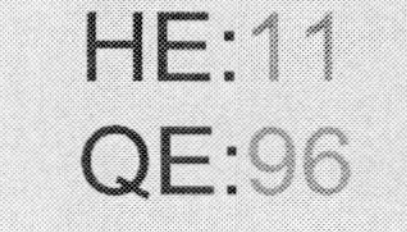

We're aware of this issue and are working to fix it as soon as possible.	Somos conscientes de este problema y estamos trabajando para solucionarlo lo antes posible.

Language Issues

What are some of the reasons for discrepancy between HE and QE?

- Mistranslations not recognized
- Terminology
- Idioms and figurative meaning
- Locale
- Placeholders
- Untranslatables
- Omissions

Proceedings of the 14th Conference of the Association for Machine Translation in the Americas
October 6 – 9, 2020, Volume 2: MT User Track

Takeaways

- The main generic QE system has aggregate scores in a similar range as HE. This is promising.

- Customization is key to QE for evaluation, to shape the output to the custom translation and evaluation guidelines

- Findings in custom data can help improve accuracy on non-custom errors

- QE is a rising technology that will be widely present in many MT uses in the near future

Future step: Use a trained engine

Proceedings of the 14th Conference of the Association for Machine Translation in the Americas
October 6 - 9, 2020, Volume 2: MT User Track

Acknowledgements

Our thanks to the language experts that worked on this:

Melany Laterman and Patricia Lawler

eBay Language Specialists

for Brazilian Portuguese and Latin American Spanish

Questions?

Proceedings of the 14th Conference of the Association for Machine Translation in the Americas
October 6 - 9, 2020, Volume 2: MT User Track

Proceedings of the 14th Conference of the Association for Machine Translation in the Americas
October 6 - 9, 2020, Volume 2: MT User Track

Machine Translation quality across demographic dialectical variation in Social Media

Adi Renduchintala and Dmitriy Genzel
Facebook AI

Proceedings of the 14th Conference of the Association for Machine Translation in the Americas
October 6 - 9, 2020, Volume 2: MT User Track

Biases in Machine Learning

- Machine learning systems can encode harmful societal biases.
- Widespread use of machine learning systems amplify these biases.

Proceedings of the 14th Conference of the Association for Machine Translation in the Americas
October 6 - 9, 2020, Volume 2: MT User Track

Biases in Machine Learning (in NLP)

- Machine learning systems can encode harmful societal biases
- Widespread use of machine learning systems amplify these biases.

$$\overrightarrow{\text{man}} - \overrightarrow{\text{woman}} \approx \overrightarrow{\text{computer programmer}} - \overrightarrow{\text{homemaker}}$$

Bolukbasi et al. Man is to Computer Programmer as Woman is to Homemaker? Debiasing Word Embeddings, Advances in neural information processing systems, 2016

Proceedings of the 14th Conference of the Association for Machine Translation in the Americas
October 6 - 9, 2020, Volume 2: MT User Track

Biases in Machine Learning (in Vision)

- Machine learning systems can encode harmful societal biases
- Widespread use of machine learning systems amplify these biases.

Study finds gender and skin-type bias in commercial artificial-intelligence systems

Examination of facial-analysis software shows error rate of 0.8 percent for light-skinned men, 34.7 percent for dark-skinned women.

http://gendershades.org/ &
news.mit.edu

Proceedings of the 14th Conference of the Association for Machine Translation in the Americas
October 6 - 9, 2020, Volume 2: MT User Track

Biases in Machine Learning (in Vision)

- Machine learning systems can encode harmful societal biases
- Widespread use of machine learning systems amplify these biases.

Study finds
commercial

Examination of fac
for light-skinned m

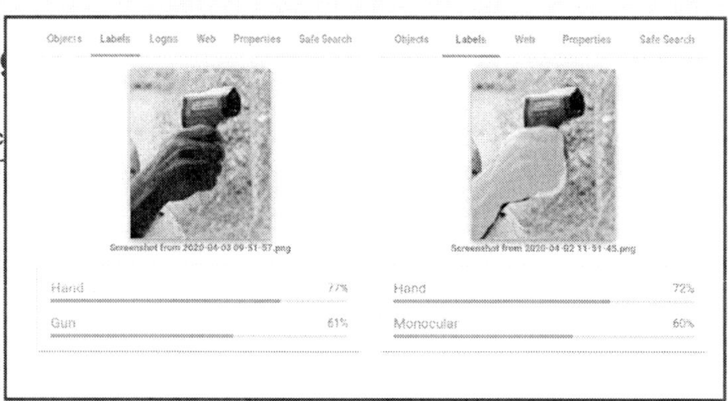

Image Credit:
@bjnagel &
algorithmwatch.org

Proceedings of the 14th Conference of the Association for Machine Translation in the Americas
October 6 - 9, 2020, Volume 2: MT User Track

Biases in Machine Learning (in Vision)

- Machine learning systems can encode harmful societal biases
- Widespread use of machine learning systems amplify these biases.

Proceedings of the 14th Conference of the Association for Machine Translation in the Americas
October 6 - 9, 2020, Volume 2: MT User Track

Biases in Machine Learning (in Vision)

- Machine learning systems can encode harmful societal biases
- Widespread use of machine learning systems amplify these biases.

Proceedings of the 14th Conference of the Association for Machine Translation in the Americas
October 6 - 9, 2020, Volume 2: MT User Track

Biases in Machine Learning (in Vision)

- Machine learning systems can encode harmful societal biases
- Widespread use of machine learning systems amplify these biases.

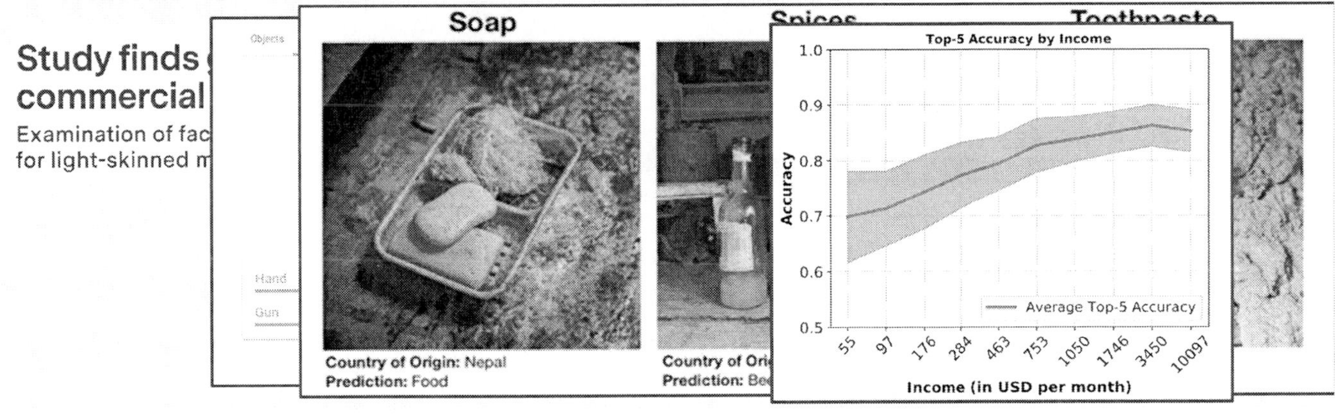

Proceedings of the 14th Conference of the Association for Machine Translation in the Americas
October 6 - 9, 2020, Volume 2: MT User Track

Biases in Machine Learning (in ASR)

- Machine learning systems can encode harmful societal biases
- Widespread use of machine learning systems amplify these biases.

There Is a Racial Divide in Speech-Recognition Systems, Researchers Say

Technology from Amazon, Apple, Google, IBM and Microsoft misidentified 35 percent of words from people who were black. White people fared much better.

Proceedings of the 14th Conference of the Association for Machine Translation in the Americas
October 6 - 9, 2020, Volume 2: MT User Track

Biases in Machine Learning (in MT?)

- Machine learning systems can encode harmful societal biases
- Widespread use of machine learning systems amplify these biases.

Goal: Investigate if modern machine translation systems amplify racial biases?

Proceedings of the 14th Conference of the Association for Machine Translation in the Americas
October 6 - 9, 2020, Volume 2: MT User Track

Proposal

- Use twitter posts which have demographic dialect information associated.
- Translate these tweets with 3 "off-the-shelf" machine translation models
- Do we notice disparity in translation quality?

Proceedings of the 14th Conference of the Association for Machine Translation in the Americas
October 6 - 9, 2020, Volume 2: MT User Track

Data

- We use data that was released in **prior work** by:
  - Blodgett, et al. *Demographic dialectal variation in social media: A case study of African-American English.* EMNLP, 2016
- This data was automatically annotated with racial dialectal labels by the same authors.

Proceedings of the 14th Conference of the Association for Machine Translation in the Americas
October 6 - 9, 2020, Volume 2: MT User Track

Data

- We use data that was released in prior work by:
  - Blodgett, et al. *Demographic dialectal variation in social media: A case study of African-American English.* EMNLP, 2016
- This data was ⚠️ **automatically annotated** ⚠️ with racial dialectal labels by the same authors.

Proceedings of the 14th Conference of the Association for Machine Translation in the Americas
October 6 - 9, 2020, Volume 2: MT User Track

Data

- We use data that was released in prior work by:
  - Blodgett, et al. *Demographic dialectal variation in social media: A case study of African-American English.* EMNLP 2016
- This data was ⚠ **automatically annotated** ⚠ with racial dialectal labels by the same authors.
  - A weakly supervised mixed-membership model was used.
  - The authors generated a posterior distribution over 4 categories for each tweet:
    - African-American English (AAE)
    - Hispanic English (H)
    - White-aligned English (W)
    - Other

Proceedings of the 14th Conference of the Association for Machine Translation in the Americas
October 6 - 9, 2020, Volume 2: MT User Track

Data

Examples	AAE	H	W
Either yu gone get yo fkn life or get out my fkn life	0.82	0.004	0.142
When you got somebody good, you hold on to ' em .	0.45	0.016	0.527
My sister asked me if the lions are in the playoffs..	0.011	0.023	0.965
I'm too sad to stay up and im tired and i have church so night	0.006	0.873	0.12

Proceedings of the 14th Conference of the Association for Machine Translation in the Americas
October 6 - 9, 2020, Volume 2: MT User Track

Profanity and Predictions

- The weakly supervised model seems to think that profanity is a feature of the AAE dialect.
- This is not observed in any of the other dialects.
- we filter out all tweets with profanity, to not be influenced by the weakly supervised model's (potentially) spurious correlations.

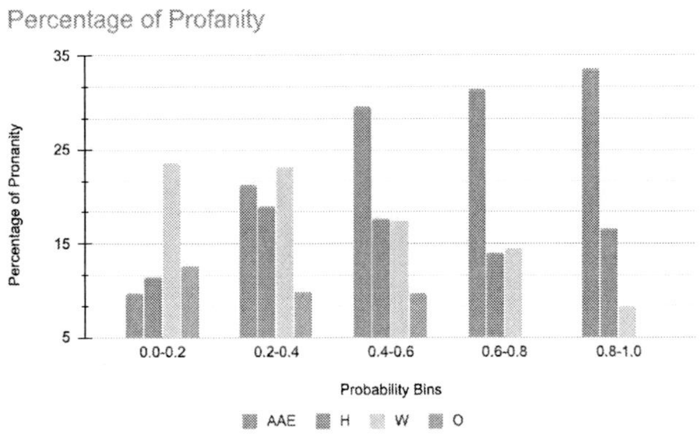

Proceedings of the 14th Conference of the Association for Machine Translation in the Americas
October 6 - 9, 2020, Volume 2: MT User Track

Data Challenges

- The dataset definitely has some flaws (correlating profanity with a demographic dialect is one example)
- However, the lack of expert annotated data to conduct analysis of this nature is also an issue.

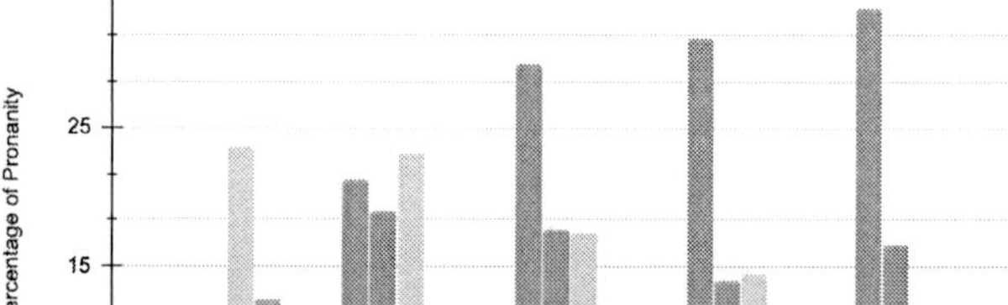

Experimental Setup

- For each category we subdivide the tweets into 5-bins based on the posterior probability (0.0 - 0.2, 0.2 - 0.4, … 0.8 - 1.0)
- From each bin in each category we sample ~30 tweets and have then translated into French by professional translators.
- We then used 3 "off-the-shelf" translation systems to translate the ~600 tweets using an English->French model.
- We plot the quality of the translation against the posterior probability of being a demographic category.

Proceedings of the 14th Conference of the Association for Machine Translation in the Americas
October 6 - 9, 2020, Volume 2: MT User Track

Results

- We plot BLEU/ (num. Reference-tokens) along the y-axis and the posterior probability of the tweet belonging to a demographic dialect category.

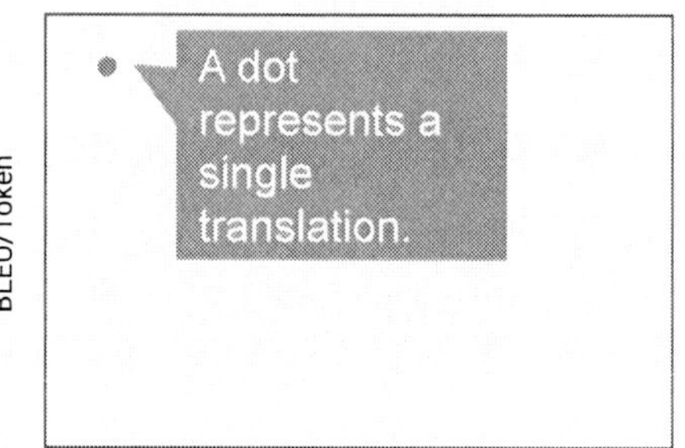

Results

- We plot BLEU/ num. Reference-tokens along the y-axis and the posterior probability of the text belonging to a demographic dialect category.

Results

- We plot BLEU/ num. Reference-tokens along the y-axis and the posterior probability of belonging to a demographic dialect category.

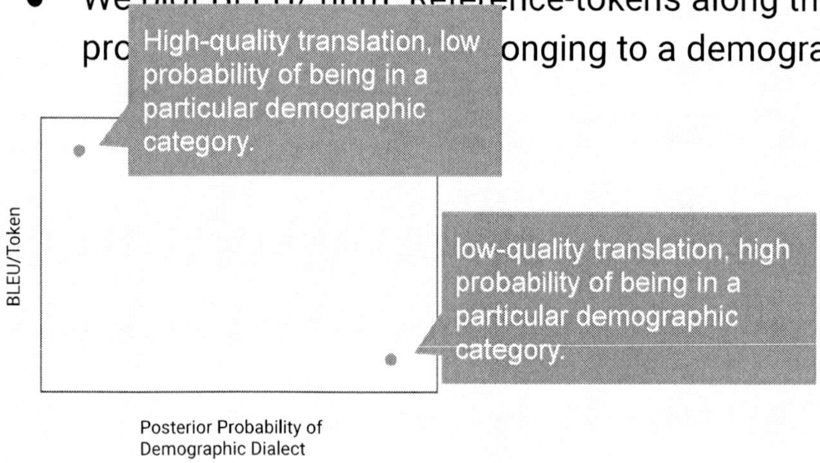

Results

- We plot BLEU/ num. Reference-tokens along the y-axis and the posterior probability of the tweet belonging to a demographic dialect category.

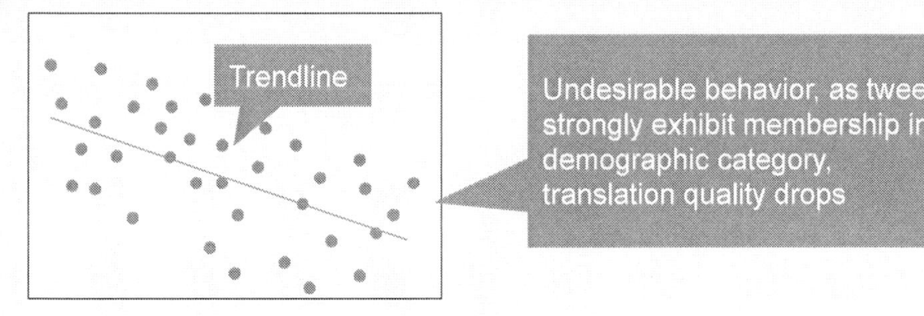

Proceedings of the 14th Conference of the Association for Machine Translation in the Americas
October 6 - 9, 2020, Volume 2: MT User Track

Results

- We plot BLEU/ num. Reference-tokens along the y-axis and the posterior probability of the tweet belonging to a demographic dialect category.

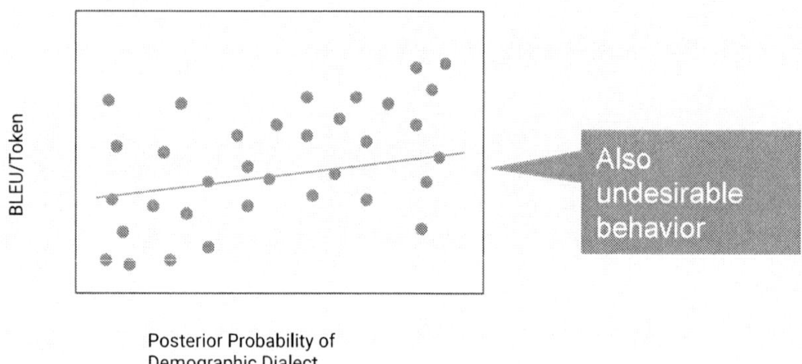

Proceedings of the 14th Conference of the Association for Machine Translation in the Americas
October 6 - 9, 2020, Volume 2: MT User Track

Results

- We plot BLEU/ num. Reference-tokens along the y-axis and the posterior probability of the tweet belonging to a demographic dialect category.

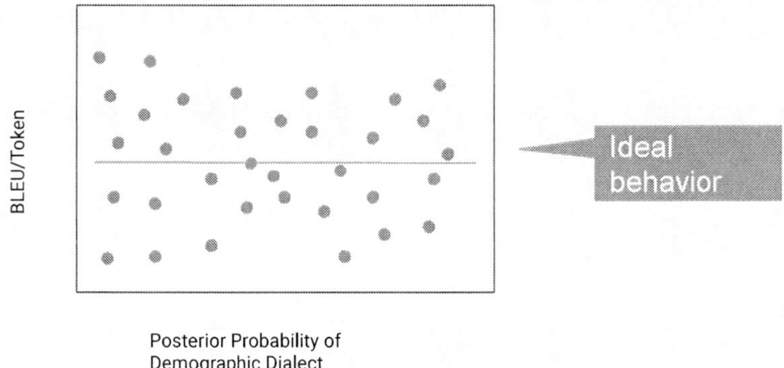

Proceedings of the 14th Conference of the Association for Machine Translation in the Americas
October 6 ~ 9, 2020, Volume 2: MT User Track

Results

System A. H

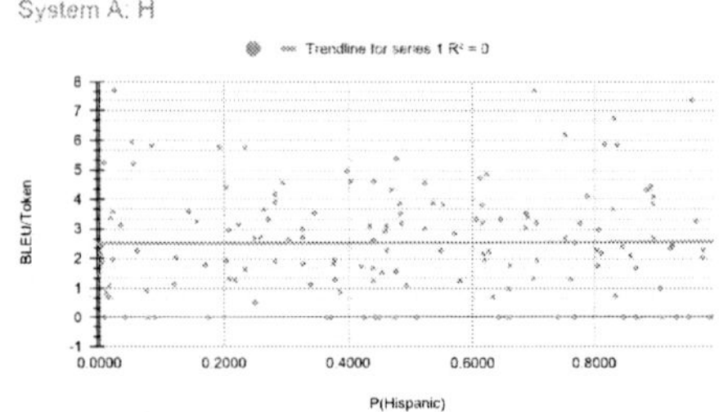

System A: AAE

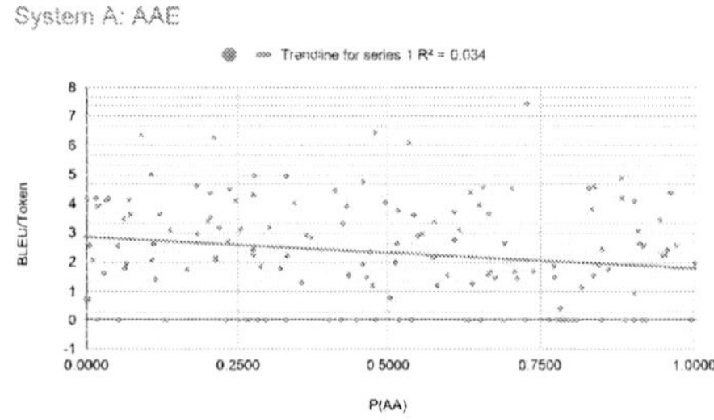

System A: W

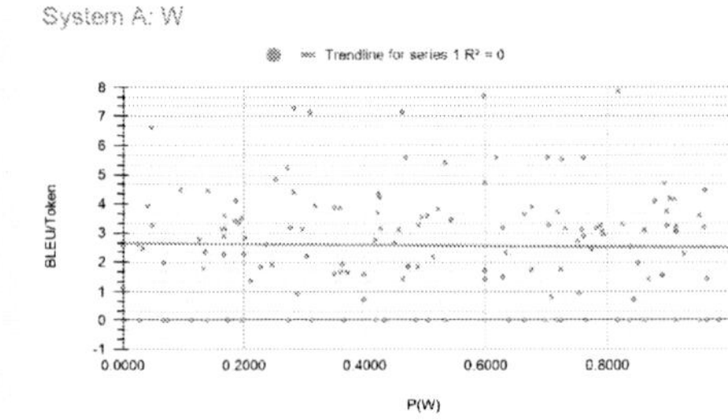

Results

System B: H

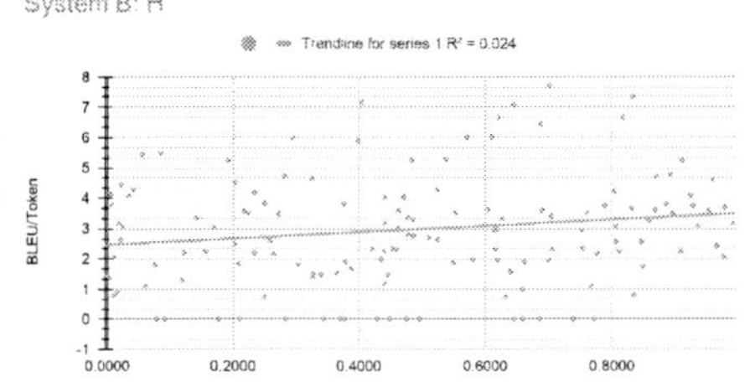

System B: AAE

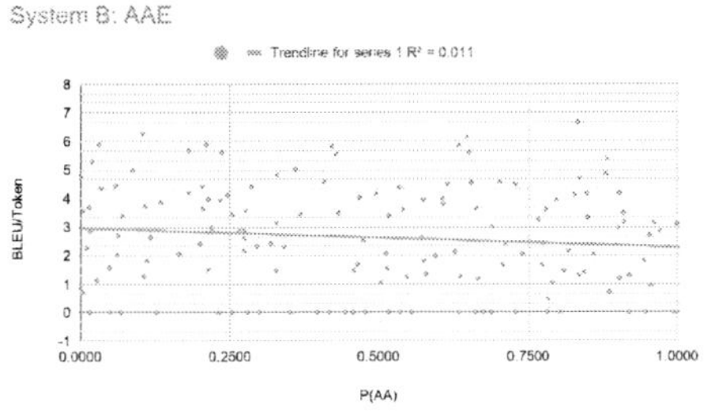

System B. W

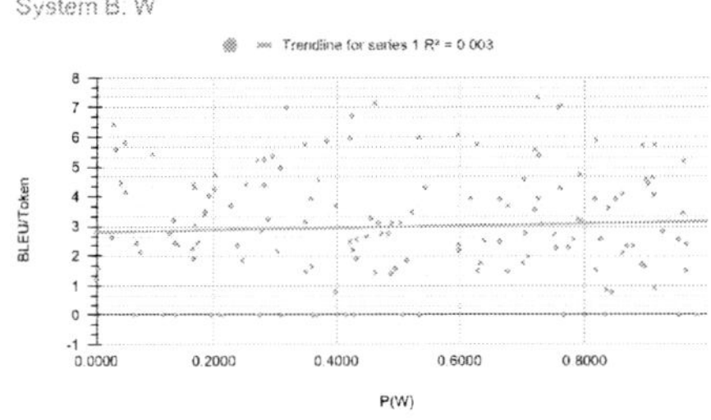

Results

System C: H

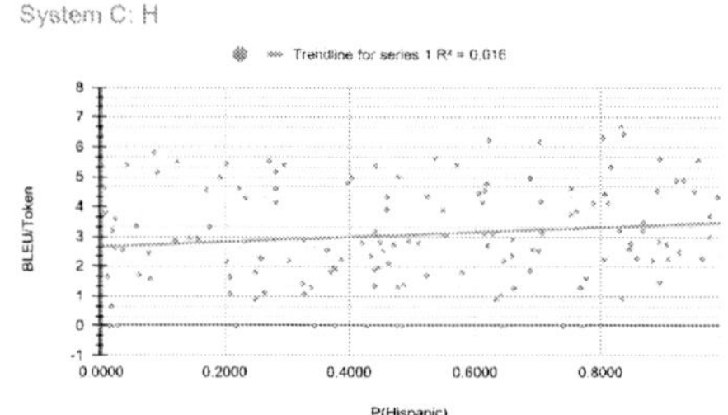

System C: AAE

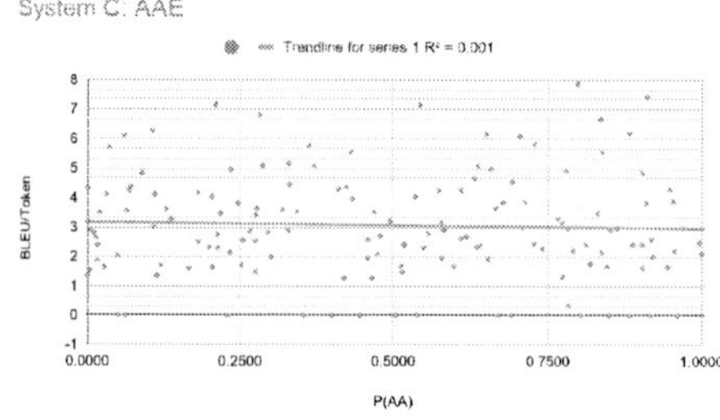

System C: W

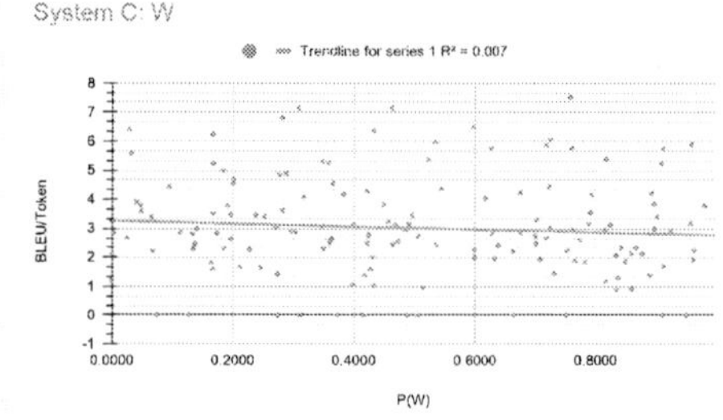

Proceedings of the 14th Conference of the Association for Machine Translation in the Americas
October 6 - 9, 2020. Volume 2: MT User Track

Conclusion

- Our experiments suggest that modern NMT systems exhibit undesirable behavior when dealing with input associated with AAE dialects.
- Further work is needed to understand this phenomenon better. Ideally, analysis should be conducted on expert annotated data.
- Our hope is that this work is a call to action to consider this a serious problem and mitigate the amplification of biases via AI systems.
- One concrete recommendation is to include analysis like this into model evaluation.

CAPITA Translation and interpreting Simplifying complex global communications

"Making the business case for adopting MT"

14th biennial conference of the AMTA

Rodrigo Cristina

October 2020

Delivering value.
Understanding ROI.

We understand

| The complexity of your organisation | The challenges to mitigate risk and avoid liability | The impact our work has on brand and reputation |

We drive cost efficiencies in everything that we do to make sure that you always achieve the expected return on your investment.

MT @ Capita TI - SmartMATE

CAPITA

Traditional Language Service Providers
- Low development capabilities
- Immature post editing language resources
- Low security

MT

Traditional MT Technology Providers
- Little or no language capabilities
- Low capitalisation - financially weak
- Little integration with translation workflows

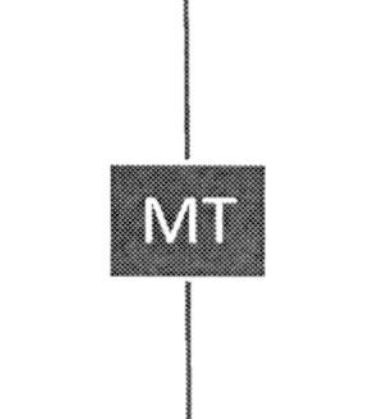

https://capitatranslationinterpreting.com

The omnipresent problem

Localization ROI is traditionally complex to measure, many times subjective

The budget holder and the localization manager don't always speak the same language

Tough and frustrating conversations to secure the budget
Localization is all about building bridges between people that speak different languages

Why not apply the same principle?

The NPV (Net Present Value) approach

- Investment analysis framework used since the 1950's
- The NPV is one of the most widely used tools in investment analysis.
- Quantifiable => better quality localization business cases
- Easier conversations and less frustration
- Potentially higher success rate
- Not the "silver bullet" but a clearer framework to discuss ROI for MT programs

"Win-Win"

CAPITA

I_0
initial investment
(The number to beat)

CF
Investment's annual net cashflow (revenues and savings – running costs)

$(1+RR)$
the discount factor; return rate of best available investment alternative

Net present value (NPV) is an investment analysis methodology that measures the difference between the initial project investment and the net present value of cash flows generated by that investment over a period of **time**, using the **DCF (Discounted Cash Flow)** methodology.

The following formula is used to calculate the NPV: $\displaystyle \text{NPV} = \sum_{t=1}^{n} \frac{CF_t}{(1+rr)^n} - I_0$

Decision criteria:
If NPV > 0 then invest
If NPV < 0 then do not invest

Time and DCF in the NPV model

- Time and DCF (Discounted Cash Flow) are key concepts in understanding the model's dynamic

- 1$ today is different from 1$ tomorrow (inflation, interest rate)

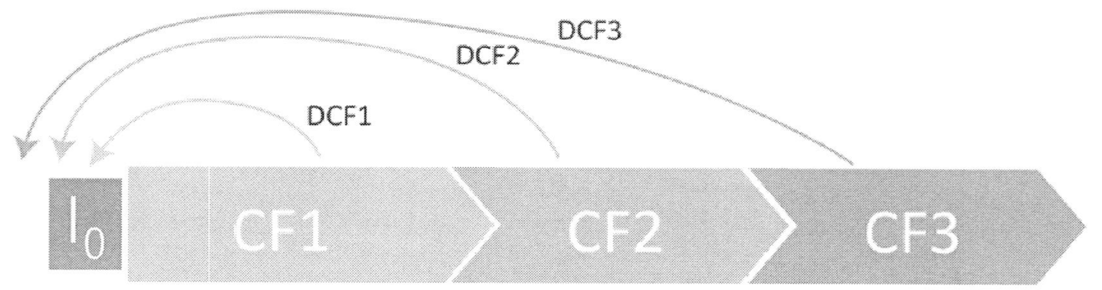

CAPITA

I_0
deployment investment for MT program

- Annual license for year 1
- Hosting costs year 1
- Software deployment costs
- Includes data cleansing and language asset optimisation (TMs, glossaries and monolingual content) and make them available for engine creation
- Includes building and setting up the engines for production and gisting purposes
- Includes testing and evaluating the best engine options (on real projects)
- Includes fine tuning the chosen engine before the "go live" stage
- Includes any integration required

CF
annual net cashflow (return and savings – running costs)

Return and savings:

- Includes the PEMT savings effect on current translation rates
- Includes the effect of faster time to market for your products that will generate more sales
- Includes savings based on an Enterprise MT service managed solution

Annual costs:

- Includes building new engines for new languages
- Includes retraining of the existing ones
- Add specific features (for example a specific glossary for a specific product line)
- Annual licenses for years 2 and 3
- Engine hosting for subsequent years

(1+RR)
return rate of best available option

What would you alternatively do with the funds available to optimise your localisation output and what return rate you would expect from it.

- For example, the cost of an authoring tool to improve TM matching that would save you 10%
- The estimated return of another (best) available MT option
- The estimated return of training the technical writing team to improve source content
- Return of cleaning and optimising the language assets (TMs, glossaries)
- Return of hiring additional internal translators

$$NPV = \frac{CF_1}{(1+rr)} + \frac{CF_2}{(1+rr)^2} + \frac{CF_3}{(1+rr)^3} - I_0$$

Like in any investment project, there are a number of assumptions we have to make, namely that the MT program will reach its maturity in 3 years. This is debatable but our data gives us some hints in that direction.

Decision criteria:

If NPV > 0 then invest on MT

If NPV < 0 then do not invest in MT

MT ROI measurement model – client case

CAPITA

Context:
- Large European Manufacturer with global footprint
- Mature and centralised localisation model
- Localising tech pubs content into 20+ languages
- Increasing volumes in top 10 languages
- Long-time user of a translation management system
- Mature terminology management (high quality glossaries)
- Large amount of content stored in translation memories
- TEP applied to technical content
- Average volume per language 800000 words
- TM leverage 68%
- New words: 32% of total
- Average NW rate 0.145$ + 5% PM fee (top 10 languages)

- **Evaluating deploying a global MT program across 10 of the 20 languages**
- **Evaluating other mutually exclusive investments (authoring tool and TM clean-up)**
- **Client wants to know the MT program's expected ROI => sell internally**

MT ROI measurement model – client case

CAPITA

I_0 – Initial investment

- Year 1 software license
- Client's language assets preparation, cleansing and optimisation
- Building several customised candidate engines
- Testing and evaluating engine performance - Automatic and Human evaluation (DQF)
- Detailed findings report
- Pre deployment systems configuration
- Engine deployment costs
- Total initial investment 93000$ (all languages)

CAPITA

MT ROI measurement model – client case

MT program Annual benefits and costs (Annual Net Cash Flow $)

Benefits (Cash inflow)
- Expected annual savings in NW rates through PEMT is 25% (92800$ across all 10 languages)
- LSP PM fee decrease from 5% to 3% (9540$ savings across all 10 languages)
- **Annual MT running benefits 102340$**

Costs (Cash outflow)
- MT license annual cost (unlimited use)
- Engine retraining (all 10 languages, once a year)
- Annual Hosting cost (10 engines)
- **Annual MT running costs 44000$**

Benefits of the alternative investment to MT program (discount factor rr in %)

- New authoring tool, will increase TM matching/leverage in 9%
- Major review/cleaning TMs and glossaries, estimated 13% more leverage from TMs
- 22% better matching is estimated to produce **8% of budget savings per language**

Proceedings of the 14th Conference of the Association for Machine Translation in the Americas
October 6 – 9, 2020, Volume 2: MT User Track

MT ROI measurement model – client case

CAPITA

$$NPV = \frac{CF_1}{(1+rr)} + \frac{CF_2}{(1+rr)^2} + \frac{CF_3}{(1+rr)^3} - I_0$$

$$NPV = \frac{(102340\$-44000\$)}{(1+8\%)} + \frac{(102340\$-44000\$))}{(1+8\%)^2} + \frac{(102340\$-44000\$))}{(1+8\%)^3} - 93000\$$$

$NPV = 57347.84\$$ (ROI for Global MT Program)

$NPV > 0$ the decision is to move ahead with the MT program

Notes:

rr is 8% and represents the expected return of the alternative investment

I_0 - All initial costs of the MT program

CF_1 (Savings – yearly costs) will be (102340\$–44000\$ = 58340\$)

CF_2 (Savings – yearly costs) will be (102340\$–44000\$ = 58340\$)

CF_3 (Savings – yearly costs) will be (102340\$–44000\$ = 58340\$)

CAPITA

CAPITA

Translation and interpreting — Simplifying complex global communications

THANK YOU!

 https://www.linkedin.com/in/rodrigo-cristina-3144377

 rodrigo.cristina@capita.com

https://capitatranslationinterpreting.com

Flexible Customization of a Single Neural Machine Translation System with Multi-dimensional Metadata Inputs

Evgeny Matusov, Patrick Wilken, Christian Herold
{ematusov,pwilken,cherold}@apptek.com
AppTek, Aachen, Germany

Abstract

Advances in neural machine translation (NMT) technology not only significantly raised machine translation quality for general-purpose, out-of-the-box systems, but also provided a way for additional input signals to an NMT model to effectively influence its output for a given translation unit, so that a single NMT system can serve different customer needs. At the same time, language service providers, media companies, and other businesses started to systematically store metadata associated with their translatable content. In this work, we show how these metadata can be used both for training and at inference time to flexibly customize a given NMT system to produce somewhat different translations of the same translation unit. The metadata as an extra input to NMT can enable such customization across multiple dimensions and at different levels of input granularity: for individual documents or their collections, for a given post-editing session of a professional translator, or even for individual sentences.

1 Introduction

The following meta-information can be "mixed in" to influence the translation output of a single neural machine translation system:

- Domain, genre, and topic can be provided either in terms of fixed labels (e.g. "patents", "contracts", "news"), or can be inferred as topic embeddings from the content of the given or similar document(s).

- In a multilingual NMT model, the language (variety) or dialect metadata not only augments the representation of corresponding input documents or sentences, but can also specify the desired target language or dialect. Post-editing tools can implement a flexible switch between supported languages/dialects for mixed-language text or speech input.

- Document-level context of different size (e.g. previous/next N sentences) can be "turned on" for better word disambiguation and pronoun resolution.

- Machine translation (MT) output length can be influenced without significant information loss. This is important in applications like subtitling and software localization where translations sometimes have to fit into a given fixed-size template.

- Translation style can be adjusted with a simple "switch" between (binary) classes (e.g. with/without profanities; informal vs. formal "you" forms in languages like German).

- The gender of the speaker/author may be important for a correct, unbiased translation in target languages like Czech where past tense verb forms have different endings depending whether a male or a female is talking about his or her actions. In speech translation, speaker gender labels can be inferred automatically from the upstream speech recognition. Post-editing applications can pre-fetch translations of all styles and genders so that a post-editor can instantaneously switch from e.g. a formal to informal translation with a single click.

- Finally, document- or user-specific terminology glossary entries can accompany each translation request to the NMT system so that for any matched source-language glossary entry it has to produce the translation from the glossary. The challenge here is how to generate this translation in a grammatically correct form, which is especially difficult for morphologically rich target languages.

All of these customizations of a single NMT model are very much suitable for commercial settings. Instead of deploying multiple different NMT models for each domain, style, length, dialect, etc., ideally we deploy a single system. Thus, not only we save on computational resources, reducing the environmental footprint of the MT technology. We also save time and machine and human power necessary for fine-tuning or otherwise adapting each of these customized systems, save on measures to counteract over-fitting, organization of parallel deployment and elaborate load balancing, etc.

In the following section, we will give an overview in which ways additional meta-information can flow into the training and inference of a single NMT system. In Section 3 we will revisit the above meta-information types and show, in many cases supported by experimental findings and/or examples, as well as citations of related work, the positive influence of meta-information on translation quality. We will also provide tips for a practical implementation of metadata-based "switches" in MT applications such as post-editing tools.

2   Using Meta-information for NMT Customization

The meta-information accompanying a source sentence or document can be incorporated into the NMT training in different ways.

The most straightforward way that does not require any changes to the NMT architecture is the use of source-side pseudo-tokens, usually in the beginning of a sentence, that correspond to a (discrete) meta-information. Pseudo-tokens are most widely used in multilingual systems (Johnson et al., 2017; Ha et al., 2016) with multiple target languages: the pseudo-token with the language code, such as @es@, signals that a translation into a particular language, in this case Spanish, is desired. Pseudo tokens were also successfully used for specifying the translation style (Sennrich et al., 2016) and for domain adaptation (Tars and Fishel, 2018). Alternatively, pseudo-tokens can be used as prefix constraints in the beginning of the (generated) target sentence (Takeno et al., 2017).

The disadvantage of pseudo-tokens is that they only encode one piece of information, and their influence on the produced NMT output is limited, especially in cases where the differentiating power of the additional meta-information is small, e.g. when the meta-information encodes domains/topics which are similar. In such cases it is advisable to use factored machine translation and encode the extra meta-information as an additional factor for each source word (García-Martínez et al., 2016; Wilken and Matusov, 2019). In this way, the meta-information will have a stronger influence, since the NMT encoder would then be able to learn for which words the meta-information factor is more important than for the other words. For some types of meta-information, like speaker gender, the factor (e.g. male/female gender) can be assigned to the relevant words only (e.g. personal pronouns and verbs whose translation may be different depending on the speaker/author gender). All other words in this case can be assigned a third, "neutral" value.

When the meta-information about a sentence or document is automatically predicted with a certain probability, it is advisable to directly include this probability into the NMT training. Thus, in case of genre prediction, assuming 20 different genres, the additional input can be a 20-dimensional vector with probabilities for each genre given the input source sentence or document. This dense representation can then be associated with a genre embedding and included in the NMT architecture in a variety of ways, e.g. via a separate attention component to the genre/topic embedding. A stronger influence of meta-information on the decoder can be achieved by concatenating each current state with the genre/topic embedding before the next decoder state is predicted. Details can be found e.g. in (Chen et al., 2016).

At inference time, we assume that the extra meta-data is provided by the user/customer or is automatically generated by an upstream component (such as speaker gender classifier or a topic classifier). At training time, the meta-information can also be already available (e.g. domain of a document or a whole collection of documents, language or language variety, or even style). This is especially true of recent customer-specific data, since a lot of companies, language service providers in particular, have started to pay attention to consistent storage of meta-data that accompanies their translation content. Other types of meta-information can be directly computed for each pair of parallel sentences in the training data, like the length ratio between the source and the target sentence which can be used to classify translations into short, medium-length, and long (see Section 4). Or, it can be derived using regular expressions or more complex tools such as syntactic parsers and part-of-speech taggers. A "garbage" class can be assigned to sentences which do not match any of the regular expressions. See Section 3.1 for more details.

For more complex types of meta-information that is not available for a given set of parallel training sentence pairs, a classifier can be trained that predicts this information either on the sentence-level or document-level. To reduce error propagation, the vector of posterior probabilities for all the predicted classes can be directly used in NMT as opposed to the first-best predicted label. For example, the genre and topic of a document can be predicted automatically with a trained classifier, but also e.g. its dialect or language variety. External monolingual labeled data can be used to select the label set and train the classifier. Usually, the classifier is trained for the source language so that it can be applied both at training time and at inference time as described above. More elaborate approaches such as the work of Zeng et al. (2018) jointly model NMT with monolingual attention-based classification tasks (in this particular case, domain classification).

3   Types of Customization

3.1   Style

The style or tone of a translation is very important for its acceptance. Thus, it is not appropriate to use an informal style in legal documents, etc. At the same time, a formal, polite style can not be used in translations of movie dialogs, chat messages, and other cases with colloquial language.

A single NMT system can be trained to support multiple styles. In what style the translation is generated depends on the additional input (selector) from the user, also called side constraints (Sennrich et al., 2016; Feely et al., 2019). In our experiments with English as the source language, we differentiated in particular between a formal style that uses a polite version of the second-person pronoun "you" (which is different from the informal pronoun in many languages such as German, Russian, French, Greek, etc.). The parallel training data was partitioned into 3 classes based on whether the formal or informal version of the pronoun was used in the target language sentence, or none at all. For corpora where document identity was available

System	BLEU [%]
AppTek baseline	27.9
AppTek style token informal	28.7
AppTek style token formal	26.7
On-line G 2020-06-18	21.8
On-line B 2020-06-18	27.3

Table 1: BLEU scores in % on an English-to-Greek subtitle test set of 50K running words, 5.5K sentences (held-out for the AppTek systems).

source	I am at your service.
formal	Ich stehe **Ihnen** zu Diensten.
informal	Ich stehe zu **deinen** Diensten.
source	I see you all are interested in media and subtitling.
formal	Ich sehe, **Sie** alle interessieren sich für Medien und Untertitelung.
informal	Ich sehe, **ihr seid** alle an Medien und Untertitelung interessiert.
source	Please hold the balls in your hands.
formal	Bitte **halten Sie** die **Bälle** in **Ihren** Händen.
informal	Bitte **halte** die **Eier** in **deinen** Händen.

Table 2: Translation examples for English-to-German NMT with formal vs. informal meta-information provided as pseudo-tokens. All of the NMT-generated translations are correct for these examples.

for each sentence, we assigned the whole document to the formal/informal class if the majority of its target sentences contained the formal/informal pronoun. This is a simple, yet effective rule-based approach; for a more sophisticated method, cf. (Niu and Carpuat, 2019).

We experimented with two language pairs: English-to-German and English-to-Greek. In both cases we used state-of-the-art NMT systems trained with Transformer architectures using millions of sentence pairs. For English-to-Greek, the MT quality as measured with the BLEU score (Papineni et al., 2002) on a held-out test set of movie subtitles (Table 1) shows that our systems compare favorably to two major online translation providers. The style information was provided to the system as a pseudo-token (one of 3) both at training and at inference time. At inference time, we always used either the formal or the informal pseudo-token for all sentences in the test set. Since the test set mostly includes popular movies with informal style, the improvement in BLEU when using the informal style token was expected.

We let a professional Greek-native translator check the output of the baseline system that does not use style tokens, compared to the systems that use the formal or informal style token. This was done on a subset of a held-out subtitle file that contains informal dialogs. Whereas no quantitative evaluation was conducted, the translator noted a generally good quality of all outputs. She found that the grammatical part of style adaptation, i.e. the correct second-person pronouns, seemed to work, with the formal version using mostly the formal form, correctly per the style chosen, despite the informal material it was applied on. She also noted that "the vocabulary choices in the MT output depending on the style chosen were fascinating". This underlines the other interesting aspect of style transfer: although not explicitly modelled when partitioning the training data, the vocabulary choice for the informal vs. formal style seems to correlate with the usage of the second-person pronouns.

Similar findings were made for English-to-German. Examples of formal vs. informal style are given in Table 2. Note that both singular and plural second-person pronouns (including

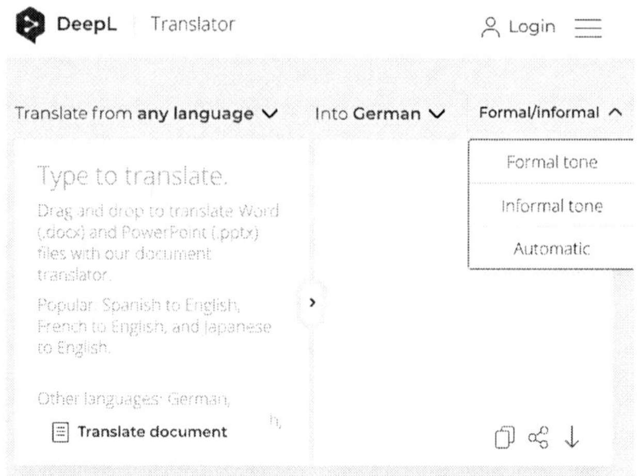

Figure 1: An example of a style switch menu in the on-line UI of the MT provider deepl.com (screenshot from August 28, 2020).

possessive ones) are translated correctly w.r.t. the requested style (Ihnen vs. deinen, Sie vs. ihr), correct auxiliary verb forms corresponding to these pronouns are used. The sentence structure is in some cases significantly different. The last anecdotal example in Table 2 where in case of the informal style the English word "balls" is translated in its profane meaning into "Eier" shows that style adaptation and transfer is also about lexical choice and meaning disambiguation. In particular, it is also possible to introduce additional constraints on the style, e.g. informal without obscene language, informal with obscene language, etc.

In practical applications of post-editing by professional translators the information about style can be provided for the whole document in advance before NMT is used to translate the document. However, in many cases style can change within a given document. For example, subtitles of a given film can include formal dialogs using the polite form of "you" as well as informal dialogs (or dialogs with a child) using the informal second-person pronouns. A button in the user interface can be implemented to help the post-editor instantly switch the translation of a single sentence to a different style when he or she notices such style changes. Of course, multiple translations for different styles would have to be pre-fetched in the background in order for this to work seamlessly.

Buttons or menu items for style switches in on-line translation tools for free text translation have started to appear already, as illustrated in Figure 1.

3.2 Domain, Genre and Topic

Domain, genre, and topic are almost synonyms in the sense that they refer to sometimes minuscule, sometimes large differences in content, combined with stylistic differences which are much harder to grasp or explain than the formal/informal style differences. Yet any information about such "world context" that goes beyond the context of the given and surrounding sentences is very important for correct translation, both by humans and by machines. For some genres it is all about correct terminology translation, whereas for others the differences are more subtle.

Usually, no fixed definitions or taxonomy of domains and genres are available. Nevertheless, the sources of monolingual and bilingual data often give a hint at the genre and domain. Yet in many cases especially the parallel data is crawled from multiple sources, often individ-

source	You need an **apple product** to obtain the best shape.
prose	Du brauchst ein **Apfelprodukt**, um die beste Form zu bekommen.
manuals	Sie brauchen ein **Apple-Produkt**, um die beste Form zu erhalten.
source	The bushing 20 is inserted in a **hole** 21 of the cover 12 of the **base** 11.
news texts	Die Buchse 20 wird in ein **Loch** 21 des Deckels 12 der **Basis** 11 eingesetzt.
patents	Die Buchse 20 ist in eine **Bohrung** 21 des Deckels 12 des **Sockels** 11 eingesetzt.
source	He came here to look for **food**.
documentary	Er kam her, um nach **Nahrung** zu suchen.
talks	Er kam her, um nach **Essen** zu suchen.

Table 3: Examples of translations by the same NMT system which change depending on additional meta-information about the input genre (English-to-German).

ual sentence pairs are taken from an unknown bilingual document or are even extracted from non-parallel, comparable corpora. Furthermore, genre can slightly vary even within a single document, or can be a new genre that has traces of the previously observed genres. Also, we would like that at inference time the genre/domain is either provided by the user, or automatically predicted for a given input sentence or document, or is not provided (and then the NMT system falls back to genre-agnostic translation). Most closely related work to our approach is by Kobus et al. (2017).

In our experiments, we decided to focus on genres. Some of them were defined in international MT research projects like GALE (Olive et al., 2011): newswire text, web (blog) text, broadcast news and conversations. We identified further genres based on the available English data. These include chat messages and comments, e-commerce product descriptions, customer product reviews, subtitles (film dialogs), documentary subtitles, emails, government texts, legal texts, software and hardware manuals, marketing material, military-related texts, non-fiction books, fiction (prose), poetry, patents, religious texts, educational (school) material, scientific texts including research papers, as well as parliamentary speeches and public talks.

We sampled 10M English sentences per genre and trained a bidirectional 1-layer LSTM classifier to predict the genre labels on a sentence level. The classifier obtained an accuracy of 77% on a held-out set of 6000 sentences that contained 250 sentences of each genre.

As mentioned in Section 2, the best way to integrate the genre information would be to change the architecture to include the predicted genre distribution as an embedding vector. In preliminary experiments, however, we converted this prediction into a single label using a heuristic – if a single label was predicted with a probability of more than 0.5, we assigned this label to a given training sentence pair. In cases when none of the labels had such a high probability, we assigned a "no genre" label. We then used this label as a pseudo-token similarly to the style pseudo-tokens described in Section 3.1.

We trained an English-to-German system with genre pseudo-tokens and first verified that its quality as measured with BLEU on multiple test sets with different domains did not significantly degrade as compared to a baseline system that does not use any pseudo-tokens. For this sanity check, we prepended each sentence with the "no genre" pseudo-token. Then, we manually checked the system performance on a number of examples.

Generally, the effect of using just the pseudo token was minimal - the translation in many cases remained the same. That is why in our future work we would like to explore a stronger signal from the predicted genre distribution. However, if there was significant change in the output, it was always in the right direction for our examples, as can be observed in Table 3. In some cases, though, a more fine-grained distinction between genres may be desirable, leading to prediction of a topic distribution/profile of a given sentence or document. For instance, to

System	BLEU [%]
baseline	35.5
concatenate in training	36.3
concatenate in training + inference	37.0
on-line G 2020-06-18	33.2
on-line D 2020-08-12	34.9

Table 4: Translation results for MT with extended context on the English-to-German subtitle test set of 2378 sentences, 18K running words.

disambiguate the translation of "Apple" it is not enough to know whether the system deals with prose or marketing content, since in almost all of the defined genres both the fruit and the brand meaning can occur with high frequency. Topic modeling usually requires unsupervised clustering methods to obtain the right number of topics with as little overlap in their distributed representations as possible. In some applications like e-commerce, however, fine-grained topic taxonomies are already defined (e.g. for product categories and sub-categories) and can be used directly as supervising labels (Chen et al., 2016).

3.3 Extended Context

Topic modeling flows into the research on extended context for NMT and is related to document-level translation. Recently, there have been advances in this area, showing that additional context in the form of encoded previous and subsequent sentences from the same document is beneficial for improved MT quality (Werlen et al., 2018; Kim et al., 2019). In particular it can help with pronoun resolution (Müller et al., 2018). We argue that it is also possible to train a single NMT system that can either consume the additional context or can translate a single sentence without it, depending on the user request.

Table 4 summarizes the results of our experiments for English-to-German. In all cases we follow the simple concatenation approaches of Tiedemann and Scherrer (2017) and Junczys-Dowmunt (2019). We concatenate subsequent sentences appearing consecutively in the same document (subtitles for a single film) if the resulting sequence does not exceed a certain number of tokens (50). Multiple sentences on source and target side are concatenated using a special symbol `@sep@` so that the NMT system learns to generate such separator symbols. The concatenated data is added to the original training data; thus some of the sentences appear in the training data twice: on their own and concatenated with surrounding sentences. The test data is augmented in a similar way, except every sentence is translated exactly once.

AppTek's baseline state-of-the-art English-to-German system was trained on ca. 20M sentence pairs, including subtitle data. As can be inferred from Table 4, its performance on a held-out subtitle test set is better in terms of BLEU than when translating with two major on-line MT services. After augmentation via concatenation of some of the sentences which had document information associated with them, the total number of lines in the training data increased to 39M.

We observed significant increases in BLEU from doing the concatenation in training only, which shows that the proposed method does not harm the baseline translation quality. When short sentences are concatenated at inference time, the translation quality increases further. A detailed analysis of sentences of different lengths showed that in particular translations of very short segments benefited from the context of the previous and next sentences. The absolute BLEU improvement for sentences of length one (individual words) was 11% absolute, and for sentences of length from 2 to 9 words it was 2% absolute. But even for long sentences, a marginal BLEU score improvement was observed.

source	I found a watch and returned it to the owner.
pseudo-token male	Našel jsem hodinky a vrátil je majiteli.
pseudo-token female	Našla jsem hodinky a vrátila je majiteli.

Table 5: An example of two translations into Czech of the same sentence by a single NMT system, the first time with the gender meta-information "male", the second time with the gender meta-information "female".

For real-life use, this means that an MT application can be programmed to use the additional document-level context (or simply put, the context of the surrounding sentences) on demand, when the context of a given sentence is not enough as determined by some objective criterion, the simplest of which can be input sentence length.

3.4 Speaker/Author Gender

In some languages, the morphological realizations of certain parts-of-speech depend on the gender of the speaker/author. Examples include past-tense singular verb forms in Russian, Czech, etc. When translating from languages such as English where this is mostly not the case, the NMT system chooses one of the gender-specific forms. With the absence of supporting gender-relevant context (e.g. "she said" vs. "he said"), it makes its decision mostly based on the examples that were observed in training. Usually, but not always, the training data is biased towards male word forms. Biased or not, however, an incorrect word form in the automatically generated translation is annoying and yet hard to fix; it can appear again and again throughout a given text or speech that, for instance, is a first-person narrative with many forms starting with the pronoun "I".

To explicitly use the information about the speaker or the author, we again propose to partition the training data into "male", "female", and "neutral" sentence pairs depending whether or not the corresponding male or female word forms are used throughout the target sentence (almost) exclusively. We realize that such a method requires many heuristics, but in the absence of data labeled with speaker gender that was used in related research of Vanmassenhove et al. (2018) it is difficult to come up with a better solution.

So far, we conducted only preliminary experiments for English-to-Czech, using 3 types of pseudo-tokens as described above. Table 5 shows an example where the correct gender forms are used in the Czech translation when the information about gender is provided to the system. This is a step in the right direction. We envision that especially for applications involving speech translation, speaker gender can be automatically predicted with high confidence and passed on to NMT for use as an additional signal. Also, in personalized translation applications, the correct gender can be set by the app user, and then her/his texts and messages would be translated from English using the right gender form of a given target language.

3.5 Length

In some applications it is desirable to control the length of MT output, as measured in words or characters, while minimizing any information loss. For instance, subtitle templates are usually created in the source language and have a fixed number of subtitles with a fixed duration of their appearance on the screen. Thus, a translation of a sentence in a subtitle that is significantly longer than the original sentence can only be inserted without changing the template by using more than the allowed number of lines per subtitle (usually two). This means that a faster reading speed is necessary to finish reading the text before the subtitle disappears, and should be avoided as much as possible. That is why shorter translations (from English) are preferred.

Another application is translation of user interface elements/menus in a software compo-

source	¿No te vas a sentir incómodo?
baseline	You're not gonna feel uncomfortable?
shortened	Won't you be uneasy?
source	Se llevan muy bien y la verdad es que me da mucha pena.
baseline	They get along very well, and the truth is, I feel very sorry for them.
shortened	They get along very well and I'm really sorry.
source	De ninguna manera me sentiré incómodo ni tengo problema en verla.
baseline	There's no way I'm gonna feel uncomfortable and I don't have a problem seeing her.
shortened	There's no way I'll feel uncomfortable or have a problem seeing her.

Table 6: Examples of translations shortened by N-best list rescoring aimed at penalizing long translations (Spanish-to-English subtitles).

nent. There, the maximum length may be technically limited by the width of the menu or a text field.

A number of research publications appeared recently which target length control, starting with the seminal work on length control in encoder-decoder architectures by Kikuchi et al. (2016). In (Lakew et al., 2019), the pseudo-tokens for short, medium, and long translations are assigned at training time. These labels are derived from the length ratios between each training source sentence and its target language translation. At inference time, the user provides the desired label, e.g. requesting a short translation. An approach with length constraints learned end-to-end in an unsupervised way is presented by (Niehues, 2020).

Another method that we tested tailored specifically to subtitle translation is to re-score the N-best output of the NMT system using a linear combination of the original NMT model score and a score derived from the the length of an N-best list hypothesis and the duration of the subtitle in which the source sentence, and thus also its translation, is to appear on the screen.

Since for judging the translation quality in cases of e.g. shortened MT output it is not reasonable to use the original reference translations created without such length constraints for computation of automatic MT error measures, we only conducted a small-scale manual evaluation of the resulting output.

We translated the content of 64 subtitles from Spanish to English with AppTek's state-of-the-art NMT system, performing N-best list rescoring aimed at penalizing all translations with a reading speed of 17 chars or more per second[1]. As a result, the average reading speed of the file reduced from 19.3 to 17.23 chars/s and the number of frames with a reading speed of more than 20 chars/s dropped from 33 to 13.

A professional translator noted that the shorter automatic translation versions "are mostly great, exactly what a subtitler would do". In very few cases, they do change the meaning, which is not acceptable, but can usually be fixed by quick post-editing.

Table 6 shows examples of translations shortened with the above approach, for which the meaning of the translation did not change.

3.6 Language Variety and Multilinguality

Multilingual NMT systems have shown to be effective in using parallel training data from high-resource language pairs to improve the quality of translation from or to a low-resource language (Firat et al., 2016; Johnson et al., 2017).

In case of multiple target languages, it is often sufficient to use a pseudo-token at the beginning of the source sentence that signals to what language it should be translated. With this

---

[1] The reading speed is defined as the subtitle length in characters (e.g. a maximum of 2 lines with a maximum of 42 characters per line) divided by the subtitle duration (usually 2-5 seconds).

simple approach, already an acceptable level of MT quality can be reached. Thus, a multilingual system can be viewed also a customization of a single NMT system with meta-information about the target language.

At AppTek, we use the multilingual approach also for language varieties or dialects, following also the work of Lakew et al. (2018). The main challenge is how to partition the training data: in most cases no reliable information about the used dialect is available, and automatic dialect prediction is a hard task. Following a pragmatic approach for English-to-Spanish translation of movie subtitles, we labeled those film subtitles in the training data as European Spanish which contained words and phrases used only in Spain. The rest was labeled as Latin American Spanish. We then trained a multilingual system with the two labels. Our customers can choose the language variety via an API parameter and obtain a possibly different translation for a given sentence using the same system. More details can be found in Matusov et al. (2019).

In case of multilingual, dialectal, or even mixed-language input, it is possible to train an NMT model which is sensitive to the meta-information about the input language or dialect. Again, in practical applications, such as computer-assisted translation from Arabic to English, a general translation can be generated prior to post-editing (assuming e.g. Modern Standard Arabic or MSA), together with translations for (a subset of) the Arabic dialects. Then, the professional translator can change the MT in the post-editing window when she or he notices that the language switched from MSA to a dialect. This can happen in particular when someone's dialectal speech is quoted in a news article written in MSA.

At the same time, for such multilingual or multi-dialect many-to-one systems it is advisable to use a "garbage" label which is associated randomly with a subset of the training data in any language or dialect. Providing this label may help when the dialect or language of the input is not known, or it is a mixed-language input. For instance, AppTek's multilingual NMT system that can translate from any of 12 Slavic languages into English is also able to translate mixed-language sentences like the following one which is a mix of Ukrainian and Russian (typical for messages and speech of a significant part of the population of Ukraine). Хлопці были у меня дома, но про дівчин они ничего не пліткували is correctly translated as "The boys were at my house, but they didn't say anything about the girls." (Ukrainian words in the otherwise Russian sentence are Хлопці, дівчин, and пліткували).

3.7 Glossaries

Terminology glossary entries or translation memory matches can accompany each translation request to an NMT system so that for any matched entry the translation from the glossary is forced to be used in-context in the MT system output. This so called glossary transfer or override is another user-specific customization of a given NMT system and can be implemented in professional post-editing UIs by e.g. giving the user the possibility to upload a glossary prior to populating the output window with the automatic translation. In other cases the glossary can be automatically created in a computer-assisted translation environment by memorizing past user translation corrections and choices.

In its simplest form, glossary transfer "as is", i.e. the exact copy of the target side of the glossary entry, is implemented using placeholder tokens. In training, a source word or phrase is replaced by such a placeholder token; the same token replaces the (consecutive sequence of) words in the target sentence which are word-aligned to this particular source word or phrase. If there are multiple replacements within a given sentence pair, different placeholder tokens are used. Thus, a system learns to translate (and thus also correctly position, if reordering is involved) a given placeholder token to itself in all cases.

At inference time, a matched glossary entry in the source sentence is replaced with such a placeholder token in preprocessing, and then the same token in the generated translation is replaced with the target side of the corresponding glossary entry in postprocessing. The obvious disadvantage of this approach is that the context in the form of the glossary entry itself is lost during translation, since it is generalized to the placeholder token.

More complex algorithms involve encoding of the desired target translation in the source sentence using special markers (Dinu et al., 2019). Other methods try to use constrained decoding (Hasler et al., 2018) or NMT-internal attention mechanisms to override the translation of the next word if the current focus of the attention is on the corresponding matched source glossary entry (Dahlmann et al., 2017). With such approaches it is not guaranteed that the desired translation from the glossary will be used, but at the same time, it is possible that the system will learn that the glossary translation has to be used in a morphological form that is different from the (base) form present in the glossary because of the surrounding context.

To illustrate the basic approach and the challenges that the more advanced approaches can rarely master, we present two examples. In the first one, the sentence `Jack, when are you going back to Vienna?` is correctly translated into German as `Jack, wann fahren Sie zurück nach Wien?`. However, this translation is not correct if Vienna is referring to a city in the United States. Here, the simple approach of the "as is" glossary override via placeholder tokens can already enforce a glossary entry `Vienna → Vienna`. In the second example for English-to-Russian translation, the sentence `The Hatter put the Dormouse's head in a teapot and winked to the March Hare` from *Alice in Wonderland* by Lewis Carol can be translated with the help of the following glossary[2]:

```
Doormouse == Sonya
March Hare == Martovskiy Zayats
Hatter == Shlyapnik
```

However, the Russian translations of these fictional characters are given in the nominative case, whereas in a translation of the sentence some of them must be used in other cases with different suffixes/endings: "Shlyapnik polozhil golovu Son**i** v chainik i podmignul Martovsk**omu** Zayt**su**". The changed suffixes are marked in bold. To the best of our knowledge, state-of-the-art glossary transfer methods for NMT are not able to satisfactorily address this task of glossary override for morphologically rich languages, which opens up possibilities for future work.

4 Conclusion

In this paper, we provided an overview of different customization opportunities so that a single neural machine translation system can be trained to accept additional meta-information as input and thus produce different translations of a given sentence based on the additional metadata. We showed how meta-information about style, genre, topic, and speaker/author gender can be obtained from customer databases or derived automatically, and then used in training and at inference to produce better, in-context translations with correct style, grammar, and correct word sense disambiguation. We discussed how extra context in the form of surrounding sentences from the same document can be "turned on" to improve the translation of a given sentence. Furthermore, we showed that translation length can be effectively controlled if necessary without significant information loss. We also showed how customization works in the context of multilinguality, language varieties and dialects, and even mixed-language input. Finally, we elaborated on the practical applications of single customizable NMT systems in several usage scenarios, with focus on user interfaces for efficient MT post-editing.

Of course, it is possible to combine all or some of the different types of metadata inputs described in this paper in a single NMT system. Our future plans are to train such a system and successfully use it for AppTek's customers.

---

[2] Transliteration of Russian is used here for better understanding.

References

Chen, W., Matusov, E., Khadivi, S., and Peter, J.-T. (2016). Guided alignment training for topic-aware neural machine translation. *AMTA 2016, Vol.*, page 121.

Dahlmann, L., Matusov, E., Petrushkov, P., and Khadivi, S. (2017). Neural machine translation leveraging phrase-based models in a hybrid search. In *Proceedings of the 2017 Conference on Empirical Methods in Natural Language Processing*, pages 1411–1420, Copenhagen, Denmark. Association for Computational Linguistics.

Dinu, G., Mathur, P., Federico, M., and Al-Onaizan, Y. (2019). Training neural machine translation to apply terminology constraints. In *Proceedings of the 57th Annual Meeting of the Association for Computational Linguistics*, pages 3063–3068, Florence, Italy. Association for Computational Linguistics.

Feely, W., Hasler, E., and de Gispert, A. (2019). Controlling Japanese honorifics in English-to-Japanese neural machine translation. In *Proceedings of the 6th Workshop on Asian Translation*, pages 45–53, Hong Kong, China. Association for Computational Linguistics.

Firat, O., Cho, K., and Bengio, Y. (2016). Multi-way, multilingual neural machine translation with a shared attention mechanism. In *Proceedings of the 2016 Conference of the North American Chapter of the Association for Computational Linguistics: Human Language Technologies*, pages 866–875.

García-Martínez, M., Barrault, L., and Bougares, F. (2016). Factored neural machine translation architectures. In *International Workshop on Spoken Language Translation (IWSLT'16)*.

Ha, T.-L., Niehues, J., and Waibel, A. (2016). Toward multilingual neural machine translation with universal encoder and decoder. In *International Workshop on Spoken Language Translation (IWSLT'16)*.

Hasler, E., de Gispert, A., Iglesias, G., and Byrne, B. (2018). Neural machine translation decoding with terminology constraints. In *Proceedings of the 2018 Conference of the North American Chapter of the Association for Computational Linguistics: Human Language Technologies, Volume 2 (Short Papers)*, pages 506–512, New Orleans, Louisiana. Association for Computational Linguistics.

Johnson, M., Schuster, M., Le, Q. V., Krikun, M., Wu, Y., Chen, Z., Thorat, N., Viégas, F., Wattenberg, M., Corrado, G., et al. (2017). Google's multilingual neural machine translation system: Enabling zero-shot translation. *Transactions of the Association for Computational Linguistics*, 5:339–351.

Junczys-Dowmunt, M. (2019). Microsoft Translator at WMT 2019: Towards large-scale document-level neural machine translation. In *Proceedings of the Fourth Conference on Machine Translation (Volume 2: Shared Task Papers, Day 1)*, pages 225–233.

Kikuchi, Y., Neubig, G., Sasano, R., Takamura, H., and Okumura, M. (2016). Controlling output length in neural encoder-decoders. In *Proceedings of the 2016 Conference on Empirical Methods in Natural Language Processing*, pages 1328–1338, Austin, Texas. Association for Computational Linguistics.

Kim, Y., Tran, D. T., and Ney, H. (2019). When and why is document-level context useful in neural machine translation? In *Proceedings of the Fourth Workshop on Discourse in Machine Translation (DiscoMT 2019)*, pages 24–34.

Kobus, C., Crego, J., and Senellart, J. (2017). Domain control for neural machine translation. In *Proceedings of the International Conference Recent Advances in Natural Language Processing, RANLP 2017*, pages 372–378, Varna, Bulgaria. INCOMA Ltd.

Lakew, S. M., Di Gangi, M. A., and Federico, M. (2019). Controlling the output length of neural machine translation. In *16th International Workshop on Spoken Language Translation*.

Lakew, S. M., Erofeeva, A., and Federico, M. (2018). Neural machine translation into language varieties. In *Proceedings of the Third Conference on Machine Translation: Research Papers*, pages 156–164, Brussels, Belgium. Association for Computational Linguistics.

Matusov, E., Wilken, P., and Georgakopoulou, Y. (2019). Customizing neural machine translation for subtitling. In *Proceedings of the Fourth Conference on Machine Translation (Volume 1: Research Papers)*, pages 82–93, Florence, Italy. Association for Computational Linguistics.

Müller, M., Gonzales, A. R., Voita, E., and Sennrich, R. (2018). A large-scale test set for the evaluation of context-aware pronoun translation in neural machine translation. In *Proceedings of the Third Conference on Machine Translation: Research Papers*, pages 61–72.

Niehues, J. (2020). Machine translation with unsupervised length-constraints. *arXiv preprint arXiv:2004.03176*.

Niu, X. and Carpuat, M. (2019). Controlling neural machine translation formality with synthetic supervision. *arXiv preprint arXiv:1911.08706*.

Olive, J., Christianson, C., and McCary, J. (2011). *Handbook of natural language processing and machine translation: DARPA global autonomous language exploitation*. Springer Science & Business Media.

Papineni, K., Roukos, S., Ward, T., and Zhu, W.-J. (2002). BLEU: a Method for Automatic Evaluation of Machine Translation. In *Proceedings of the 41st Annual Meeting of the Association for Computational Linguistics*, pages 311–318, Philadelphia, Pennsylvania, USA.

Sennrich, R., Haddow, B., and Birch, A. (2016). Controlling politeness in neural machine translation via side constraints. In *Proceedings of the 2016 Conference of the North American Chapter of the Association for Computational Linguistics: Human Language Technologies*, pages 35–40.

Takeno, S., Nagata, M., and Yamamoto, K. (2017). Controlling target features in neural machine translation via prefix constraints. In *Proceedings of the 4th Workshop on Asian Translation (WAT2017)*, pages 55–63, Taipei, Taiwan. Asian Federation of Natural Language Processing.

Tars, S. and Fishel, M. (2018). Multi-domain neural machine translation. *arXiv preprint arXiv:1805.02282*.

Tiedemann, J. and Scherrer, Y. (2017). Neural machine translation with extended context. In *Proceedings of the Third Workshop on Discourse in Machine Translation*, pages 82–92.

Vanmassenhove, E., Hardmeier, C., and Way, A. (2018). Getting gender right in neural machine translation. In *Proceedings of the 2018 Conference on Empirical Methods in Natural Language Processing*, pages 3003–3008.

Werlen, L. M., Ram, D., Pappas, N., and Henderson, J. (2018). Document-level neural machine translation with hierarchical attention networks. In *Proceedings of the 2018 Conference on Empirical Methods in Natural Language Processing*, pages 2947–2954.

Wilken, P. and Matusov, E. (2019). Novel applications of factored neural machine translation. *arXiv preprint arXiv:1910.03912*.

Zeng, J., Su, J., Wen, H., Liu, Y., Xie, J., Yin, Y., and Zhao, J. (2018). Multi-domain neural machine translation with word-level domain context discrimination. In *Proceedings of the 2018 Conference on Empirical Methods in Natural Language Processing*, pages 447–457, Brussels, Belgium. Association for Computational Linguistics.

Customized Neural Machine Translation Systems for the Swiss Legal Domain

Rubén Martínez Domínguez   ruben.martinez@tilde.com
Matīss Rikters   matiss.rikters@tilde.lv
Artūrs Vasiļevskis   arturs.vasilevskis@tilde.com
Mārcis Pinnis   marcis.pinnis@tilde.com
Tilde, Vienības gatve 75A, Riga, Latvia, LV-1004

Paula Reichenberg   paula.reichenberg@hieronymus.ch
Hieronymus, Stauffacherstrasse 100 CH-8004 Zürich, Switzerland

Abstract

This paper describes Tilde's work on the development of a Neural Machine Translation (NMT) platform for Hieronymus, a Switzerland-based boutique legal and financial translation provider, giving particular attention to the increase in efficiency as regards internal translation processes, as well as NMT's impact on the customer experience of their partners. The NMT tool was developed by combining a set of domain-adapted NMT systems with a customized translation platform, both of which were built and developed by Tilde. The central aim of the solution is to assist Hieronymus translators and to create LexMachina, a secure, do-it-yourself NMT solution for Swiss lawyers. The current paper outlines the workflow used to collect, filter, clean, normalize, and pre-process data for the NMT systems, as well as the methods utilized to train and adapt the NMT systems for Hieronymus. The current paper also sheds light on the needs of Tilde's partner, from approaches to resolving the challenges they faced to the implementation process itself.

1 Introduction

As a steadily growing company in a highly competitive language service industry, Tilde's partner, Hieronymus[1], was eager to adopt an innovative Neural Machine Translation (NMT) strategy to ensure its long-term growth while vastly improving the translation customer experience, as well as gaining the loyalty of their customers via a 'self-service' tool made to cover their needs. Much to their surprise the absence of readily available solutions on the market coupled with the Swiss-specific language context posed considerable challenges when adopting the chosen NMT strategy. Namely, language tools and NMT systems required by Hieronymus had to account for the linguistic specifics of Switzerland's local languages: Swiss-German, Swiss-French and Swiss-Italian. Unsurprisingly, most of the parallel data available for NMT training is in standard German, French, and Italian. Furthermore, Hieronymus' interests lie translation for highly-technical domains: criminal law, tax law, banking, and finance. The NMT systems used by Hieronymus must therefore be able to deliver reliable and trustworthy translations of highly technical domain-specific terminology. Additionally, the NMT systems must be fully integrated into their translation workflows, so as to boost both the internal and external opera-

---

[1] www.hieronymus.ch

tional efficiency. The NMT integration sought to provide Hieronymus with a competitive edge by streamlining the translation processes while enhancing quality and terminological accuracy.

Another priority of Hieronymus' NMT development was to offer a new product to their clients, mainly law firms, it being a way to enhance the customer experience. Central to this new product was a self-service legal machine translation infrastructure that their partners could independently access with the guarantee of full confidentiality and the "Swiss touch"—two essential elements for Hieronymus' clients.

With the above elements in mind, Tilde combined its language and client-oriented approach with the latest, AI-driven natural language processing technology to develop *Lex-Machina* [2]. The development of LexMachina was a joint effort between Tilde and Hieronymus, where much attention was placed on the selection and preparation of the right data, as well as the testing and improvement of the same. *LexMachina* is a customized translation platform that guarantees the security and confidentiality throughout the translation process. It has been launched as a collection of 10 customized NMT systems and will be extended to include new domain-specific NMT systems in the near future.

The platform is based on the Tilde MT platform (Pinnis et al., 2018) and LetsMT technology (Vasiļjevs et al., 2012). It supports multiple input formats and maintains tag and formatting integrity when translating documents. Additionally, the translation platform integrates Hieronymus translation memories (TMs), supports integration of NMT systems into the most commonly used computer-assisted translation (CAT) tools, and allows for integration of the NMT engines into Microsoft Outlook. As a result, the *LexMachina* platform allows Swiss lawyers to instantly translate legal documents in the necessary confidential environment while reaping the benefits of customized NMT technologies. The solution developed by Tilde and Hieronymus may also be adapted to the specific needs of Swiss banks, insurance companies and major advisory and accounting companies.

All NMT systems were tailor-made to conform to Hieronymus' requirements regarding Swiss local language and domain-specific terminology. To that end, we set out to acquire, classify, and align Swiss domain data, reviewing the main details and preparing the correct training formula for the customization thereafter. As a result, alongside Hieronymus, we developed generic Swiss legal engines. Further development on this project will see the release of additional Swiss legal engines specialized in various sub-domains (criminal law, financial law, tax law, etc.).

The current paper describes the development of *LexMachina*, and how Hieronymus leveraged their machine translation capability to increase both productivity and efficiency, allowing them to streamline translation processes and become the first provider to offer a do-it-yourself, legal machine translation solution for Swiss lawyers. In presenting this use case, we bring to light the details of the technological, infrastructural, and linguistic challenges we have experienced, and indeed overcome, while creating and implementing this NMT project. The application of the developed NMT systems aim at facilitating the vision of Tilde's partner, and enable the desired innovation with the creation of customized NMT systems and a self-service translation platform.

2 Requirements

Hieronymus' demand for NMT solutions were not satisfied with those currently available on the market. Most available engines are based on standard German, French, and Italian, omitting essential local elements such as punctuation, vocabulary, lexicon, style, register, grammar structure, and terminology. These differences between Swiss local and standard languages were of particular concern to Hieronymus' customers, among which are local law firms, banks, in-

---

[2] www.lex-machina.ch

surance companies, and other financial institutions, all of which consider the accuracy of terminology essential.

Thus Hieronymus presented Tilde with a list of requirements that the NMT and translation platform had to meet to be considered adapted to their customers' needs. These needs were primarily a question of data; the NMT systems should be built using in-domain terminology, such as legislative acts and laws, and financial and tax content, adapting them to the specificities of the Swiss-German, Swiss-French, and Swiss-Italian languages.

Due to the nature of work of Hieronymus' customers, all information and documents had to be translated securely. Specifically, it was paramount that the MT system guarantee the confidentiality of sensitive data at all times, and that all data be stored within a Swiss infrastructure environment never to be transferred outside of Switzerland. To reinforce the confidentiality of the translation process, the NMT engines and the *LexMachina* translation platform are hosted in a secure, Swiss-based cloud environment controlled by Hieronymus.

To address the above requirements, Tilde and Hieronymus developed *LexMachina*. *LexMachina* is a set of adapted NMT systems which are integrated into a customized translation platform based on Tilde's MT platform. *LexMachina* provides the following functionalities:

- translation of text snippets (words, sentences, up to several paragraphs);

- translation of documents by preserving formatting and document formats;

- translation of websites by preserving website structure and design;

- CAT tool plug-ins for SDL Tradus Studio and Wordbee.

3 Machine Translation Systems

A typical development cycle of domain-specific MT systems involves MT training on general domain data and adaptation on domain-specific data. The Hieronymus case is different, as the final quality and appropriateness of the MT systems depend not only on their ability to translate domain-specific texts, but also on their being tailored to Swiss language specificities. The following section (3.1) describes how we tackled additional challenges posed by data sparsity, which is result of both occupying a niche domain and Swiss language needs.

3.1 Data Collection

To develop NMT systems for the Swiss legal domain, we used three types of data:

- **Publicly available parallel corpora**. Most publicly available parallel data comprise texts in standard French, Italian, and German. These data are not necessarily of Swiss origin and usually do not contain texts of Swiss German, Swiss Italian, and Swiss French. However, such data are available in large proportions and can help to form baseline models. The largest of such is available from the DGT Translation Memories (Steinberger et al., 2012), Digital Corpus of the European Parliament (Hajlaoui et al., 2014), the Tilde MODEL corpus (Rozis and Skadiņš, 2017), Europarl (Koehn, 2005), and other sources available from the Tilde Data Library[3].

- **Parallel data crawled and extracted from legal-domain Web sites** of institutions of Swiss origin. Having four official languages, many Swiss institutions provide multilingual information on their Websites, making it a valuable asset for machine translation. Therefore, we crawled public institution websites using a parallel data crawler, downloaded

---

[3]https://www.tilde.com/products-and-services/data-library

monolingual documents, and performed cross-lingual alignment with consecutive parallel data extraction to acquire parallel corpora.

- **Translation memories from Tilde's partner**. The in-domain data that were used to fine-tune NMT systems were provided by Hieronymus, thereby ensuring that the trained NMT systems are tailored specifically to the Swiss language context.

3.2 NMT System Training and Domain Adaptation

For the training of NMT models, we use the Marian NMT toolkit (Junczys-Dowmunt et al., 2018) as it provides the most efficient implementation for training and inference of any standard NMT model. We use Marian's standard configuration[4] of the *transformer-base* model (Vaswani et al., 2017). We select training batch sizes dynamically so that they fit in a workspace of 9,000-22,500 MB (depending on GPU specification). We train models with early stopping (Prechelt, 1998), using ten consecutive evaluations with no improvement in translation quality on the development set as the stopping criterion. The high level view of NMT system training:

1. First, pre-process all data using Tilde's parallel data pre-processing pipeline (Pinnis et al., 2018), which involves custom-made processes for parallel data filtering, normalization, non-translatable entity identification, tokenization, and truecasing, as well as standard processes for word splitting, and cross-lingual word alignment.

2. Then, for each domain, we perform careful data selection. We split data into four parts: out-of-domain colloquial data, out-of-domain formal language data, out-of-domain Swiss data, in-domain Swiss data. All Swiss data are up-sampled while the colloquial data are down-sampled or discarded. See Table 1 for the summary of training data size for each language pair.

3. Before training, we separate random subsets of 2000 and 1000 parallel sentences from the in-domain Swiss data to be used as development and evaluation data sets, respectively.

4. To make MT models more robust against incomplete or incorrect input, we synthesize additional training data by randomly replacing 1-3 content words in sentences with a placeholder (Pinnis et al., 2017).

5. We train baseline Transformer NMT models with guided alignment using the Marian NMT toolkit. We provide subword-unit-based statistical alignments as an additional input data stream for learning guided alignments, which are important for formatting-rich document translation and integration in computer-assisted translation tools.

6. Finally, we adapt the systems, thereby ensuring conformity to Swiss language specificities and style. Domain adaptation is performed using a 1-1 mix of in-domain Swiss data with an equal amount randomly sampled from the remaining data.

3.3 NMT System Quality

Figure 1 gives results of automatic evaluation of translation quality of *LexMachina* MT systems using BLEU (Papineni et al., 2002) metric. The performance of publicly available Google Translate general domain systems is given for the reference. Results show that *LexMachina* MT systems yield substantially better quality (12.3 BLEU higher on average) than the publicly available counterparts. The substantial difference in performance suggests that the strategy to approaching Hieronymus' requirements for Swiss language and domain-specific MT systems as a two-fold domain adaptation problem has been successful.

---

[4]https://github.com/marian-nmt/marian-examples/tree/master/transformer

			Baseline Data		Domain Adaptation Data	
			Parallel	**Synthetic**	**Parallel**	**Synthetic**
FR	↔	**EN**	53.5	50.7	0.24	0.22
DE	↔	**IT**	15.1	13.4	0.17	0.14
IT	↔	**FR**	16.6	16.2	0.17	0.16
FR	↔	**DE**	9.6	7.6	1.8	1.4

Table 1: Training data sizes in millions of sentences.

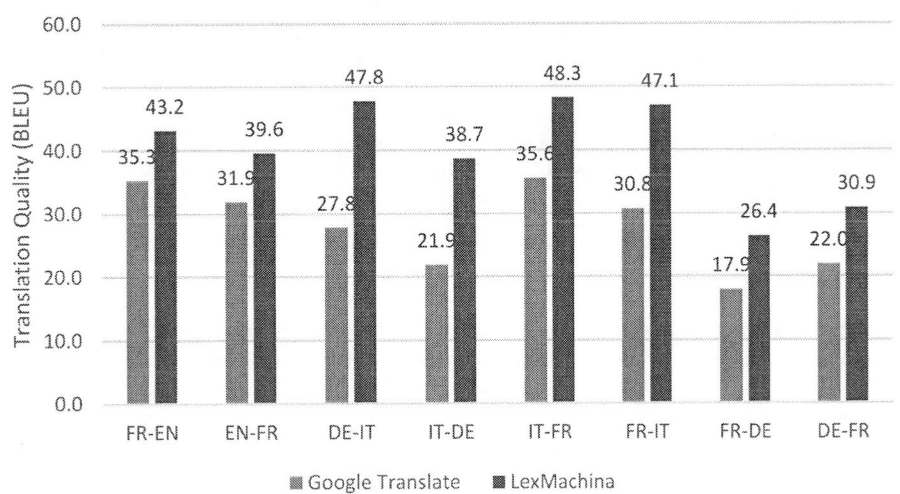

Figure 1: Results of automatic evaluation of translation quality measured in BLEU scores. *LexMachina* in-domain MT systems compared against publicly available general domain MT systems by Google Translate. The comparison was made in February 2020.

4 Implementation

The implementation process for the project was divided in four steps: 1) a pilot to assess NMT capabilities for one language pair, 2) NMT system training, 3) development of the *LexMachina* platform, and 4) deployment of the *LexMachina* platform in Hieronymus' infrastructure. The pilot allowed us to better understand the domain, identify data sources, and establish the domain adaptation strategy for NMT system training. Once satisfied with the results of the pilot, we trained all remaining NMT systems using the strategy established in the pilot phase. The NMT systems were at first deployed on the Tilde MT platform to allow instant access to testing and evaluation of the NMT systems and features of the MT platform. All systems were tested and custom-tweaked by adjusting data pre-processing and post-processing rules. The platform was simultaneously developed according to Hieronymus' requirements. Finally, the platform was deployed in a Switzerland-based, secure data center to comply with the security requirements of Hieronymus and their customers.

The project allowed Hieronymus to reach the following milestones:

- to integrate custom NMT engines in their workflow, which allows their translators to increase productivity and efficiency;

- to become the first provider to offer a self-service, legal machine translation solution for Swiss lawyers;

- to become the first provider to offer a fully secure NMT solution deployed in the Swiss Azure cloud for banks, insurance companies, and major advisory and accounting companies.

5 Conclusions

In response to growing interest from the Swiss banking and insurance industry, both of which want their own specialized NMT engines, Hieronymus and Tilde have developed a common solution to cater for the industry's urgent NMT needs – the current *LexMachina* infrastructure is a proof-of-concept. As a result of the joint project between both parties, Hieronymus can build on the deployed solution and offer on-premises custom NMT engines using both precious corpora developed by Hieronymus, as well as Tilde's extensive experience in setting-up secure infrastructures. Custom-made NMT solutions will allow banks, insurance companies, and large consulting and accounting firms to reduce their translation costs by 30%-50%, improving the quality and speed of delivery - all while maintaining security and confidentiality.

6 Acknowledgements

We would like to acknowledge the contribution, support, and involvement of Hieronymus in the project described in this paper, especially to Orane Laeri and Lauren Spencer, who managed the project on Hieronymus' side. We would also like to thank our colleagues Roberts Rozis, Valters Šics, Igors Zotovs and Viktorija Kononova for their contribution to the project described in this paper.

References

Hajlaoui, N., Kolovratnik, D., Väyrynen, J., Steinberger, R., and Varga, D. (2014). DCEP-Digital Corpus of the European Parliament. In *Proceedings of the Ninth International Conference on Language Resources and Evaluation (LREC'14)*.

Junczys-Dowmunt, M., Grundkiewicz, R., Dwojak, T., Hoang, H., Heafield, K., Neckermann, T., Seide, F., Germann, U., Fikri Aji, A., Bogoychev, N., Martins, A. F. T., and Birch, A. (2018). Marian: Fast neural machine translation in C++. In *Proceedings of ACL 2018, System Demonstrations*, pages 116–121, Melbourne, Australia. Association for Computational Linguistics.

Koehn, P. (2005). Europarl : A Parallel Corpus for Statistical Machine Translation. In *Proceedings of the 10th Machine Translation Summit (MT Summit)*, pages 79–86.

Papineni, K., Roukos, S., Ward, T., and Zhu, W.-J. (2002). BLEU: a Method for Automatic Evaluation of Machine Translation. In *Proceedings of the 40th annual meeting on association for computational linguistics*, pages 311–318. Association for Computational Linguistics.

Pinnis, M., Krišlauks, R., Deksne, D., and Miks, T. (2017). Neural Machine Translation for Morphologically Rich Languages with Improved Sub-word Units and Synthetic Data. In *Proceedings of the 20th International Conference of Text, Speech and Dialogue (TSD2017)*, volume 10415 LNAI, Prague, Czechia.

Pinnis, M., Vasiļjevs, A., Kalniņš, R., Rozis, R., Skadiņš, R., and Šics, V. (2018). Tilde MT Platform for Developing Client Specific MT Solutions. In *Proceedings of the Eleventh International Conference on Language Resources and Evaluation (LREC 2018)*, Miyazaki, Japan. European Language Resources Association (ELRA).

Prechelt, L. (1998). Early Stopping- but When? In *Neural Networks: Tricks of the trade*, pages 55–69. Springer.

Rozis, R. and Skadiņš, R. (2017). Tilde MODEL - Multilingual Open Data for EU Languages. In *Proceedings of the 21st Nordic Conference on Computational Linguistics*, pages 263–265.

Steinberger, R., Eisele, A., Klocek, S., Pilos, S., and Schlüter, P. (2012). DGT-TM: A Freely Available Translation Memory in 22 Languages. In *Proceedings of the Eighth International Conference on Language Resources and Evaluation (LREC'12)*, pages 454–459.

Vasiļjevs, A., Skadiņš, R., and Tiedemann, J. (2012). LetsMT!: a Cloud-Based Platform for Do-It-Yourself Machine Translation. In *Proceedings of the ACL 2012 System Demonstrations*, pages 43—-48, Jeju Island, Korea. Association for Computational Linguistics, Association for Computational Linguistics.

Vaswani, A., Shazeer, N., Parmar, N., Uszkoreit, J., Jones, L., Gomez, A. N., Kaiser, Ł., and Polosukhin, I. (2017). Attention Is All You Need. In *Advances in neural information processing systems*, pages 5998–6008.

RWS
Moravia
Machine Translation Hype
Crash-Tested by Translation Students
www.rws.com/moravia

1

Since 2016 I have been treating the last four weeks of my
Translation Technology course as a testing laboratory...
PERCEIVED QUALITY OF RAW MT OUTPUT
ACROSS ALL LANGUAGE COMBINATIONS
2018
SYSTRAN
Translator Hub
Google Translate
BASED ON TAUS
(ACCURACY &
FLUENCY SCORES
4-POINT SCALE
Below 3.0 = poor
3.0 - 3.5 = good
Greater then 3.5
excellent
SPRING, SUMMER & FALL OF 2018
Spanish
(Español)
Simplified Chinese
(简体中文)
Statistical (Customized)
Neural (Baseline)
BASED ON EDIT
DISTANCE SCORES
...BUT...

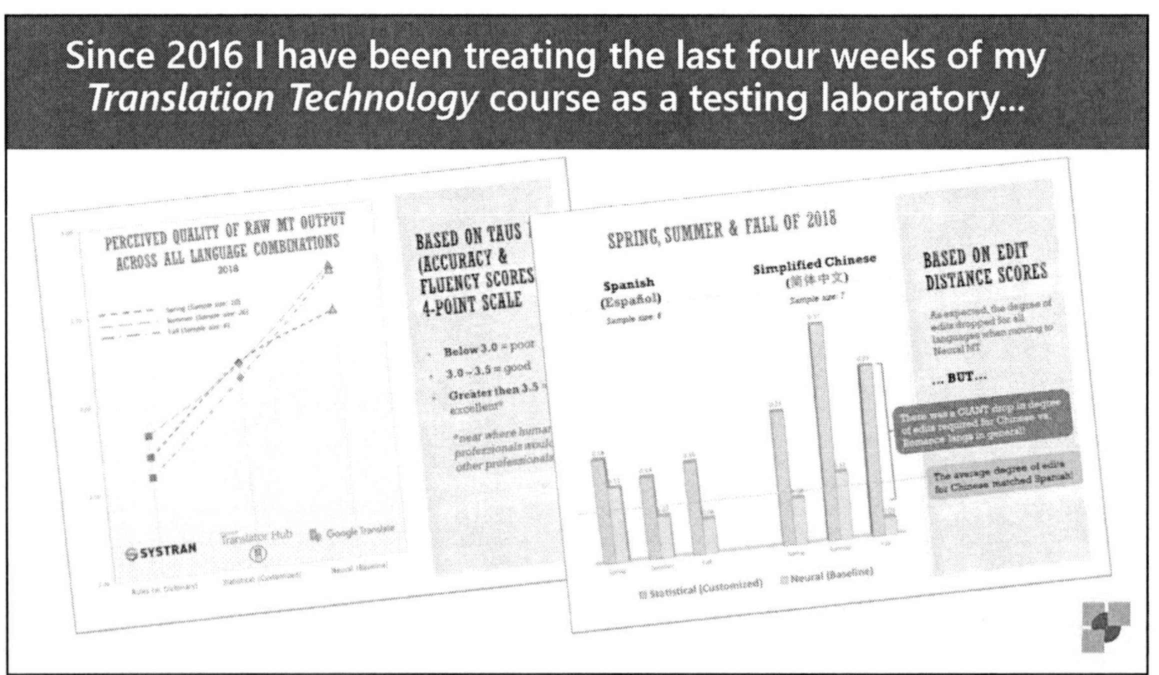

2

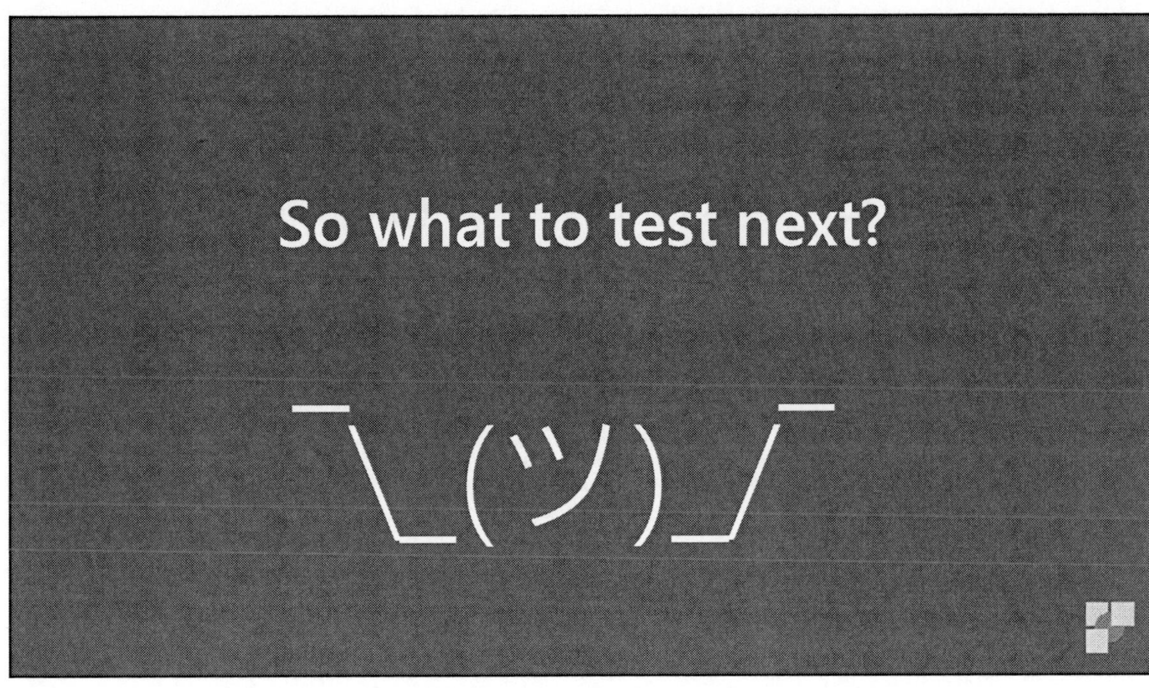

So what to test next?
¯_(ツ)_/¯

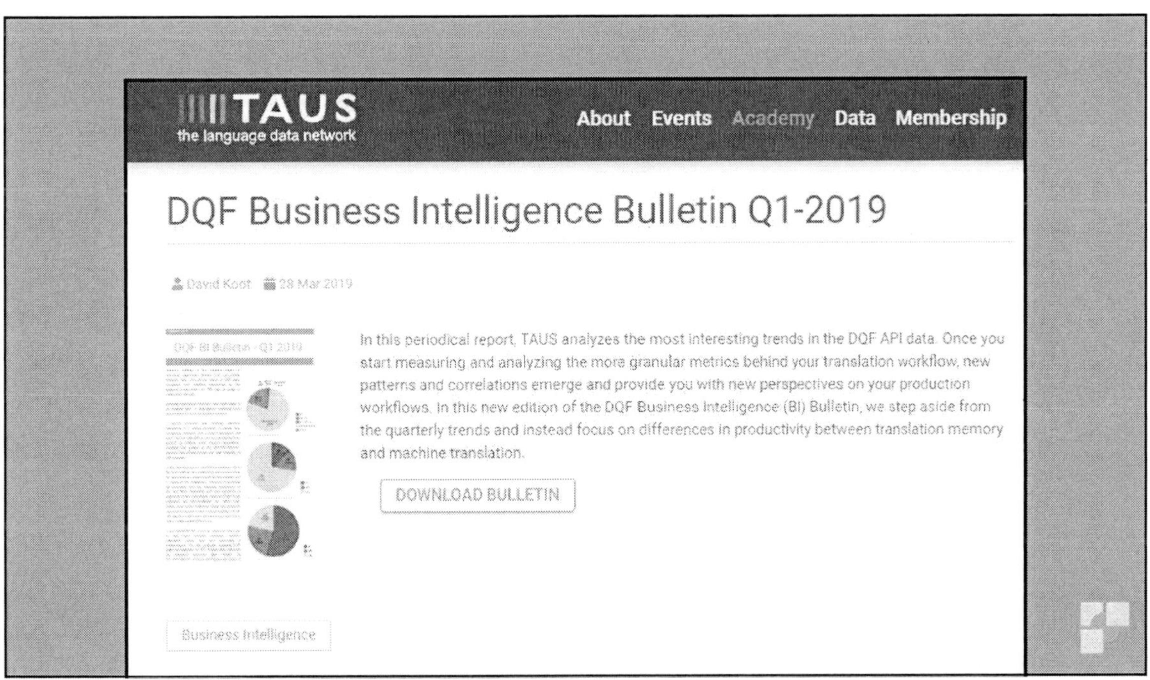

TAUS
the language data network
About   Events   Academy   Data   Membership
DQF Business Intelligence Bulletin Q1-2019
David Koot   28 Mar 2019
In this periodical report, TAUS analyzes the most interesting trends in the DQF API data. Once you start measuring and analyzing the more granular metrics behind your translation workflow, new patterns and correlations emerge and provide you with new perspectives on your production workflows. In this new edition of the DQF Business Intelligence (BI) Bulletin, we step aside from the quarterly trends and instead focus on differences in productivity between translation memory and machine translation.
DOWNLOAD BULLETIN
Business Intelligence

Differences Between the Languages Are Substantial

The trends in MT productivity have a quite stable pattern over time, as the trend reports show. But that does not mean that machine translation is equally productive across different languages. There are considerable differences between languages when it comes to the average time that is needed to edit a machine translation for every 100 characters of the source text. Again we took the same sample, and filtered on a few of the bigger target languages that used MT and had English as the source language.

As shown in figure 10, it appears that the MT productivity in the Western-European languages is twice or almost three times as high as in the Asian languages.

Brazilian Portuguese and Spanish being the MT champions in DQF, how do MT and TM compare in these languages? MT here is on par with fuzzy matches between 75 and 85%, and it shows that the sweet spot for switching to machine translation might move up to the higher TM match rates.

5

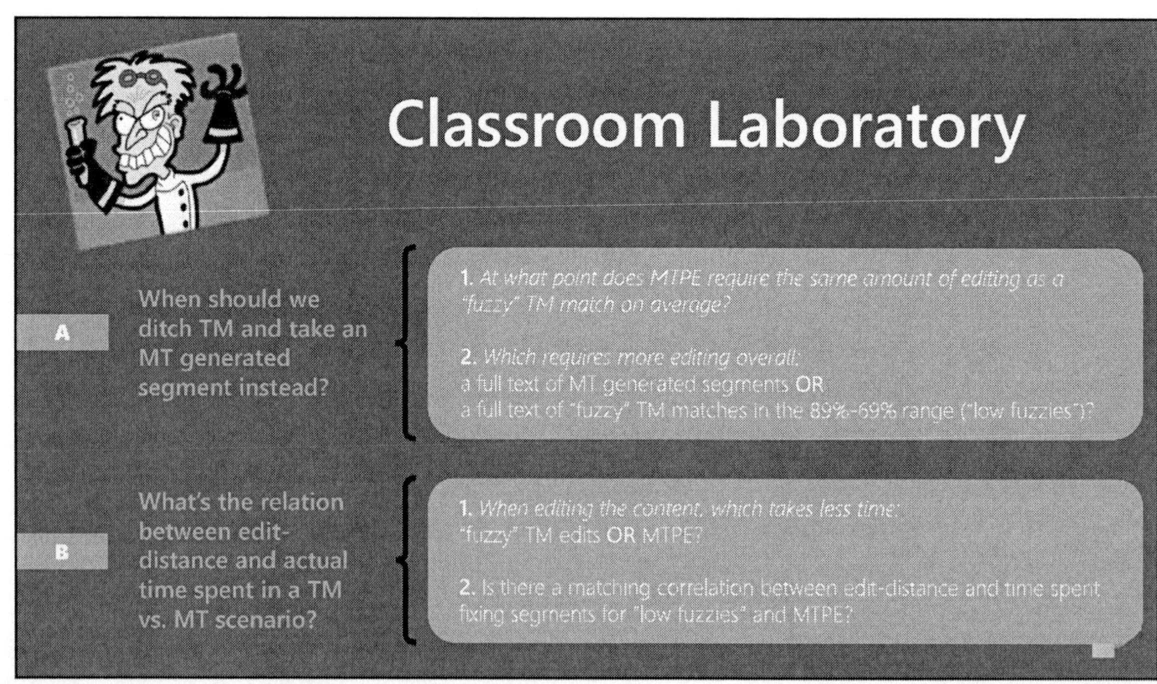

6

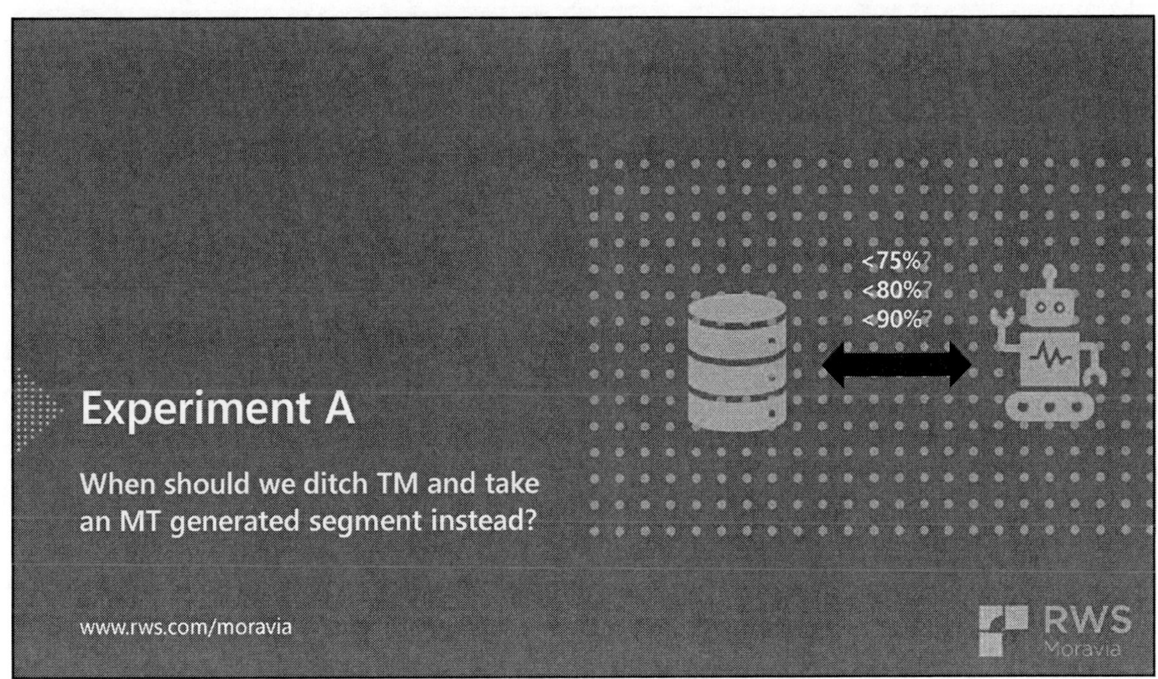

7

Methodology

- 8 students; en-US > 3 target language groups (es-419 (es-LA), zh-CN, zh-TW)

- There are 22 source segments in total split equally into "Set A" and "Set B"

- All are *full* sentences from older (2015 or earlier) Apple iOS documentation (pulled from PDFs) with an average length of 15 wds

- For **TM**, pre-populate with fuzzy matches in the 89%-69% range (avg. match across Set A = 79%, Set B = 78%)

- For MT, pre-populate with Google Translate generated sentences

- One student *per language* will complete Set A with a "fuzzy match TM" and Set B as MTPE; the other student will do the reverse. Then they will switch.

- Edit distance will be measured for every segment

- NOTE: Students can be unpredictable on occasion, so the official Apple translations were added as a "control group" to minimize this risk

For every language...

MT (G⅔)	Set B - 161 wds - 11 sentences; avg. 15 wds long	Set A
Fuzzies TM	Set A - 165 wds - 11 sentences; avg. 15 wds long	Set B

9

At what point does MTPE require the same amount of editing as a fuzzy TM match on average?

> Organize segments by original TM match categories

> Calculate location of point based on average edit-distance for total sampled segments by language

> Do this both for fuzzy TM edited & MTPE segments

> Plot the trendlines for both

> Find intersection

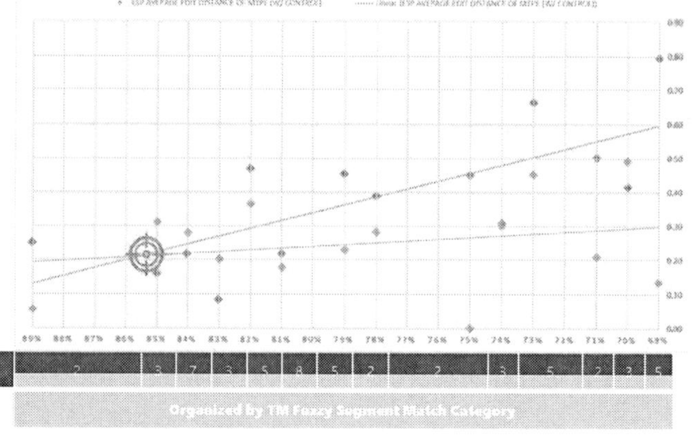

At what point does MTPE require the same amount of editing as a fuzzy TM match on average?

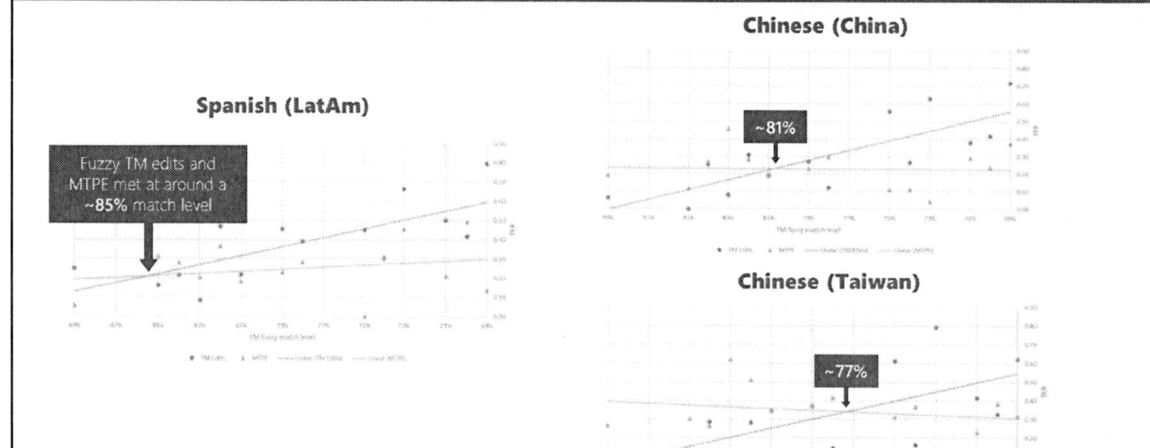

2
Which requires more editing overall:
MT generated segments OR
"fuzzy" TM matches in the
AND YOU CALL MT
"UNPREDICTABLE"
Spanish (LatAm)
TM Edits   MTPE
0.90
0.80   0.79
0.70
0.60
0.50   0.49
0.40   0.38
0.30   0.25
0.20
0.10   0.08
0.00   0.00
TER
Chinese (China)
TM Edits   MTPE
0.90
0.80
0.70   0.72
0.60
0.50   0.46
0.40
0.30   0.30
0.20   0.23
0.10
0.00   0.00   0.04
TER
0.62
0.60
0.50   0.51
0.40   0.34
0.30   0.32
0.20
0.10   0.13
0.05
0.00
TER

13

Experiment B
What's the relation between edit-
distance and actual time spent in a
TM vs. MT scenario?

www.rws.com/moravia

RWS
Moravia

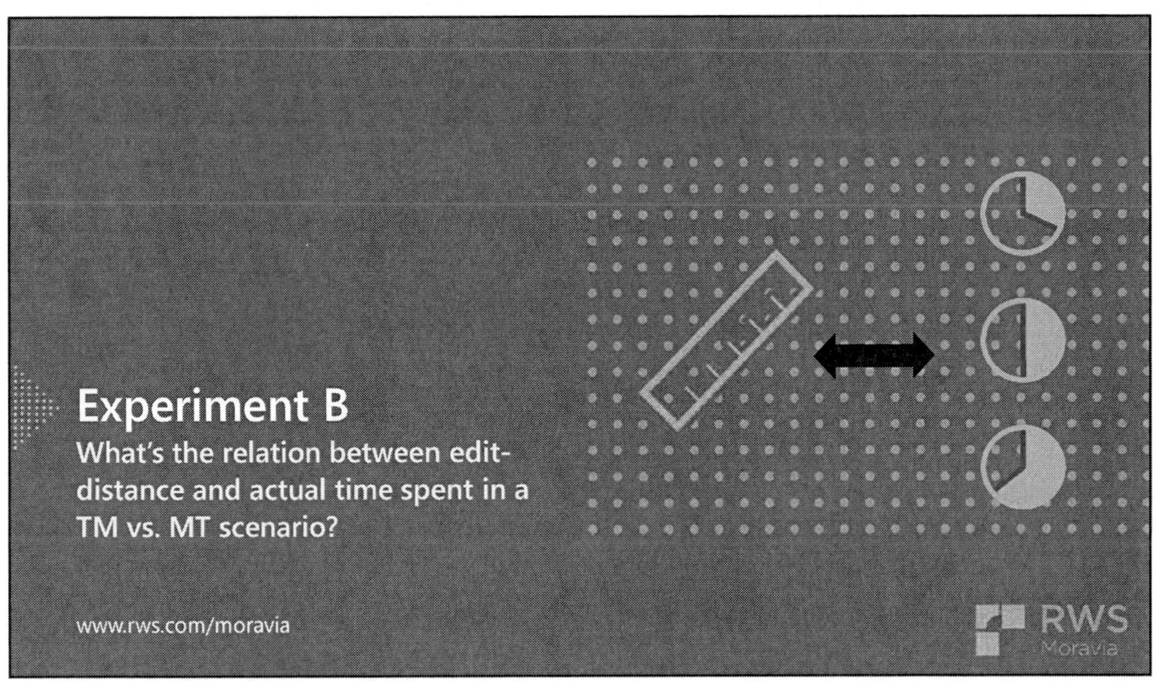

16

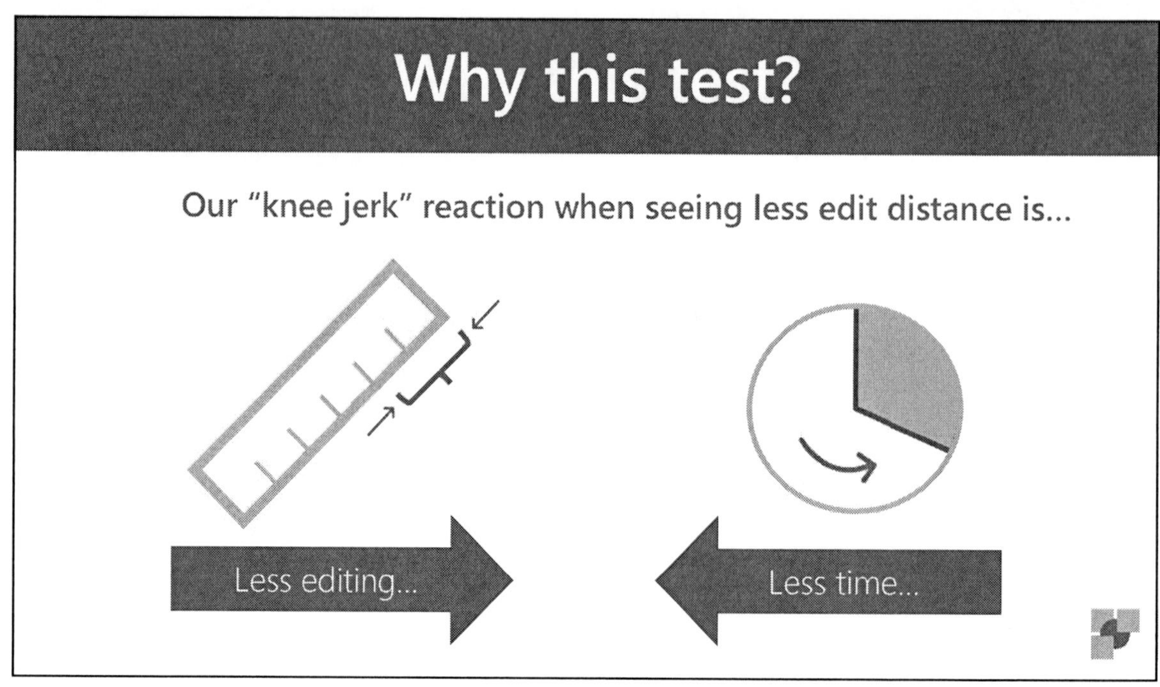

Why this test?
Our "knee jerk" reaction when seeing less edit distance is...
Less editing...
Less time...

17

SDL* Blog   Topics   About   SDL Trados Blog
Machine Translation
Edit Distance: Not a Miracle Cure
by Izabella Izuka
March 13, 2019 · read time: 10 min
With the current rapid developments in Neural Machine Translation (NMT), discussions on its market impact are gathering pace particularly around post-editing. While some suggest that paying by the hour – rather than the traditional per-word rate – is the way to go, others feel that translators should only be paid for actual changes to the MT output. This second option is usually operationalized by using what's known as an edit distance metric.
Edit distance metrics have also been suggested as a means to replace or support BLEU (bilingual evaluation understudy), which is an algorithm for evaluating the quality of text that has been machine-translated from one natural language to another and is used for assessing MT quality - thus support MT engine development. These discussions are not necessarily new; however, edit distances have not become mainstream as of yet. Why? The apparent ease of this solution does in fact hide a lot of complications. Let's take a closer look.
What is edit distance?
There are various ways to measure edit distance, with Levenshtein distance and TER(p) among the best-known. In essence, all edit distance metrics work on the same principle: they measure the minimal number of edits necessary to change one string (in this case, the MT output) into another string (in this case, the final translation). An edit can

18

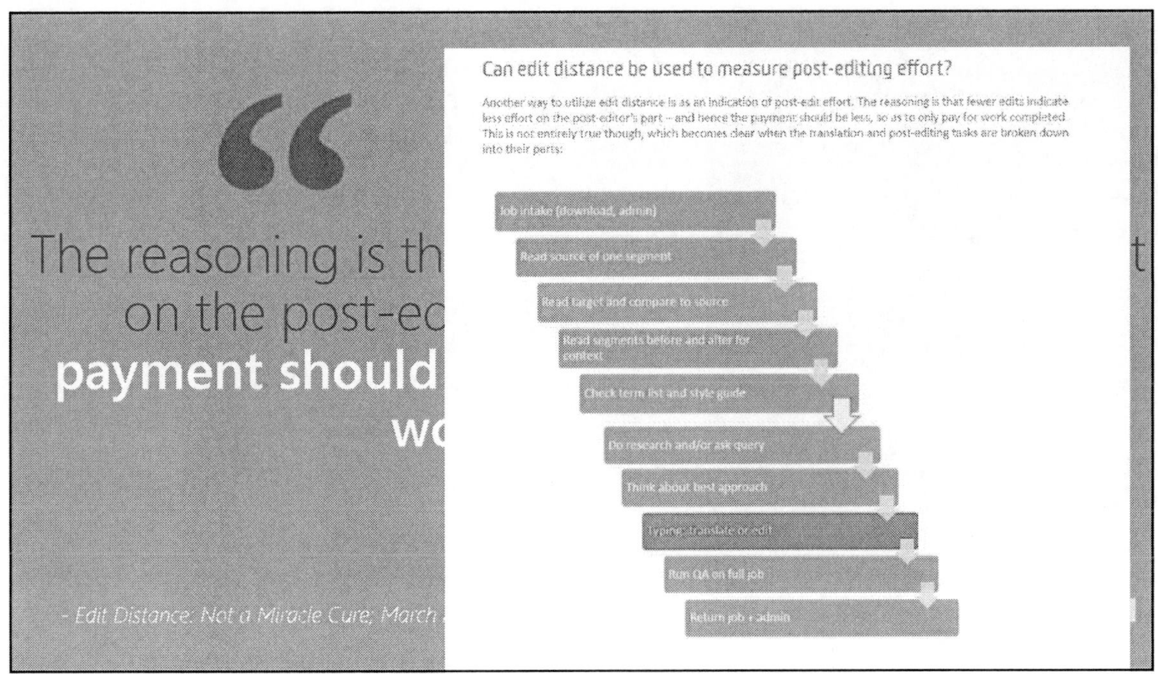
Can edit distance be used to measure post-editing effort?
Another way to utilize edit distance is as an indication of post-edit effort. The reasoning is that fewer edits indicate less effort on the post-editor's part – and hence the payment should be less, so as to only pay for work completed. This is not entirely true though, which becomes clear when the translation and post-editing tasks are broken down into their parts:
Job intake (download, admin)
Read source of one segment
Read target and compare to source
Read segments before and after for context
Check term list and style guide
Do research and/or ask query
Think about best approach
Typing: translate or edit
Run QA on full job
Return job + admin
The reasoning is th
on the post-ed
payment should
wo
- Edit Distance: Not a Miracle Cure; March

19

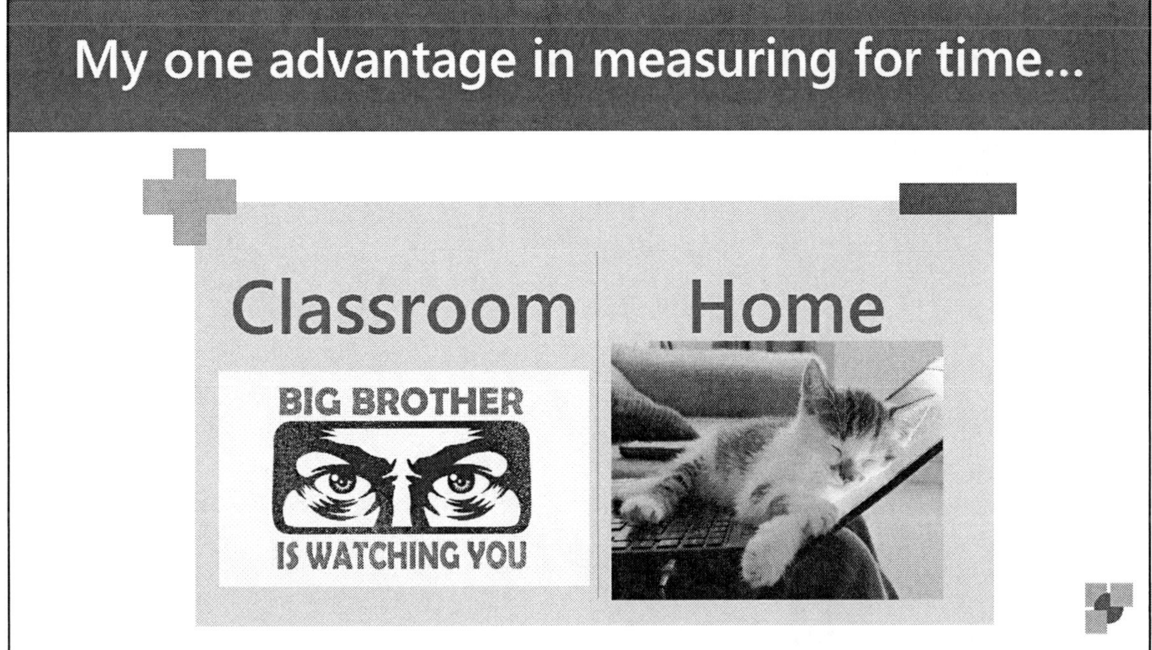
My one advantage in measuring for time...
Classroom
Home
BIG BROTHER
IS WATCHING YOU

20

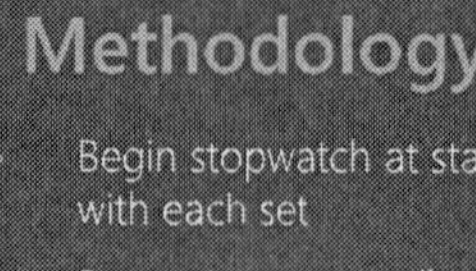

Methodology

> Begin stopwatch at start of translation with each set

> Pause timer and call instructor over when...
>> All segments confirmed
>> All terminology checks against the term database were cleared out (or personally verified as a "non-error")
>> All other automated quality checks that could be cleared out were completed (*capitalization, punctuation, number mismatches, etc*).

> If issue was spotted, unpause the timer and call instructor over again when fixed.

> Instructor writes down time of completion

> NOTE: there is no "control group" for this experiment

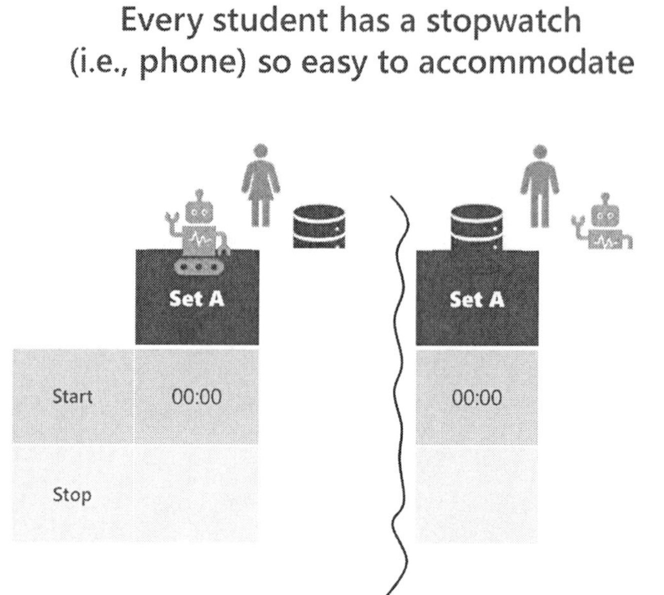

22

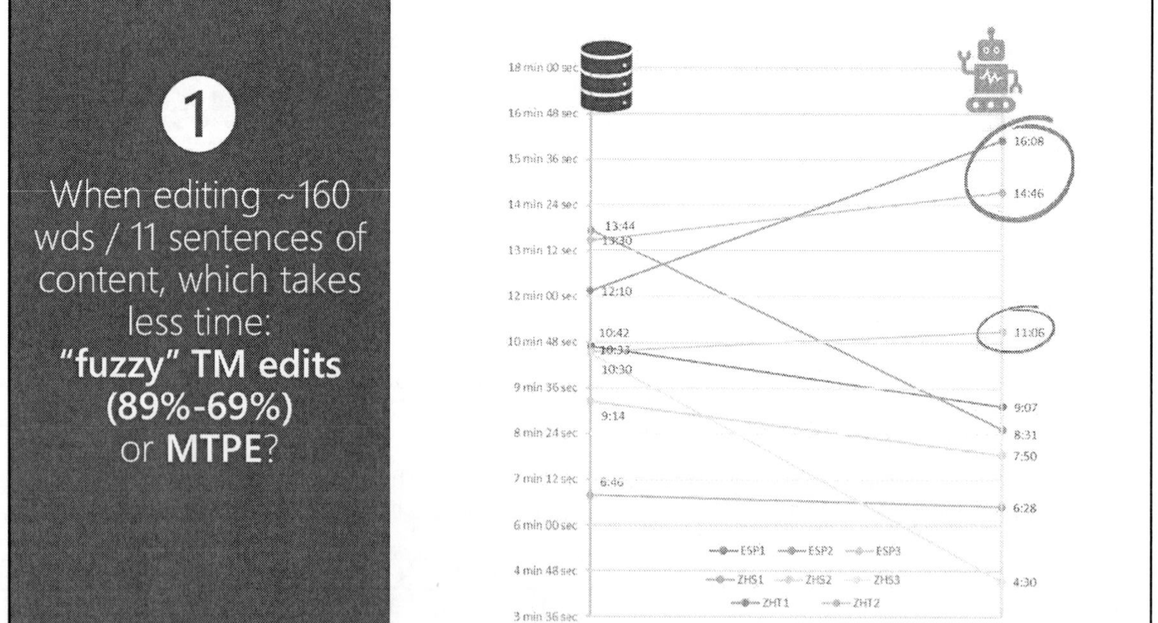

23

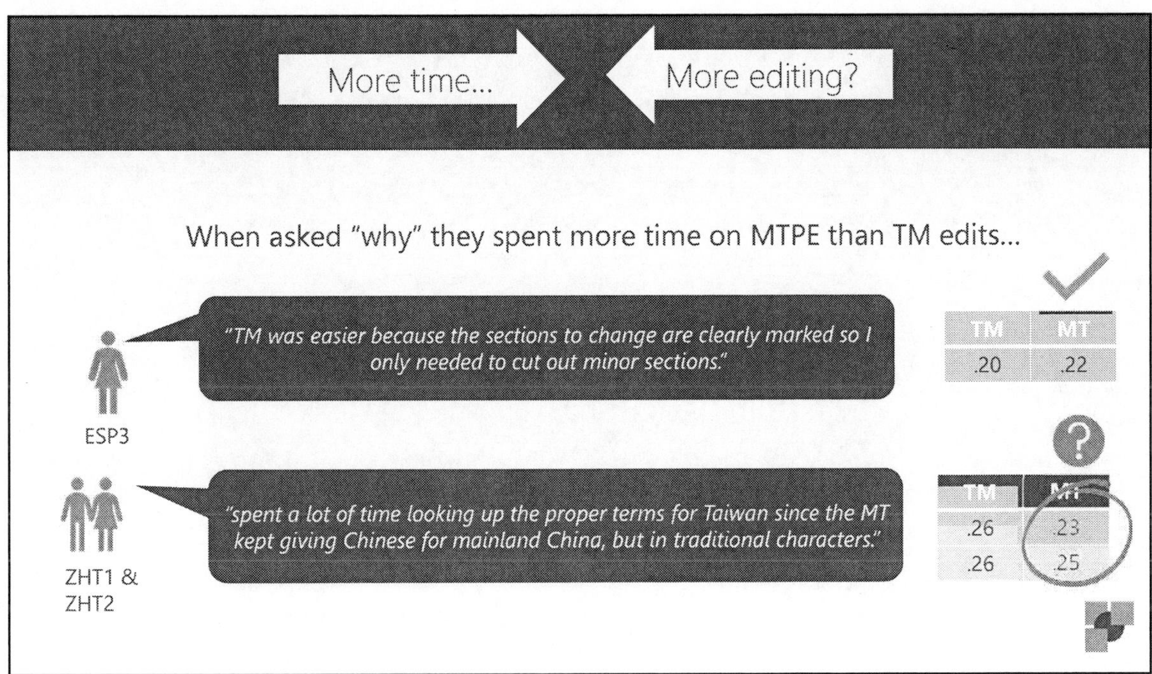

24

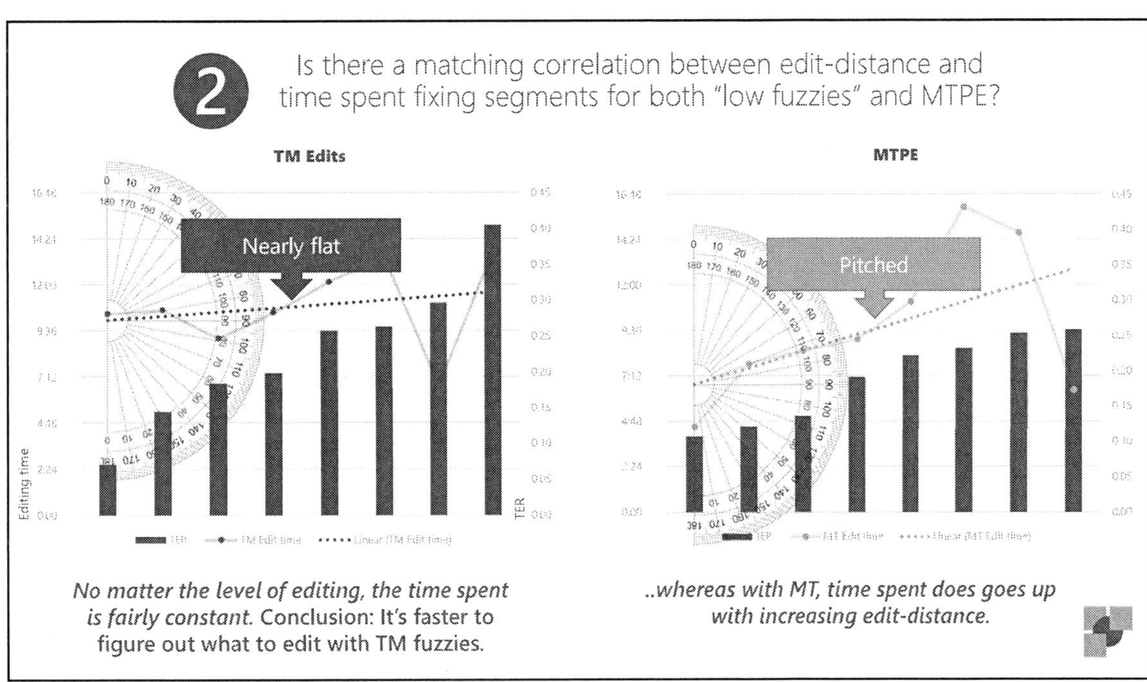

No matter the level of editing, the time spent is fairly constant. Conclusion: It's faster to figure out what to edit with TM fuzzies.

..whereas with MT, time spent does goes up with increasing edit-distance.

26

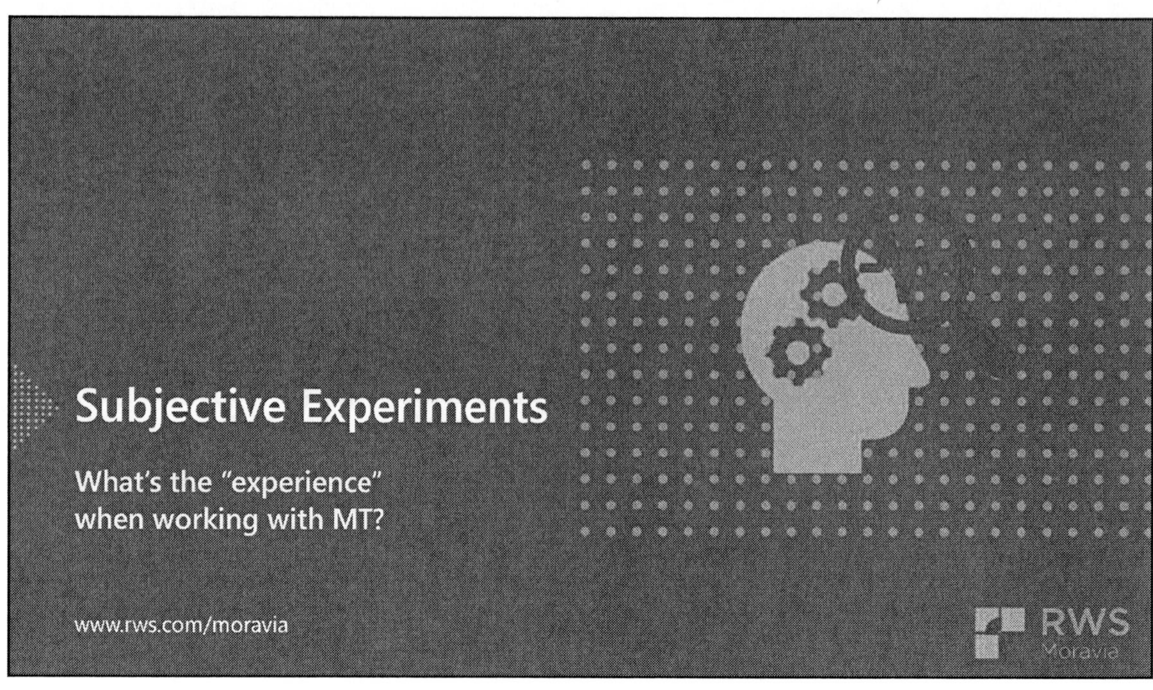

Subjective Experiments
What's the "experience"
when working with MT?
www.rws.com/moravia
RWS
Moravia

27

What did you prefer?
PE of wholly generated raw MT output OR
a trained "adaptive" MT system where you had control over the output
Nearly 50/50 in a show of hands every year since 2016

...those who prefer "adaptive MT" are nearly always
Romance language speakers

28

I've mixed the reference translations in with raw MT from 4 major engines.
Which do you think is human?

Students are given homework the week before to provide multiple sentences of human-made content (bilingual) that _they believe_ will be "tough" for MT.

Poor Tom Fool, yonder behind the wagon, mumbling his bone with the honest family which lives by his tumbling.	可憐的湯姆 姑爾，馬車後面的遠處，他的骨頭與他的離眾生活的誠實家庭喃喃自語。	可憐的湯姆 傻瓜，就在馬車後面，嘟囔著他的骨頭和靠他跌倒生活的誠實家庭。	可憐的湯姆·富爾 (Tom Fool) 身處馬車後面，與誠實的家庭咀嚼骨頭，誠實的家庭靠他的翻滾生活。	可憐的湯姆 愚人，在馬車後面，嘟囔自語和誠實的家庭，這是由他的翻滾。	再過去是可憐的小丑湯姆倚靠在貨車後頭帶著一家老小啃骨頭，這些老實人就靠他翻筋斗賺來的錢過活。
The young lady's countenance, which had before worn an almost livid look of hatred, assumed a smile that perhaps was scarcely more agreeable.	只是這笑容比起方才惡狠狠嫉青的臉色來，也好看不了多少。	這位年輕女士的臉容，曾經穿著一種幾乎鮮豔的仇恨外表，假設一個微笑，也許幾乎沒有比較愉快。	這位年輕女士的面容，以前帶著近乎憤怒的神情，露出了一絲可能更討人喜歡的微笑。	這位年輕女士的臉上以前帶著幾分仇恨的嫩青色，現在露出了一種也許再好不過討人喜歡的微笑。	這位年輕女士的容顏曾帶過幾乎幾乎是充滿生氣的仇恨表情，倨露出了微笑，這也許簡直讓人難以接受。
The world is a looking-glass, and gives back to every man the reflection of his own face.	這世界是一面鏡子，每個人都可以在裡面看見自己的影子。	這個世界是一個眾望的玻璃，並將自己臉上的反射回饋給每個人。	世界是一面鏡子，把自己臉上的倒影還給每個人。	這個世界是一個鏡像機，並且將每個人的面孔反射給每個人。	世界是一個看起來玻璃，並回饋每個人自己的臉的反射。
A very stout, puffy man, in buckskins, and Hessian boots, with several immense neckcloths that rose almost to his nose.	他穿著鹿皮褲子，簡上有流蘇的靴子，圍著好幾條寬大的領巾，幾乎直豎到鼻子。	一個非常健壯，浮腫的男人，鹿皮，黑森靴，幾條幾乎高到鼻子的大領巾。	一個非常粗壯，浮腫的人，在鹿皮和黑森靴子，與幾個巨大的領布，幾乎上升到他的鼻子。	一個非常粗壯，浮腫的男人，在牛皮和黑森靴子，幾乎上升到他的鼻子幾乎巨大的領口。	一個非常矮胖，蝴蝶的人，穿著鹿皮和黑森州的靴子，蝴蝶巨大的圍巾圍在他的鼻子上。

Fall 2019 = 1st time students in a language group (Spanish) chose MT generated output over the human reference text

29

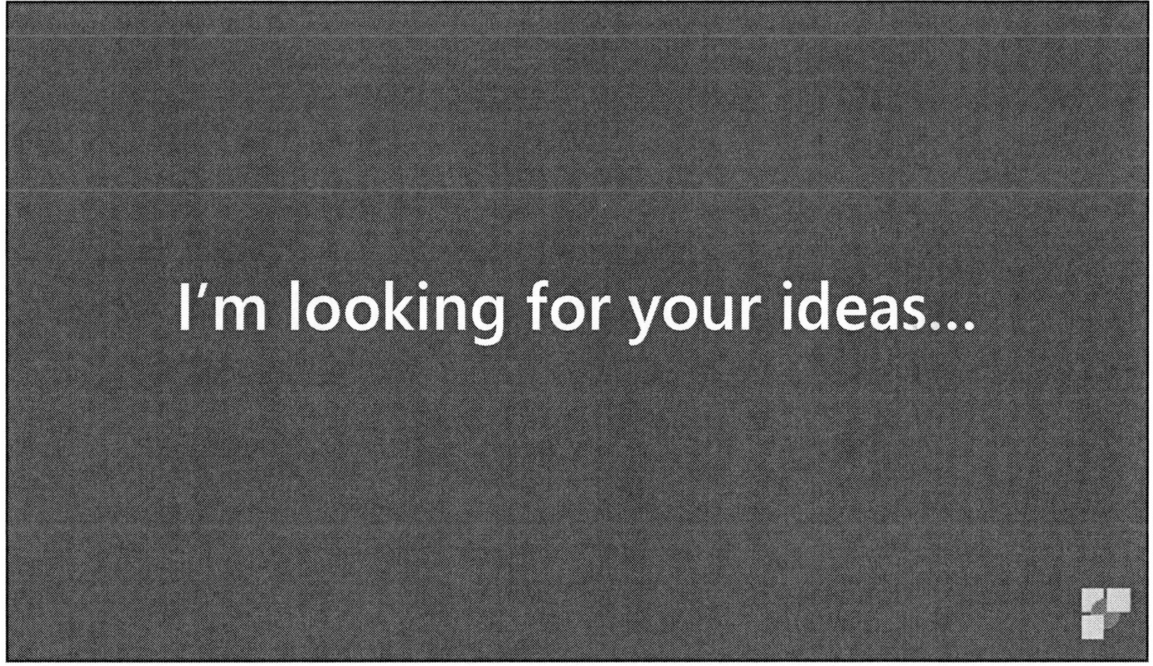

30

31

Use MT to Simplify and Speed Up Your Alignment for TM creation

Judith Klein, STAR Group

Judith.Klein@star-group.net

Proceedings of the 14th Conference of the Association for Machine Translation in the Americas
October 6 – 9, 2020, Volume 2: MT User Track

- Motivation

- TMs for CAT Tools

- MT-based Alignment

- Workflow for MT-Aligned TM

- Conclusion

Proceedings of the 14th Conference of the Association for Machine Translation in the Americas
October 6 - 9, 2020, Volume 2: MT User Track

STAR Group (since 1984)

➢ Translation Services & Translation Technology

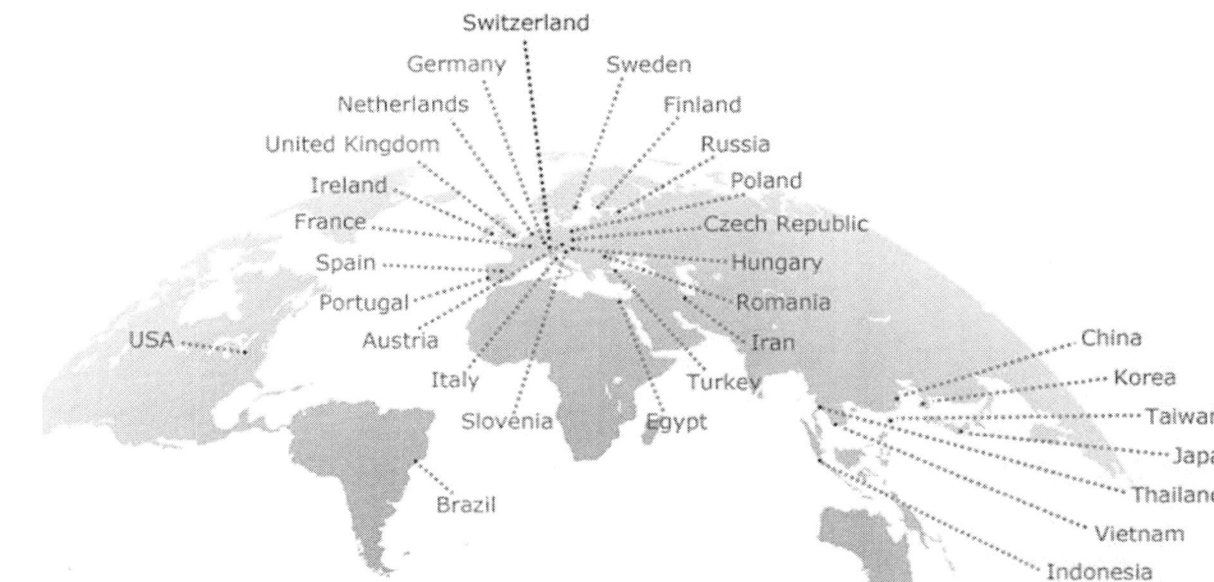

Proceedings of the 14th Conference of the Association for Machine Translation in the Americas
October 6 – 9, 2020, Volume 2: MT User Track

STAR's Translation Technology

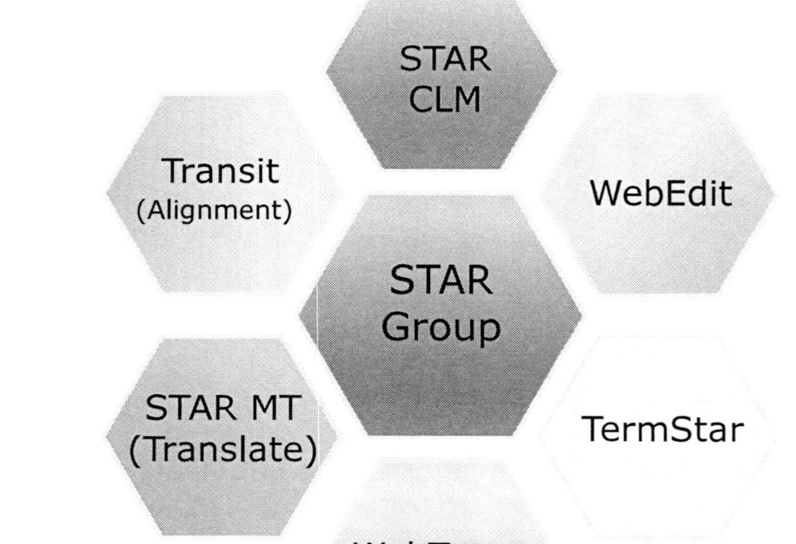

Proceedings of the 14th Conference of the Association for Machine Translation in the Americas
October 6 - 9, 2020, Volume 2: MT User Track

Swiss Federal Administration (Bund)

- 8 departments, 80 offices, 450 language experts
  - Federal Chancellery (BK)
  - Foreign Affairs (EDA)
  - Home Affairs (EDI)
  - Finance (EFD)
  - Justice and Police (EJPD)
  - Environment, Transport, Energy and Communications (UVEK)
  - Defense, Civil Protection and Sport (VBS)
  - Economic Affairs, Education and Research (WBF)
- German, French, Italian, Rhaeto-Romanic, English
- Different tools
- Huge amounts of language resources (translation pools, termbases)

Proceedings of the 14th Conference of the Association for Machine Translation in the Americas
October 6 – 9, 2020, Volume 2: MT User Track

Systematic Collection of Legislation (SR)

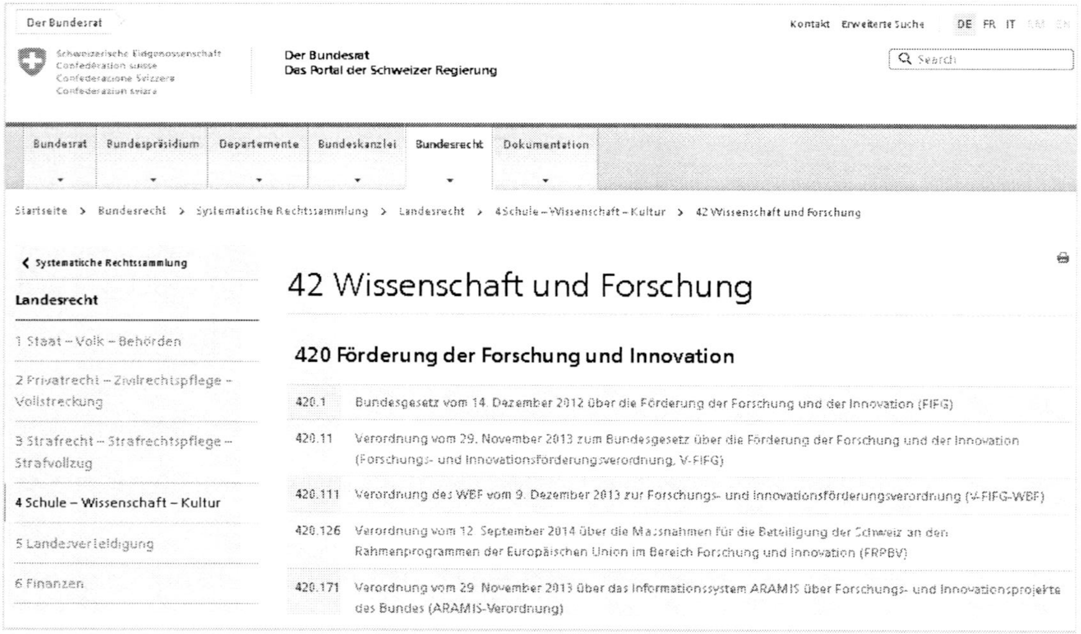

Der Bundesrat

Schweizerische Eidgenossenschaft
Confédération suisse
Confederazione Svizzera
Confederaziun svizra

Der Bundesrat
Das Portal der Schweizer Regierung

Kontakt   Erweiterte Suche   DE FR IT RM EN

Search

| Bundesrat | Bundespräsidium | Departemente | Bundeskanzlei | Bundesrecht | Dokumentation |

‹ Systematische Rechtssammlung

Landesrecht

1 Staat – Volk – Behörden

2 Privatrecht – Zivilrechtspflege – Vollstreckung

3 Strafrecht – Strafrechtspflege – Strafvollzug

4 Schule – Wissenschaft – Kultur

5 Landesverteidigung

6 Finanzen

42 Wissenschaft und Forschung

420 Förderung der Forschung und Innovation

420.1	Bundesgesetz vom 14. Dezember 2012 über die Förderung der Forschung und der Innovation (FIFG)
420.11	Verordnung vom 29. November 2013 zum Bundesgesetz über die Förderung der Forschung und der Innovation (Forschungs- und Innovationsförderungsverordnung, V-FIFG)
420.111	Verordnung des WBF vom 9. Dezember 2013 zur Forschungs- und Innovationsförderungsverordnung (V-FIFG-WBF)
420.126	Verordnung vom 12. September 2014 über die Massnahmen für die Beteiligung der Schweiz an den Rahmenprogrammen der Europäischen Union im Bereich Forschung und Innovation (FRPBV)
420.171	Verordnung vom 29. November 2013 über das Informationssystem ARAMIS über Forschungs- und Innovationsprojekte des Bundes (ARAMIS-Verordnung)

Proceedings of the 14th Conference of the Association for Machine Translation in the Americas
October 6 - 9, 2020, Volume 2: MT User Track

Systematic Collection of Legislation (SR)

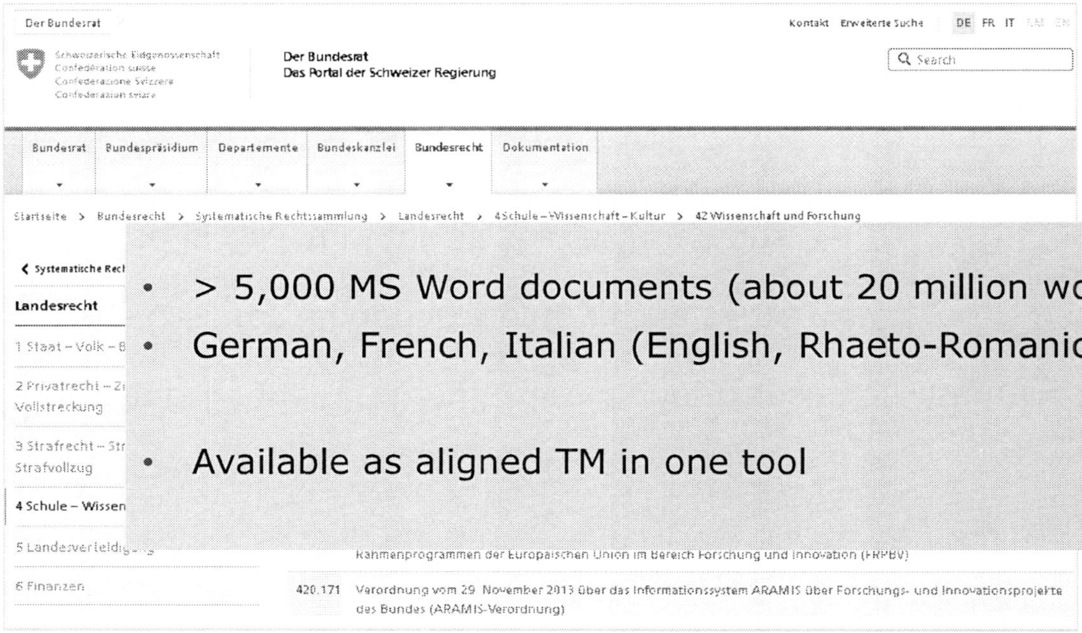

- > 5,000 MS Word documents (about 20 million words)
- German, French, Italian (English, Rhaeto-Romanic)
- Available as aligned TM in one tool

SR as TM for all Departments

- Aim
  - Multi-lingual and multi-directional translation memory
  - Access for all departments in the same way
  - Use in CAT tool for all search functions
- Solution
  - Standard translation workflow solution
  - Fully automated machine alignment
  - Fully automated update-workflow every three month

Proceedings of the 14th Conference of the Association for Machine Translation in the Americas
October 6 – 9, 2020, Volume 2: MT User Track

Standard Translation Workflow Solution

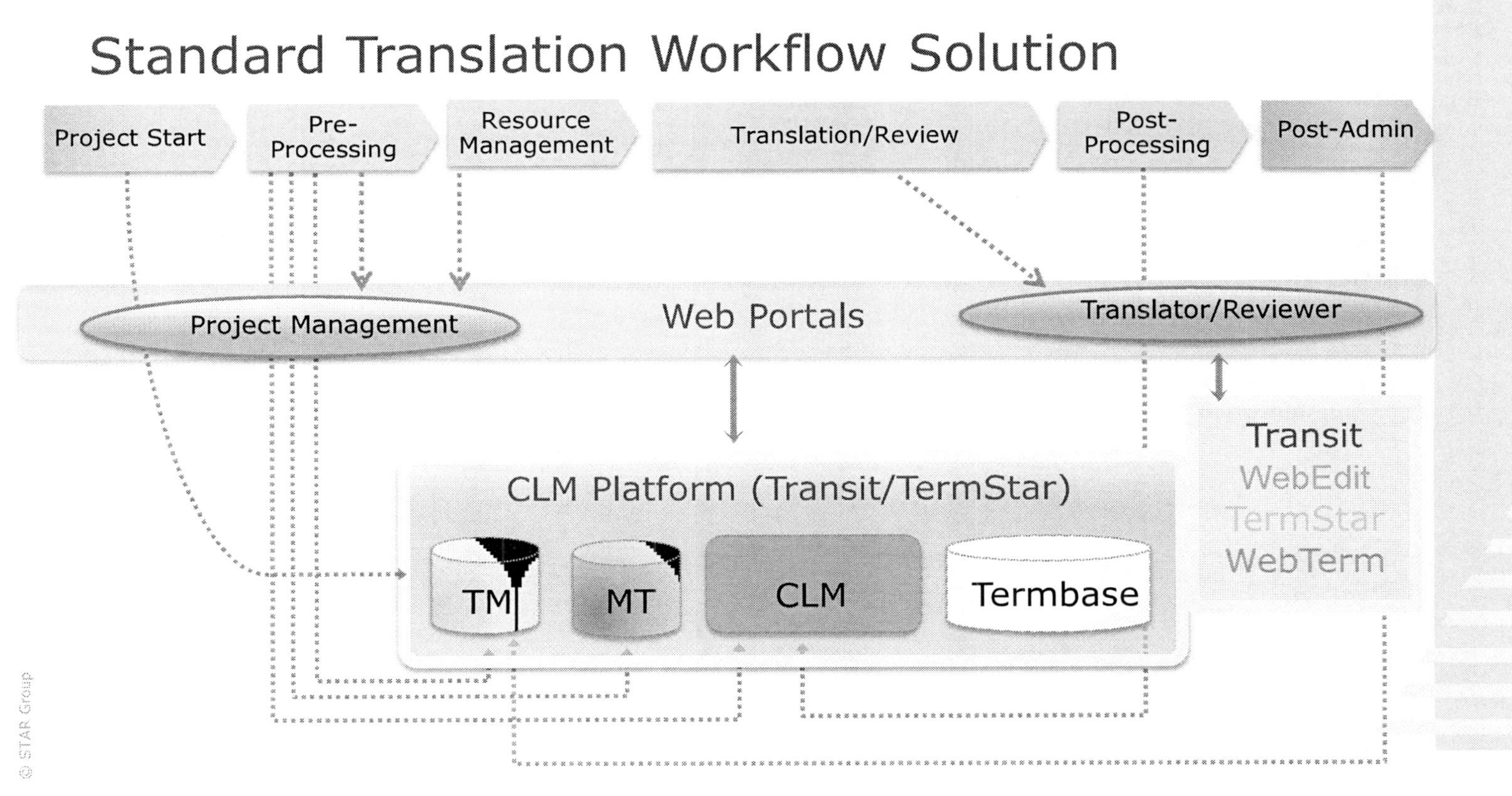

Proceedings of the 14th Conference of the Association for Machine Translation in the Americas
October 6 – 9, 2020, Volume 2: MT User Track

Standard Translation Workflow Solution

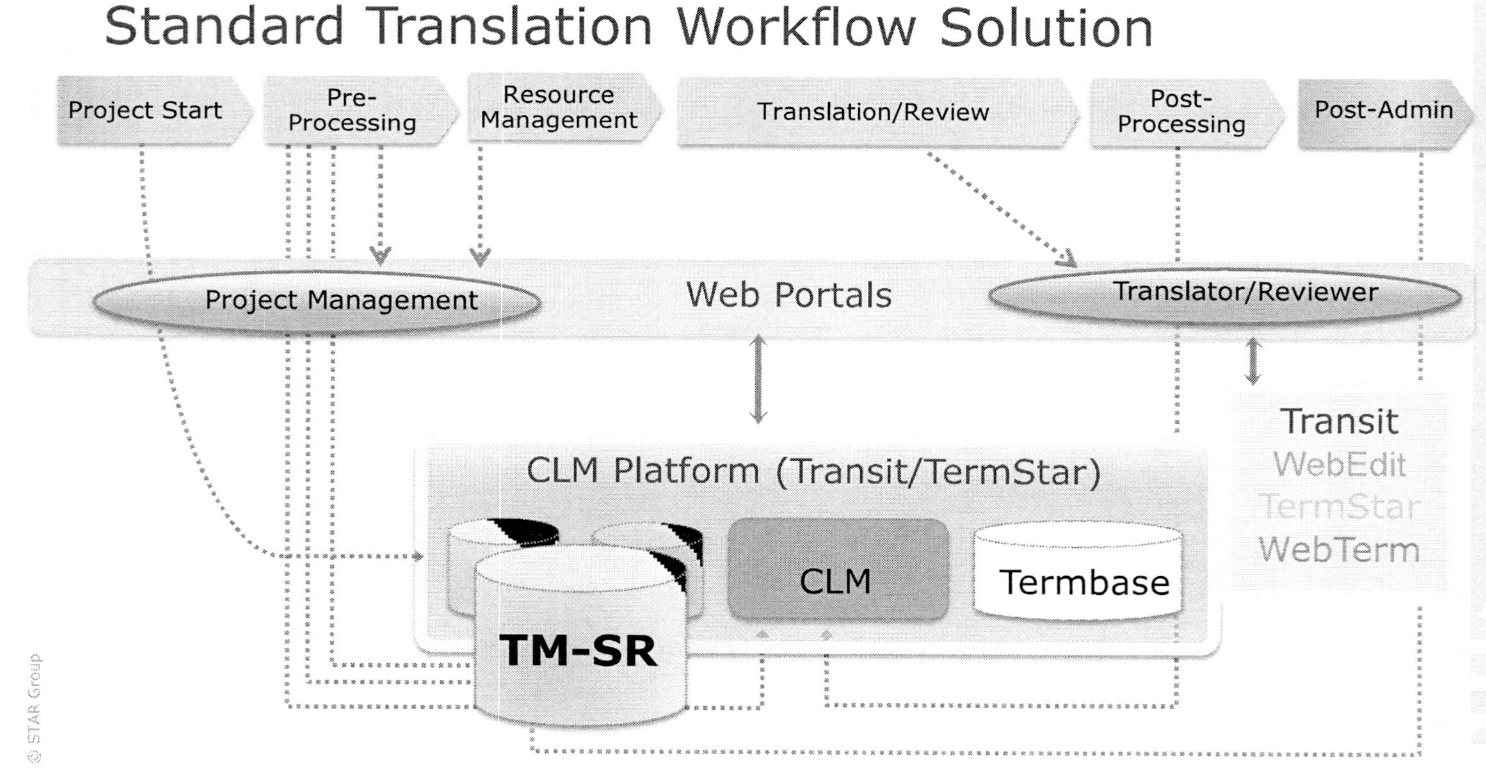

Proceedings of the 14th Conference of the Association for Machine Translation in the Americas
October 6 – 9, 2020, Volume 2: MT User Track

CAT Tool – Segments & Document Context

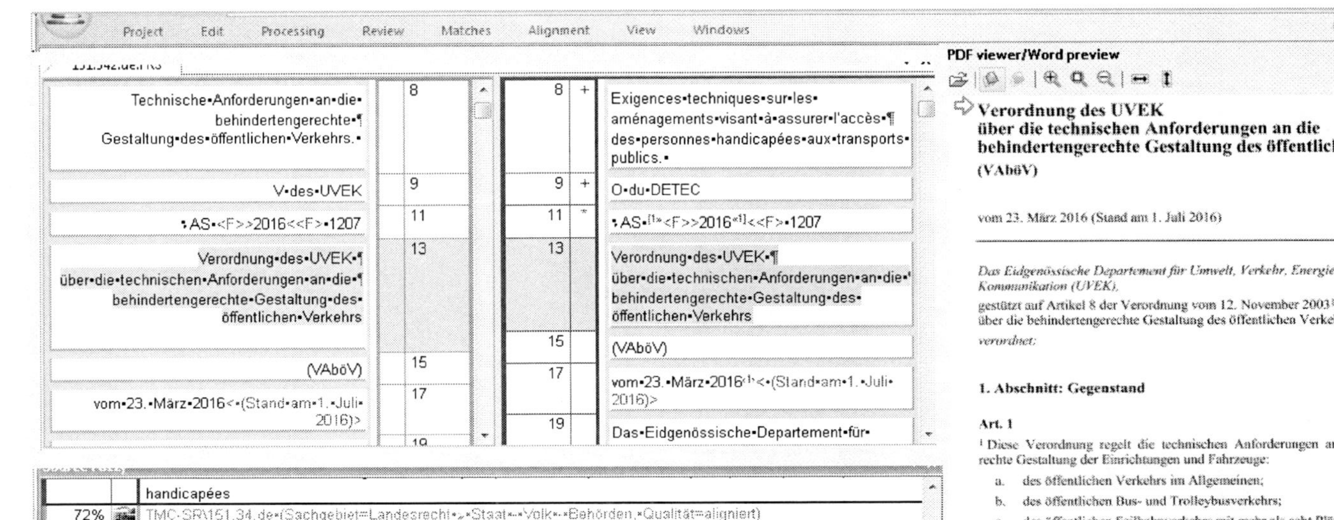

CAT Tool – 100% Matches & Pretranslation

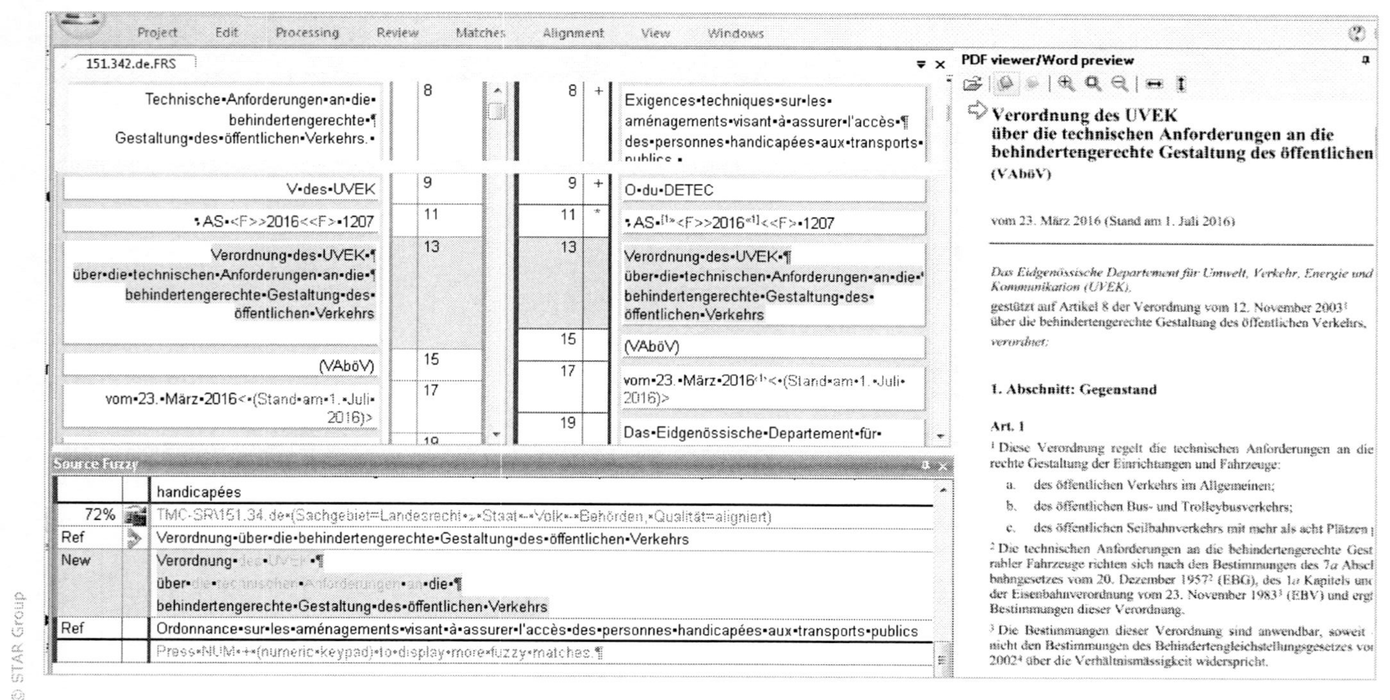

CAT Tool – Fuzzy Matches

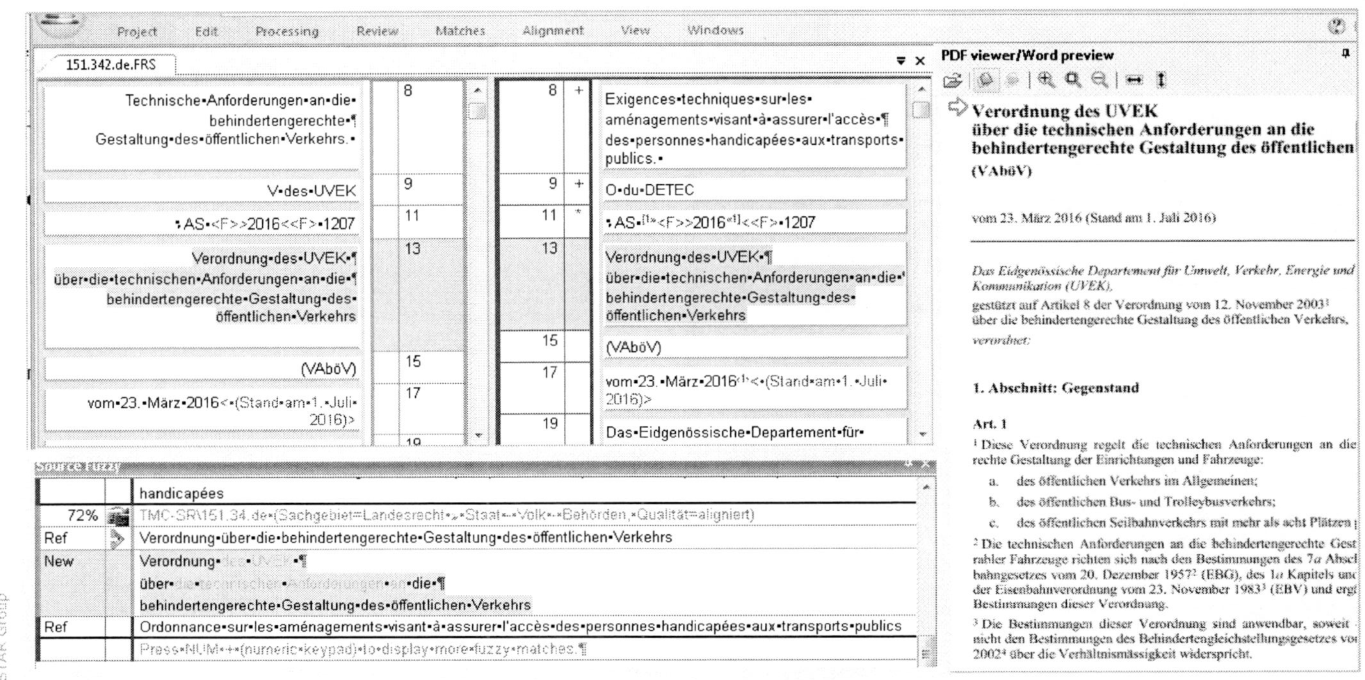

CAT Tool

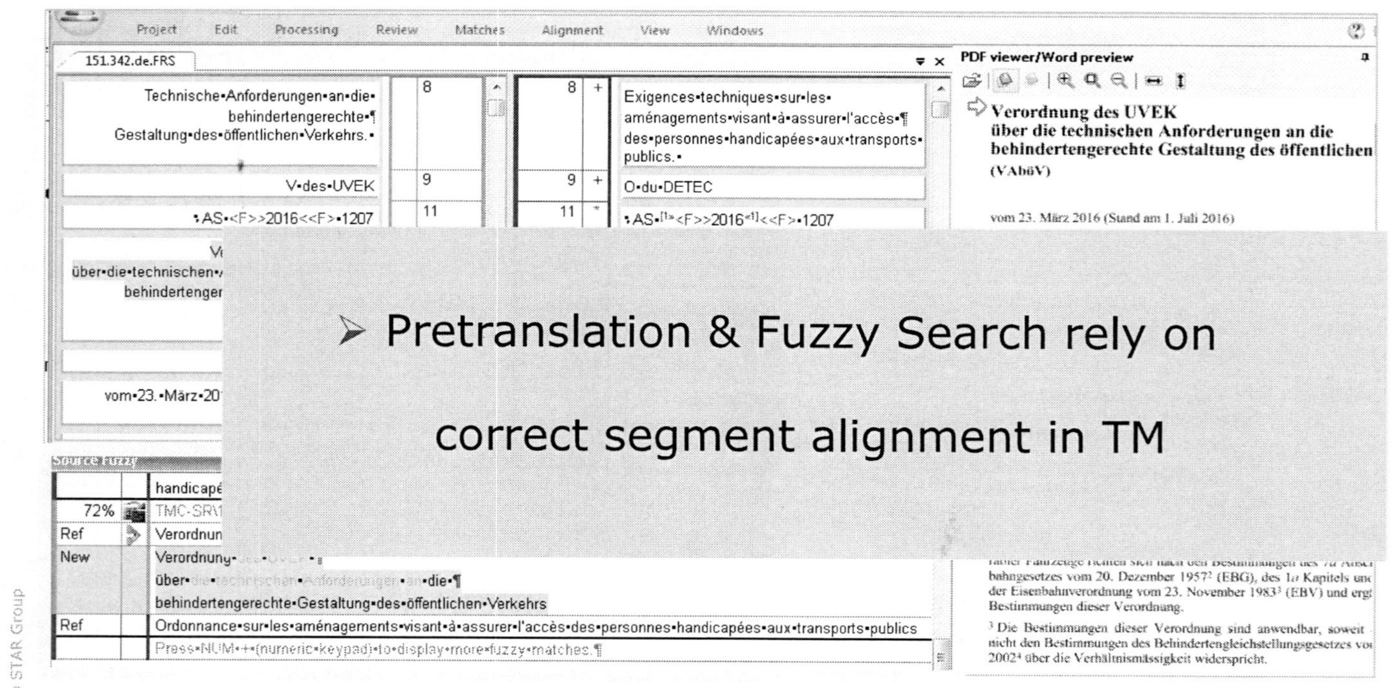

Pretranslation & Fuzzy Search rely on

correct segment alignment in TM

CAT Tool – Concordance Search

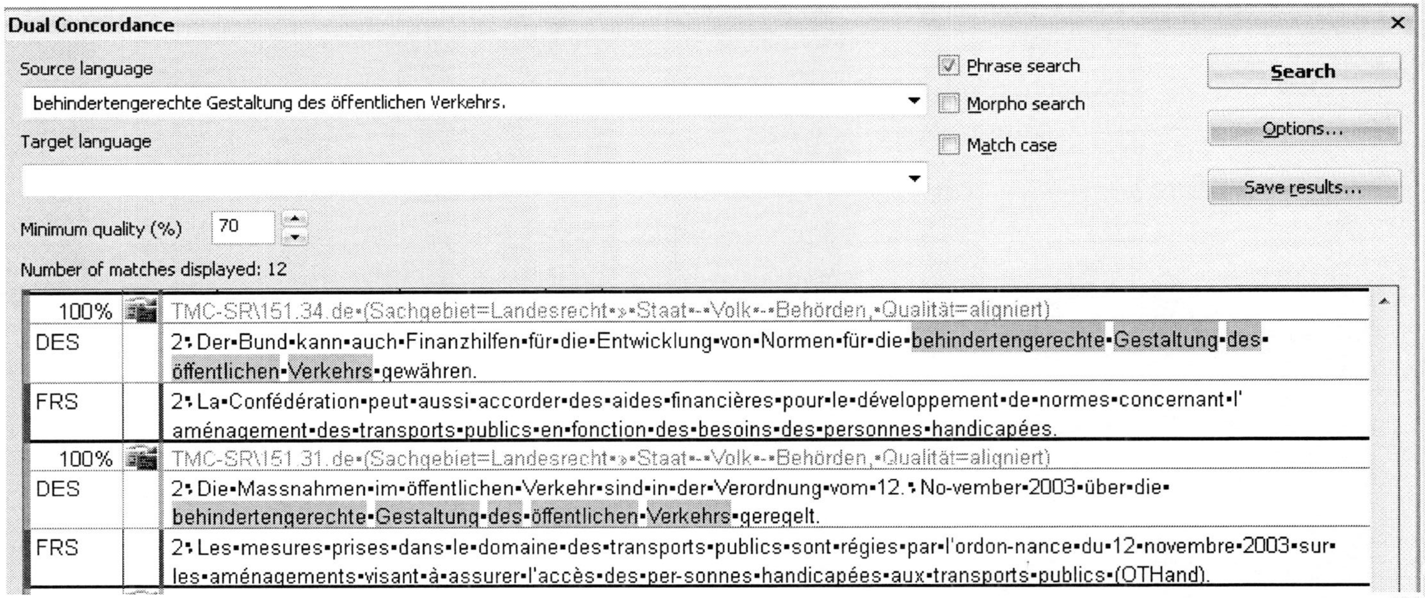
Dual Concordance
Source language
behindertengerechte Gestaltung des öffentlichen Verkehrs.
Target language
Minimum quality (%)
70
Number of matches displayed: 12
Phrase search
Morpho search
Match case
Search
Options...
Save results...
100%
TMC-SR\151.34.de•(Sachgebiet=Landesrecht•»•Staat•-•Volk•-•Behörden,•Qualität=aligniert)
DES
2• Der•Bund•kann•auch•Finanzhilfen•für•die•Entwicklung•von•Normen•für•die•behindertengerechte•Gestaltung•des•öffentlichen•Verkehrs•gewähren.
FRS
2• La•Confédération•peut•aussi•accorder•des•aides•financières•pour•le•développement•de•normes•concernant•l'aménagement•des•transports•publics•en•fonction•des•besoins•des•personnes•handicapées.
100%
TMC-SR\151.31.de•(Sachgebiet=Landesrecht•»•Staat•-•Volk•-•Behörden,•Qualität=aligniert)
DES
2• Die•Massnahmen•im•öffentlichen•Verkehr•sind•in•der•Verordnung•vom•12.• No-vember•2003•über•die•behindertengerechte•Gestaltung•des•öffentlichen•Verkehrs•geregelt.
FRS
2• Les•mesures•prises•dans•le•domaine•des•transports•publics•sont•régies•par•l'ordon-nance•du•12•novembre•2003•sur•les•aménagements•visant•à•assurer•l'accès•des•per-sonnes•handicapées•aux•transports•publics•(OTHand).

CAT Tool – Concordance Search

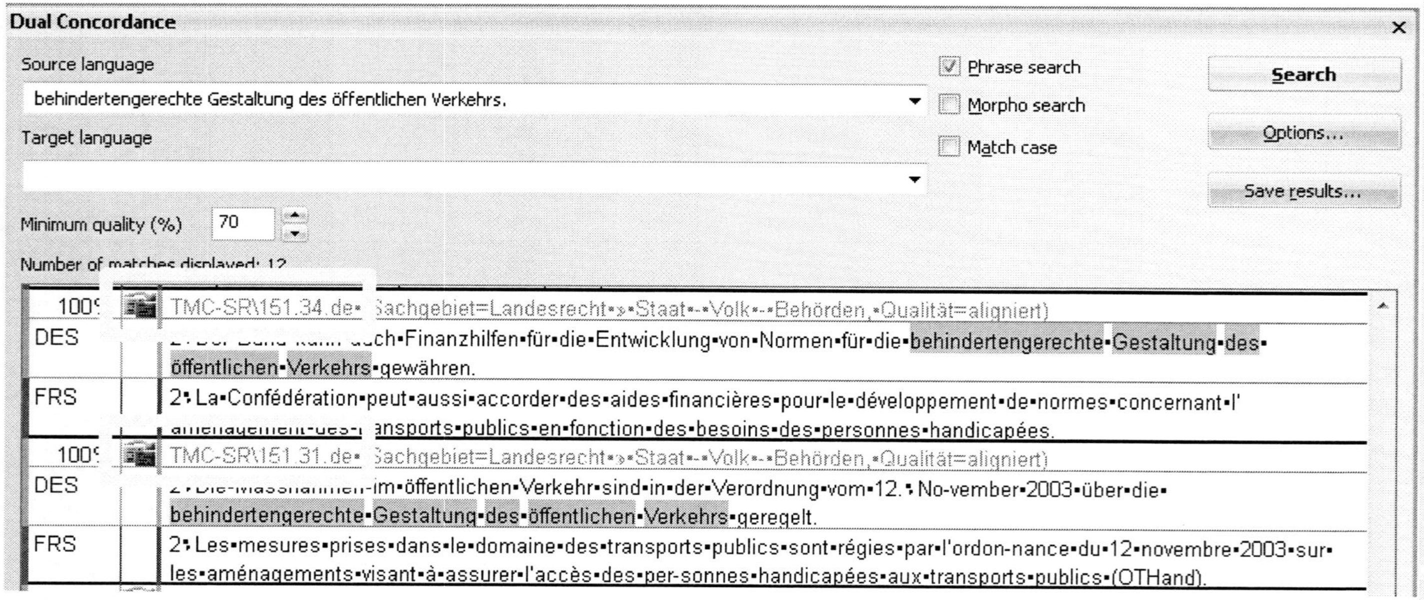

© STAR Group

CAT Tool – Matches & Document Context

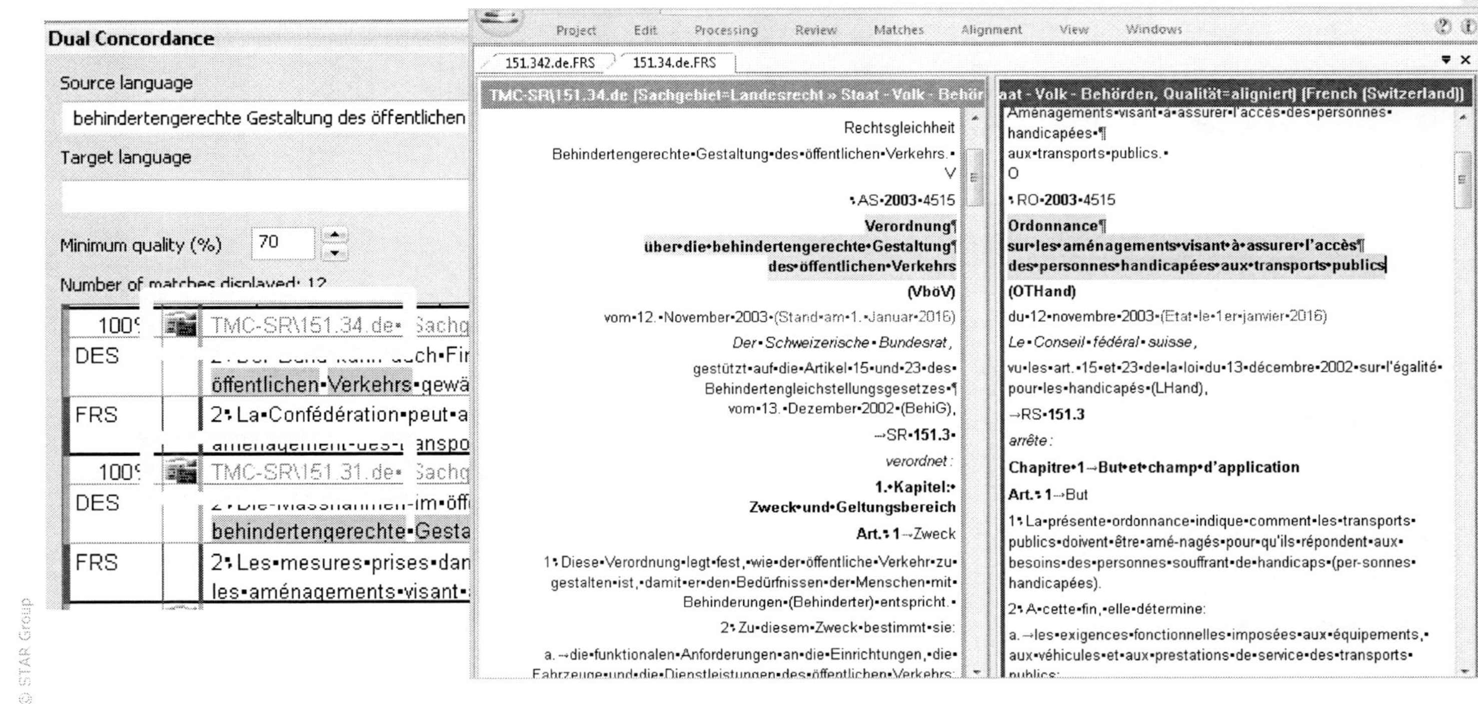

Alignment 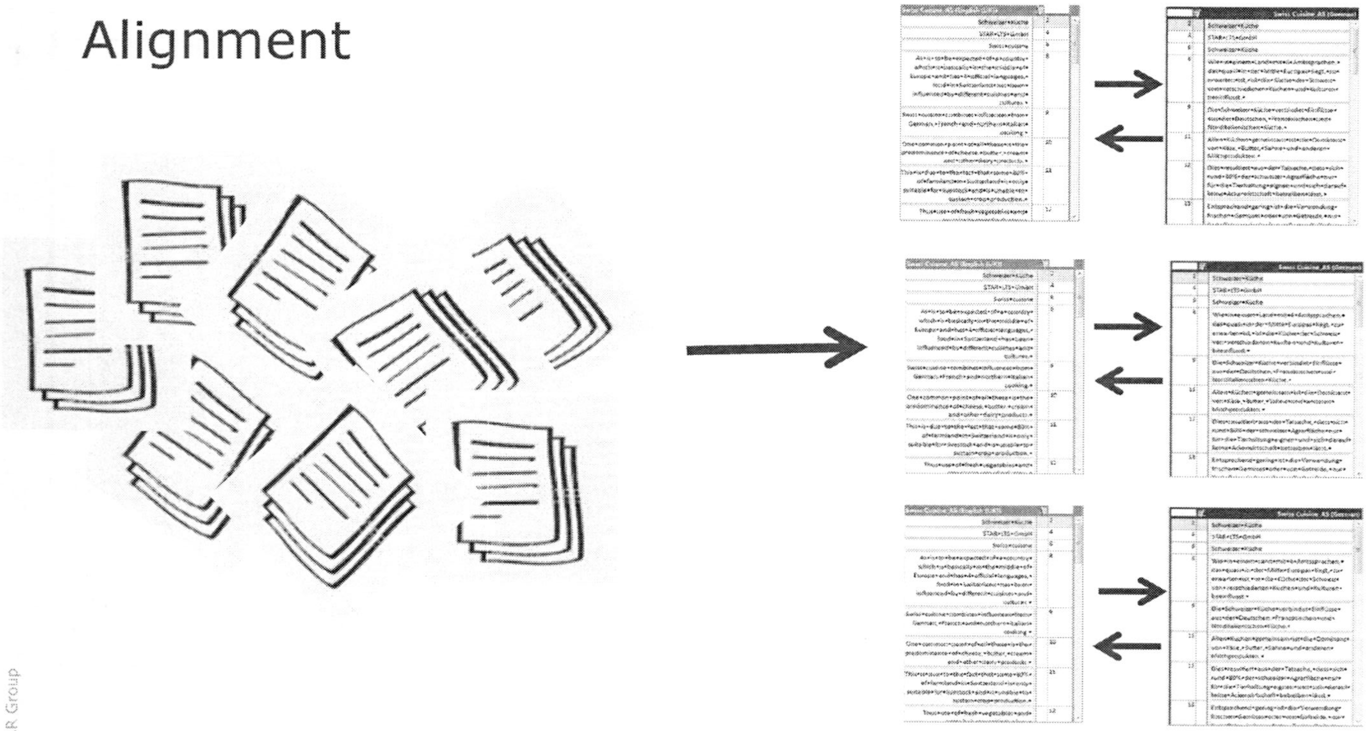
© STAR Group

Why not MT instead?

- Documents approved by linguists and law professionals
- Specific terminology usage and meaning depending on sub-areas
- Consistent translation required for same/similar sentences
- Look-up text and translation of specific law (e.g. file 151.342)

- MT often very well – but different
- MT can be identical by chance – but not reliably so

- Systematic Collection of Legislation must be available as it is!

CAT Tool & Alignment

- Formatting

- Linguistic

- 1 <> many, 0<> 1 , different order

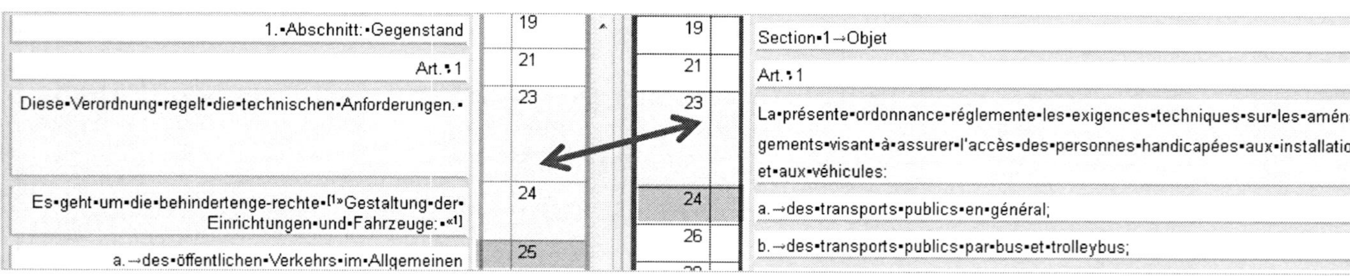

Proceedings of the 14th Conference of the Association for Machine Translation in the Americas
October 6 – 9, 2020, Volume 2: MT User Track

CAT Tool & Alignment

➤ Alignment projects with file alignment

➤ Import and calculate alignment probability

➤ Formal (sentence length, numbers, formating, characters,…)

➤ Lexical (unchanged words, dictionary entries, word lists)

Proceedings of the 14th Conference of the Association for Machine Translation in the Americas
October 6 - 9, 2020, Volume 2: MT User Track

STAR Transit & TM-based Alignment

- Translation Memory segments for alignment

  - Search in TM for segment that is to be aligned

  - Compare translation from TM with alignment candidate

  - Use similarity score as most important value for probability

  - Transit fuzzy algorithms to calculate the similarity

- But – no TM available for the Systematic Collection of Legislation

Proceedings of the 14th Conference of the Association for Machine Translation in the Americas
October 6 – 9, 2020, Volume 2: MT User Track

STAR Transit & MT-based Alignment

- Use MT !
- Transit fuzzy algorithm as with TM segments
  - MT-based sentence alignment (Sennrich & Volk, AMTA 2010)
  - BleuAlign used in BiTextor within Paracrawl project

- MT quality per se not so important
- Similarity to decide if two sentences are translation of each other

- MT interfaces available
- MT system selection (DeepL)

Proceedings of the 14th Conference of the Association for Machine Translation in the Americas
October 6 - 9, 2020, Volume 2: MT User Track

Interactive Alignment

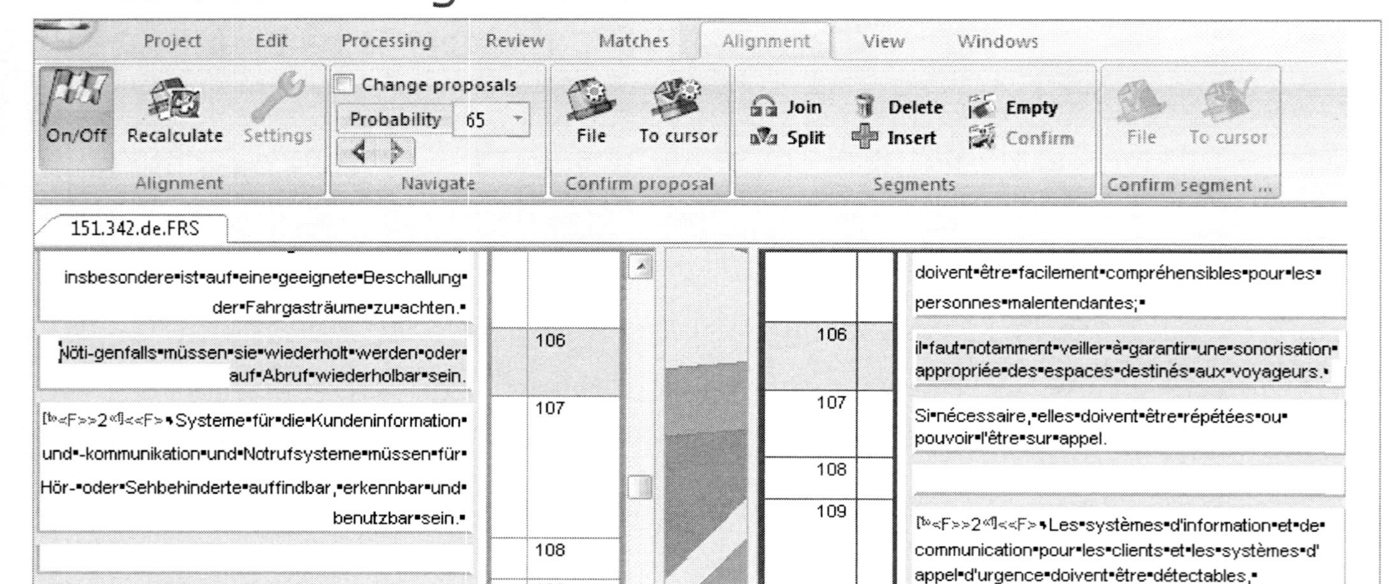

Interactive Alignment

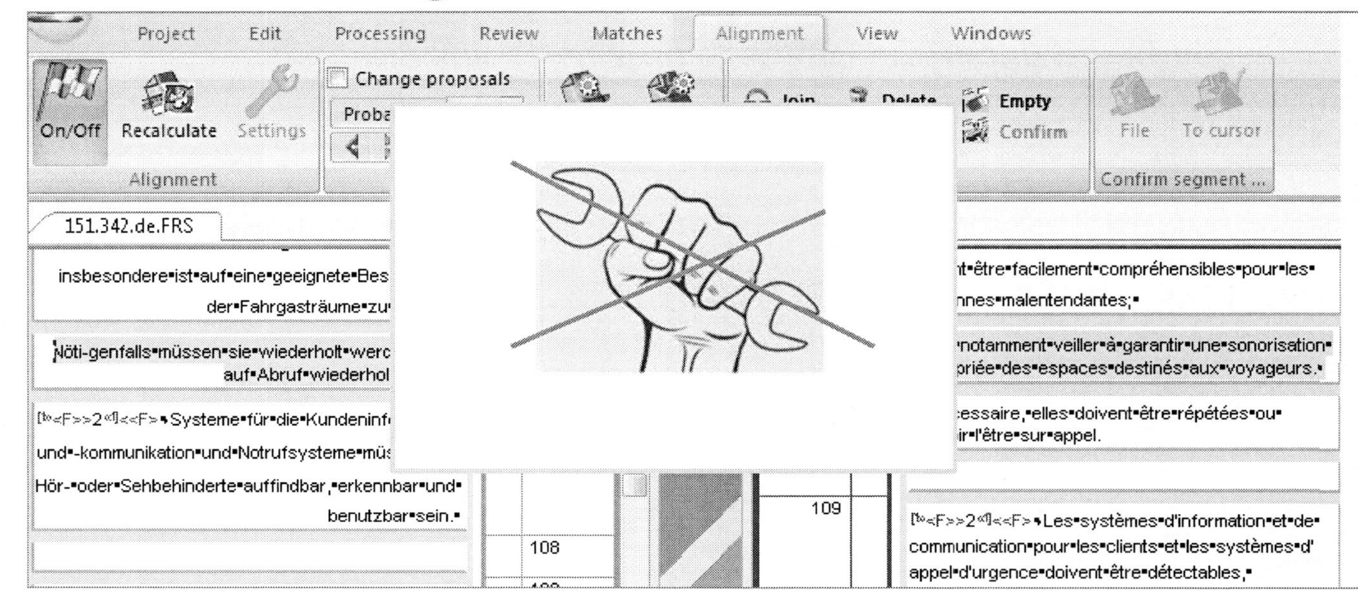

Machine Alignment in Transit

- One environment, no separate tool necessary
  - Transit & Alignment tool for project specification
  - Transit MT interface for fast processing
- Steps:
  - Import, machine translation, translation comparison, calculation
  - Automatic alignment
    - top-down process
    - paragraph tags as anchors
    - 100% similarity as strongest anchors within paragraphs

Proceedings of the 14th Conference of the Association for Machine Translation in the Americas
October 6 – 9, 2020, Volume 2: MT User Track

Machine Alignment

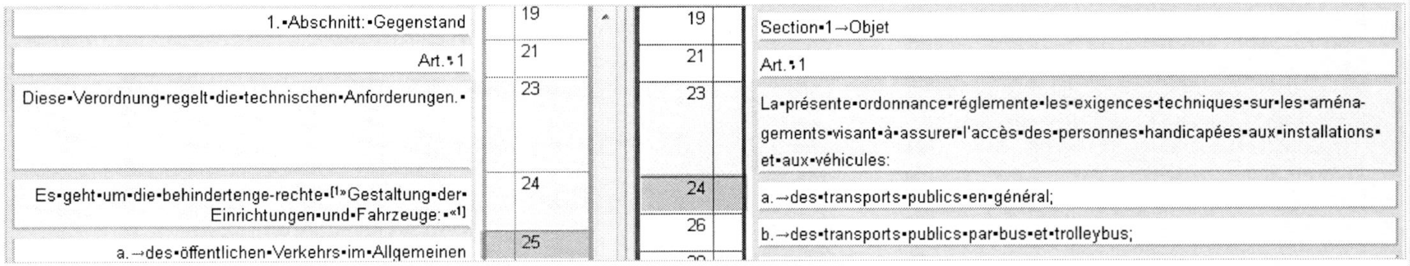

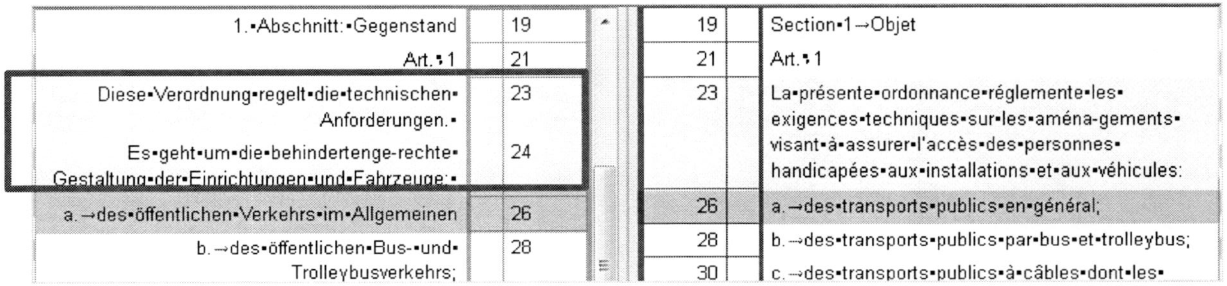

Machine Alignment

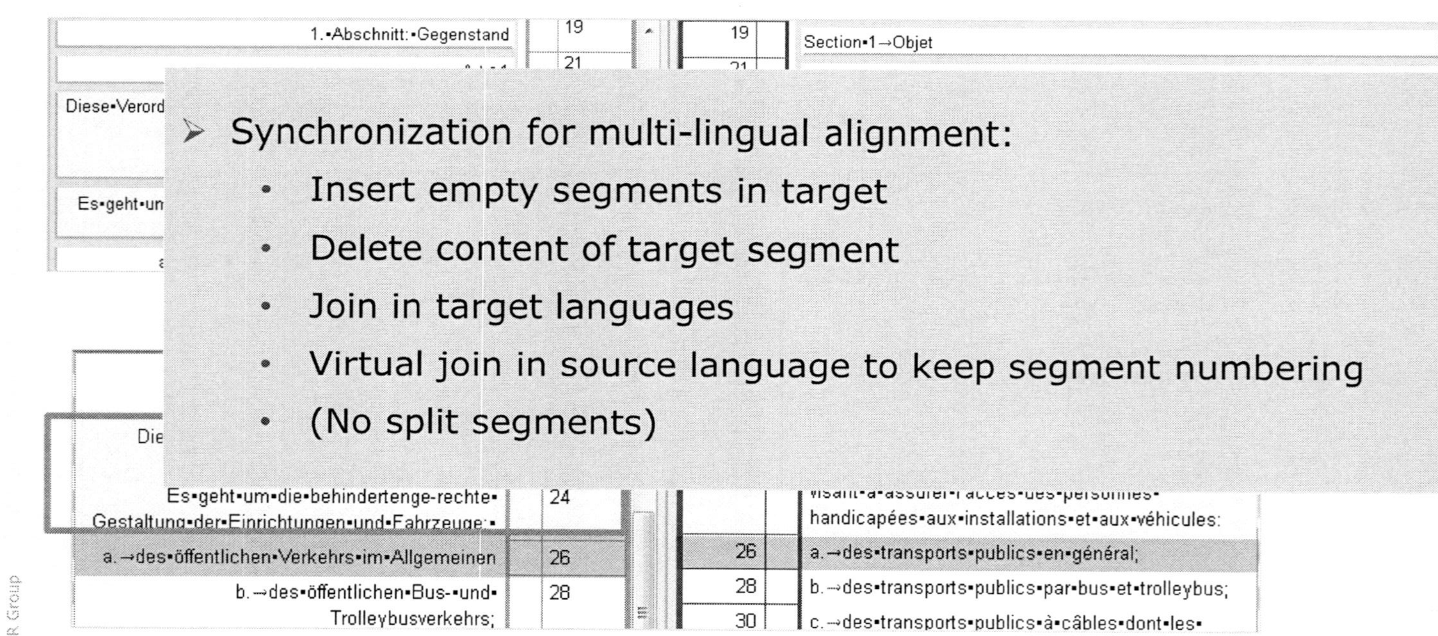

> Synchronization for multi-lingual alignment:
> - Insert empty segments in target
> - Delete content of target segment
> - Join in target languages
> - Virtual join in source language to keep segment numbering
> - (No split segments)

Workflow for MT-Aligned TM-SR

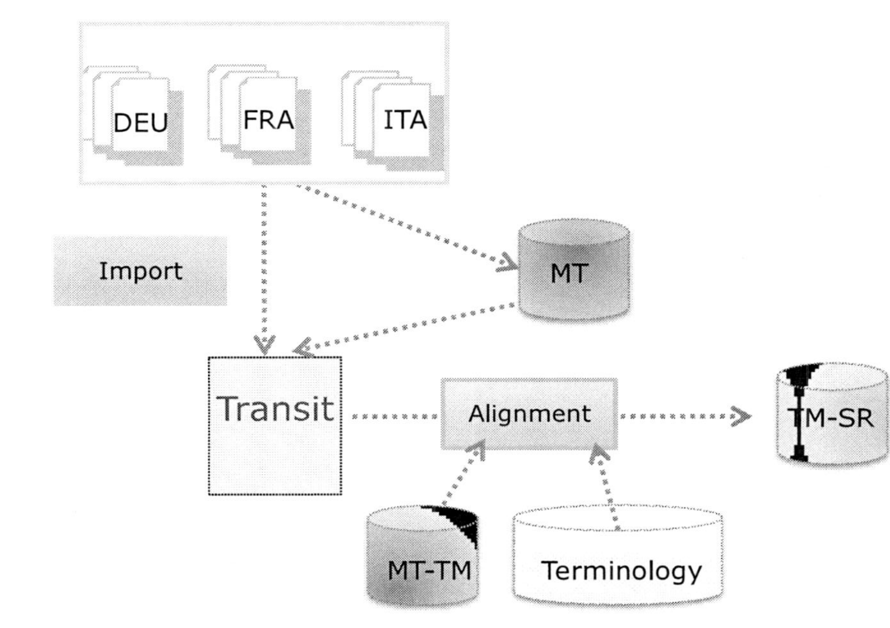

Proceedings of the 14th Conference of the Association for Machine Translation in the Americas
October 6 – 9, 2020, Volume 2: MT User Track

Workflow for MT-Aligned TM-SR

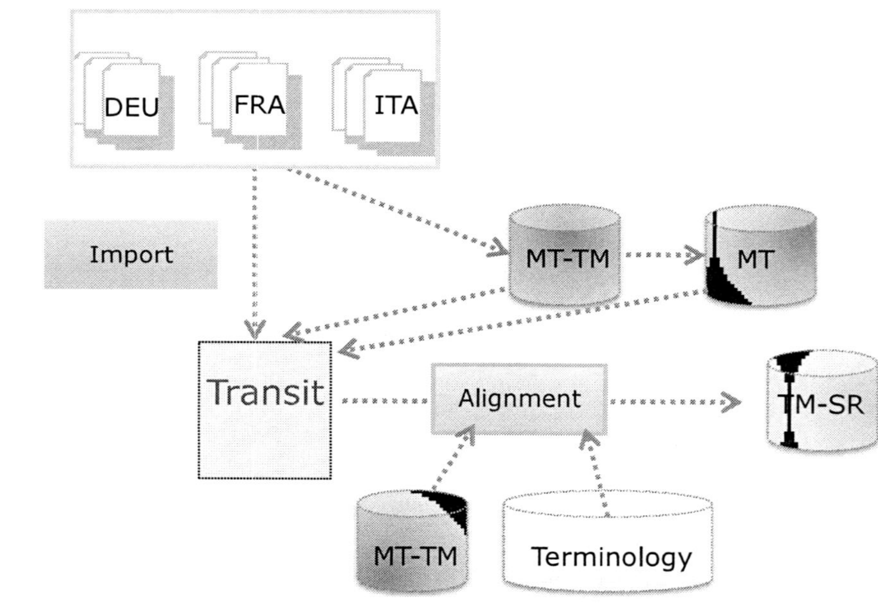

Proceedings of the 14th Conference of the Association for Machine Translation in the Americas
October 6 – 9, 2020, Volume 2: MT User Track

Workflow for MT-Aligned TM-SR

➢ Delta process for next delivery

- Automatic file comparison
- Only new and modified documents are processed
- Deleted files automatically deleted from TM-SR

Proceedings of the 14th Conference of the Association for Machine Translation in the Americas
October 6 – 9, 2020, Volume 2: MT User Track

Conclusion

> ➢ Machine alignment integrated Transit feature

> ➢ Smooth interaction of Transit, Alignment tool and MT interface

> ➢ Random evaluation of machine aligned documents promising

> ➢ Use for search functions in CAT tool possible but restricted

> ➢ TM-SR is available for all users in standard translation environment

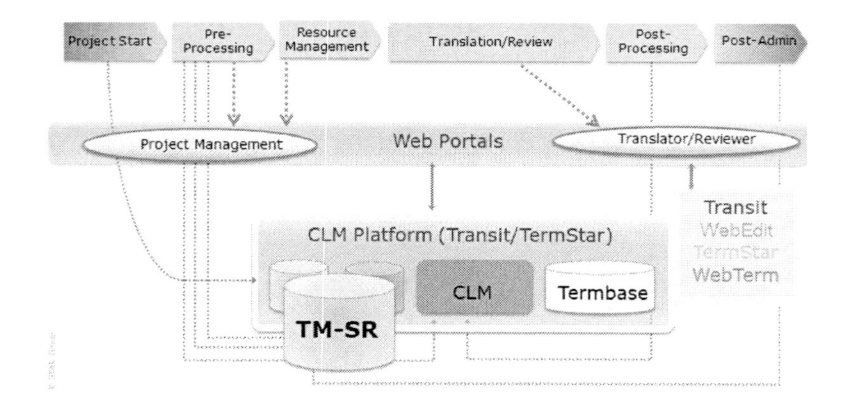

Proceedings of the 14th Conference of the Association for Machine Translation in the Americas
October 6 – 9, 2020, Volume 2: MT User Track

Selection of MT Systems in Translation Workflows

Proceedings of the 14th Conference of the Association for Machine Translation in the Americas
October 6 – 9, 2020, Volume 2: MT User Track

OUTLINE

- Introduction, motivation

- MT Quality Across Domains

- Approaches to MT Selection

- Conclusion

Proceedings of the 14th Conference of the Association for Machine Translation in the Americas
October 6 – 9, 2020, Volume 2: MT User Track

INTRODUCTION

- MT quality has been steadily improving in the past few years

- MT can be very beneficial in translation
  - In some scenarios, MT can be used with little or no post-editing
  - MT can be a useful starting point for post-editing

- There are many commercial MT providers to choose from
  - Quality of MT systems varies across languages or domains
  - It is difficult to decide ahead of time which system is optimal for a project

Proceedings of the 14th Conference of the Association for Machine Translation in the Americas
October 6 – 9, 2020, Volume 2: MT User Track

ABOUT MEMSOURCE

- Cloud-based translation management system

- Customers use Memsource to manage the localization process and to produce translations

- We want to provide high-quality MT by default so that our users can benefit from MT as much as possible

Proceedings of the 14th Conference of the Association for Machine Translation in the Americas
October 6 – 9, 2020, Volume 2: MT User Track

MT Quality Across Domains

Proceedings of the 14th Conference of the Association for Machine Translation in the Americas
October 6 - 9, 2020, Volume 2: MT User Track

METHODOLOGY

- Domains were defined using unsupervised machine learning on aggregate customer data, labels assigned manually
    - For non-English source languages, internal MT into English is applied first

- Domains contain data from multiple customers

- MT engines are assigned to documents using Memsource Translate
    - Eliminates bias of customer preference for specific engines
    - Given enough data points, we can assume inputs for each MT system are i.i.d.

Proceedings of the 14th Conference of the Association for Machine Translation in the Americas
October 6 – 9, 2020, Volume 2: MT User Track

DOMAINS

Domain	Keywords
Medical	'study', 'patients', 'patient', 'treatment', 'dose', 'mg', 'clinical'
Travel and Hospitality	'km', 'hotel', 'guests', 'room', 'accommodation'
Business and Education	'team', 'business', 'work', 'school', 'students',
Legal and Finance	'agreement', 'company', 'contract', 'services', 'financial'
Software User Documentation	'click', 'select', 'data', 'text', 'view', 'file',
Consumer Electronics	'power', 'battery', 'switch', 'sensor', 'usb',
User Support	'please', 'email', 'account', 'domain', 'contact',
Cloud Services	'network', 'server', 'database', 'sql', 'data'
Industrial	'mm', 'pressure', 'valve', 'machine', 'oil'
Software Development	'value', 'class', 'type', 'element', 'string'
Entertainment	'game', 'like', 'get', 'love', 'play', 'go', '

Proceedings of the 14th Conference of the Association for Machine Translation in the Americas
October 6 – 9, 2020, Volume 2: MT User Track

RESULTS: ENGLISH-RUSSIAN

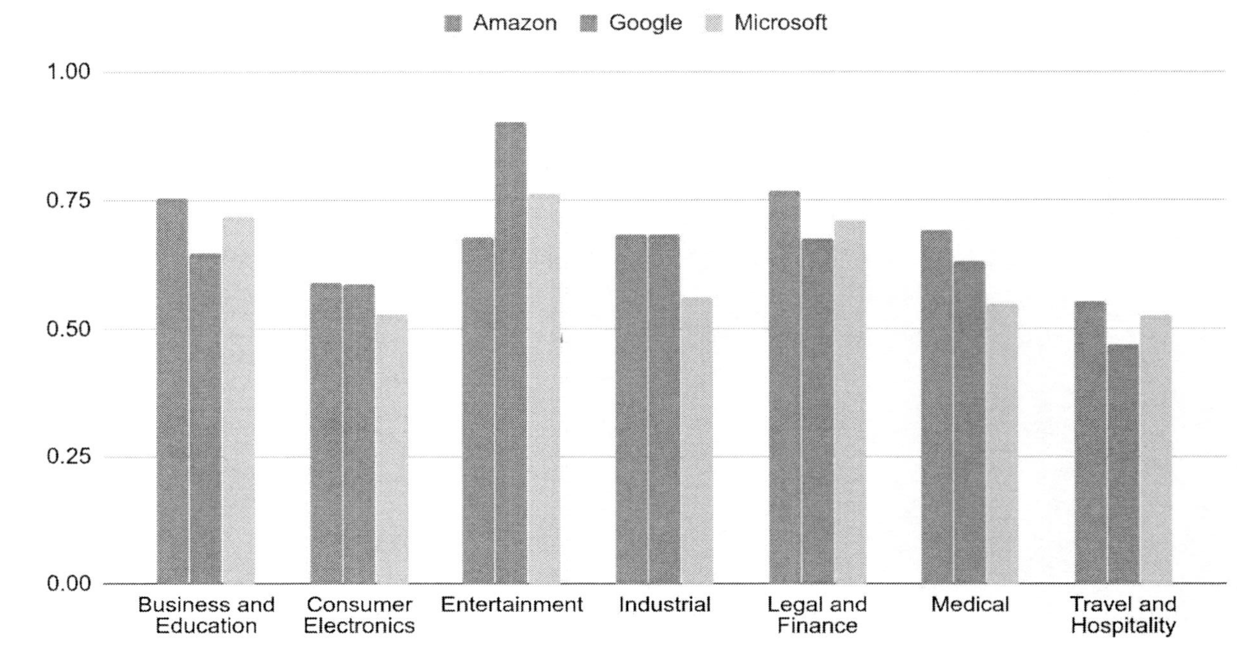

Proceedings of the 14th Conference of the Association for Machine Translation in the Americas
October 6 – 9, 2020, Volume 2: MT User Track

RESULTS: ENGLISH-FRENCH

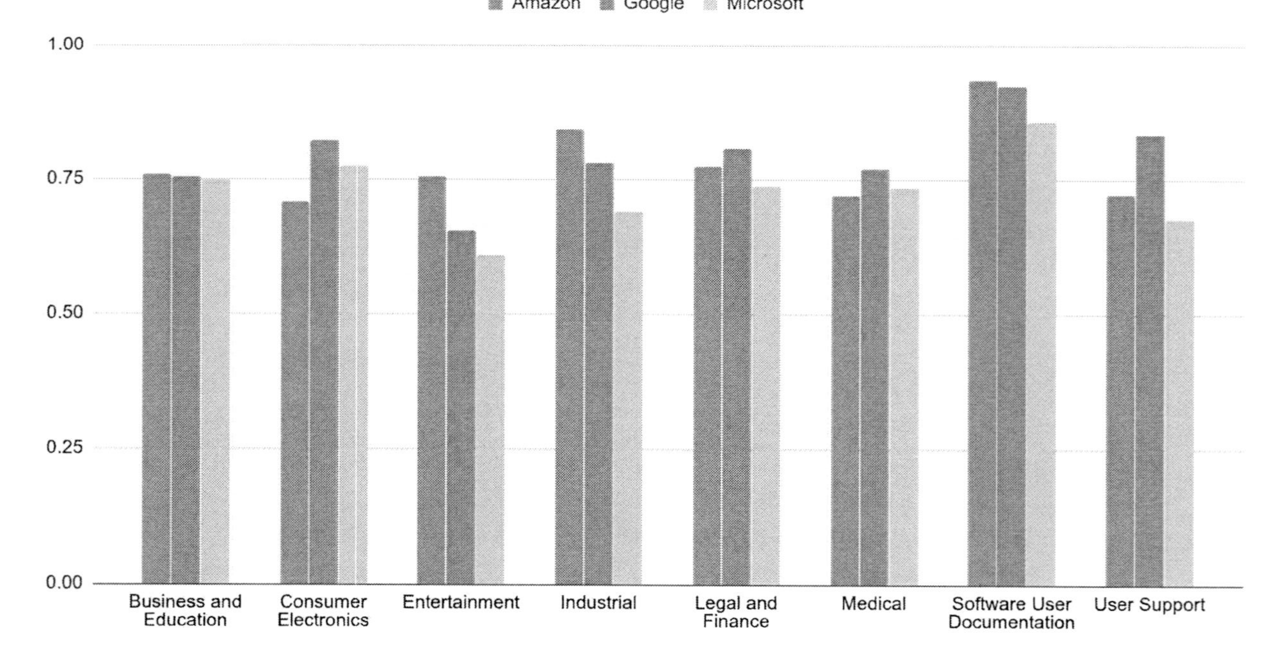

Proceedings of the 14th Conference of the Association for Machine Translation in the Americas
October 6 – 9, 2020, Volume 2: MT User Track

RESULTS: SINGLE DOMAIN, MULTIPLE LANGUAGES

Domain: Legal and Finance

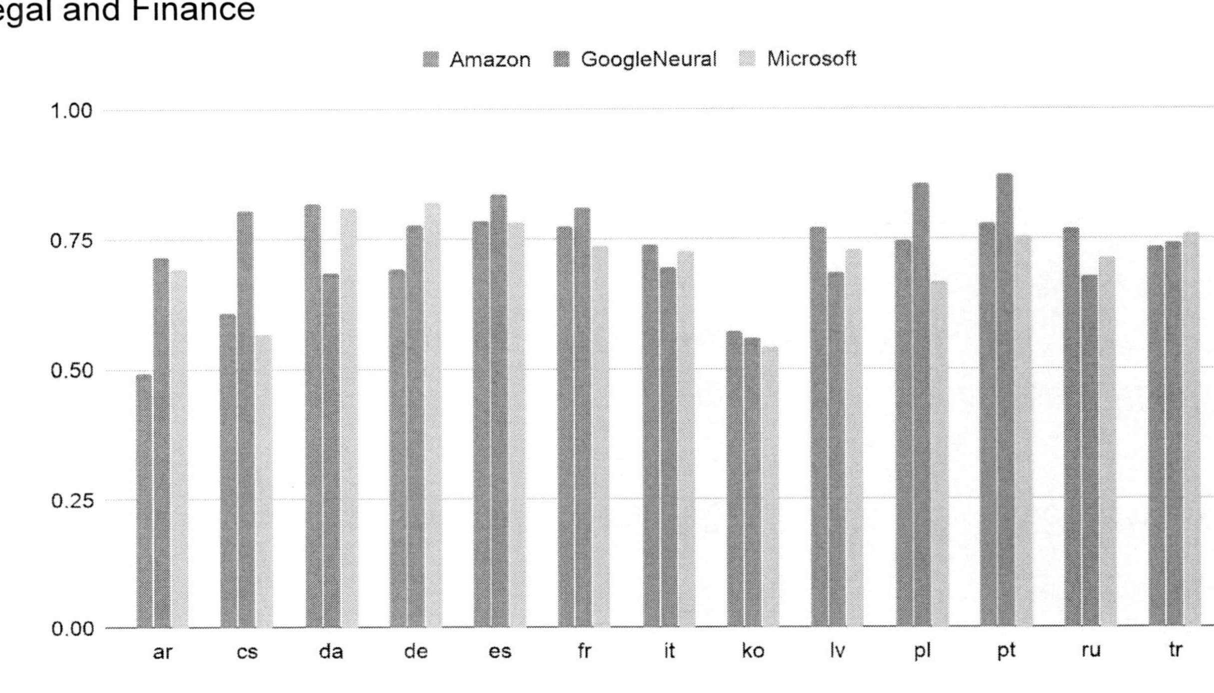

Proceedings of the 14th Conference of the Association for Machine Translation in the Americas
October 6 – 9, 2020, Volume 2: MT User Track

IMPORTANCE OF SELECTING OPTIMAL MT ENGINES

- Given that all MT systems perform relatively well, does it matter which system is used?

- Sanchez-Torron and Koehn, 2016 show that *"for each 1-point increase in BLEU, there is a PE [post-editing] time decrease of 0.16 seconds per word, about 3-4%".*

  - There is a clear correlation between MT quality and translator productivity.
  - The exact number may be different today due to specifics of NMT.

Proceedings of the 14th Conference of the Association for Machine Translation in the Americas
October 6 – 9, 2020, Volume 2: MT User Track

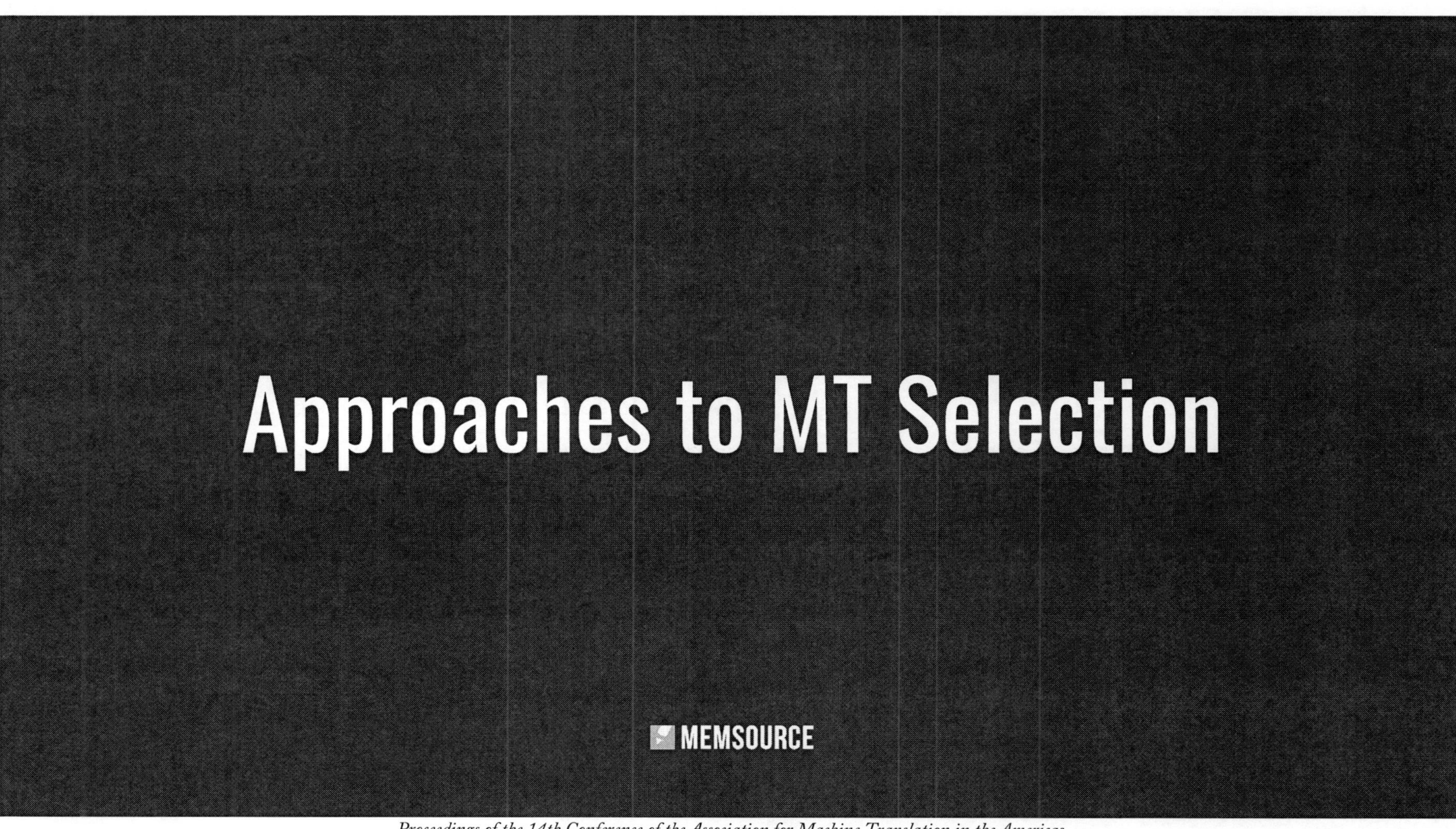

Proceedings of the 14th Conference of the Association for Machine Translation in the Americas
October 6 – 9, 2020, Volume 2: MT User Track

PILOT STUDY

- High-level overview:
    - Create a sample dataset from the project
    - Translate the sample using multiple MT engines
    - Linguists are asked to post-edit the samples
    - Measure required amount of post-editing, time

- Robust, sound method but costly. Only makes sense for large projects/customers.
    - Needs to be re-done for every project (potential of data drift).

Proceedings of the 14th Conference of the Association for Machine Translation in the Americas
October 6 – 9, 2020, Volume 2: MT User Track

MT QUALITY ESTIMATION

- Similar to pilot study but no manual post-editing.

- High-level overview:
  - Create a sample dataset from the project
  - Translate the sample using multiple MT engines
  - Measure MT quality using MTQE (manual translation is not required)

- Quick, cheap but still requires some manual steps (data preparation, evaluation).
  - Needs to be re-done for every project.

- MTQE may not be reliable enough for some domains/language combinations.

Proceedings of the 14th Conference of the Association for Machine Translation in the Americas
October 6 – 9, 2020, Volume 2: MT User Track

MULTI-ENGINE MT

- Since multiple MT engines are available, use all of them.
  - MT system combination, not selection

- There are methods and for combining multiple MT outputs into a single translation, see e.g. Heafield and Lavie 2010, Freitag et al. 2014, Zhou et al. 2017

- More difficult to implement, costly (all engines used for all inputs), potentially the most robust option.

MACHINE-LEARNING BASED SELECTION

- Use ML directly for recommending optimal MT engines based on translated content
- Only the selected MT engine is used (reduced costs)
- Fully automated for users, no manual steps are involved

- Commercial solutions:
  - Memsource Translate
  - Smartling MT Auto Select
  - Intento Smart Routing*

- Academic work is limited
  - At this conference though: Naradowsky et al. 2020, Machine Translation System Selection from Bandit Feedback

* It is not clear whether recommendations are based on ML or rather static benchmarks.

Proceedings of the 14th Conference of the Association for Machine Translation in the Americas
October 6 – 9, 2020, Volume 2: MT User Track

MEMSOURCE TRANSLATE

- Automated selection of optimal MT system based on language pair and domain
- For every input document:
  - Analysis of content → domain label
  - Recommendation of MT system based on MT engine statistics
  - Once manual post-editing is completed, MT score is calculated → estimate update

- Recommendations driven by a standard algorithm for Bayesian multi-armed bandits
  - Model is continuously learning and improving
  - MT engine statistics are based on more than 100K documents (and growing)

- Simple, interpretable, fully automated
- A flexible framework, supports custom MT engines

Proceedings of the 14th Conference of the Association for Machine Translation in the Americas
October 6 – 9, 2020, Volume 2: MT User Track

RECOMMENDED SYSTEMS IN TIME

English-Spanish, domain: User support

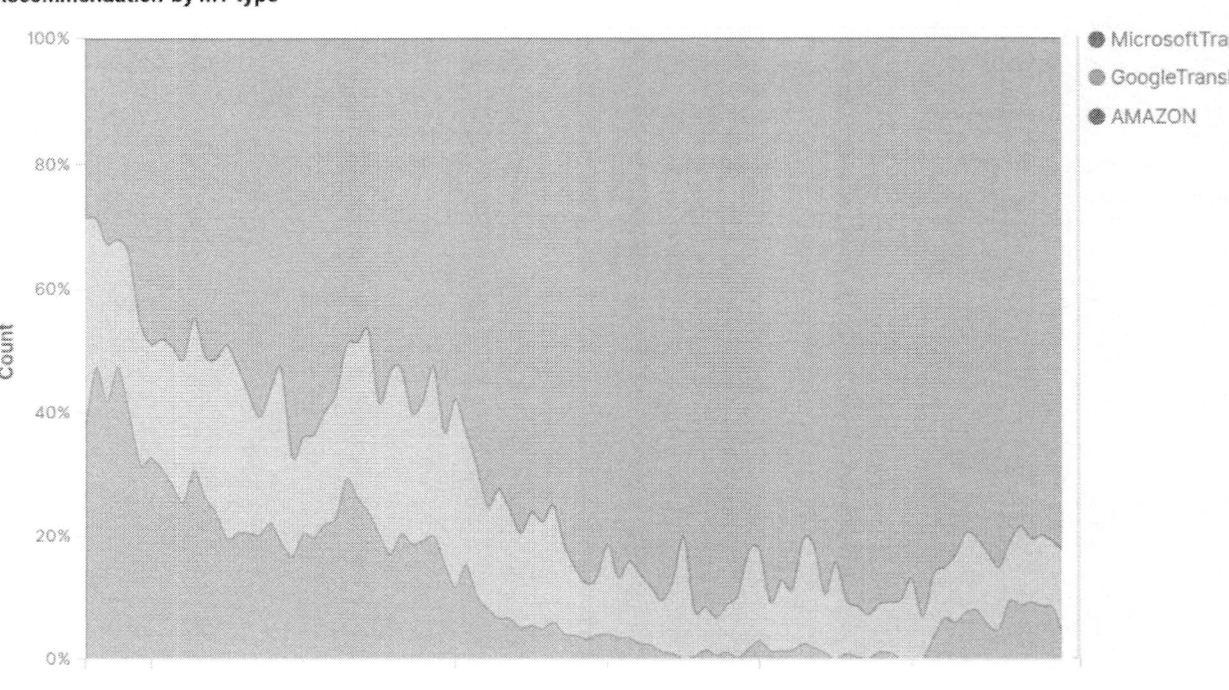

Proceedings of the 14th Conference of the Association for Machine Translation in the Americas
October 6 – 9, 2020, Volume 2: MT User Track

Conclusion

MEMSOURCE

Proceedings of the 14th Conference of the Association for Machine Translation in the Americas
October 6 – 9, 2020, Volume 2: MT User Track

CONCLUSION

- MT can be very useful in localization

- Considerations:
    - Landscape of MT providers difficult to navigate
    - MT system quality varies across languages but also across domains
    - MT systems evolve over time

- Various approaches to MT selection exist
    - Manual evaluations work well for large, well-defined projects
    - Machine learning can allow to automate the process

REFERENCES

- Axelrod, Amittai, Xiaodong He, and Jianfeng Gao. "Domain adaptation via pseudo in-domain data selection." In *Proceedings of the 2011 Conference on Empirical Methods in Natural Language Processing*, pp. 355-362. 2011.
- Freitag, Markus, Matthias Huck, and Hermann Ney. "Jane: Open source machine translation system combination." In *Proceedings of the Demonstrations at the 14th Conference of the European Chapter of the Association for Computational Linguistics*, pp. 29-32. 2014.
- Heafield, Kenneth, and Alon Lavie. "Combining machine translation output with open source: The Carnegie Mellon multi-engine machine translation scheme." *The Prague Bulletin of Mathematical Linguistics* 93, no. 2010 (2010): 27-36.
- Naradowsky, Jason, Xuan Zhang, and Kevin Duh. "Machine Translation System Selection from Bandit Feedback." *arXiv preprint arXiv:2002.09646* (2020).
- Sanchez-Torron, Marina, and Philipp Koehn. "Machine translation quality and post-editor productivity." In *Proceedings of AMTA*, vol. 1, pp. 16-26. 2016.
- Van der Wees, Marlies, Arianna Bisazza, Wouter Weerkamp, and Christof Monz. "What's in a domain? Analyzing genre and topic differences in statistical machine translation." In *Proceedings of the 53rd Annual Meeting of the Association for Computational Linguistics and the 7th International Joint Conference on Natural Language Processing (Volume 2: Short Papers)*, pp. 560-566. 2015.
- Zhou, Long, Wenpeng Hu, Jiajun Zhang, and Chengqing Zong. "Neural system combination for machine translation." *arXiv preprint arXiv:1704.06393* (2017).

Proceedings of the 14th Conference of the Association for Machine Translation in the Americas
October 6 – 9, 2020, Volume 2: MT User Track

Beyond MT: Opening Doors for an NLP Pipeline

Alex Yanishevsky

Senior Manager, AI Deployments

Proceedings of the 14th Conference of the Association for Machine Translation in the Americas
October 6 – 9, 2020, Volume 2: MT User Track

Overview

Primary Use Cases of MT

MT for NLP Pipeline

- Why?
- Before MT: Language identification
- After: MT Quality Estimation
- After MT: Social Listening
- After MT: Named Entity Recognition
- After MT: Dependency Parsing
- After MT: Keyword Search

Case Studies

Proceedings of the 14th Conference of the Association for Machine Translation in the Americas
October 6 – 9, 2020, Volume 2: MT User Track

Primary Use Cases of MT

Proceedings of the 14th Conference of the Association for Machine Translation in the Americas
October 6 - 9, 2020, Volume 2: MT User Track

Primary Use Cases of MT

- From and into English
- Generic or trained engines (domain, product, etc.)
- Informational (raw MT) including chat, forums, knowledge bases
- Post-editing (light, medium, full)
- Via MT connectors in TMS or CAT tools
- MT Quality Estimation

MT for NLP Pipeline

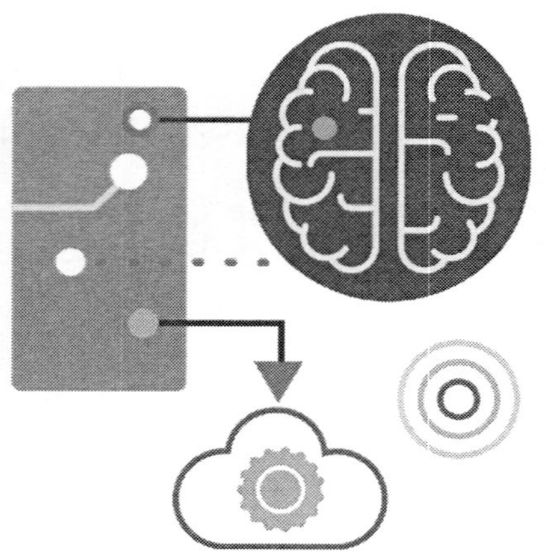

Proceedings of the 14th Conference of the Association for Machine Translation in the Americas
October 6 - 9, 2020, Volume 2: MT User Track

Why?

- Many NLP packages (such as NTLK, Stanford CoreNLP or spaCy) not available or lag behind for non-English languages, e.g. readability for Flesch-Kincaid, POS tagging, dependency parsing, named entity recognition, stemming, lemmatization

- Insufficient data to train models

Source: Memsource, AMTA 2020, Session C14

- Domains were defined using unsupervised machine learning on aggregate customer data, labels assigned manually
  - For non-English source languages, internal MT into English is applied first

NLP Pipeline

- Before MT: Language identification
- Machine Translation (generic or trained)
- After: MT Quality Estimation
- After MT: Social Listening
- After MT: Named Entity Recognition*
- After MT: Dependency Parsing
- After MT: Keywords

* Can also be done Before MT

Proceedings of the 14th Conference of the Association for Machine Translation in the Americas
October 6 - 9, 2020, Volume 2: MT User Track

Before MT:
Language Identification

For some domains such as litigation, a file or email may be multi-lingual. Thus, we need a way to identify the language(s) and pass them to MT in one request.

How to deal with this?

Language ID suite with **five** algorithms and majority polling Identification, MT and reassembly on a segment basis.

Example

Программное обеспечение защищено законодательством и международными соглашениями об авторском праве, а также законодательством и соглашениями о защите интеллектуальной собственности. Программное обеспечение не продается, а предоставляется в пользование по лицензии. Puede activar cierto software mediante una clave de licencia proporcionada por el servicio de soporte técnico de Luminex, enviando un mensaje a support@luminexcorp.com o llamando al 1-877-785-2323 o al 1-512-381-4397. 경기 부천에 있는 쿠팡 물류센터 관련 신종 코로나바이러스 감염증(코로나19) 환자가 급속도로 늘어나자, 정부는 내달 14일까지 수도권 내 모든 다중이용시설 운영을 한시적으로 중단하기로 했다. 다만, 수도권 내 조·중·고 등교 수업은 증지 없이 진행된다.

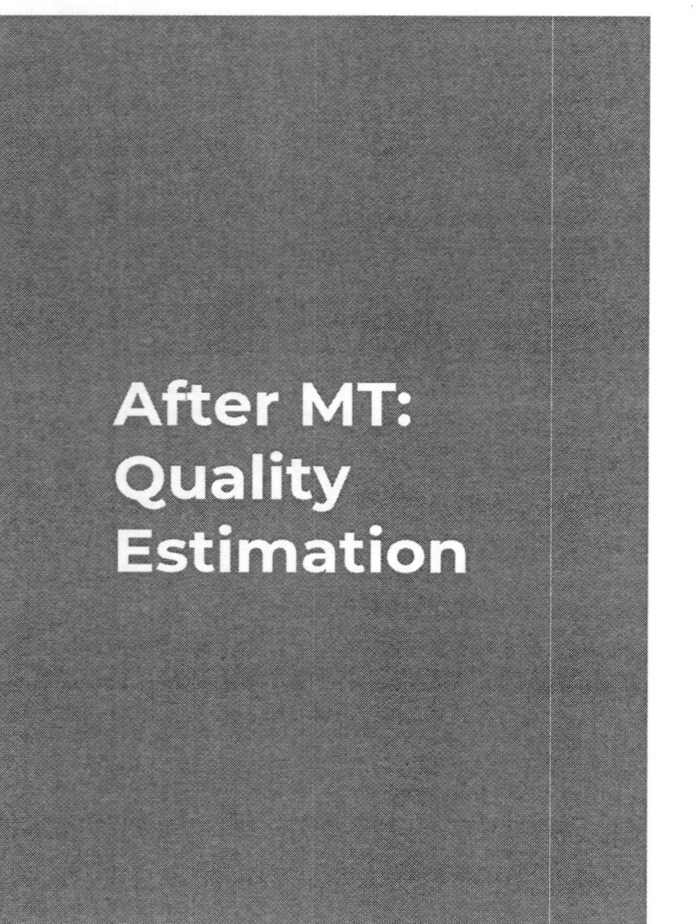

Proceedings of the 14th Conference of the Association for Machine Translation in the Americas
October 6 - 9, 2020, Volume 2: MT User Track

After MT: Social Listening

Brand Health

Evaluating public perception of brand and/or products.

Industry Insights

Analyzing discussions or hashtags related to specific industry.

Competitive Analysis

Analyzing competing brands or products.

Campaign Analysis and Event Monitoring

- Evaluating public perception of a campaign.
- Monitoring audience responses to a conferences and/or events.

Proceedings of the 14th Conference of the Association for Machine Translation in the Americas
October 6 - 9, 2020, Volume 2: MT User Track

After MT:
Named Entity
Recognition*

Recognition (Identification)
Deanonymization
Reassembly

GDPR Compliance
HIPAA Compliance
Responsive (hot) document for litigation

* Can be done before MT

After MT: Dependency Parsing

1. What is it?

2. How to do it? Dependency Parse Tree, Head-Dependent

3. Why do it?

Relation	Examples with *head* and **dependent**
NSUBJ	**United** *canceled* the flight.
DOBJ	United *diverted* the **flight** to Reno.

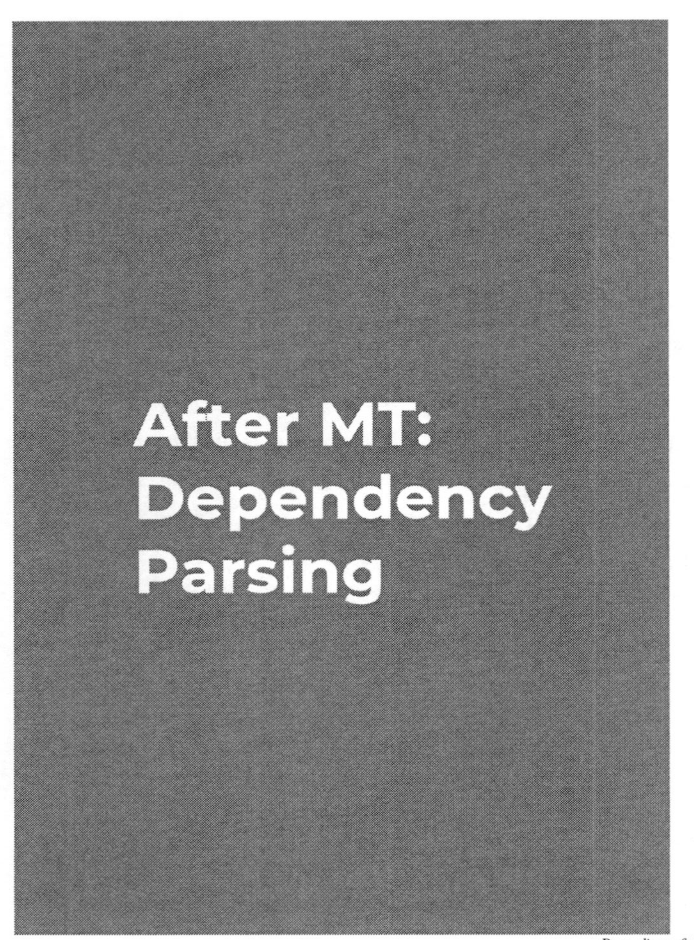

Source: https://medium.com/data-science-in-your-pocket/dependency-parsing-associated-algorithms-in-nlp-96d65dd95d3e

After MT: Keyword Search

- An example of a word cloud with salient terms for side effects of a drug

Proceedings of the 14th Conference of the Association for Machine Translation in the Americas
October 6 - 9, 2020, Volume 2: MT User Track

Case Studies

Proceedings of the 14th Conference of the Association for Machine Translation in the Americas
October 6 - 9, 2020, Volume 2: MT User Track

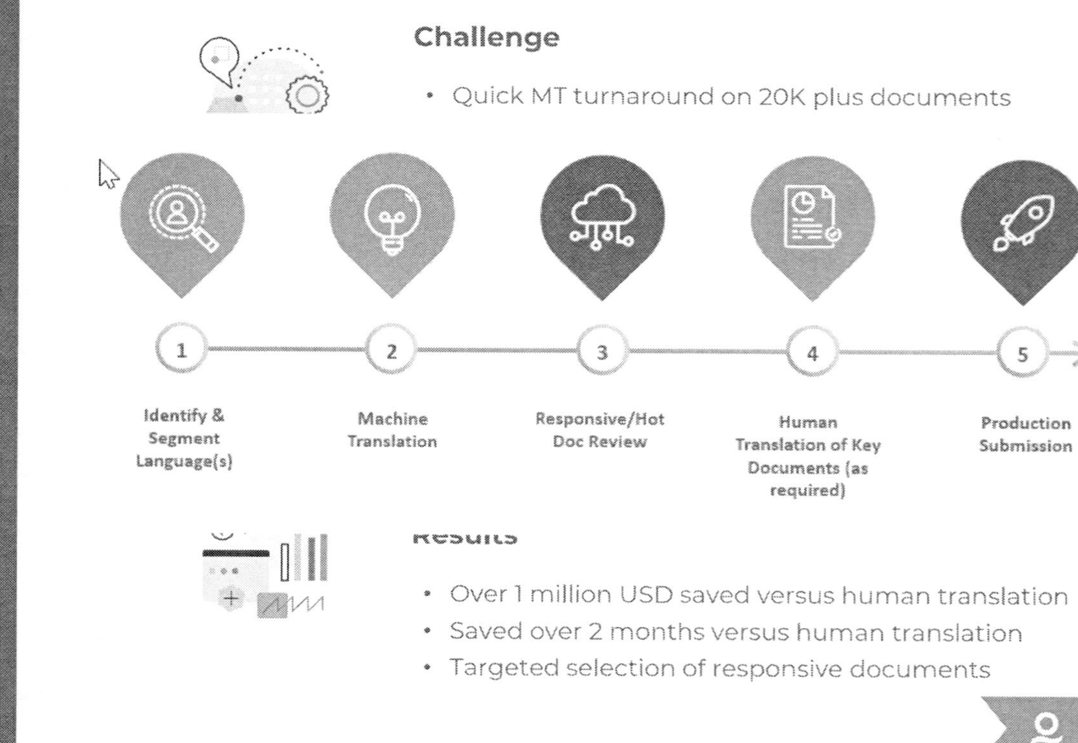

Challenge

- Quick MT turnaround on 20K plus documents

Results

- Over 1 million USD saved versus human translation
- Saved over 2 months versus human translation
- Targeted selection of responsive documents

Challenge

- Social listening for FR and ES
- Monitor responses of patients taking medication on social media channels

Solution

- Normalization of UGC
- Named Entity Recognition
- Customized sentiment analysis models including parsing ironic and sarcastic comments

Results

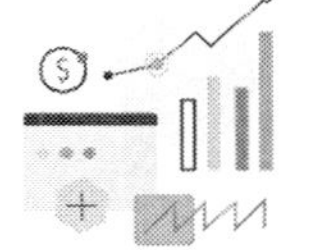

- Respond to patients' concerns
- Monitor and take action on adverse side effects
- Geographical, product and context distributions

Proceedings of the 14th Conference of the Association for Machine Translation in the Americas
October 6 - 9, 2020, Volume 2: MT User Track

AMTA VIRTUAL 2020

aws

Building
A Multi-Purpose
MT Portfolio

INTENTO

© Intento, Inc. / September 2020

AGENDA

Multi-Purpose MT?

MT usage scenarios and requirements

Case Study 1: **Entity Protection**

Case Study 2: **Custom Terminology**

Case Study 3: **Tone of Voice**

Key Takeaways

Intento

Proceedings of the 14th Conference of the Association for Machine Translation in the Americas
October 6 – 9, 2020, Volume 2: MT User Track

MULTI-PURPOSE MT?

© Intento, Inc. / September 2020

Proceedings of the 14th Conference of the Association for Machine Translation in the Americas
October 6 – 9, 2020, Volume 2: MT User Track

Proceedings of the 14th Conference of the Association for Machine Translation in the Americas
October 6 – 9, 2020, Volume 2: MT User Track

BRIDGING THE GAP BETWEEN
MT CAPABILITIES AND ADOPTION

MT Procurement

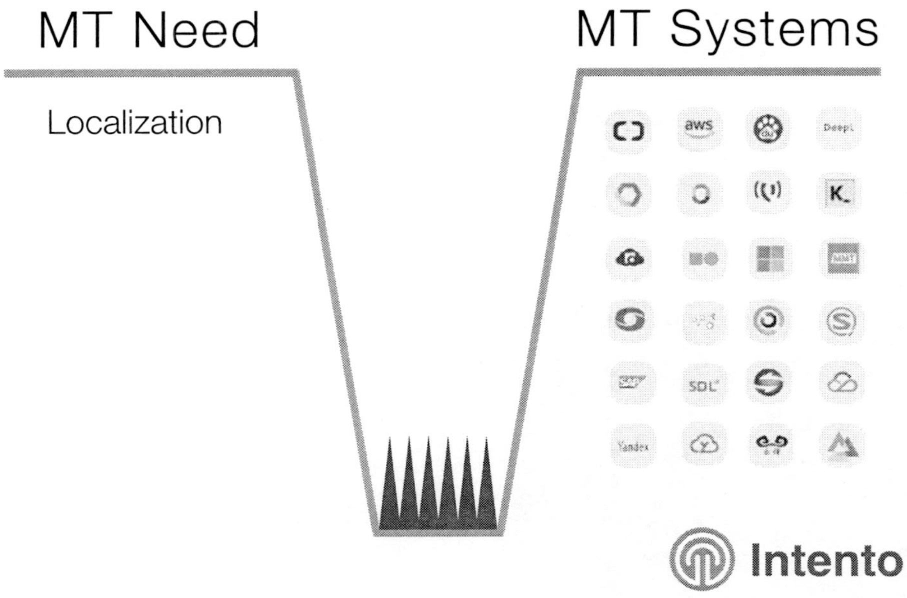

MT Need

MT Systems

© Intento, Inc. / September 2020

Proceedings of the 14th Conference of the Association for Machine Translation in the Americas
October 6 – 9, 2020, Volume 2: MT User Track

BRIDGING THE GAP BETWEEN
MT CAPABILITIES AND ADOPTION

MT Procurement

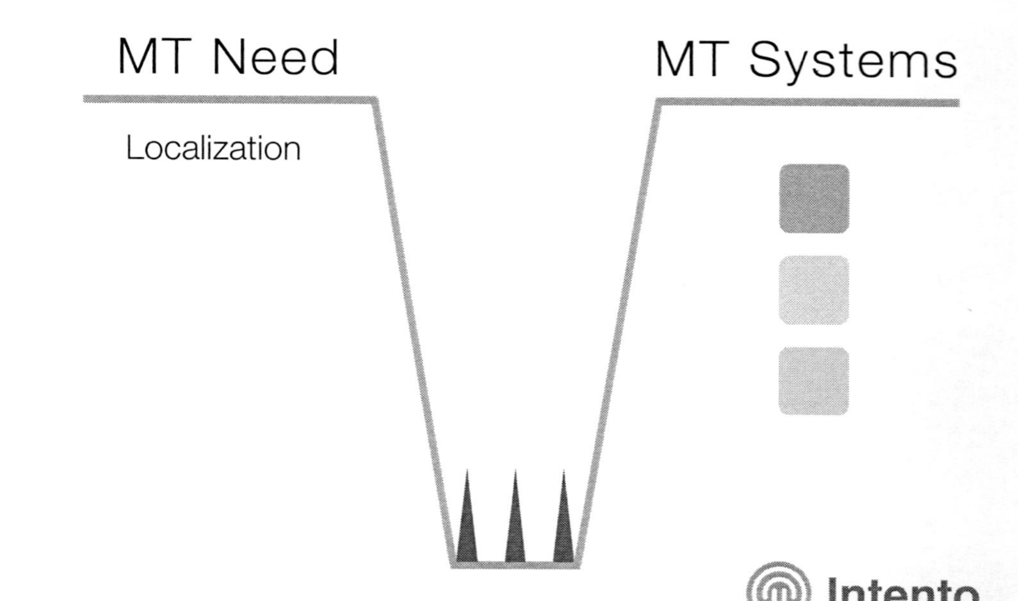

Proceedings of the 14th Conference of the Association for Machine Translation in the Americas
October 6 – 9, 2020, Volume 2: MT User Track

BRIDGING THE GAP BETWEEN
MT CAPABILITIES AND ADOPTION

MT Procurement

MT Curation

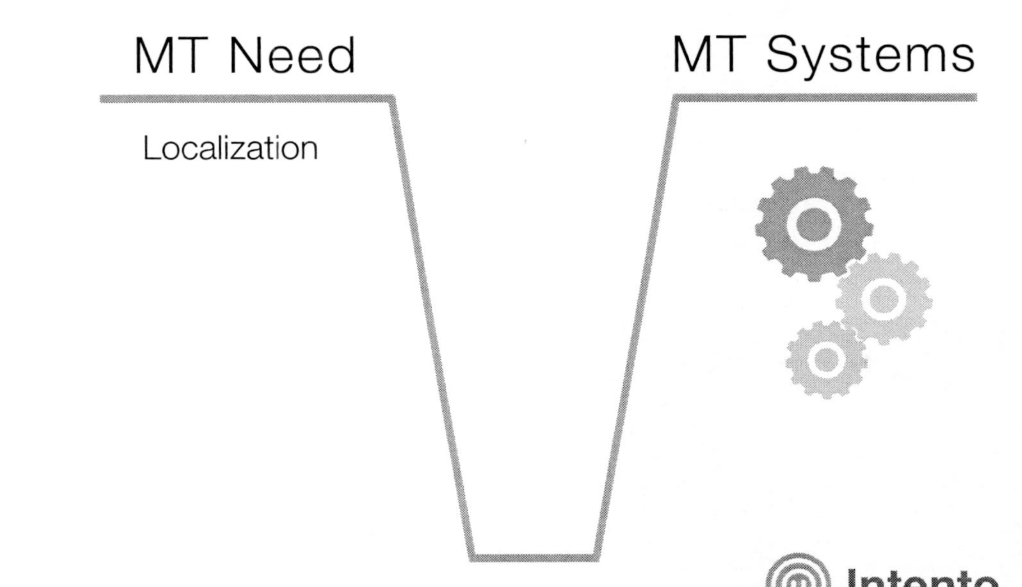

Proceedings of the 14th Conference of the Association for Machine Translation in the Americas
October 6 – 9, 2020, Volume 2: MT User Track

BRIDGING THE GAP BETWEEN
MT CAPABILITIES AND ADOPTION

MT Procurement

—

MT Curation

—

Multi-Engine MT

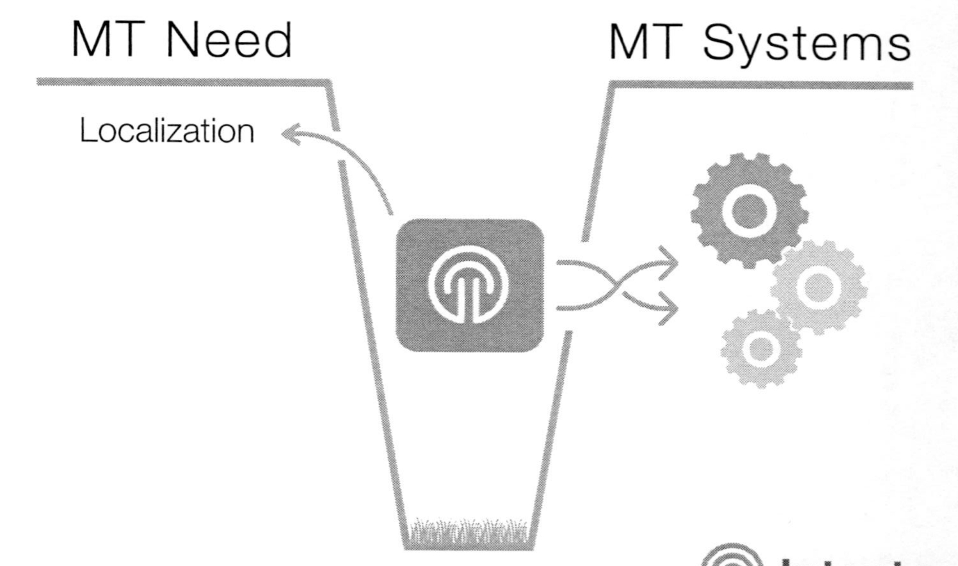

© Intento, Inc. / September 2020

Intento

Proceedings of the 14th Conference of the Association for Machine Translation in the Americas
October 6 – 9, 2020, Volume 2: MT User Track

BRIDGING THE GAP BETWEEN
MT CAPABILITIES AND ADOPTION

MT Procurement

MT Curation

Multi-Engine MT

Multi-Purpose MT

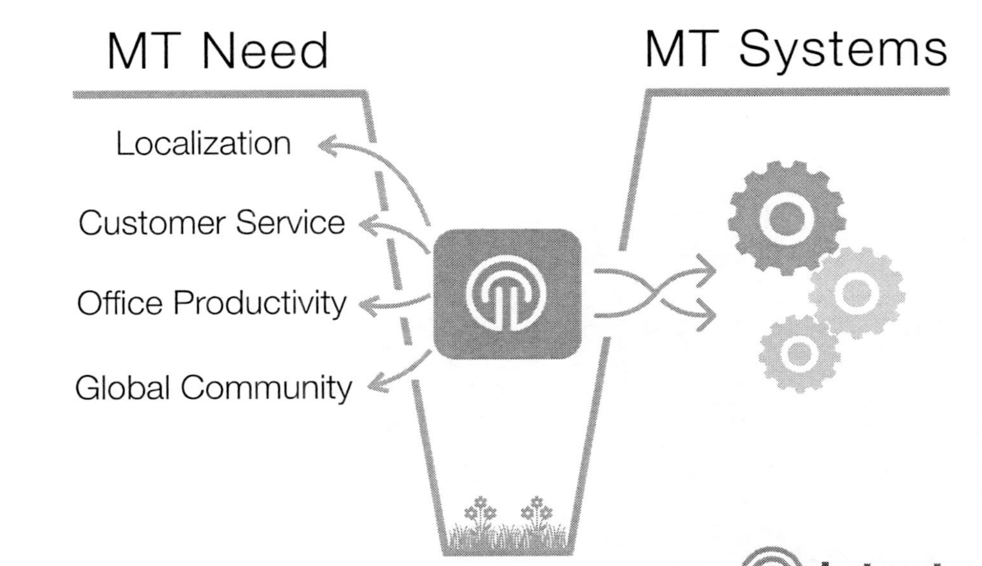

© Intento, Inc. / September 2020

Proceedings of the 14th Conference of the Association for Machine Translation in the Americas
October 6 – 9, 2020, Volume 2: MT User Track

MULTI-PURPOSE MT

Instant ROI on the investments already made

Combining resources of multiple stakeholders to benefit everyone

MT Requirements beyond the objective linguistic quality

Optimizing for features may compromise the quality

Proceedings of the 14th Conference of the Association for Machine Translation in the Americas
October 6 – 9, 2020, Volume 2: MT User Track

MT USAGE SCENARIOS AND REQUIREMENTS

Intento

Proceedings of the 14th Conference of the Association for Machine Translation in the Americas
October 6 – 9, 2020, Volume 2: MT User Track

MULTI-PURPOSE MT

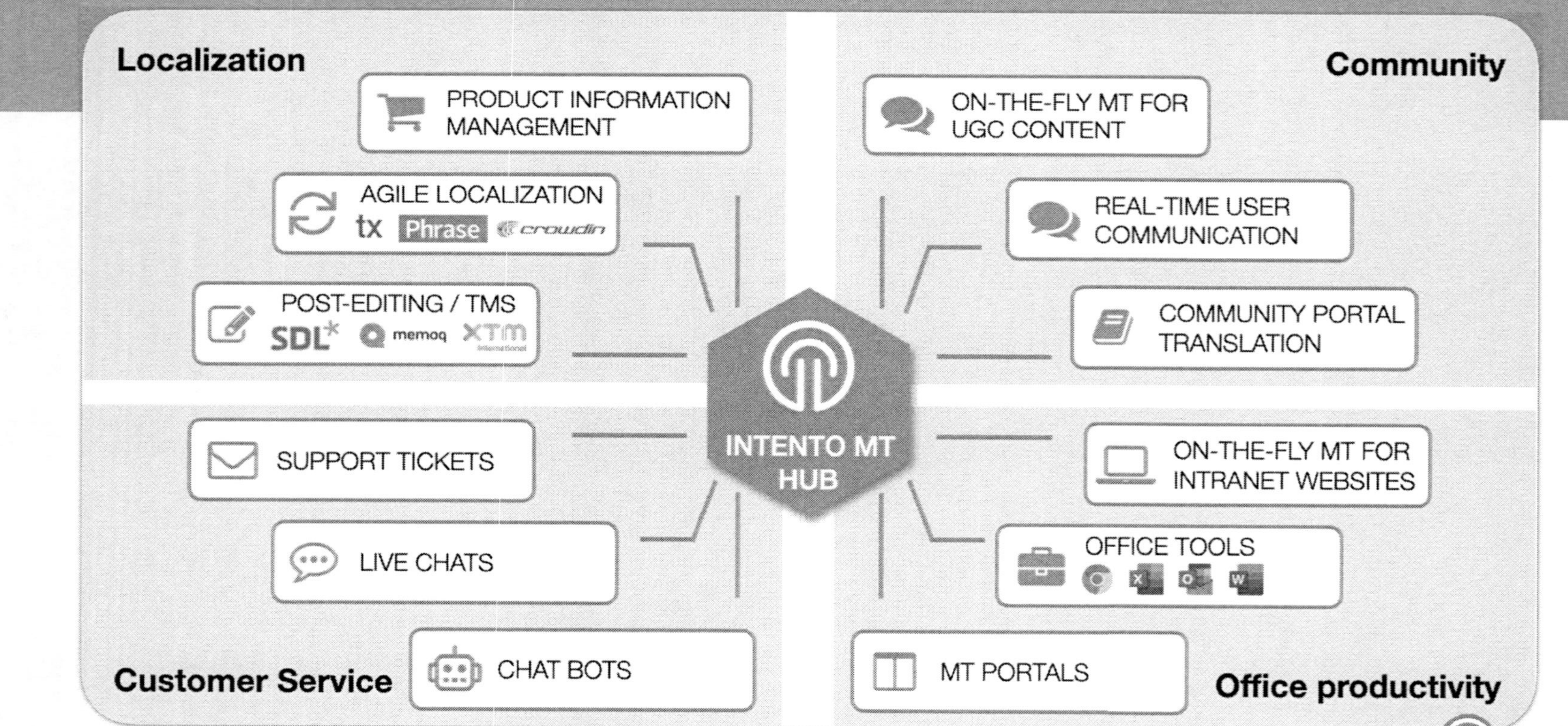

Proceedings of the 14th Conference of the Association for Machine Translation in the Americas
October 6 – 9, 2020, Volume 2: MT User Track

MULTI-PURPOSE MT
REQUIREMENTS BEYOND QUALITY

large text translation

batch translation

latency and jitter

tolerance to bad source

language detection

tag support

multilingual source

profanity control

metadata protection

entity protection

custom terminology

tone of voice consistency

Intento

Proceedings of the 14th Conference of the Association for Machine Translation in the Americas
October 6 – 9, 2020, Volume 2: MT User Track

ADDITIONAL CHALLENGES
WITH SPECIFIC COMBINATIONS

large text translation + HTML support

—

source language detection + multilingual source

—

…

Proceedings of the 14th Conference of the Association for Machine Translation in the Americas
October 6 – 9, 2020, Volume 2: MT User Track

MT REQUIREMENTS MATRIX
EVERY CASE HAS ITS OWN NEEDS

	large text translation	batch translation	latency and jitter	tolerance to bad source	language detection	tag support	multilingual source	profanity control	metadata protection	entity protection	custom terminology	tone of voice control
Post-editing / TMS		●				●					●	
Support tickets	●				●		●	●	●	●	●	
Live chats			●	●	●			●		●	●	●
Chatbots			●	●	●	●		●		●	●	●
On-the-fly UGC		●	●	●	●	●	●	●		●		●
Real-time communication			●	●						●		●
Knowledge bases	●					●			●		●	

Intento

Proceedings of the 14th Conference of the Association for Machine Translation in the Americas
October 6 – 9, 2020, Volume 2: MT User Track

MT REQUIREMENTS MATRIX
SAMPLE

ALSO

different for inbound and outbound…

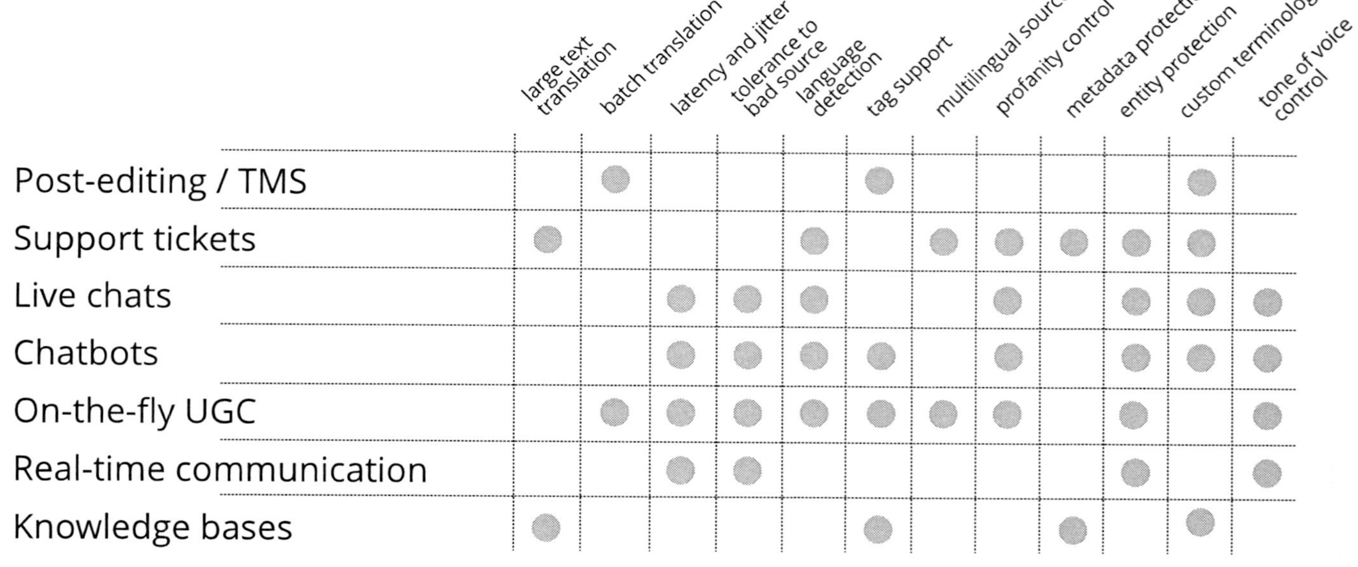

	large text translation	batch translation	latency and jitter	tolerance to bad source	language detection	tag support	multilingual source	profanity control	metadata protection	entity protection	custom terminology	tone of voice control
Post-editing / TMS		●			●						●	
Support tickets	●				●		●	●	●	●	●	
Live chats			●	●	●			●		●	●	●
Chatbots			●	●	●	●		●		●	●	●
On-the-fly UGC		●	●	●	●	●	●	●		●		●
Real-time communication			●	●						●		●
Knowledge bases	●					●			●		●	

Intento

16

Proceedings of the 14th Conference of the Association for Machine Translation in the Americas
October 6 – 9, 2020, Volume 2: MT User Track

MT REQUIREMENTS SUPPORT
BY POPULAR MT ENGINES

Legend:
- ● supported
- ○ support or its quality depends on the language pair / model

	large text translation	batch translation	latency and jitter	tolerance to bad source	language detection	tag support	multilingual source	profanity control	metadata protection	entity protection	custom terminology	tone of voice control
Amazon Translate	●		○	○	○	○	○		○	○	●	
Google Translate Advanced	●	●	○	○	○	○	○		○	○	●	
DeepL Pro API	●	●	○	○	○	○	○		○	○		●
IBM Watson Translator	●	●	○	○	○	○	○		○	○	●	
Microsoft Text Translator		●	○	○	○	○	○	●	○	○	●	
ModernMT		●	○	○	○	○	○		○	○		
Systran PNMT	●	●	○	○	○	○	○		○	○	●	

Intento

Proceedings of the 14th Conference of the Association for Machine Translation in the Americas
October 6 – 9, 2020, Volume 2: MT User Track

CASE STUDY 1: ENTITY PROTECTION

ENTITY PROTECTION
SOME SAMPLES

Simplest cases:
protecting email,
URLs, phone
numbers, file paths

———

Crucial for Customer
Service

———

Easily broken by MT

Source text (English)	Machine Translation
I just want to let you know about a spam mail I have received on Friday - it's in D:\Drv\Prt\Epson\Universal driver x64\ABC6\eeecu120m.inf	Я просто хочу уведомить вас о спаме, который я получил в пятницу - он здесь D:\Drv\Prt\Epson\Универсальный драйвер x64\ABC6\eeecu120m.inf
It has been Ivan Mitrich (ASAP, email.some+plus@example.com.tr) from Belgrad, but in the future it will be me.	Bio je to Ivan Mitrich (ASAP, email.some+plus@ekample.com.tr) iz Belgrada, ali u budućnosti to ću biti ja.
Would you like to help with a new phone for the ABC department - (772) 194 59 65 ext 4406/4408).	Desideri aiutarti con un nuovo telefono per il dipartimento ABC - (772) 194 59 65 ext 406/4408).
You must submit such a request via ABC-portal, attached link: www.example.com/en/submit	Deve enviar o pedido de tal atraves do ABC-portal, link anexo: www.example.com/pt/submit

© Intento, Inc. / September 2020

Proceedings of the 14th Conference of the Association for Machine Translation in the Americas
October 6 – 9, 2020, Volume 2: MT User Track

ENTITY PROTECTION
EXPERIMENTAL RESULTS

Selecting the MT based on the default entity protection may compromise the quality

What if we enforce protection via MT-agnostic NLP?

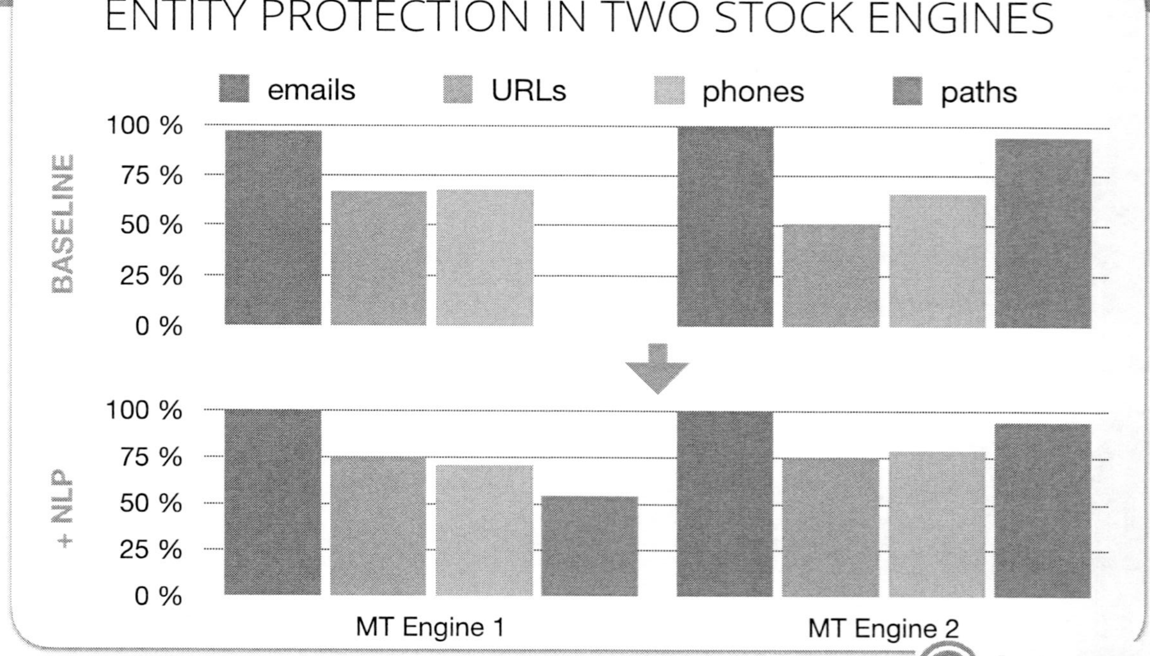

Intento

Proceedings of the 14th Conference of the Association for Machine Translation in the Americas
October 6 – 9, 2020, Volume 2: MT User Track

CASE STUDY 2: CUSTOM TERMINOLOGY

Proceedings of the 14th Conference of the Association for Machine Translation in the Americas
October 6 – 9, 2020, Volume 2: MT User Track

CUSTOM TERMINOLOGY
IMPROVES FIDELITY

Simplest cases:
enforcing acronyms,
brand names and
other proper nouns.

—

Without Custom
Terminology support,
NMT easily breaks
them.

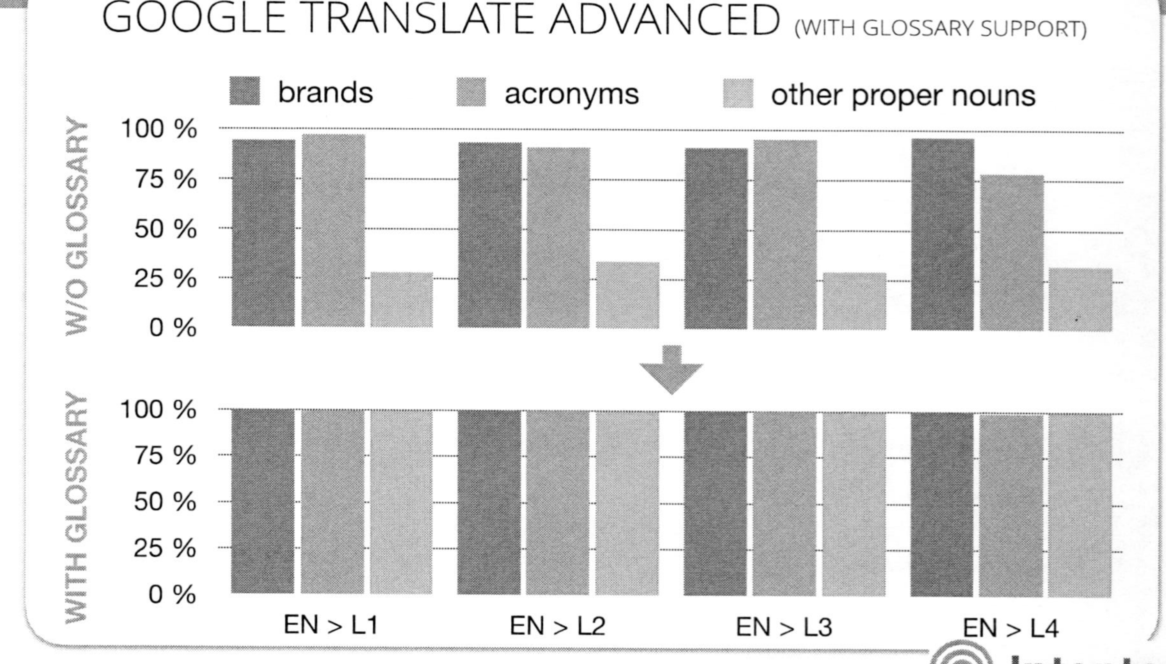

© Intento, Inc. / September 2020

Proceedings of the 14th Conference of the Association for Machine Translation in the Americas
October 6 – 9, 2020, Volume 2: MT User Track

CUSTOM TERMINOLOGY
IMPROVES FIDELITY

Selecting the MT engine by the custom terminology support may compromise MT Quality

MT-agnostic glossary on a top of NMT

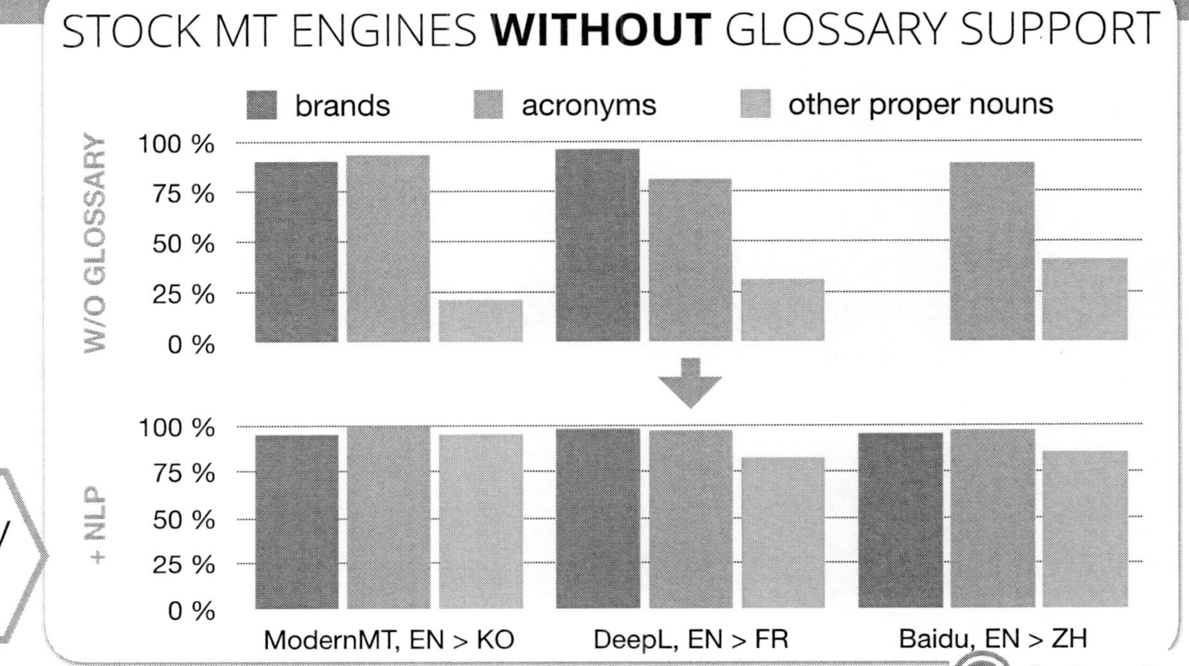

Proceedings of the 14th Conference of the Association for Machine Translation in the Americas
October 6 – 9, 2020, Volume 2: MT User Track

CASE STUDY 3: TONE OF VOICE CONTROL

Intento

Proceedings of the 14th Conference of the Association for Machine Translation in the Americas
October 6 – 9, 2020, Volume 2: MT User Track

TONE OF VOICE CONTROL
SAMPLES FROM SUPPORT CHATS

Formal vs. Informal

Crucial for Live Chats

Baseline MT engines are not consistent

Source text (English)	Machine Translation (German)	COMMENT
Can you share your screen?	Können Sie Ihren Bildschirm freigeben?	FORMAL
Could you help me?	Kannst du mir helfen?	INFORMAL
Make sure you report any of these issues.	Stellen Sie sicher, dass Sie eines dieser Probleme melden.	FORMAL
Can you give an example?	Kannst du ein Beispiel geben?	INFORMAL

© Intento, Inc. / September 2020

 Intento

TONE OF VOICE CONTROL
DEFAULT MT OUTPUT

English to German

—

210 segments

—

stock models

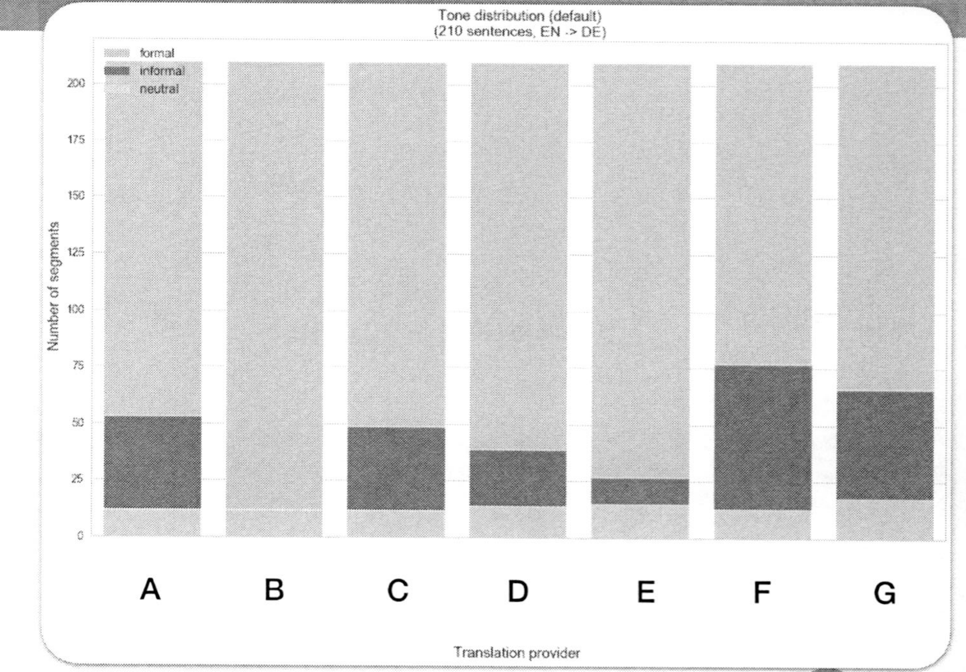

© Intento, Inc. / September 2020

Intento

TONE OF VOICE CONTROL
HOW TO MAKE IT INFORMAL?

Option 1: Use DeepL with formality=less (99.5% accuracy)

What if you need a custom model and terminology, or another MT has better linguistic quality for you?

Option 2: Generate synthetic training data, hoping translations become more informal

Expensive and time-consuming, also introduces bias into the model

Option 3: MT-agnostic NLP

Works to a certain extent, provides a wider choice of MT engines

Proceedings of the 14th Conference of the Association for Machine Translation in the Americas
October 6 – 9, 2020, Volume 2: MT User Track

TONE OF VOICE CONTROL
MT-AGNOSTIC ADJUSTMENT

English to German

210 segments

stock models

let's make it more **INFORMAL**

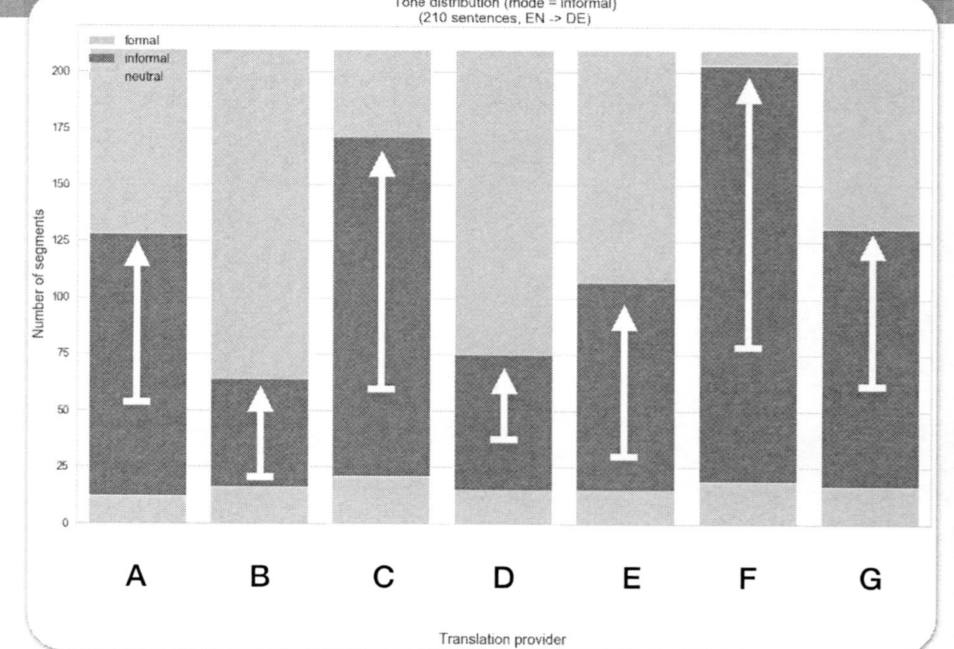

© Intento, Inc. / September 2020

Intento

Proceedings of the 14th Conference of the Association for Machine Translation in the Americas
October 6 – 9, 2020, Volume 2: MT User Track

TONE OF VOICE CONTROL
MT-AGNOSTIC ADJUSTMENT

English to German

210 segments

stock models

let's make it more
FORMAL

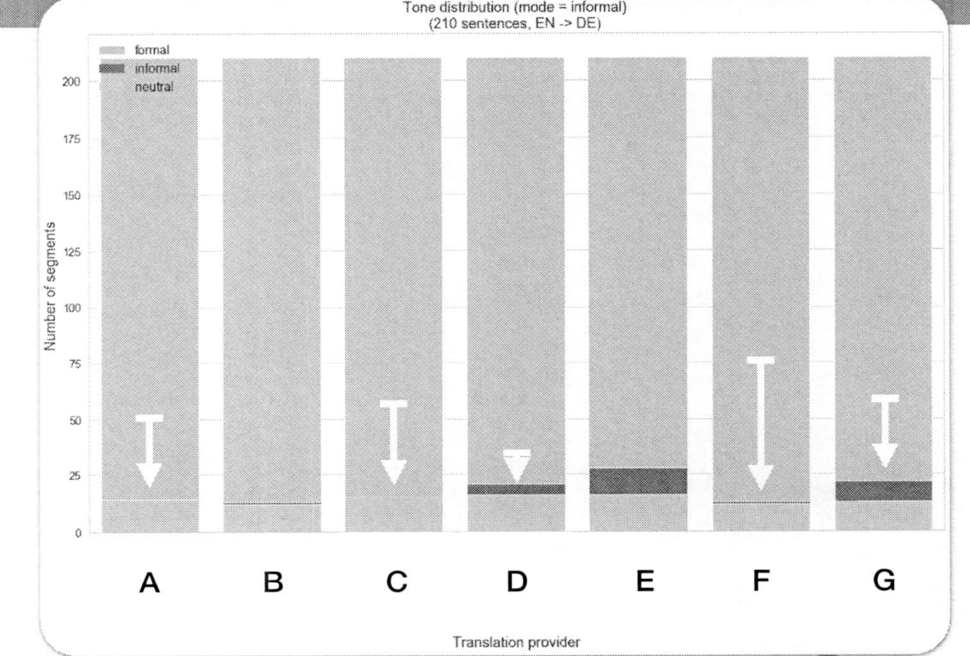

Intento

Proceedings of the 14th Conference of the Association for Machine Translation in the Americas
October 6 – 9, 2020, Volume 2: MT User Track

KEY TAKEAWAYS

Multi-Purpose MT brings an instant ROI on the MT investment already made.

Different use cases impose multiple requirements beyond the linguistic quality.

Meeting the requirements takes either the right MT engine choice or clever engineering.

We do both, by implementing MT-agnostic fine tuning algorithms to avoid compromising the MT quality.

© Intento, Inc. / September 2020

Intento

Proceedings of the 14th Conference of the Association for Machine Translation in the Americas
October 6 – 9, 2020, Volume 2: MT User Track

Proceedings of the 14th Conference of the Association for Machine Translation in the Americas
October 6 – 9, 2020, Volume 2: MT User Track

Simultaneous Speech Translation in Google Translate

Jeff Pitman <jrp@google.com>
For animations, see: t.co/mz6oZiLEP4

Google Research

Proceedings of the 14th Conference of the Association for Machine Translation in the Americas
October 6 – 9, 2020, Volume 2: MT User Track

Agenda

01 Overview

02 Long-form Audio Input

03 Streaming Translation

04 Streaming Text-to-Speech

05 Putting It Together

Google Research

01

Overview

Google Research

Proceedings of the 14th Conference of the Association for Machine Translation in the Americas
October 6 - 9, 2020, Volume 2: MT User Track

Conversational Turn-taking

2011

Components

- ASR
- MT
- TTS

Model Orchestration

Google Research

Client-based Model Orchestration

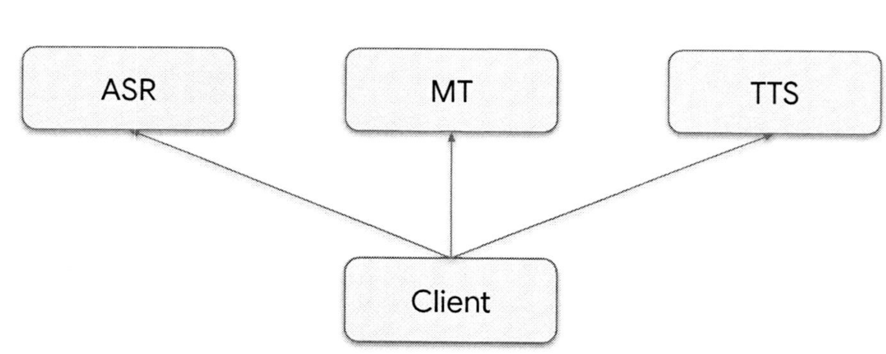

Google Research

Proceedings of the 14th Conference of the Association for Machine Translation in the Americas
October 6 – 9, 2020, Volume 2: MT User Track

(Low) Latency is a feature.

Google Research

Proceedings of the 14th Conference of the Association for Machine Translation in the Americas
October 6 – 9, 2020, Volume 2: MT User Track

Server-based Model Orchestration

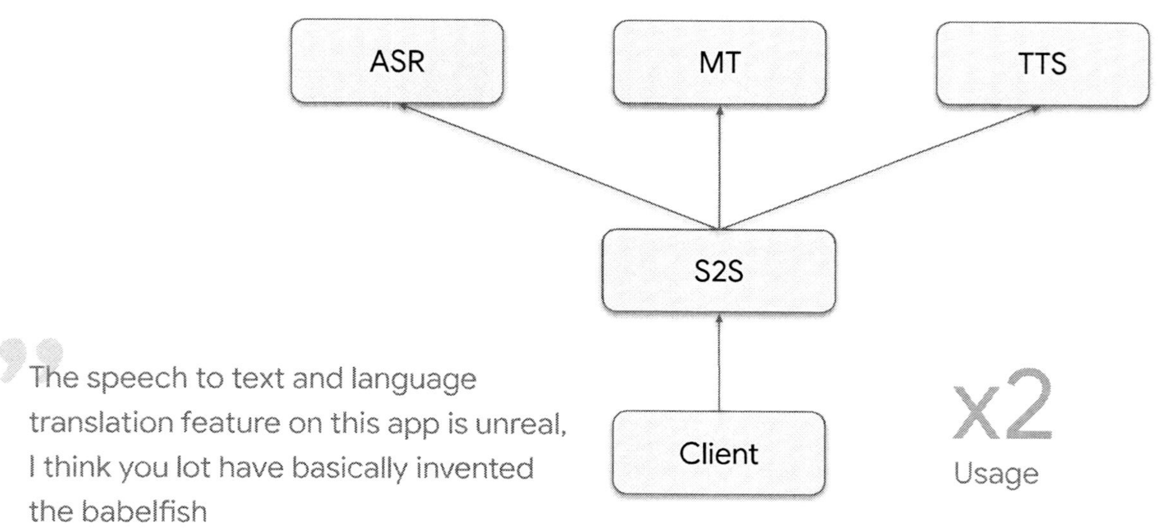

> The speech to text and language translation feature on this app is unreal, I think you lot have basically invented the babelfish

x2
Usage

Proceedings of the 14th Conference of the Association for Machine Translation in the Americas
October 6 – 9, 2020, Volume 2: MT User Track

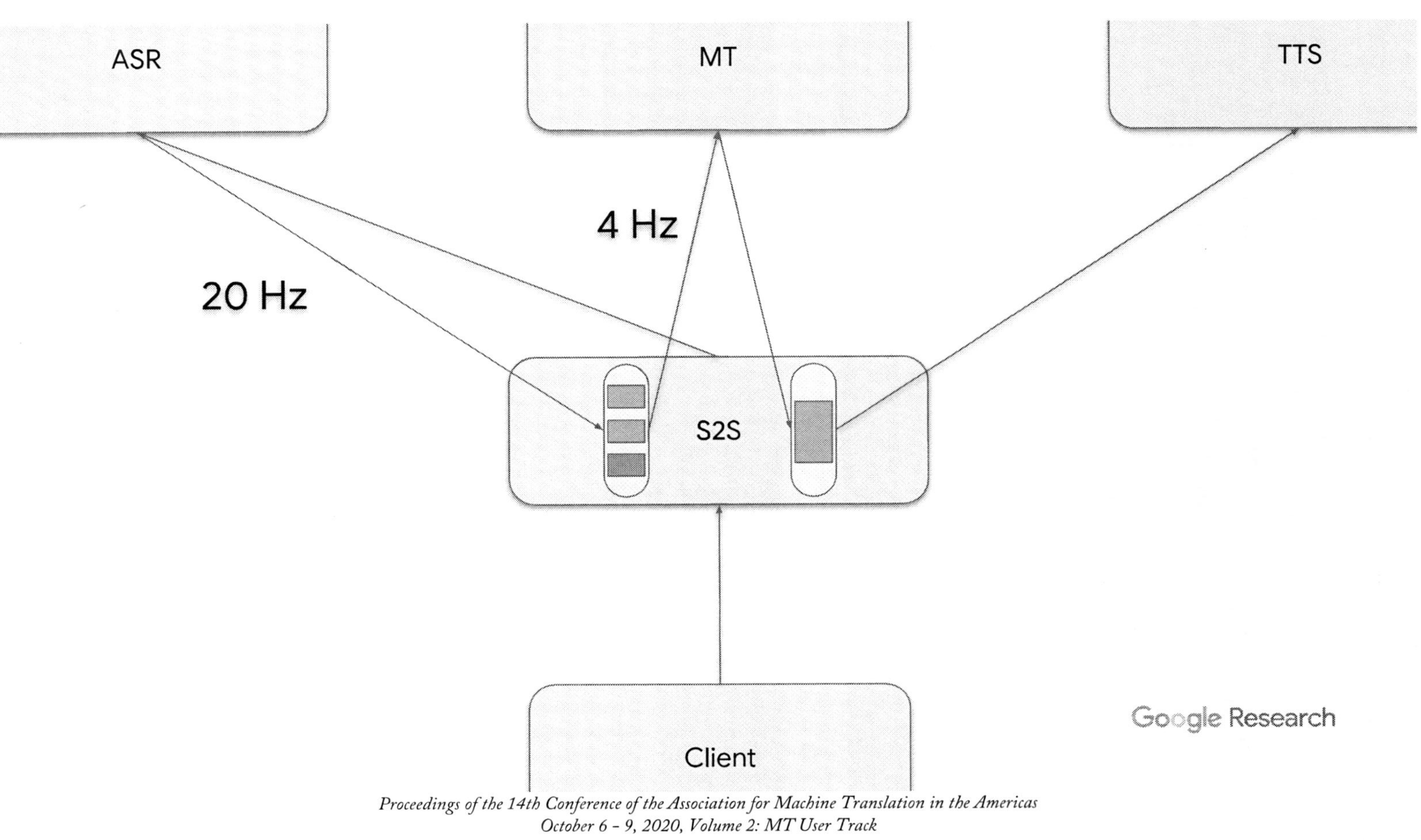

ASR
MT
TTS
20 Hz
4 Hz
S2S
Client
Google Research

Proceedings of the 14th Conference of the Association for Machine Translation in the Americas
October 6 – 9, 2020, Volume 2: MT User Track

User experience

Input interactions

- Tap and hold
- Quick tap
- Auto mic

Google Research

Proceedings of the 14th Conference of the Association for Machine Translation in the Americas
October 6 – 9, 2020, Volume 2: MT User Track

Auto Mic

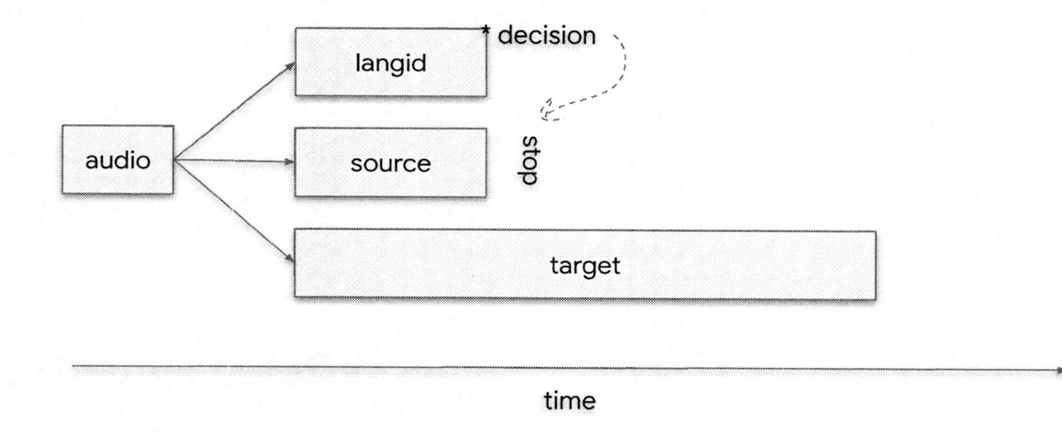

Google Research

Proceedings of the 14th Conference of the Association for Machine Translation in the Americas
October 6 – 9, 2020, Volume 2: MT User Track

What if we kept the microphone on?

Google Research

Proceedings of the 14th Conference of the Association for Machine Translation in the Americas
October 6 – 9, 2020, Volume 2: MT User Track

02

Long-form Audio Input

Codecs

The Timeout

ASR Model training

Google Research

Proceedings of the 14th Conference of the Association for Machine Translation in the Americas
October 6 – 9, 2020, Volume 2: MT User Track

Codecs

AMR-WB[1] only worked well with clean recording environments and at close distance to the microphone.

Opus[2] @24kbps performed just as well as uncompressed audio. Ended up using 32kbps.

1. Adaptive Multi-rate Wideband
2. Opus

Google Research

Proceedings of the 14th Conference of the Association for Machine Translation in the Americas
October 6 – 9, 2020, Volume 2: MT User Track

The Timeout

Problem: ASR limited to 30 second sessions. But, anything could cause a disconnection.

Solution[1]: Maintain audio buffer on client to stitch sessions together.

1. live-transcribe-speech-engine

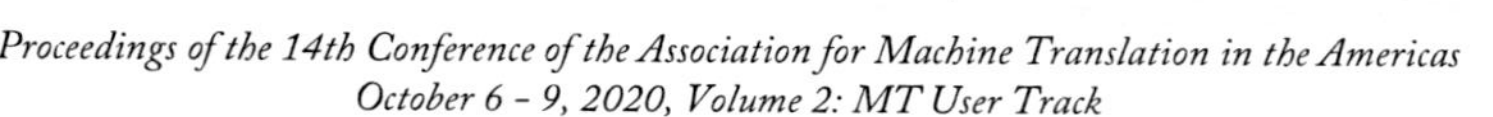

Proceedings of the 14th Conference of the Association for Machine Translation in the Americas
October 6 - 9, 2020, Volume 2: MT User Track

ASR Model

Key insight was to move
to models trained on
long-form audio.

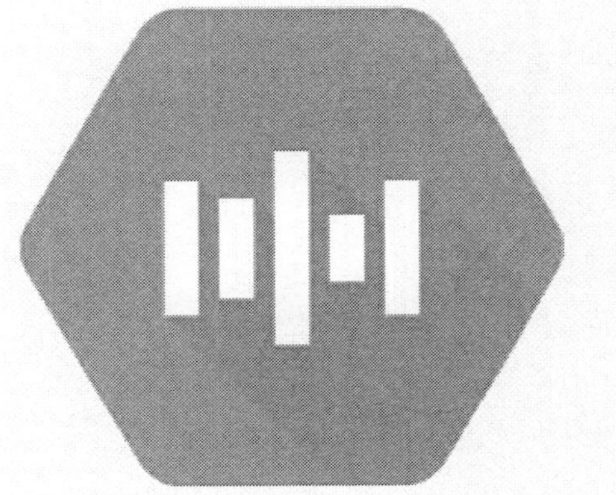

Proceedings of the 14th Conference of the Association for Machine Translation in the Americas
October 6 – 9, 2020, Volume 2: MT User Track

03

Streaming Translation

Proceedings of the 14th Conference of the Association for Machine Translation in the Americas
October 6 – 9, 2020, Volume 2: MT User Track

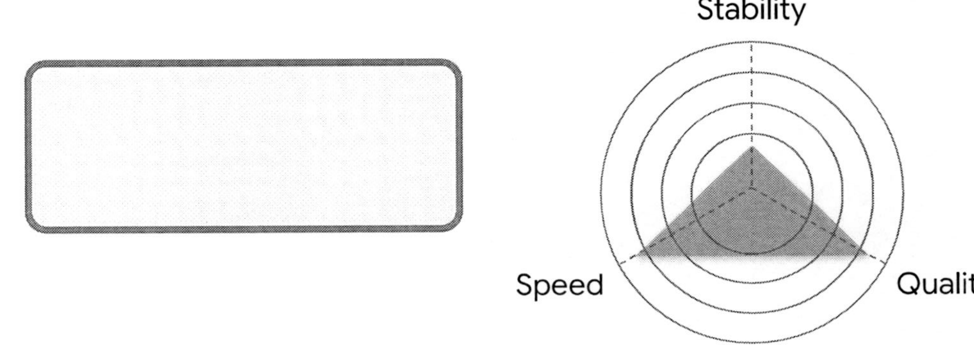

Stability
Speed
Quality
Google Research

UX Research

Participants thought that the instability of the text results were disruptive.

Without preparation, professional interpreters are roughly 60% to 70% accurate in simultaneous interpretation.

Research[1] has shown that audiences get uncomfortable if results take too long.

1. Lee, T.-H. 2002. "Ear voice span in English into Korean simultaneous interpretation." Meta 47 (4): 596–606.

"The sentence continues to change while I'm reading it and it is making me nervous."

Participant

Use case	ASR	TTS	Overall experience
Lecture	⚠	✓	⚠
Museum tour	⚠	✗	⚠
Walking city tour	⚠	✗	⚠
Boat / Bus tour	✗	⚠	✗
Airport	✗	✓	✗

Google Research

Proceedings of the 14th Conference of the Association for Machine Translation in the Americas
October 6 – 9, 2020, Volume 2: MT User Track

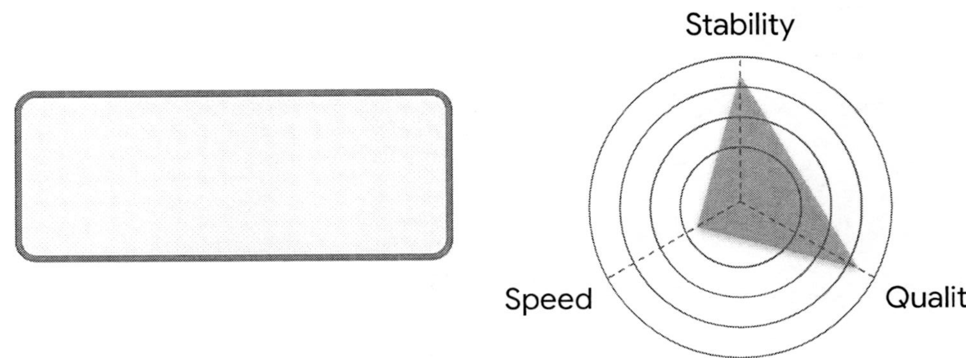

Stability
Speed
Quality
Google Research

Tech. Research

We can re-use off-the-shelf ASR and NMT systems by using edit distance heuristics to stabilize prefixes.

We can further improve stabilization by making NMT prefix-aware. Beam search is then constrained on prefixes.

We evaluate performance using a metrics triple of BLEU, Voice-to-eye Latency, and Erasure (flickering rate).

Proceedings of the 14th Conference of the Association for Machine Translation in the Americas
October 6 – 9, 2020, Volume 2: MT User Track

Monotonic Infinite Lookback Attention
for Simultaneous Machine Translation

Naveen Arivazhagan*   Colin Cherry*   Wolfgang Macherey   Chung-Cheng Chiu

Semih Yavuz   Ruoming Pang   Wei Li   Colin Raffel

Google

arXiv:1906.05218v1 [cs.CL] 12 Jun 2019

RE-TRANSLATION STRATEGIES FOR LONG FORM, SIMULTANEOUS, SPOKEN
LANGUAGE TRANSLATION

Naveen Arivazhagan*, Colin Cherry*, Te I, Wolfgang Macherey, Pallavi Baljekar and George Foster

Google Research

arXiv:1912.03393v2 [cs.CL] 7 Apr 2020

Re-translation versus Streaming for Simultaneous Translation

Naveen Arivazhagan; Colin Cherry; Wolfgang Macherey and George Foster
Google Research
{navari,colincherry,wmach,fosterg}@google.com

Abstract

There has been great progress in improving streaming machine translation, a simultaneous paradigm where the system appends to a growing hypothesis as more source content becomes available. We study a related problem in which revisions to the hypothesis beyond strictly appending words are permitted. This is suitable for applications such as live captioning an audio feed. In this setting, we compare custom streaming approaches to re-translation, a straightforward strategy where each new source token triggers a distinct translation from scratch. We find re-translation to be as good or better than state-of-the-art streaming systems, even when operating under constraints that allow very few revisions. We attribute much of this

however, the prohibition against revising output is overly stringent

The ability to revise previous partial translations makes simply re-translating each successive source prefix a viable strategy. Compared to streaming models, re-translation has the advantage of low latency, since it always attempts a translation of the complete source prefix, and high final-translation quality, since it is not restricted to preserving previous output. It has the disadvantages of higher computational cost, and a high revision rate, visible as textual *instability* in an online translation display. When revisions are an option, it is unclear whether one should prefer a specialized streaming model, or a re-translation strategy.

arXiv:1912.03393v2 [cs.CL] 14 Apr 2020

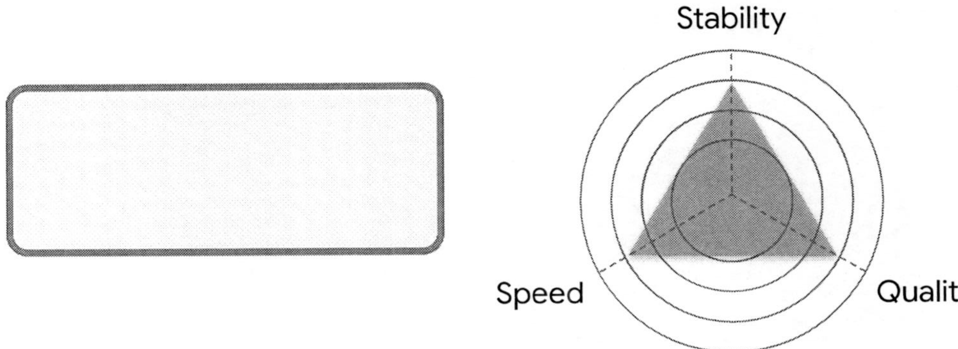

Proceedings of the 14th Conference of the Association for Machine Translation in the Americas
October 6 – 9, 2020, Volume 2: MT User Track

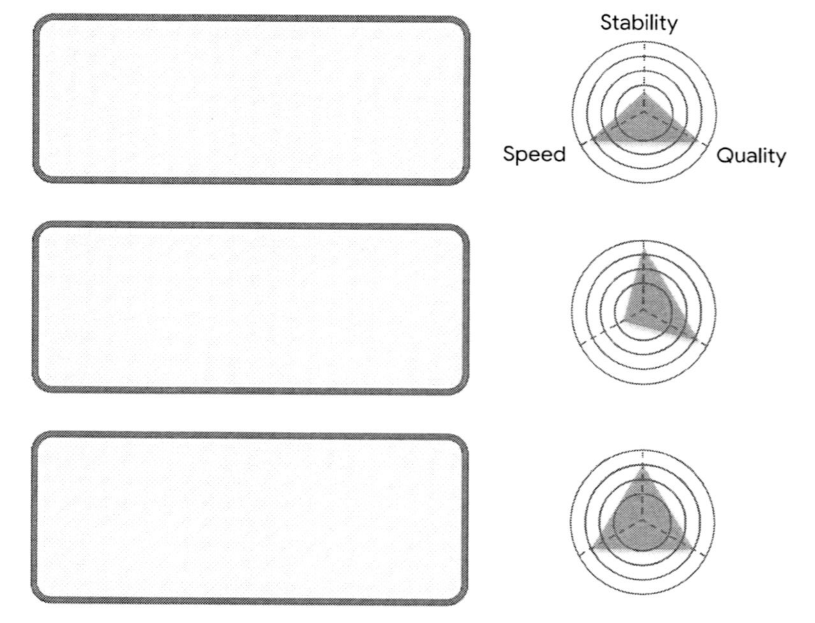

Stability
Speed
Quality
Google Research

Unspoken Punctuation

+8 BLEU

Proceedings of the 14th Conference of the Association for Machine Translation in the Americas
October 6 - 9, 2020, Volume 2: MT User Track

04

Streaming Text-to-Speech

Google Research

Proceedings of the 14th Conference of the Association for Machine Translation in the Americas
October 6 – 9, 2020, Volume 2: MT User Track

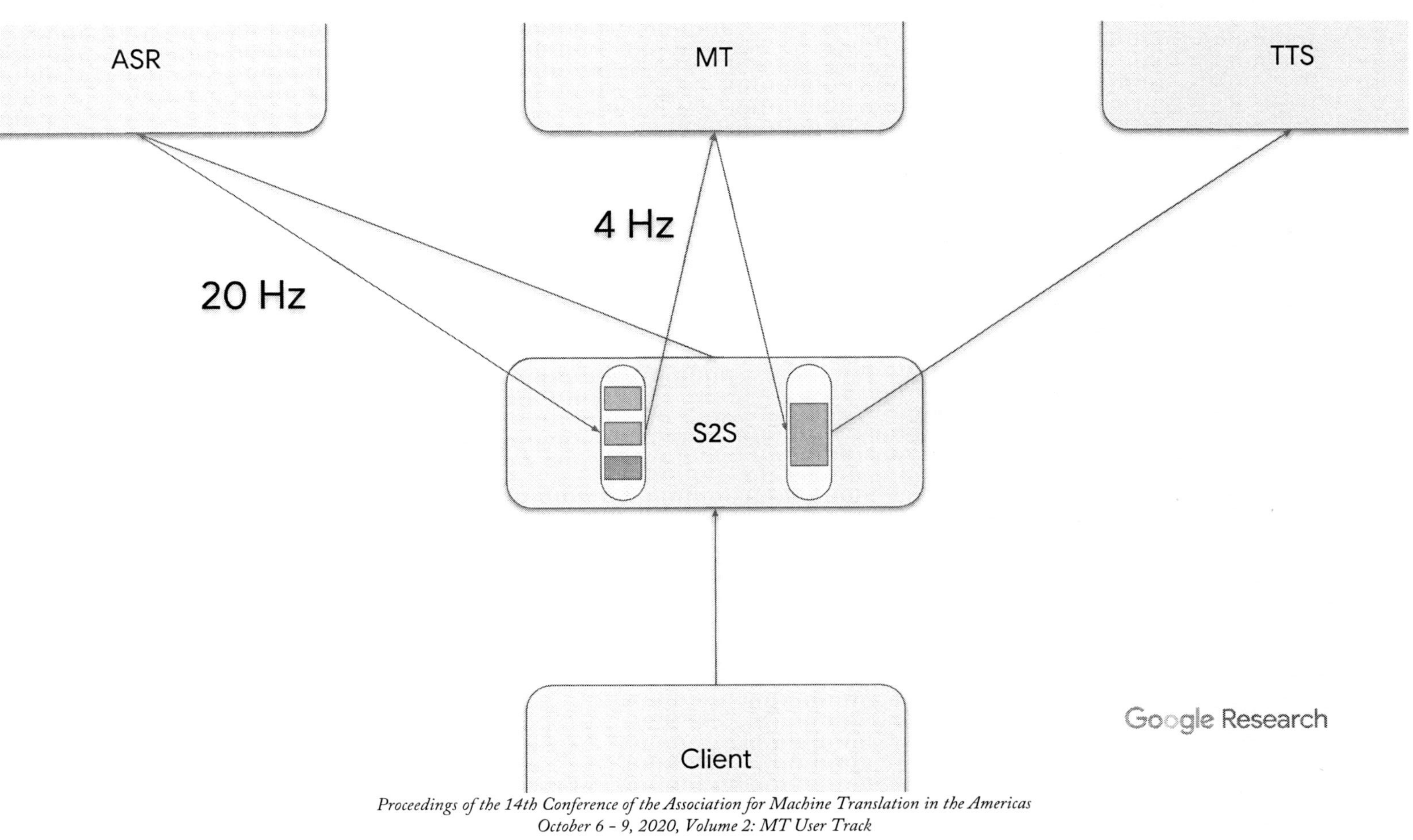

Proceedings of the 14th Conference of the Association for Machine Translation in the Americas
October 6 – 9, 2020, Volume 2: MT User Track

Goals

Voice-to-ear Latency

Prosody

Pure VUI?

Proceedings of the 14th Conference of the Association for Machine Translation in the Americas
October 6 - 9, 2020, Volume 2: MT User Track

Voice-to-ear

Slow finality of ASR results

Short-form ASR models

TTS Speed

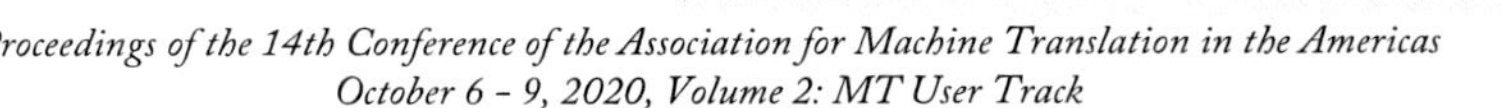

Proceedings of the 14th Conference of the Association for Machine Translation in the Americas
October 6 - 9, 2020, Volume 2: MT User Track

Prosody

TTS Speed

Length limitations

Proceedings of the 14th Conference of the Association for Machine Translation in the Americas
October 6 - 9, 2020, Volume 2: MT User Track

Pure Voice UI

Quality

Navigation

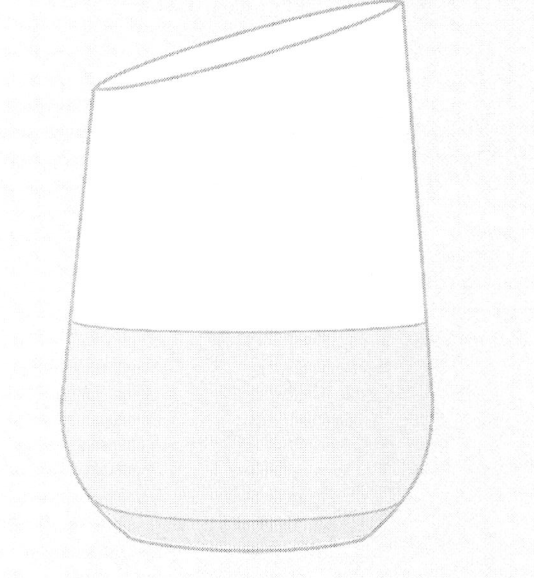

Proceedings of the 14th Conference of the Association for Machine Translation in the Americas
October 6 - 9, 2020, Volume 2: MT User Track

05

Putting It Together

Evaluation

Results

Google Research

Proceedings of the 14th Conference of the Association for Machine Translation in the Americas
October 6 – 9, 2020, Volume 2: MT User Track

Evaluation

We wanted to see if human judgement in a controlled environment can help make launch decisions.

Google Research

Proceedings of the 14th Conference of the Association for Machine Translation in the Americas
October 6 – 9, 2020, Volume 2: MT User Track

Initial setup

Asked 3 bilingual raters to watch original video, read final and static NMT output, answer adequacy/fluency and gist questions.

Lorem ipsum dolor sit amet, consectetur adipiscing elit. Praesent quis dolor lacus. Orci varius natoque penatibus et magnis dis parturient montes, nascetur ridiculus mus. In eu mi placerat, facilisis tellus vitae, efficitur nisi. Nulla placerat placerat sem, tempor vulputate libero suscipit sed. Mauris sit amet massa eu justo dignissim pharetra. Praesent sapien tortor, ornare et leo nec, aliquet suscipit nisi. Aenean egestas mauris eget hendrerit finibus. In eleifend ex pharetra tellus dignissim.

Google Research

Test set

~100 1-minute publically available videos.

Focused on clean audio with 1 person speaking.

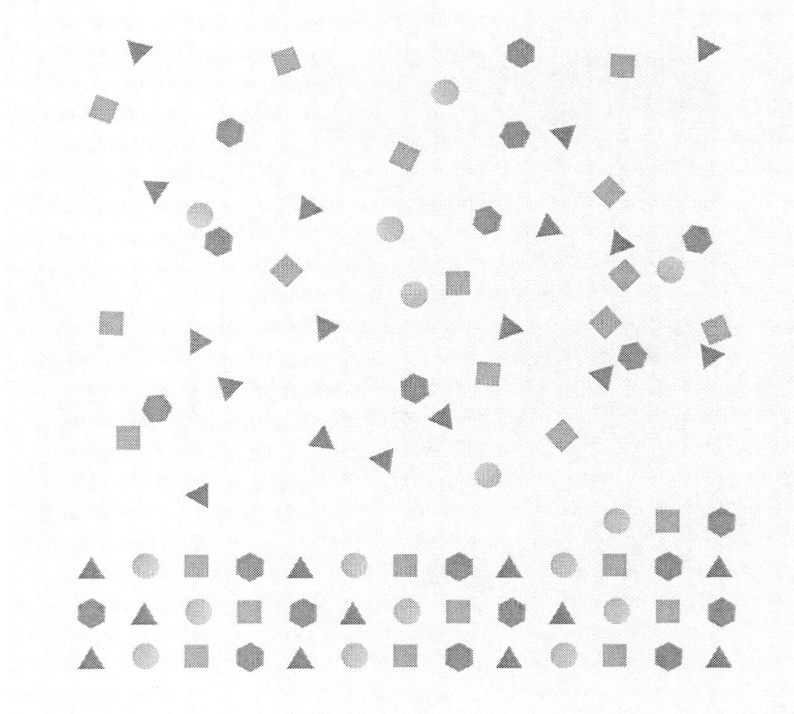

Proceedings of the 14th Conference of the Association for Machine Translation in the Americas
October 6 – 9, 2020, Volume 2: MT User Track

Problems

Domain of test sets
misaligned across languages

Raters were not trustworthy
.. understanding source
language was a bias .. just
answering yes to everything
was a bias.

Google Research

Proceedings of the 14th Conference of the Association for Machine Translation in the Americas
October 6 – 9, 2020, Volume 2: MT User Track

Improvements

Minimized video selection
bias with better QC

Minimized bilingual bias by
using a monolingual
template

Ground truth

Lorem ipsum dolor sit amet, consectetur adipiscing elit. Praesent quis dolor lacus. Orci varius natoque penatibus et magnis dis parturient montes, nascetur ridiculus mus. In eu mi placerat, facilisis tellus vitae, efficitur nisi. Nulla placerat placerat sem, tempor vulputate libero suscipit sed. Mauris sit amet massa eu justo dignissim pharetra. Praesent sapien tortor, ornare et leo nec, aliquet suscipit nisi. Aenean egestas mauris eget hendrerit finibus. In eleifend ex pharetra tellus dignissim.

System output

Lorem ipsum dolor sit amet, consectetur adipiscing elit. Praesent quis dolor lacus. Orci varius natoque penatibus et magnis dis parturient montes, nascetur ridiculus mus. In eu mi placerat, facilisis tellus vitae, efficitur nisi. Nulla placerat placerat sem, tempor vulputate libero suscipit sed. Mauris sit amet massa eu justo dignissim pharetra. Praesent sapien tortor, ornare et leo nec, aliquet suscipit nisi. Aenean egestas mauris eget hendrerit finibus. In eleifend ex pharetra tellus dignissim.

Proceedings of the 14th Conference of the Association for Machine Translation in the Americas
October 6 – 9, 2020, Volume 2: MT User Track

Results

Launched support for 10 languages.

Launched streaming TTS support for Pixel Buds.

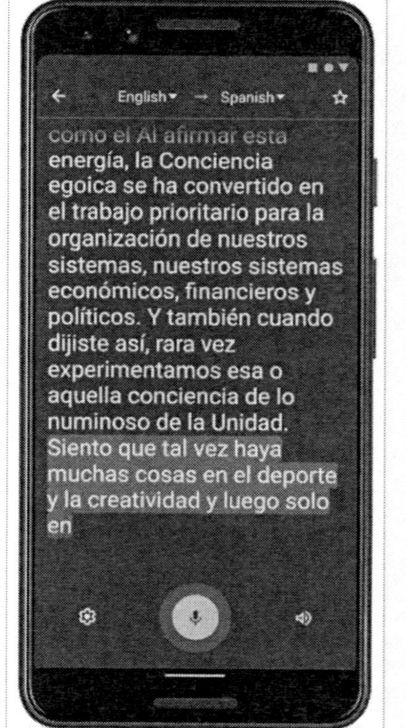

Google Research

What's next?

Google Research

Proceedings of the 14th Conference of the Association for Machine Translation in the Americas
October 6 – 9, 2020, Volume 2: MT User Track

Advancing
Speech Translation

Long-form Audio Input

Streaming Translation

Streaming Text-to-Speech

Evaluation

Google Research

Proceedings of the 14th Conference of the Association for Machine Translation in the Americas
October 6 - 9, 2020, Volume 2: MT User Track

Thank You

Jeff Pitman
Senior Staff Engineering Manager

Deck Props: Shilp Vaishnav, Tom Small, Kannu Mehta, Mengmeng Niu, Bryan Lin,
Naveen Ari, Colin Cherry

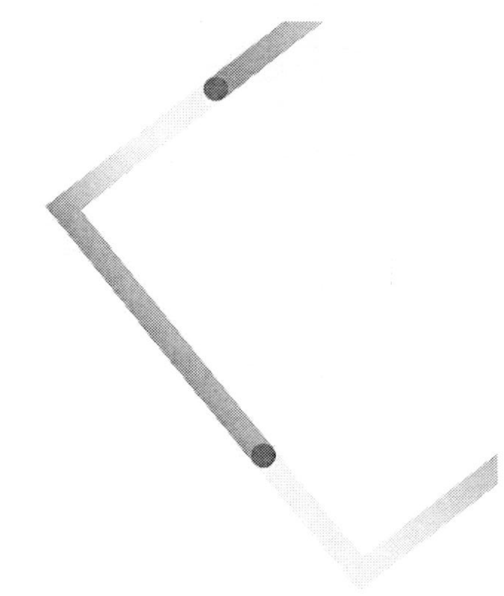

Proceedings of the 14th Conference of the Association for Machine Translation in the Americas
October 6 – 9, 2020, Volume 2: MT User Track

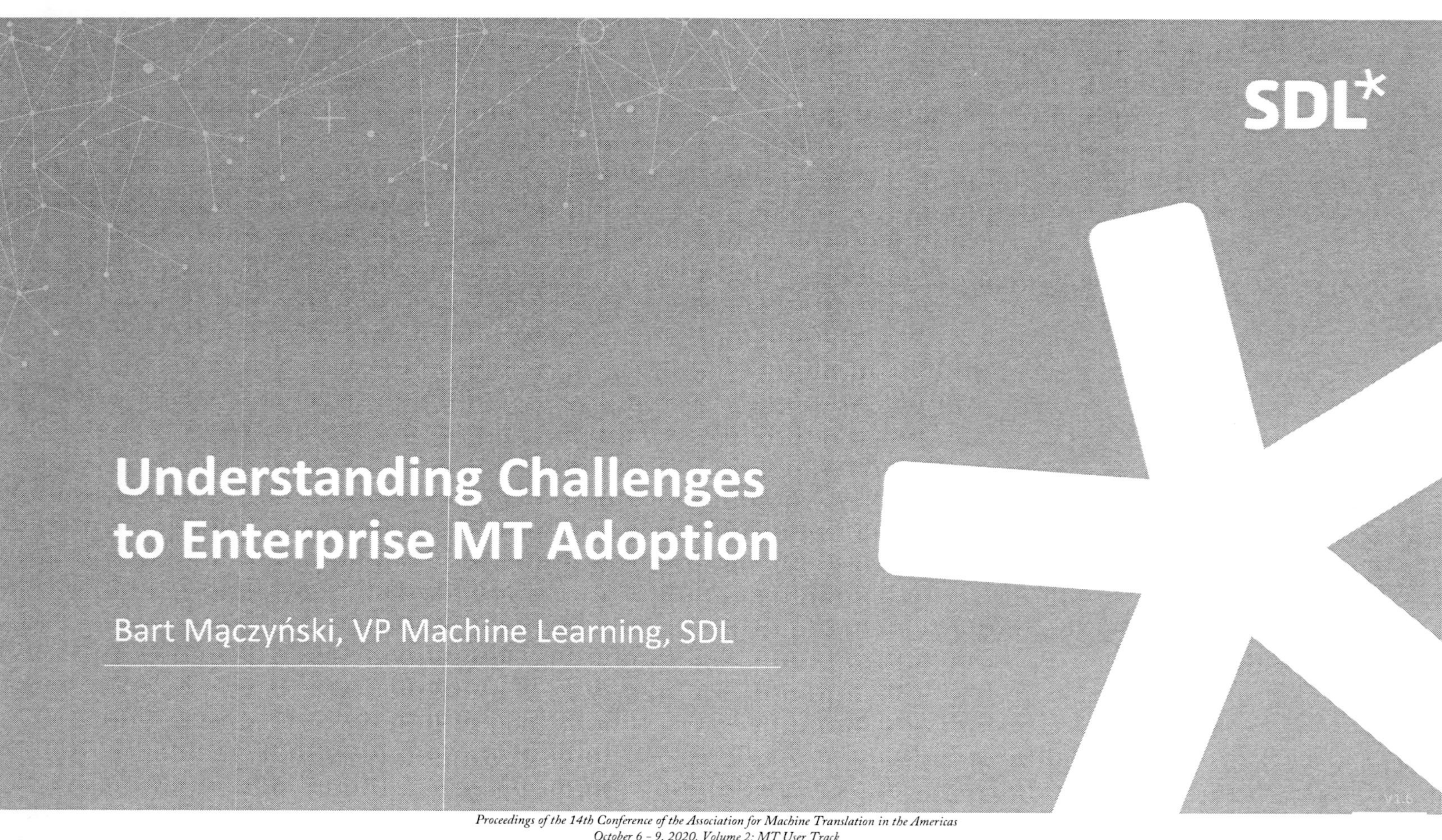

Proceedings of the 14th Conference of the Association for Machine Translation in the Americas
October 6 – 9, 2020, Volume 2: MT User Track

Agenda

- Introduction
- New Buyers, New Misconceptions
- The Challenges
    - The Use Case Challenge
    - The Technical Challenge
    - The Linguistic Challenge
- What's Next

SDL*

Proceedings of the 14th Conference of the Association for Machine Translation in the Americas
October 6 – 9, 2020, Volume 2: MT User Track

Introduction

Bart Mączyński

- VP Machine Learning, Solutions Consulting
- Expertise in translation management, TM, MT, terminology systems
- Over 20 years of experience in the field
- Focus on commercial applications of Linguistic AI

© 2020 SDL

SDL*

Background

Rise of the Machines

- MT is now a viable solution for the enterprise
- Recent advancement opened up new MT use cases
- MT is now directly exposed to new buyer communities
- These new buyers may not have much experience in translation management

SDL*

Proceedings of the 14th Conference of the Association for Machine Translation in the Americas
October 6 - 9, 2020, Volume 2: MT User Track

New Buyers, New Misconceptions

AI, ML, MT Hype

* „MT replaces human translators"
* „MT can learn from what it translates"
* „MT can handle all content"
* „MT quality is amazing across the board"
* „MT is cheap"
* „Anyone can build an MT system"
* „I've read about GPT-3, all my content issues will be solved soon"

SDL*

Proceedings of the 14th Conference of the Association for Machine Translation in the Americas
October 6 – 9, 2020, Volume 2: MT User Track

The Three Challenges

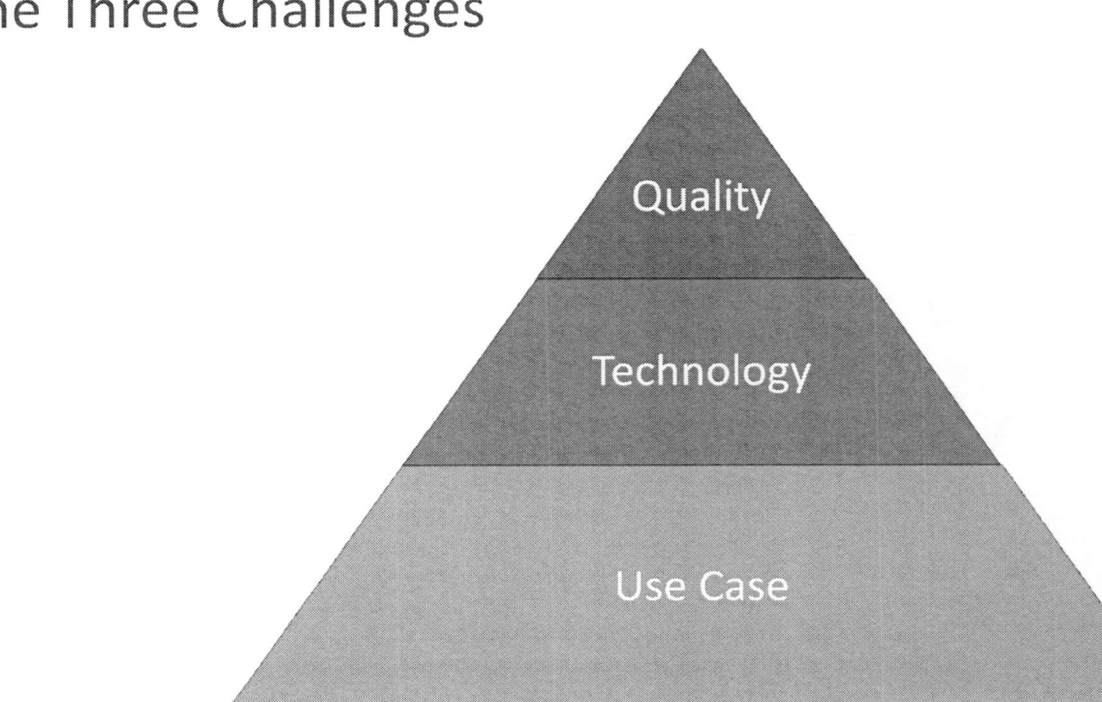

Proceedings of the 14th Conference of the Association for Machine Translation in the Americas
October 6 – 9, 2020, Volume 2: MT User Track

Proceedings of the 14th Conference of the Association for Machine Translation in the Americas
October 6 - 9, 2020, Volume 2: MT User Track

The Use Case Challenge

- Understanding if, and how, MT can be utilized
- Providing a pathway to the most optimal translation option

Things to Consider

- Language pair coverage
- Quality
- Volume
- Speed
- Security

Proceedings of the 14th Conference of the Association for Machine Translation in the Americas
October 6 – 9, 2020, Volume 2: MT User Track

Chatbot
Quality
9
8
7
6
5
4
3
2
1
0
Security
Language Coverage
Volume
Speed

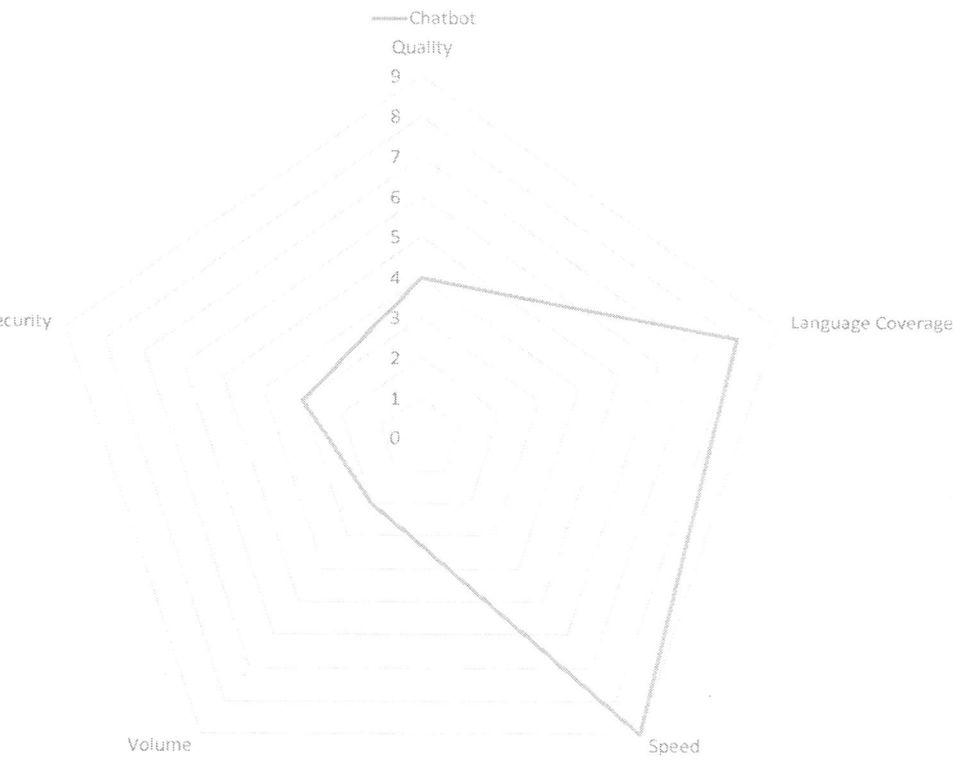

SDL*

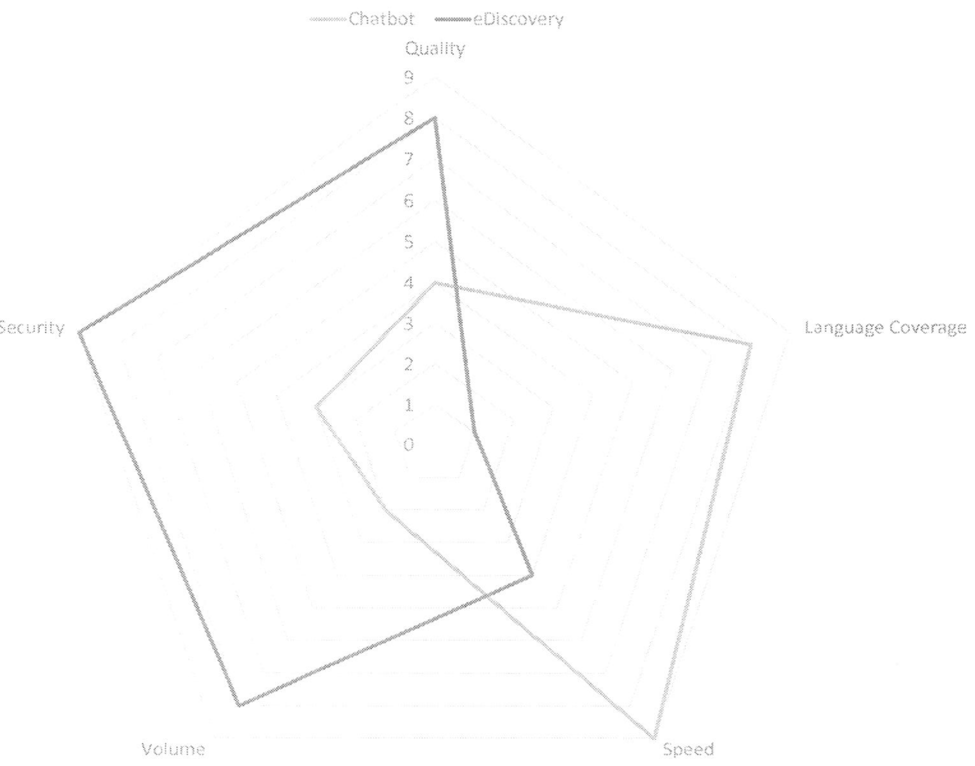

SDL*

10   © 2020 SDL

Proceedings of the 14th Conference of the Association for Machine Translation in the Americas
October 6 - 9, 2020, Volume 2: MT User Track

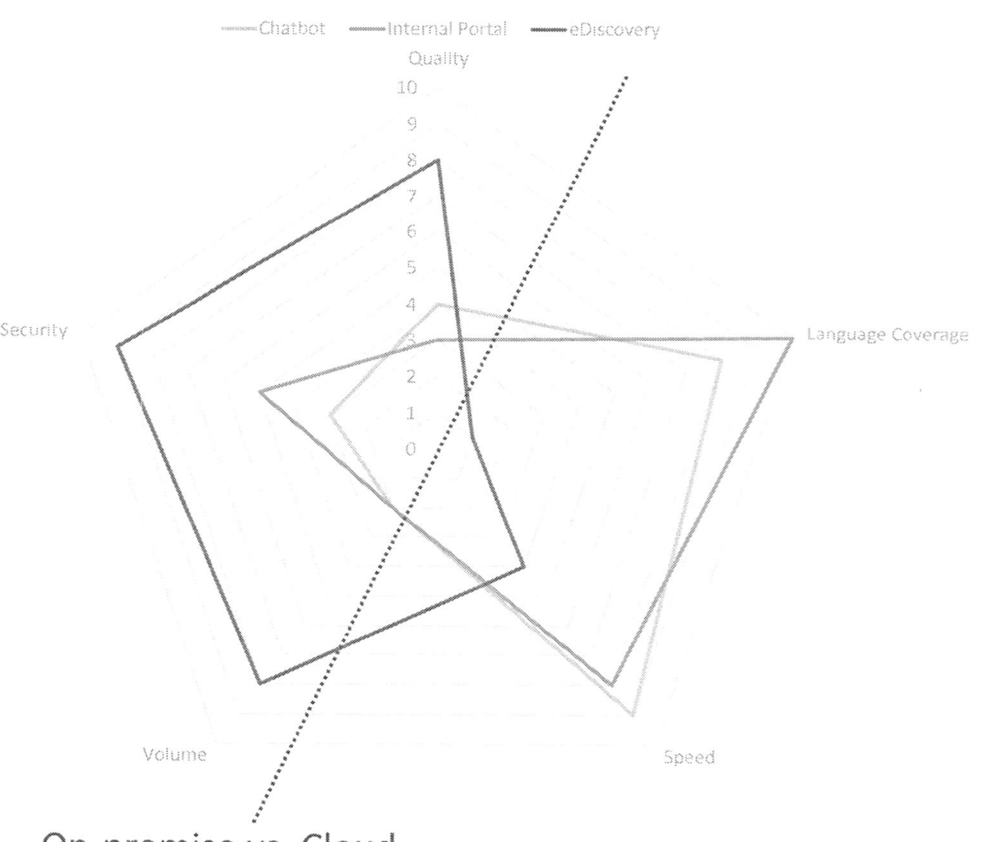

On-premise vs. Cloud

Proceedings of the 14th Conference of the Association for Machine Translation in the Americas
October 6 – 9, 2020, Volume 2: MT User Track

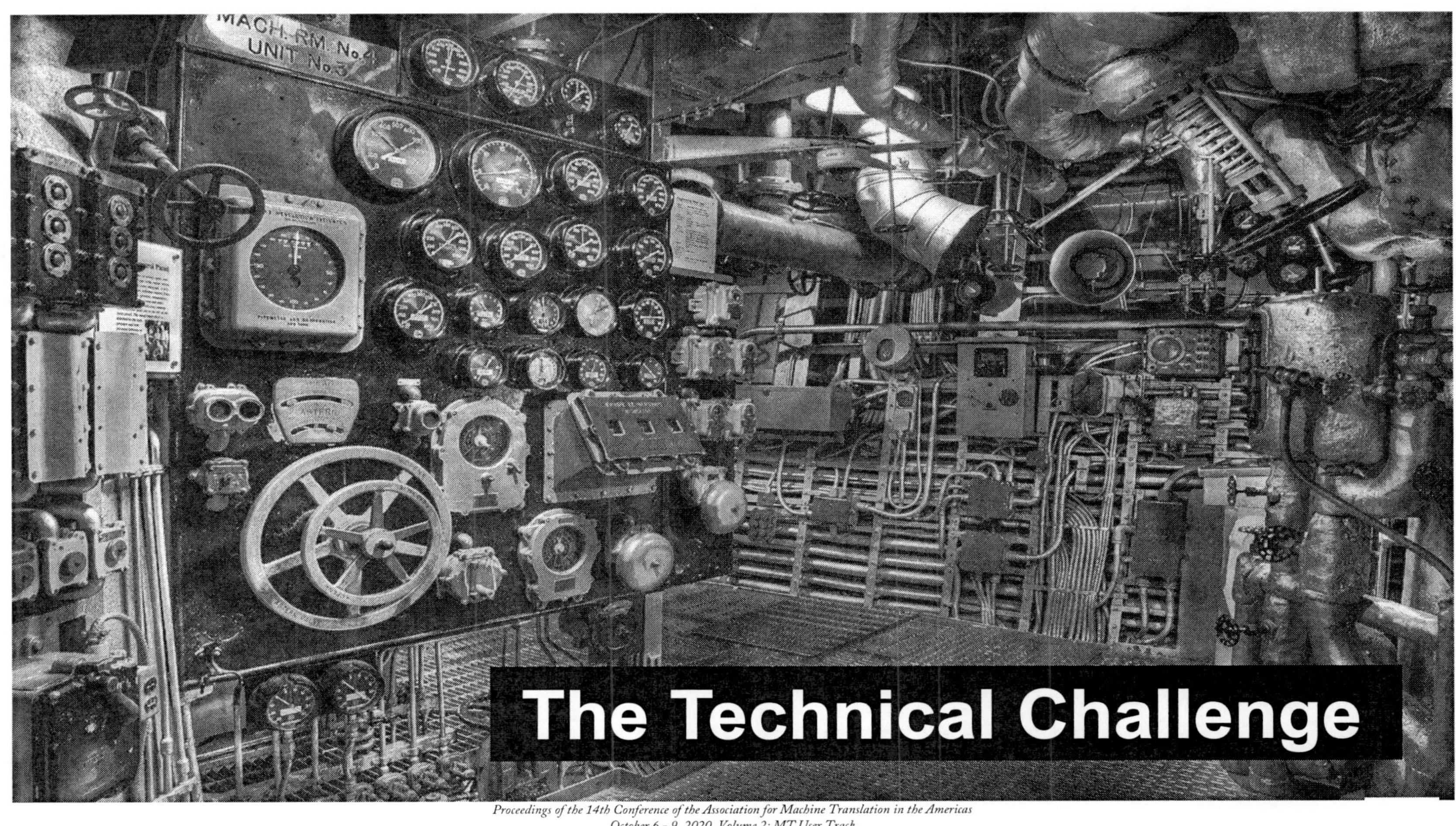

Proceedings of the 14th Conference of the Association for Machine Translation in the Americas
October 6 – 9, 2020, Volume 2: MT User Track

The Technical Challenge

- Understanding how the MT solution needs to be deployed
- Providing a pathway to acceptable TCO

Things to Consider

- Number of LPs and individual LP scalability
- Translation speed and latency
- Cost of achieving scale (hardware, hosting)
- Flexible licensing model (e.g. for seasonal peaks)
- Integrations and burden of maintenance
- Security and business continuity

SDL*

Proceedings of the 14th Conference of the Association for Machine Translation in the Americas
October 6 – 9, 2020, Volume 2: MT User Track

The Linguistic Challenge

- Understanding the current limits of MT
- Providing a pathway to sufficient quality

Things to Consider

- MT still comes out as too direct and non-idiomatic
- High level of fluency can mask other issues
- Humans excel at detecting extra-textual context
- Even commercial-grade MT systems struggle with messy inputs
- Bias in training data is reflected in MT output

15   © 2020 SDL

Example 1 – Fluent Nonsense

<u>Phototherapy exposure</u> in this range is used in the treatment of hyperbilirubinemia in newborn children.

<u>Fototerapia ekspozycji</u> w tym zakresie jest stosowana w leczeniu hiperbilirubinemii u noworodków.

fototerapia ekspozycji = phototherapy of exposure

Example 2 – Cross Domain Issues

System 1

<u>Administration</u> should be performed by an individual who has been adequately trained in <u>injection techniques</u>.

<u>Podawanie</u> powinno być wykonywane przez osobę, która została odpowiednio przeszkolona w zakresie <u>technik iniekcji</u>.

Proceedings of the 14th Conference of the Association for Machine Translation in the Americas
October 6 – 9, 2020, Volume 2: MT User Track

Example 2 – Cross Domain Issues

System 2

Administration should be performed by an individual who has been adequately trained in injection techniques.

Podawanie leku powinno być wykonywane przez osobę, która została odpowiednio przeszkolona w zakresie technik wstrzykiwania.

Example 2 – Cross Domain Issues

System 1

<u>System administration</u> should be performed by an individual who has been adequately <u>trained</u>.

<u>Podawanie systemu</u> powinno być wykonywane przez osobę odpowiednio <u>przeszkoloną</u>.

SDL

Proceedings of the 14th Conference of the Association for Machine Translation in the Americas
October 6 – 9, 2020, Volume 2: MT User Track

Example 2 – Cross Domain Issues

System 2

<u>System administration</u> should be performed by an individual who has been adequately <u>trained</u>.

<u>Administrowanie systemem</u> powinno być wykonywane przez osobę, która została odpowiednio <u>przeszkolona</u>.

SDL

Example 3 – Gender Bias

The doctor went home.

The nurse went home.

The professor went home.

The cleaner went home.

[m] Der Arzt ging nach Hause. Доктор пошел домой.

[f] Die Krankenschwester ging nach Hause. Медсестра пошла домой.

[m] Der Professor ging nach Hause. Профессор пошел домой.

[f] Die Putzfrau ging nach Hause. Уборщица пошла домой.

Example 4 – Imperfect Inputs

This is a test of the emergency alert system.

To jest test systemu alarmowego.

This is a test of the emergency alert system

To jest test systemu alarmowego w sytuacjach awaryjnych

SDL*

Proceedings of the 14th Conference of the Association for Machine Translation in the Americas
October 6 – 9, 2020, Volume 2: MT User Track

Example 5 – Missing Context

Wymiana <u>puszek</u> i <u>instalacji</u> w starym domu.

Replacement of <u>cans</u> and <u>installations</u> in an old house.

Replacement of <u>junction boxes</u> and <u>wiring</u> in an old house.

Proceedings of the 14th Conference of the Association for Machine Translation in the Americas
October 6 – 9, 2020, Volume 2: MT User Track

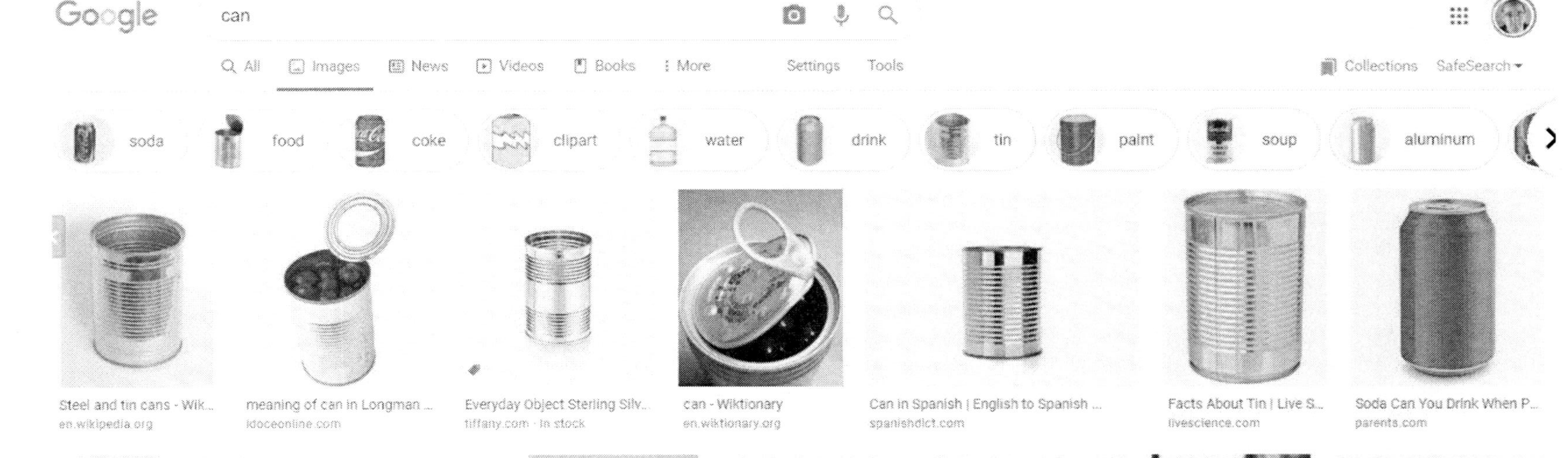

Proceedings of the 14th Conference of the Association for Machine Translation in the Americas
October 6 - 9, 2020, Volume 2: MT User Track

Google
puzzka
All   Images   Shopping   News   Maps   More   Settings   Tools
Collections   SafeSearch
pepsi   puszka hermetyczna   puszka podtynkowa   puszka metalowa   puszka instalacyjna   puszka natynkowa   puszki elektryczne   kopos puszka   farby
Puszka stalowa | różne kolory - X...
xxigastro.pl · In stock
Puszka do farby + wieczko 1L APP ...
allegro.pl · In stock
Puszka z wieczkiem do pak...
swiatwokolkuchni.pl · In stock
Puszki (puszka) na konserwy...
prepersklep.pl · In stock
Puszka 200 ml / 300 ml Dębica ...
sprzedajemy.pl
Puszka konserwowa emaliowana...
swiatdrozdzy.pl · In stock
Puszka elektryczna Simet Puszka...
ceneo.pl · In stock
Puszka elektryczna głęboka podwójna z ...
allegro.pl · In stock
Puszka instalacyjna 60 do ścian z ...
obi.pl · In stock
Puszka do konserw 650ml - Swiat ...
swiatdrozdzy.pl · In stock
Puszka na herbatę ze s...
bioherbaty.pl · In stock
Puszka podtynkowa Elektro-Plast ...
castorama.pl · In stock
© 2020 SDL
SDL

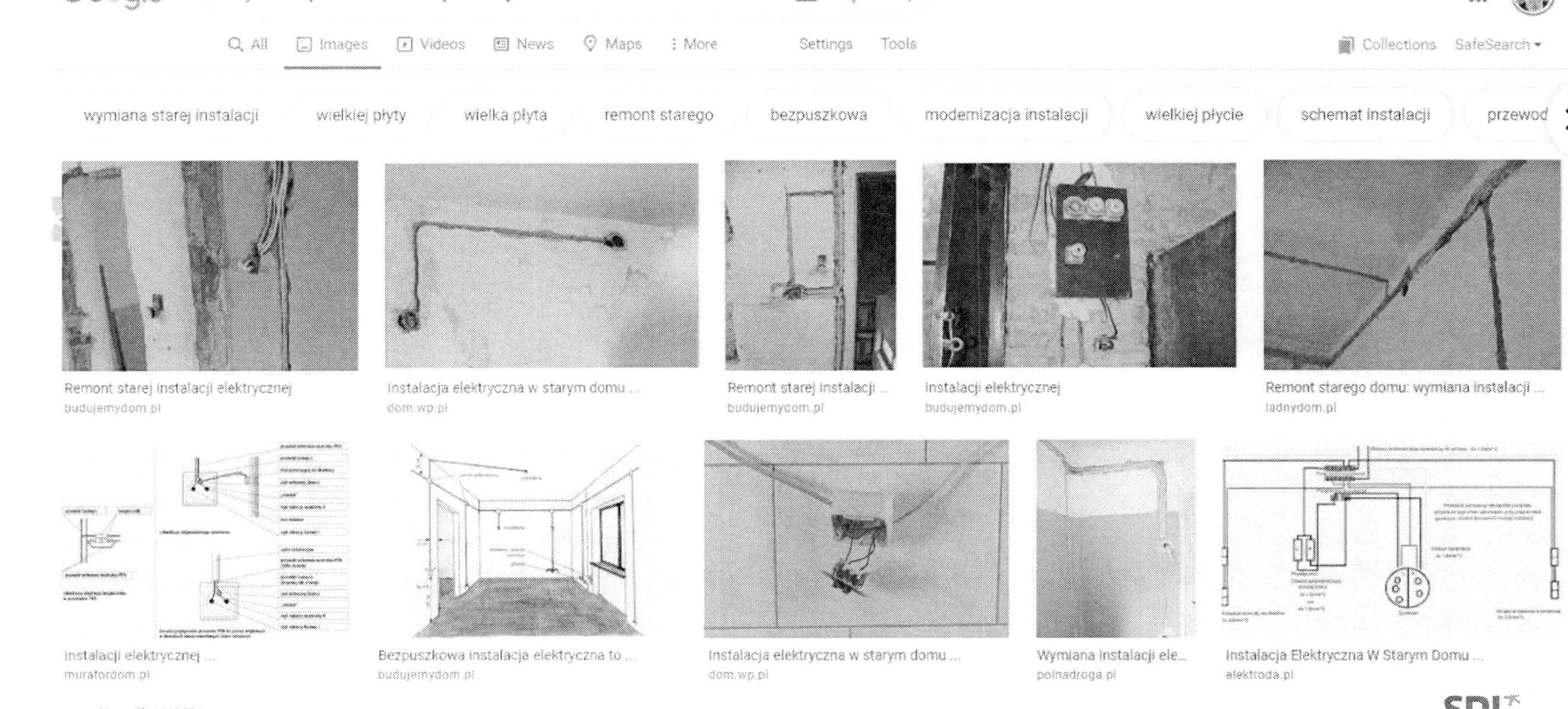

Proceedings of the 14th Conference of the Association for Machine Translation in the Americas
October 6 – 9, 2020, Volume 2: MT User Track

Linguistic AI

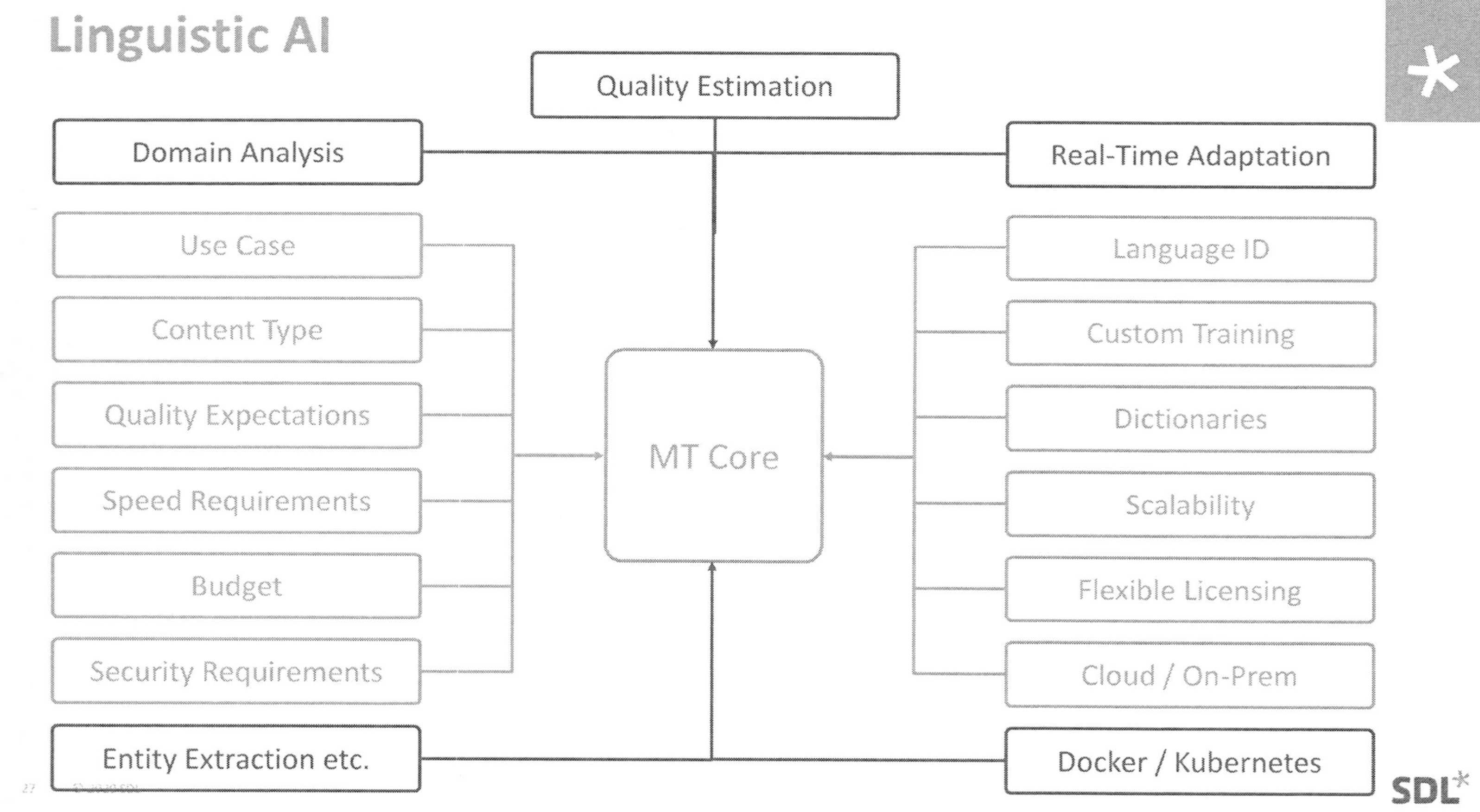

Proceedings of the 14th Conference of the Association for Machine Translation in the Americas
October 6 – 9, 2020, Volume 2: MT User Track

Proceedings of the 14th Conference of the Association for Machine Translation in the Americas
October 6 – 9, 2020, Volume 2: MT User Track

The Problem....

original	`Hello <g id="1" ctype="x-bold;">World!</g>`
after tokenization	`Hello < g id = " 1 " ctype = " x-bold ; " > World !  < / g >`
after escaping	`Hello < g id = " 1 " ctype = " x-bold ; " > World !  < / g >`
after lowercasing	`hello < g id = " 1 " ctype = " x-bold ; " > world !  < / g >`
after translation	`guten tag < code < ept id = " 1 " ctype = " " " x-bold ; " > world money < / g > !`
after recasing	`Guten Tag < Code < ept id = " 1 " ctype = " " " x-bold ; " > World Money < / G > !`
after detokenization	`Guten Tag < Code < ept id = " 1 " ctype = "" "x-bold;" > World Money < / G >!`
after unescaping	`Guten Tag < Code < ept id = " 1 " ctype = "" "x-bold;" > World Money < / G >!`

410

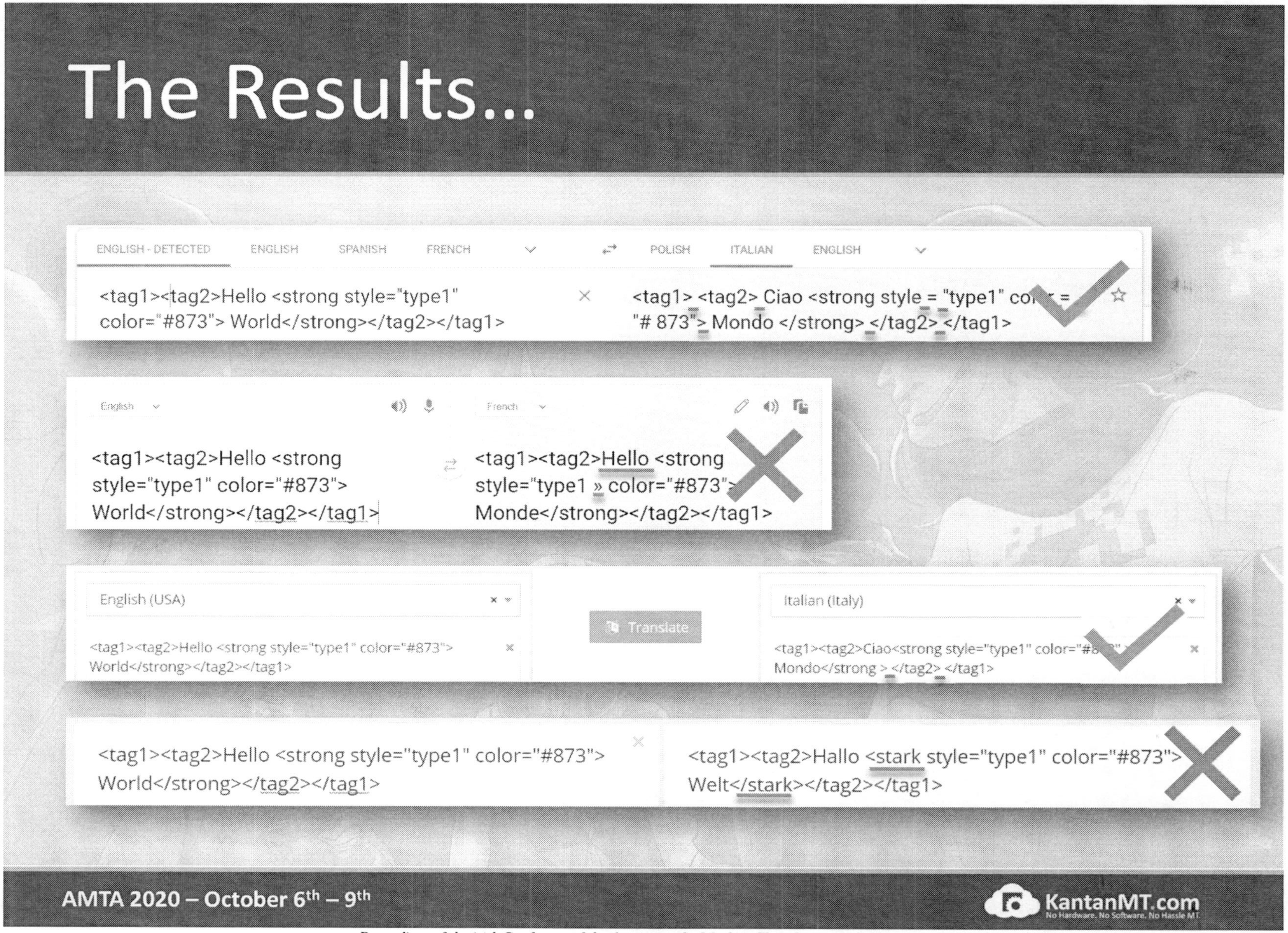
The Results...
ENGLISH - DETECTED ENGLISH SPANISH FRENCH
POLISH ITALIAN ENGLISH
<tag1><tag2>Hello <strong style="type1" color="#873"> World</strong></tag2></tag1>
<tag1> <tag2> Ciao <strong style = "type1" co
"# 873"> Mondo </strong> </tag2> </tag1>
English
French
<tag1><tag2>Hello <strong style="type1" color="#873"> World</strong></tag2></tag1>
<tag1><tag2>Hello <strong style="type1 » color="#873"
Monde</strong></tag2></tag1>
English (USA)
Translate
Italian (Italy)
<tag1><tag2>Hello <strong style="type1" color="#873"> World</strong></tag2></tag1>
<tag1><tag2>Ciao<strong style="type1" color="#
Mondo</strong > </tag2> </tag1>
<tag1><tag2>Hello <strong style="type1" color="#873"> World</strong></tag2></tag1>
<tag1><tag2>Hallo <stark style="type1" color="#873"> Welt</stark></tag2></tag1>
AMTA 2020 – October 6th – 9th
KantanMT.com
No Hardware. No Software. No Hassle MT

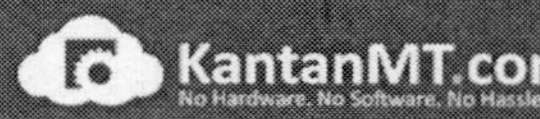

Strategy #1: Structure Forming

- ## Subtitling DFXP Format

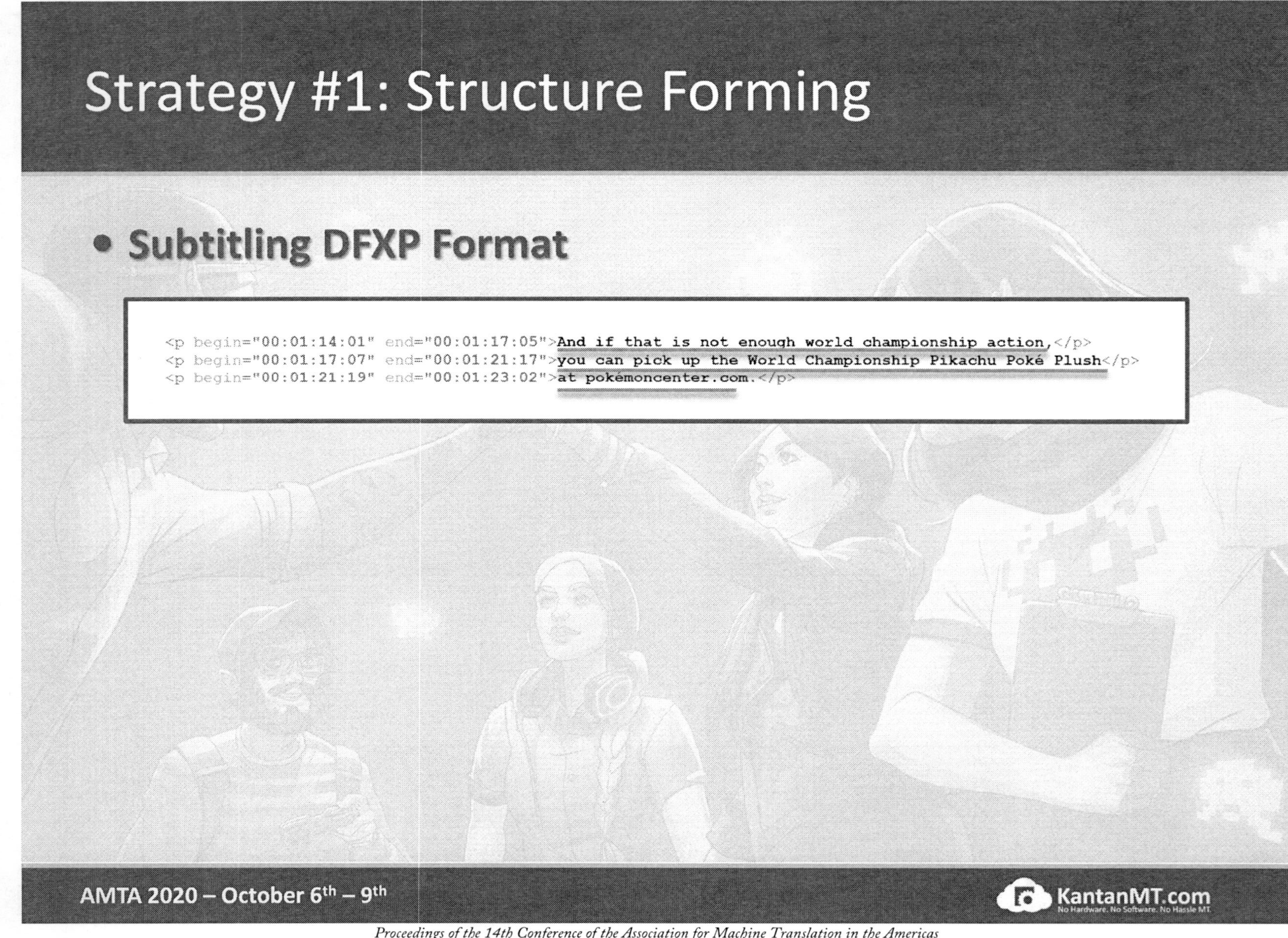

AMTA 2020 – October 6th – 9th

KantanMT.com
No Hardware. No Software. No Hassle MT.

Proceedings of the 14th Conference of the Association for Machine Translation in the Americas
October 6 – 9, 2020, Volume 2: MT User Track

Strategy #1: Structure Forming

Subtitling DFXP Format

```
<p begin="00:01:14:01" end="00:01:17:05">And if that is not enough world championship action,</p>
<p begin="00:01:17:07" end="00:01:21:17">you can pick up the World Championship Pikachu Poké Plush</p>
<p begin="00:01:21:19" end="00:01:23:02">at pokémoncenter.com.</p>
```

Step 1 - Sentence Forming

And if that is not enough world championship action, you can pick up the World Championship Pikachu Poké Plush pokémoncenter.com.

Strategy #1: Structure Forming

- ## Subtitling DFXP Format

```
<p begin="00:01:14:01" end="00:01:17:05">And if that is not enough world championship action,</p>
<p begin="00:01:17:07" end="00:01:21:17">you can pick up the World Championship Pikachu Poké Plush</p>
<p begin="00:01:21:19" end="00:01:23:02">at pokémoncenter.com.</p>
```

- ## Step 1 - Sentence Forming

And if that is not enough world championship action, you can pick up the World Championship Pikachu Poké Plush at pokémoncenter.com.

- ## Step 2 - Translate

A jeśli to nie wystarczy akcja mistrzostw świata, możesz wybrać World Championship Pikachu Poké Plush na pokémoncenter.com.

Strategy #1: Structure Forming

- ## Step 1 - Sentence Forming

  And if that is not enough world championship action, you can pick up the World Championship Pikachu Poké Plush at pokémoncenter.com.

- ## Step 2 – Translate

  A jeśli to nie wystarczy akcja mistrzostw świata, możesz wybrać World Championship Pikachu Poké Plush na pokémoncenter.com.

- ## Step 3 – Reformat & Re-insert

```
<p begin="00:01:14:01" end="00:01:17:05">И если этого недостаточно для участия в чемпионате мира,</p>
<p begin="00:01:17:07" end="00:01:21:17">вы можете забрать Pikachu Poké Plush Plush</p>
<p begin="00:01:21:19" end="00:01:23:02">pokémoncenter.com.</p>
```

Strategy #2: Zones & Walls

- **Moses decoder has the concept of**
  - **Forced Translations** – parts of the input sentence can be wrapped in <np> tags and assigned a probability

```
<np translations="Translated Term" prob="1">…</np>
```

  - **Zones**
    - Encapsulates a series of tokens that cannot be individually re-ordered, but can be re-ordered as part of the parent sequence

```
You can pick up the World Championship <zone>Pikachu Poké
Plush</zone>
```

  - **Wall**
    - A hard border that tokens cannot cross during re-ordering

KantanMT.com
No Hardware. No Software. No Hassle MT.

Strategy #3: Segmentation

And if that is not enough world championship action, you can pick up the World Championship <strong>**Pikachu Poké Plush** </strong>at pokémoncenter.com.

Strategy #3: Segmentation

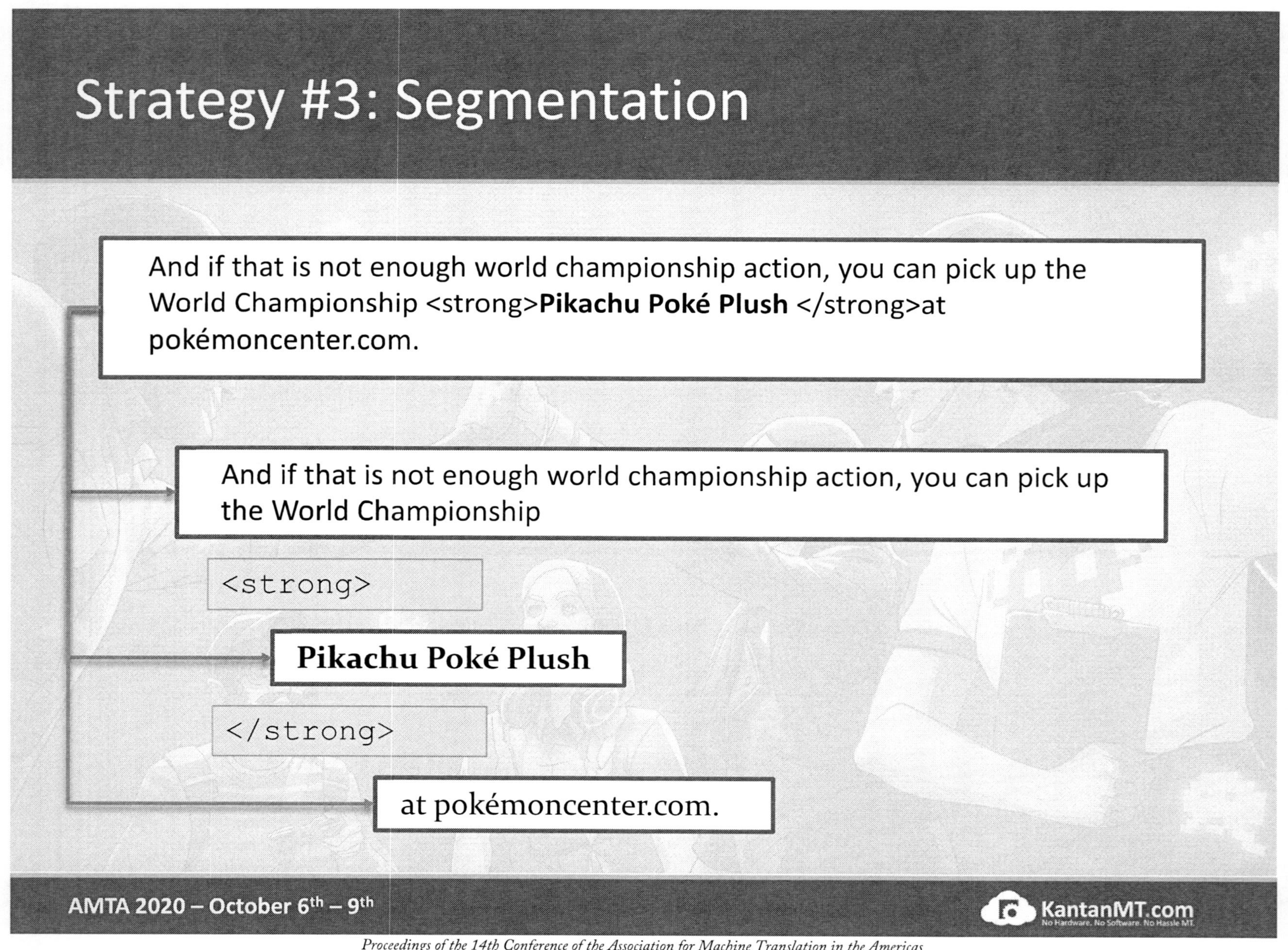

KantanMT.com
No Hardware. No Software. No Hassle MT.

Proceedings of the 14th Conference of the Association for Machine Translation in the Americas
October 6 – 9, 2020, Volume 2: MT User Track

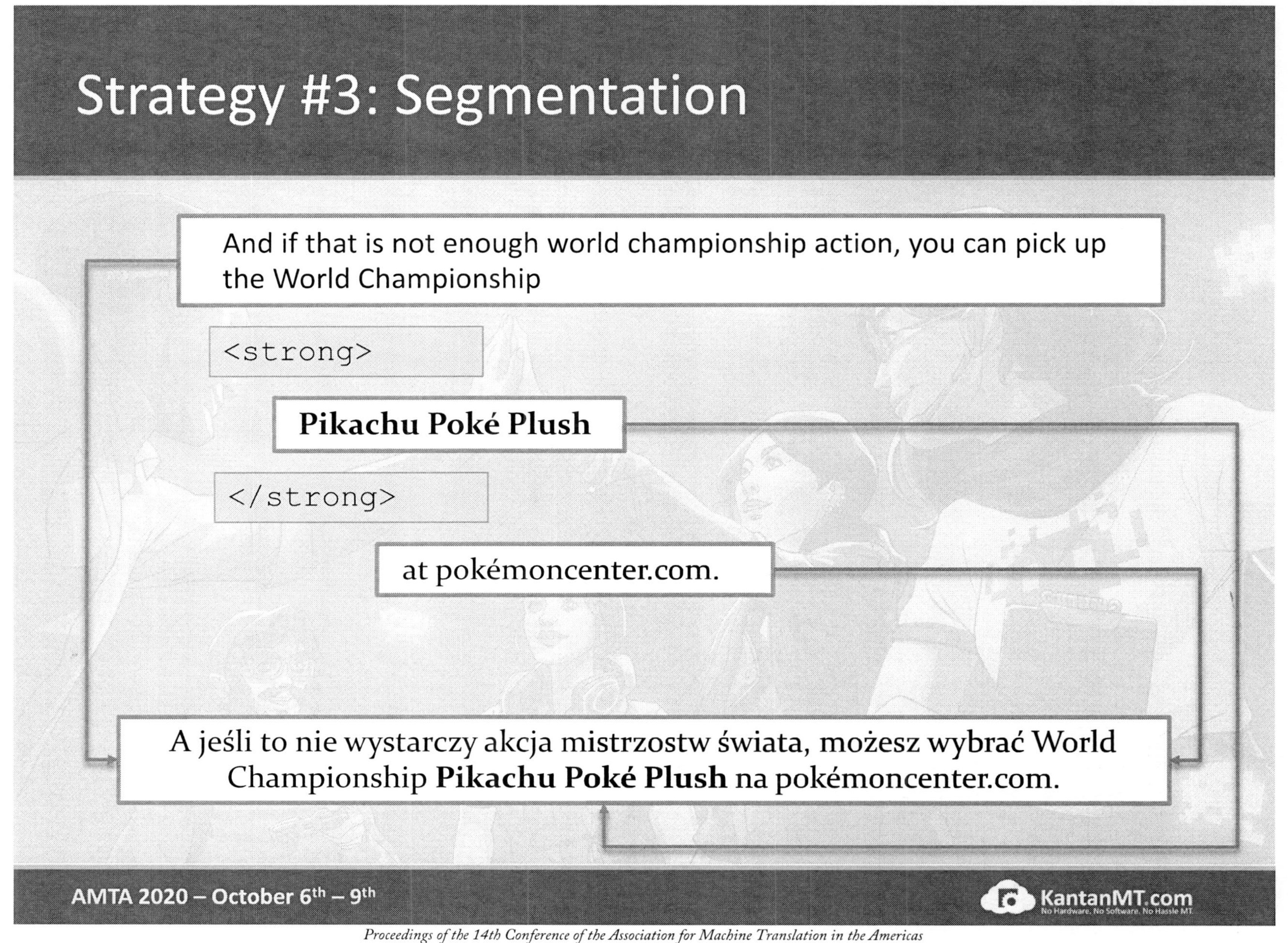

Strategy #3: Segmentation
And if that is not enough world championship action, you can pick up the World Championship
<strong>
Pikachu Poké Plush
</strong>
at pokémoncenter.com.
A jeśli to nie wystarczy akcja mistrzostw świata, możesz wybrać World Championship Pikachu Poké Plush na pokémoncenter.com.
AMTA 2020 – October 6th – 9th
KantanMT.com
No Hardware. No Software. No Hassle MT.

Strategy #4: Pass Through

And if that is not enough world championship action, you can pick up the World Championship <strong>**Pikachu Poké Plush** </strong>at pokémoncenter.com.

Strategy #4: Pass Through

And if that is not enough world championship action, you can pick up the World Championship <strong>**Pikachu Poké Plush** </strong>at pokémoncenter.com.

And if that is not enough world championship action, you can pick up the World Championship ❶ **Pikachu Poké Plush** ❷ at pokémoncenter.com.

Token	Assigned
❶	<strong>
❷	</strong>

Proceedings of the 14th Conference of the Association for Machine Translation in the Americas
October 6 – 9, 2020, Volume 2: MT User Track

Strategy #4: Pass Through

And if that is not enough world championship action, you can pick up the World Championship <strong>**Pikachu Poké Plush** </strong>at pokémoncenter.com.

And if that is not enough world championship action, you can pick up the World Championship ❶ **Pikachu Poké Plush** ❷ at pokémoncenter.com.

A jeśli to nie wystarczy akcja mistrzostw świata, możesz wybrać World Championship ❶**Pikachu Poké Plush**❷ na pokémoncenter.com.

Token	Assigned
❶	<strong>
❷	</strong>

KantanMT.com
No Hardware. No Software. No Hassle MT.

Strategy #4: Pass Through

And if that is not enough world championship action, you can pick up the World Championship <strong>**Pikachu Poké Plush** </strong>at pokémoncenter.com.

And if that is not enough world championship action, you can pick up the World Championship ❶ **Pikachu Poké Plush** ❷ at pokémoncenter.com.

Token	Assigned
❶	<strong>
❷	</strong>

A jeśli to nie wystarczy akcja mistrzostw świata, możesz wybrać World Championship <strong>**Pikachu Poké Plush**</strong> na pokémoncenter.com.

Strategy #4: Pass Through

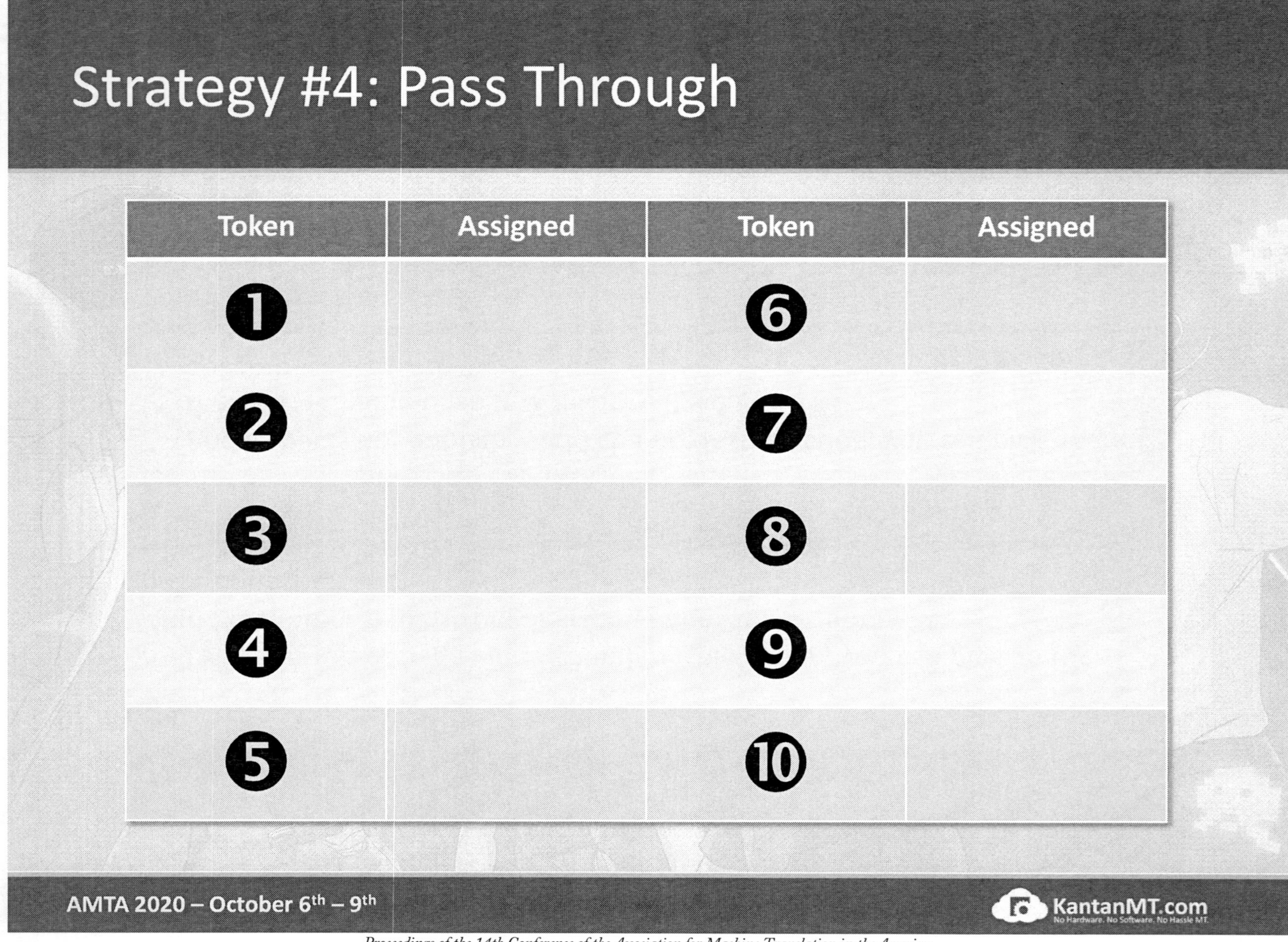

Strategy #5: Optimisation

- **Detecting lead/trail tags**

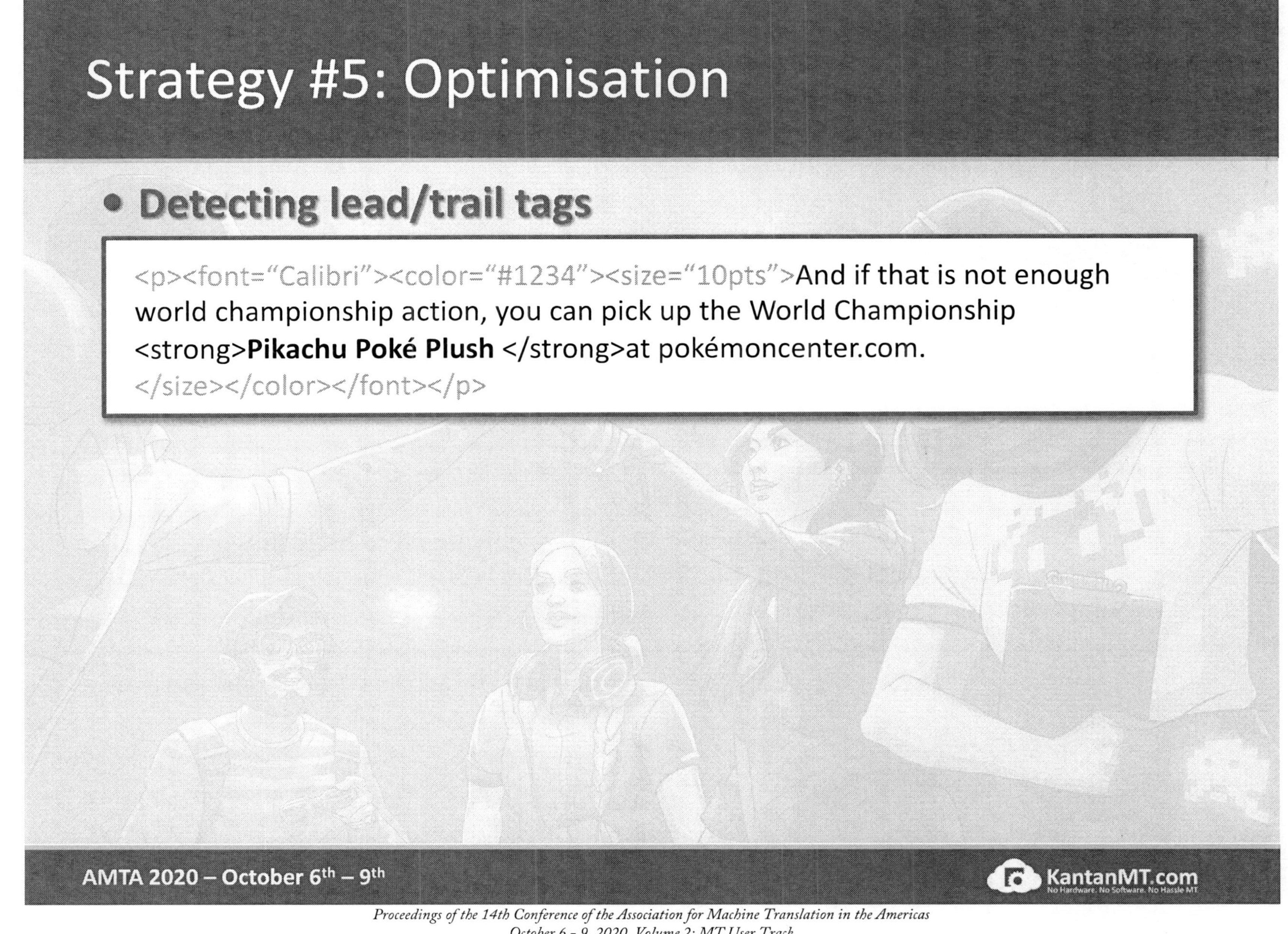

Strategy #5: Optimisation

- **Detecting lead/trail tags**

<p><font="Calibri"><color="#1234"><size="10pts">And if that is not enough world championship action, you can pick up the World Championship <strong>**Pikachu Poké Plush** </strong>at pokémoncenter.com. </size></color></font></p>

<lead/>And if that is not enough world championship action, you can pick up the World Championship ❶ **Pikachu Poké Plush** ❷ at pokémoncenter.com.<trail/>

Token	Assigned
❶	<strong>
❷	</strong>
Lead	<p><font="Calibri"><color="#1234"><size="10pts">
Trail	</size></color></font></p>

KantanMT.com
No Hardware. No Software. No Hassle MT.

Which one to work with???

- **Strategy #1**
  - Structure Forming
- **Strategy #2**
  - Zones & Walls
- **Strategy #3**
  - Segmentation
- **Strategy #4**
  - Pass-Thru
- **Strategy #5**
  - Optimisation

KantanMT.com
No Hardware. No Software. No Hassle MT.
Challenges of Terminology

Basic Levels of Terminology

- **Lexically Constrained Decoding for Sequence Generation**
  - **Level I**
    - Multi-word phrases – non-inflected
    - Nouns, Proper Nouns, Brand or Feature/Service names
    - Can be represented in simple list form

EN	FR	IT	DE
Stakataka	Ama-Ama	Stakataka	Muramura
Snorlax	Ronflex	Snorlax	Relaxo
Trainer	Dresseur	Allenatore	Trainer
Terrakion	Terrakium	Terrakion	Terrakium
Whimsicott	Farfaduvet	Whimsicott	Elfun
Gengar	Ectoplasma	Gengar	Gengar
Tapu Bulu	Tokotoro	Tapu Bulu	Kapu-Toro
Kommo-o	Ékaïser	Kommo-o	Grandiras

  - **Level II**
    - Inflected Multi-word phases
    - Cannot be represented in simple list form
    - Inflected variations to indicate number, grammatical case, or gender

What is a Glossary?

- **Terms in one or more languages**
  - With comments, and usage examples
  - **Industry Glossary**
    - Includes terms that are standard for an industry or subject/domain
      - **Example**: Banking, Cardiology, Automotive, Accounting
  - **Client Glossary**
    - Contains terms that are very specific to a company/client
      - **Example**: eBay, Adobe, BMW
  - **Project Glossary**
    - Used to maintain consistency throughout translation project
      - **Example**: Microsoft Office, Pokemon

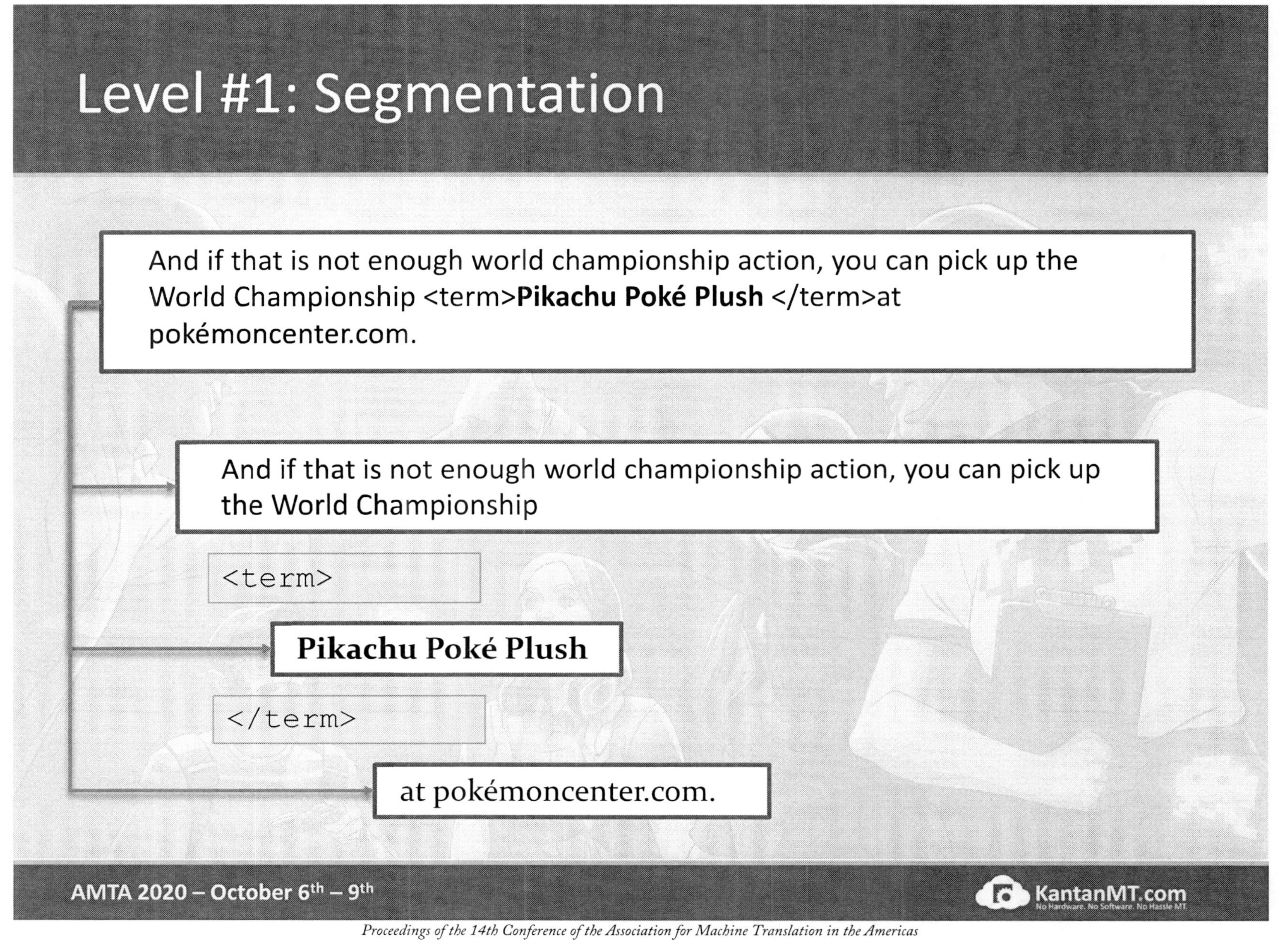

And if that is not enough world championship action, you can pick up the World Championship <term>**Pikachu Poké Plush** </term>at pokémoncenter.com.
And if that is not enough world championship action, you can pick up the World Championship
<term>
Pikachu Poké Plush
</term>
at pokémoncenter.com.

Level #1: Segmentation

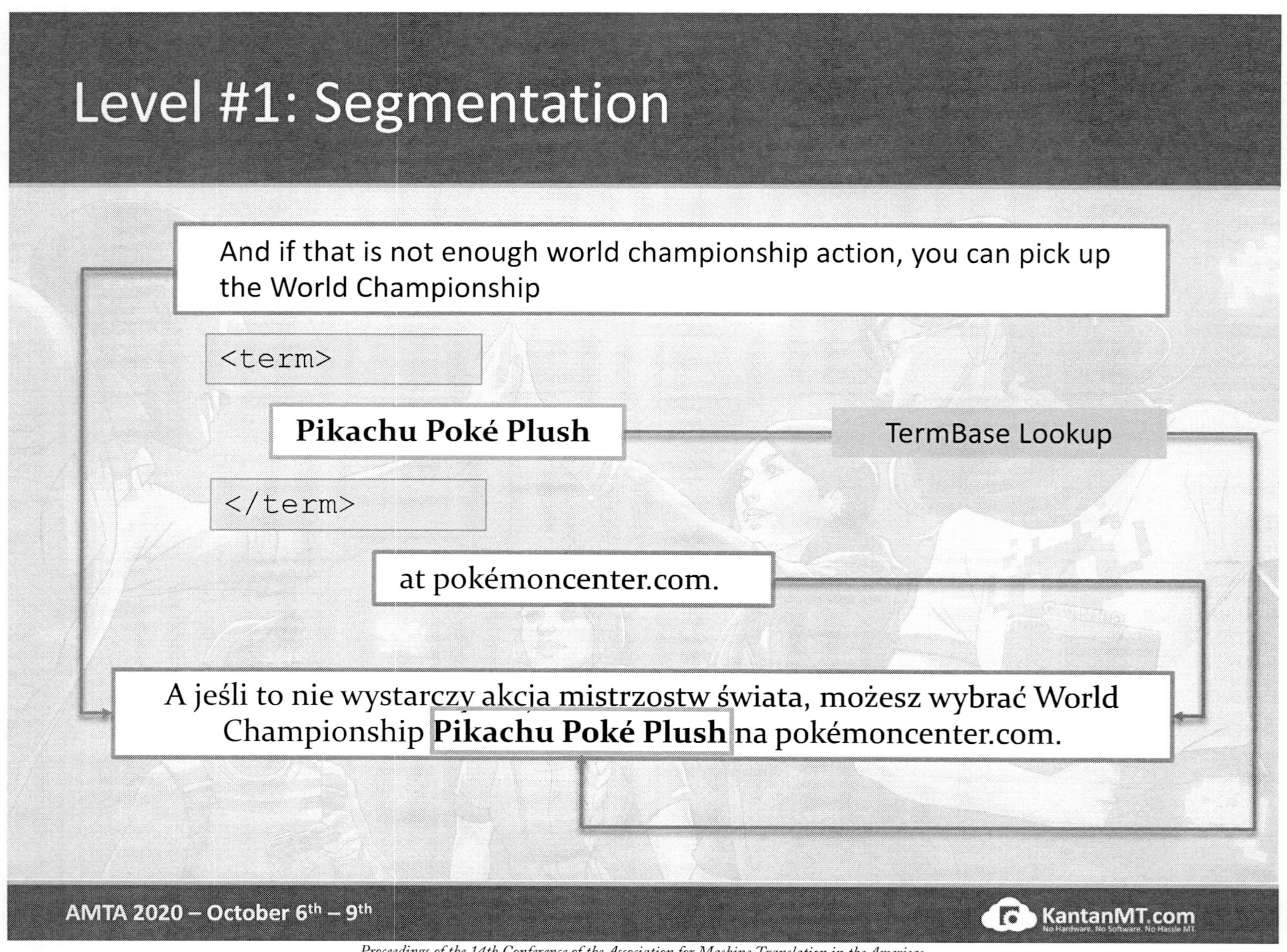

Proceedings of the 14th Conference of the Association for Machine Translation in the Americas
October 6 – 9, 2020, Volume 2: MT User Track

Level #1: Pre-process & Pass-Thru

And if that is not enough world championship action, you can pick up the World Championship **Pikachu Poké Plush** at pokémoncenter.com.

TermBase Lookup

And if that is not enough world championship action, you can pick up the World Championship **<np translations="Pikachu Poké Plush" prob="1"/>** at pokémoncenter.com.

Level #1: Pre-process & Pass-Thru

And if that is not enough world championship action, you can pick up the World Championship **Pikachu Poké Plush** at pokémoncenter.com.

TermBase Lookup

And if that is not enough world championship action, you can pick up the World Championship **<np translations="Pikachu Poké Plush" prob="1"/>** at pokémoncenter.com.

A jeśli to nie wystarczy akcja mistrzostw świata, możesz wybrać World Championship **Pikachu Poké Plush** na pokémoncenter.com.

salesforce
Building Salesforce Neural Machine Translation System
Kazuma Hashimoto, Lead Research Scientist
@ Salesforce Research
Raffaella Buschiazzo, Director, Localization
@ Salesforce R&D Localization
AMTA 2020 Commercial Track
TRAILMAP

Agenda

- Why invest in machine translation
- Salesforce online help
- What was done: Phase I
  - Technical overview
  - Example flows
- What was done: Phase II
- Roadmap

Proceedings of the 14th Conference of the Association for Machine Translation in the Americas
October 6 – 9, 2020, Volume 2: MT User Track

Why Invest in Machine Translation

A three-year collaboration between R&D Localization and Salesforce Research teams

Interesting research project
- Challenges: difficult MT languages (i.e. Finnish, Japanese), XML tagging.

Improve international customer experience by

- Reducing translation time by enhancing translator's productivity for our online help
- Increasing content accuracy/freshness by publishing updates more frequently
- Re-investing savings into high-value efforts
    - Products and product-related properties
    - Underserved localization content/efforts

Benefits

- Increase case deflection through up-to-date content for existing languages
- Increase breadth and depth of localization coverage with more flexibility by market

Proceedings of the 14th Conference of the Association for Machine Translation in the Americas
October 6 – 9, 2020, Volume 2: MT User Track

Salesforce Online Help

Primary target for our MT system

- Translated in 16 languages.

- Translations are updated per major release (3 x year).

- New feature/product terminology.

- Structured in DITA XML (200+ tags).

Documentation

Find documentation, videos, and walkthroughs to help you succeed.

VIEW DOCUMENTATION

English
Français
Deutsch
Italiano
日本語
Español (México)
Español
中文（简体）
中文（繁體）
한국어
Русский
Português (Brasil)
Suomi
Dansk
Svenska
Nederlands
ภาษาไทย
Norsk

Proceedings of the 14th Conference of the Association for Machine Translation in the Americas
October 6 - 9, 2020, Volume 2: MT User Track

What Was Done: Phase I

Linguistic testing

Built an NMT system on Salesforce domain
- Language-agnostic architecture with models for each language
- Processes whole XML files from English into 16 languages

Completed human evaluations of MTed output
- Japanese, Finnish, German, French Help subsets (500 strings)

Published paper A High-Quality Multilingual Dataset for Structured Documentation Translation (WMT 2019)

Proceedings of the 14th Conference of the Association for Machine Translation in the Americas
October 6 – 9, 2020, Volume 2: MT User Track

Technical Overview

Data and application

Dataset in our paper
- https://github.com/salesforce/localization-xml-mt

Translation of rich-formatted text
- How to preserve the structure

- Example (a)

<u>English:</u>

You can use this report on your Community Management Home dashboard or in <ph>Community Workspaces</ph> under <menucascade><uicontrol>Dashboards</uicontrol><uicontrol>Home</uicontrol></menucascade>.

<u>Japanese:</u>

このレポートは、[コミュニティ管理] のホームのダッシュボード、または <ph>コミュニティワークスペース </ph>の <menucascade><uicontrol>[ダッシュボード]</uicontrol> <uicontrol>[ホーム]</uicontrol></menucascade> で使用できます。

- Example (b)

<u>English:</u>

Results with <b>both</b><i>beach</i> and <i>house</i> in the searchable fields of the record.

<u>Japanese:</u>

レコードの検索可能な項目に <i>beach</i> と <i>house</i> の <b>両方 </b>が含まれている結果。

- Example (c)

<u>English:</u>

You can only predefine this field to an email address. You can predefine it using either T (used to define email addresses) or To Recipients (used to define contact, lead, and user IDs).

<u>Japanese:</u>

この項目 はメールアドレスに対してのみ事前に定義できます。 この項目 は [宛先] (メールアドレスを定義するために使用) または [宛先受信者] (取引先責任者、リード、ユーザ ID を定義するために使用) のいずれかを使用して事前に定義できます。

Proceedings of the 14th Conference of the Association for Machine Translation in the Americas
October 6 – 9, 2020, Volume 2: MT User Track

Technical Overview

Model

Transformer encoder-decoder (Vaswani et al., 2017)

- Input: XML-tagged text in English
- Output: XML-tagged text in another language
  - **XML-tag-aware tokenizer** is used (based on sentencepiece)
  - e.g.) <uicontrol>New Suite</uicontrol>: Create a suite of test classes that...
    - → _ <uicontrol> New _Suite </uicontrol> : _Create _a _suit e _of _test _classes _that...
- + copy mechanisms
  - Copy from source is used to **align XML tags**

- **Source to be translated (English)**
<xref>View a single feed update</xref> by clicking the timestamp below the update, *for example*, <uicontrol>Yesterday at **12:57 AM**</uicontrol>.

- **Retrieved source (English)**
In a feed, click the timestamp that appears below the post, *for example*, <uicontrol>Yesterday at 12:57 AM</uicontrol>.
- **Retrieved reference (Japanese)**
フィード内で、*たとえば*、<uicontrol>[昨日の 12:57 AM]</uicontrol> のように、投稿の下に表示されるタイムスタンプをクリックします。

- **Output of the X*rs* model (Japanese)**
<uicontrol> [昨日の 12:57 AM] </uicontrol> のように、更新の下にタイムスタンプをクリックして、<xref> 1 つのフィード更新を表示</xref>します。

Proceedings of the 14th Conference of the Association for Machine Translation in the Americas
October 6 – 9, 2020, Volume 2: MT User Track

Technical Overview

System

Training

- Construct our training data from
    - the **N-th** release
        - a later version than our published dataset
    - release notes of the new, **(N+1)-th**, release
        - to incorporate translation of new features/context in the new release
        - available for our company's top-tier languages
    - [optional and if applicable] whatever internal parallel data

Translation

- Target English strings that have **little overlap** with our translation memory
- Remove metadata from XML tags
- Run our model for each language
- Align the metadata with the translated strings by using our model's copy mechanism

Human verification and post-editing before publishing the translated online help

Proceedings of the 14th Conference of the Association for Machine Translation in the Americas
October 6 – 9, 2020, Volume 2: MT User Track

Example Flow (1)

Overview

Update basic community settings like your community URL, community name, members, login options, and general preferences in the <TAG id="1">Administration</TAG> section of <TAG id="2">Experience Workspaces</TAG> or <TAG id="3">Community Management</TAG>.

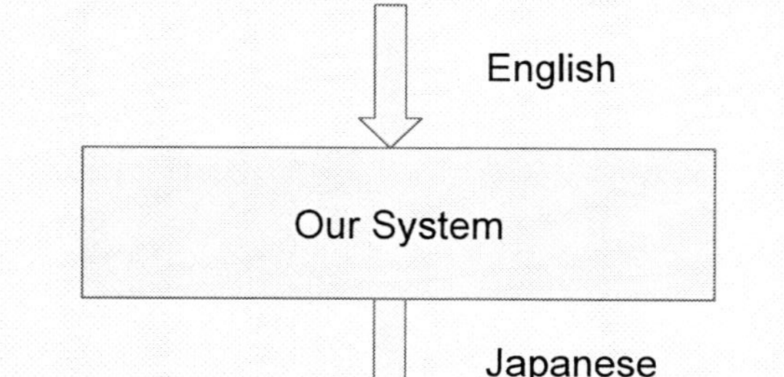

<TAG id="2">エクスペリエンスワークスペース</TAG>または <TAG id="3">[コミュニティ管理]</TAG> の <TAG id="1">[管理]</TAG> セクションで、コミュニティ URL、コミュニティ名、メンバー、ログインオプション、一般的な設定など、コミュニティの基本設定を更新します。

Example Flow (2)
Input Preprocessing

Update basic community settings like your community URL, community name, members, login options, and general preferences in the <TAG id="1">Administration</TAG> section of <TAG id="2">Experience Workspaces</TAG> or <TAG id="3">Community Management</TAG>.

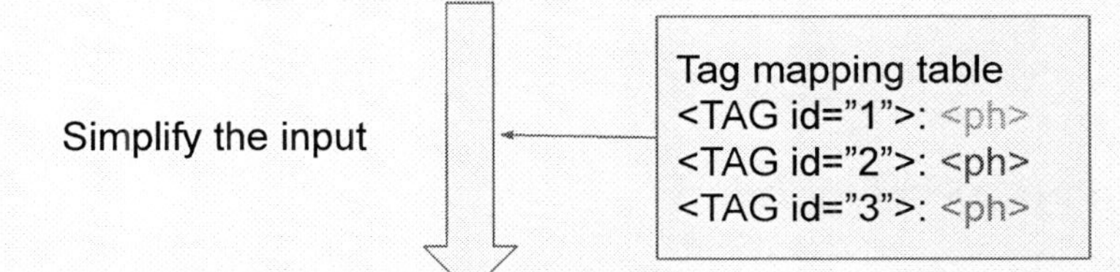

Update basic community settings like your community URL, community name, members, login options, and general preferences in the <ph>Administration</ph> section of <ph>Experience Workspaces</ph> or <ph>Community Management</ph>.

Proceedings of the 14th Conference of the Association for Machine Translation in the Americas
October 6 – 9, 2020, Volume 2: MT User Track

Example Flow (3)
Translation by our model

Update basic community settings like your community URL, community name, members, login options, and general preferences in the <ph>Administration</ph> section of <ph>Experience Workspaces</ph> or <ph>Community Management</ph>.

Translation

<ph>エクスペリエンスワークスペース</ph>または <ph>[コミュニティ管理]</ph> の <ph>[管理]</ph> セクションで、コミュニティ URL、コミュニティ名、メンバー、ログインオプション、一般的な設定など、コミュニティの基本設定を更新します。

Proceedings of the 14th Conference of the Association for Machine Translation in the Americas
October 6 – 9, 2020, Volume 2: MT User Track

Example Flow (4)
Tag Alignment

Update basic community settings like your community URL, community name, members, login options, and general preferences in the <ph>Administration</ph> section of <ph>Experience Workspaces</ph> or <ph>Community Management</ph>.

Maximize the product of the copy weights based on one-to-one mapping assumption

English \ Japanese	<ph>_ja	<ph>_ja	<ph>_ja
<ph>_en	0.01	0.05	**0.91**
<ph>_en	**0.92**	0.02	0.01
<ph>_en	0.01	**0.95**	0.01

<ph>エクスペリエンスワークスペース</ph>または <ph>[コミュニティ管理]</ph> の <ph>[管理]</ph> セクションで、コミュニティ URL、コミュニティ名、メンバー、ログインオプション、一般的な設定など、コミュニティの基本設定を更新します。

Proceedings of the 14th Conference of the Association for Machine Translation in the Americas
October 6 – 9, 2020, Volume 2: MT User Track

Example Flow (5)
Output Postprocessing

<ph>エクスペリエンスワークスペース</ph>または <ph>[コミュニティ管理]</ph> の <ph>[管理]</ph> セクションで、コミュニティ URL、コミュニティ名、メンバー、ログインオプション、一般的な設定など、コミュニティの基本設定を更新します。

Tag mapping table
<TAG id="1">: <ph>
<TAG id="2">: <ph>
<TAG id="3">: <ph>

<TAG id="2">エクスペリエンスワークスペース</TAG>または <TAG id="3">[コミュニティ管理]</TAG> の <TAG id="1">[管理]</TAG> セクションで、コミュニティ URL、コミュニティ名、メンバー、ログインオプション、一般的な設定など、コミュニティの基本設定を更新します。

Proceedings of the 14th Conference of the Association for Machine Translation in the Americas
October 6 – 9, 2020, Volume 2: MT User Track

What Was Done: Phase II

Completed 2 pilots
- MTPEd two major releases of help content in Japanese, French, German, Brazilian Portuguese, Mexican Spanish, Swedish, Danish, Norwegian.

Evaluated 500 strings: our system against uncustomized commercially available NMT system

Observations:
- Salesforce NMT is better at outputting sentences with Salesforce writing style.
- Other system is good at outputting generally well-written sentences.
- Most challenging part is translating new features/terminology.
- Including Salesforce Release Notes in training data increased score #1.

Proceedings of the 14th Conference of the Association for Machine Translation in the Americas
October 6 – 9, 2020, Volume 2: MT User Track

Roadmap

- Leveraging publicly available models
  - So far, we used our own data only
  - Fine-tune/customize general models/engines
    - Publicly available pretrained models: mBART, XLM-R, etc.
- Human-in-the-loop training
  - At every release, we can get post-edited strings
  - Can we use the feedback to train another model to refine MT output?
    - Or can we train a model to spot potentially wrong segments to help human post-editing?
- Continual learning
- Extend MT to more online languages and more use cases

Proceedings of the 14th Conference of the Association for Machine Translation in the Americas
October 6 - 9, 2020, Volume 2: MT User Track

thank you
BLAZE YOUR TRAIL
salesforce

SUCCESSFUL TECH TRANSFER
OF
OF MT RESEARCH IN
GOVERNMENT

Dr. Kathy Baker
US Dept. of Defense
AMTA
October 9, 2020

Proceedings of the 14th Conference of the Association for Machine Translation in the Americas
October 6 – 9, 2020, Volume 2: MT User Track

Background

- *Vision* – DoD Agency recognizes Neural Machine Translation (NMT) as a force multiplier for analysis

- In-house HLT Research organization: Cutting edge Artificial Intelligence/Machine Learning (AI/ML)

- "Make vs. buy" – Agency not obligated to productize in-house research

- Key selling point is *access to and understanding of government data sets*

Proceedings of the 14th Conference of the Association for Machine Translation in the Americas
October 6 – 9, 2020, Volume 2: MT User Track

What makes tech transfer successful?

- Partnerships, partnerships, partnerships!

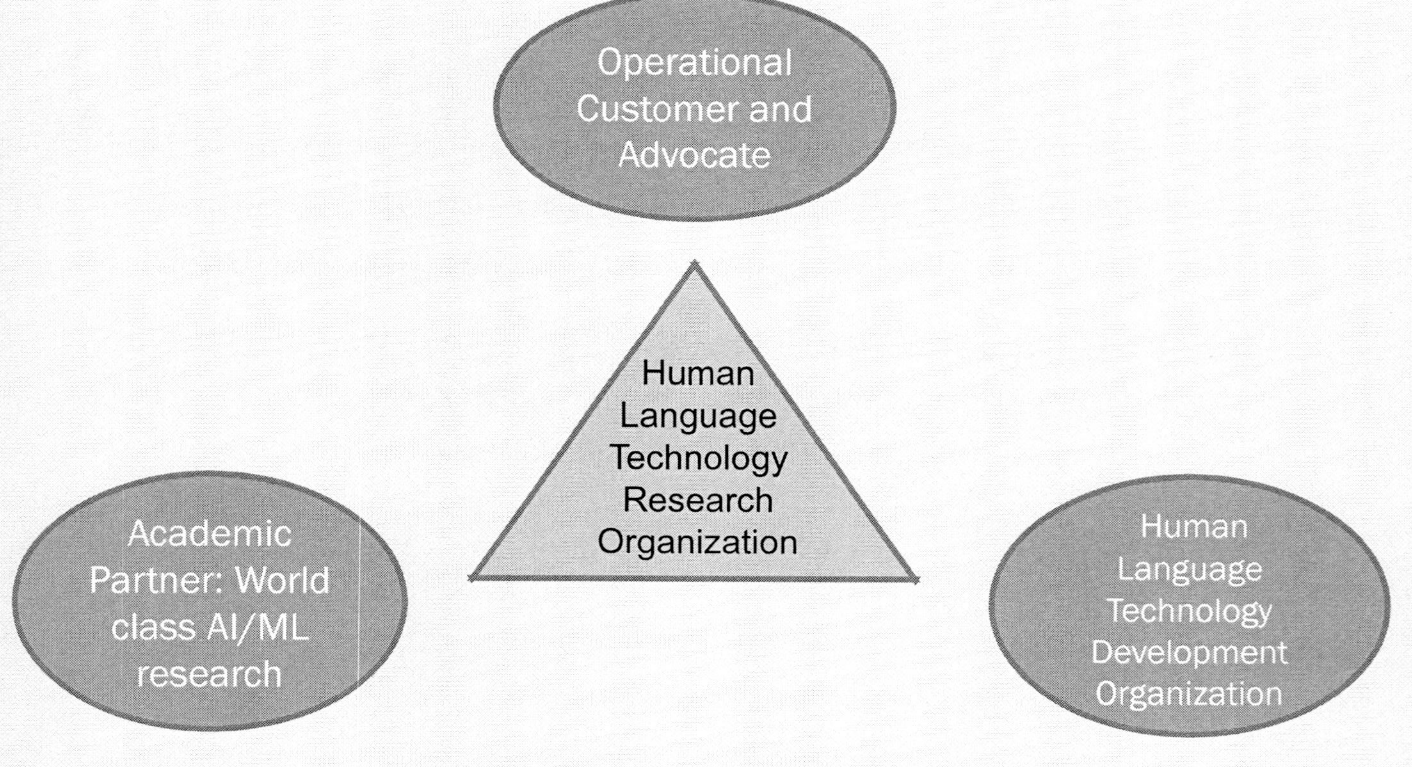

Proceedings of the 14th Conference of the Association for Machine Translation in the Americas
October 6 – 9, 2020, Volume 2: MT User Track

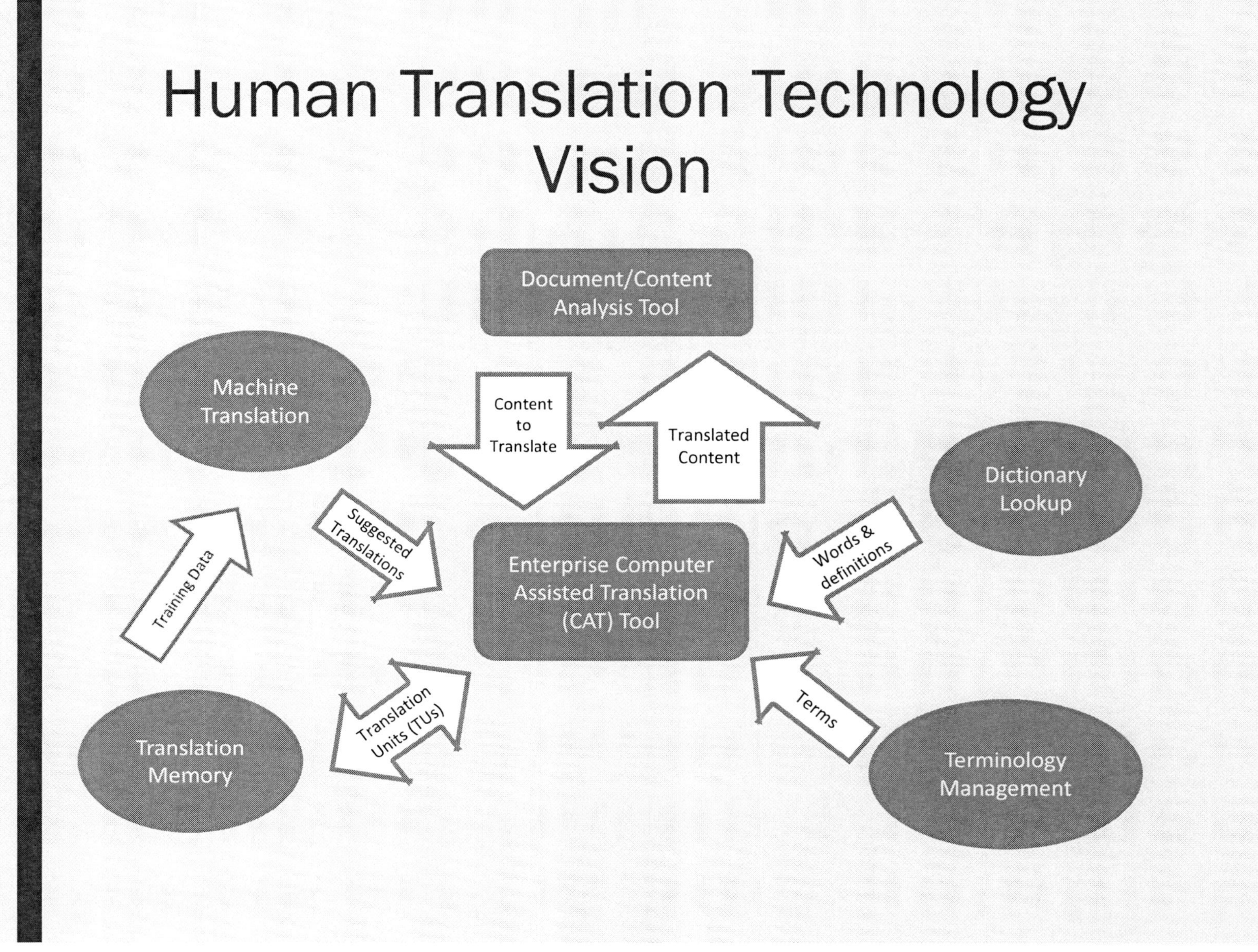

Human Translation Technology Vision
Document/Content Analysis Tool
Machine Translation
Content to Translate
Translated Content
Dictionary Lookup
Enterprise Computer Assisted Translation (CAT) Tool
Training Data
Suggested Translations
Words & definitions
Translation Memory
Translation Units (TUs)
Terms
Terminology Management

Academic Partnership

- Academic partnership with Johns Hopkins University

- Jump start research in neural MT with "dream team" of academic and industrial experts (Summer 2018 workshop)

- Adapt MT trained on general domain data for your use case with small amounts of highly technological or informal data

Proceedings of the 14th Conference of the Association for Machine Translation in the Americas
October 6 – 9, 2020, Volume 2: MT User Track

General Domain Training

General domain: News, parliamentary proceedings, movie subtitles, Wikipedia headlines, etc.

General Domain Training

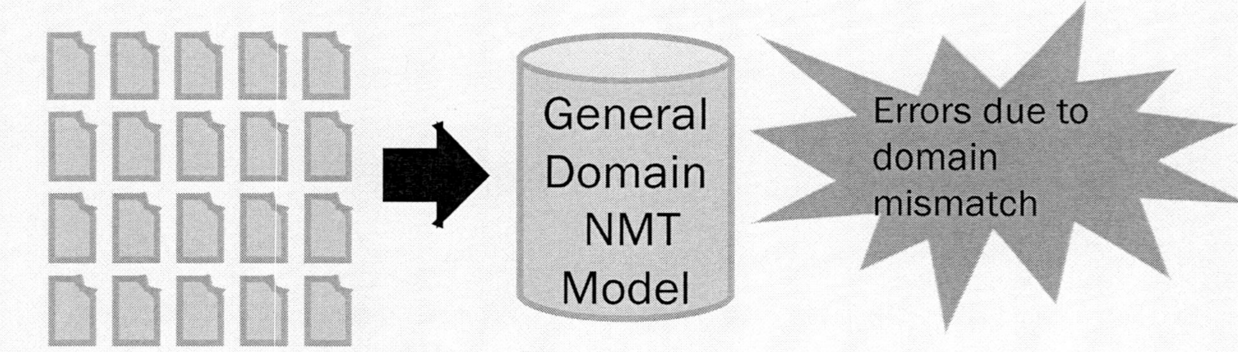

Russian patent example

Input: устройство для сбора воды с последующим её использованием для **стеклоомывателя**
Human: device for collecting water for subsequent use in a **windscreen washer**
System: water collection device and subsequent use for glazing

Proceedings of the 14th Conference of the Association for Machine Translation in the Americas
October 6 – 9, 2020, Volume 2: MT User Track

Domain Adaptation

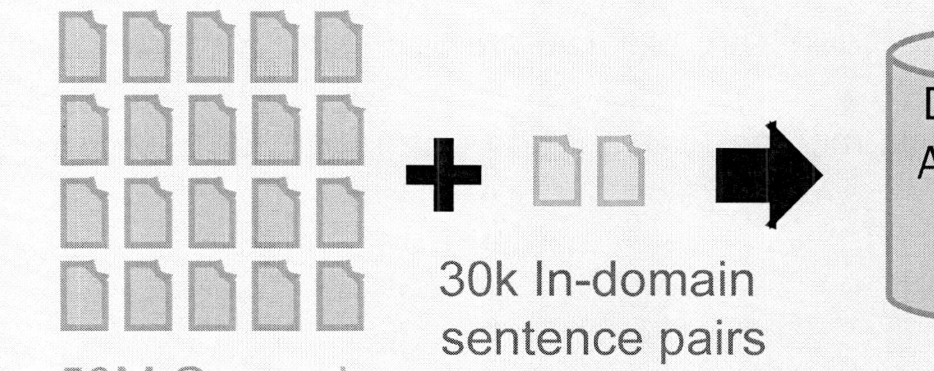

Proceedings of the 14th Conference of the Association for Machine Translation in the Americas
October 6 – 9, 2020, Volume 2: MT User Track

Domain Adaptation

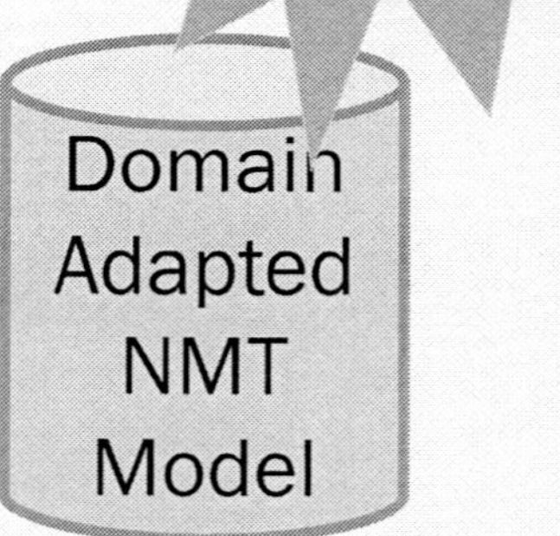

Input: устройство для сбора воды с последующим её использованием для **стеклоомывателя**
Human: device for collecting water for subsequent use in a **windscreen washer**
Output: water collecting device with subsequent use thereof for a windscreen washer

Proceedings of the 14th Conference of the Association for Machine Translation in the Americas
October 6 – 9, 2020, Volume 2: MT User Track

Continued Training

[= "Fine-tuning" in STT literature]

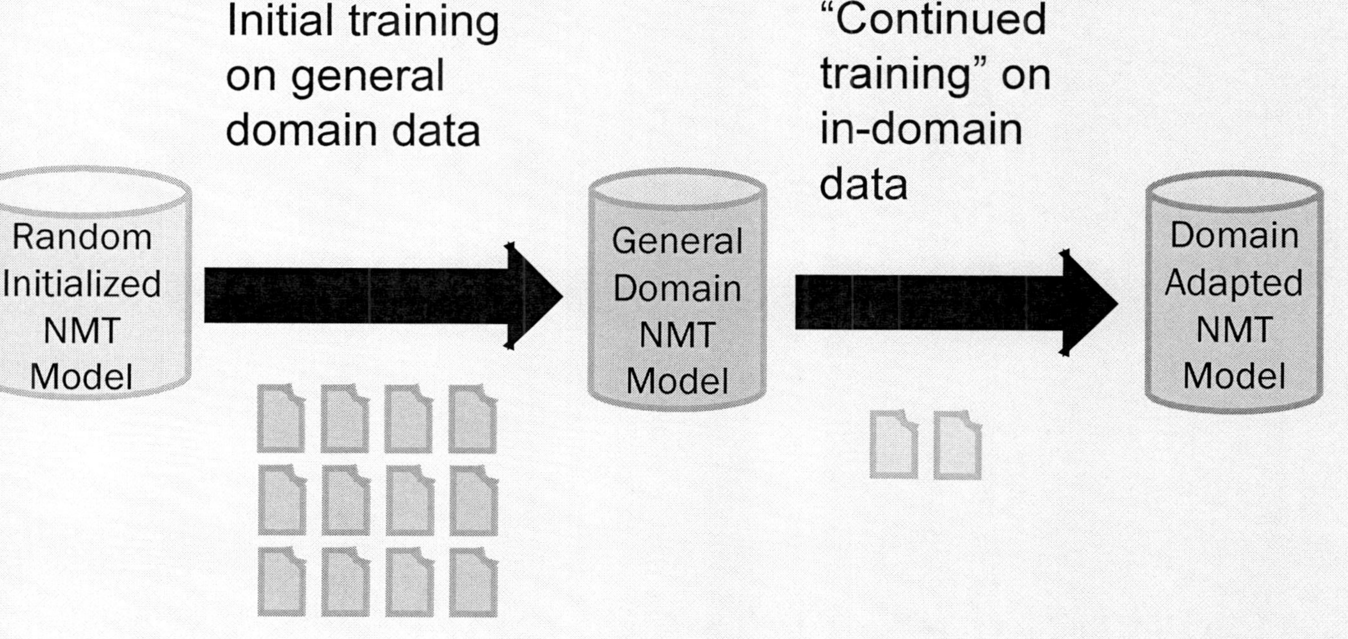

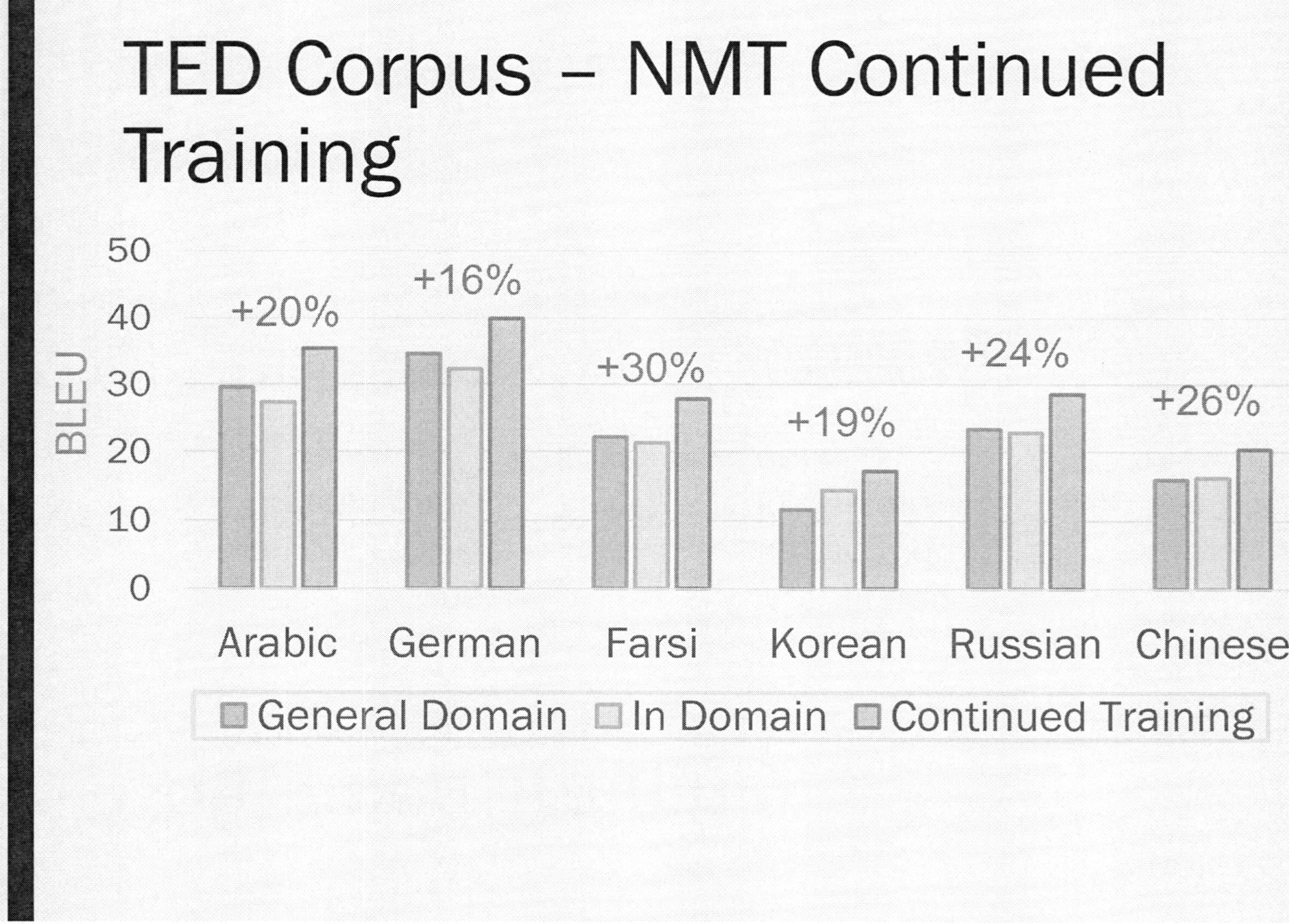

Proceedings of the 14th Conference of the Association for Machine Translation in the Americas
October 6 – 9, 2020, Volume 2: MT User Track

Patents - NMT vs Statistical MT, Out of box MT

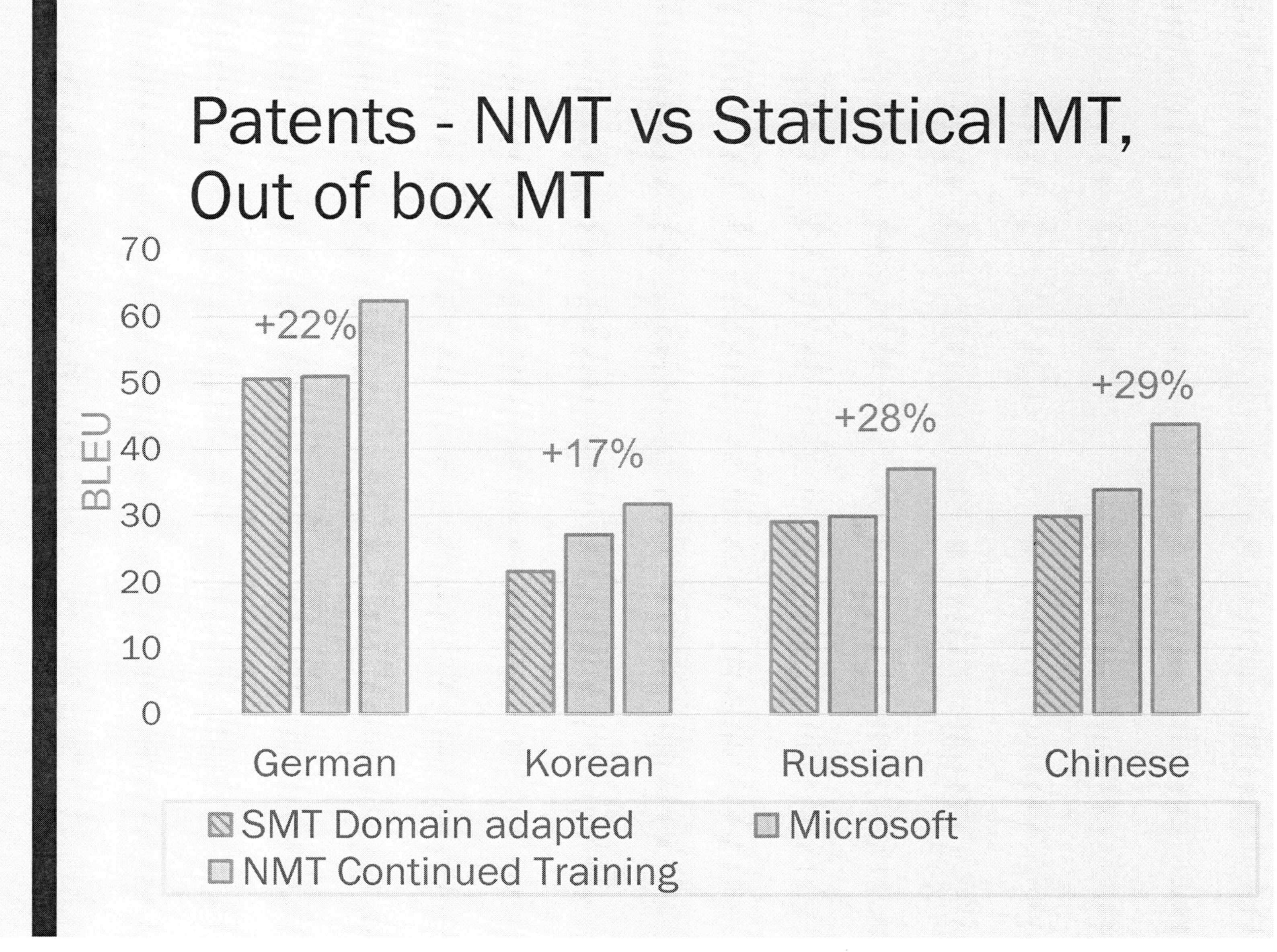

Proceedings of the 14th Conference of the Association for Machine Translation in the Americas
October 6 – 9, 2020, Volume 2: MT User Track

Sample Translations

TED Talk

- **Source:** 我遇到了霍金教授 他说他的梦想是空间旅行

- **Reference:** And I met Professor Hawking, and he said his dream was to travel into space.

- **Agency Baseline:** I ran into Professor Hodgen he saying that his dream was the spatial travel

- **DA-NMT:** I met Professor Hawking who said that his dream was space travel.

Patent

- **Source:** 一种基于纳米滤膜的废有机溶剂处理工艺及系统

- **Reference:** WASTE ORGANIC SOLVENT TREATMENT PROCESS AND SYSTEM BASED ON NANO FILTRATION MEMBRANE

- **Agency Baseline:** One kind based on nanometer filter diaphragm's waste organic solvent processing craft and system

- **DA-NMT:** Waste organic solvent treatment process and system based on nanometer filter film

Proceedings of the 14th Conference of the Association for Machine Translation in the Americas
October 6 – 9, 2020, Volume 2: MT User Track

Operational Partnership

- Customer who understands benefits of research early on contributes
  - *Advocacy*
  - *Funding*
  - *Personnel with language expertise*
  - *Operational Data*

Proceedings of the 14th Conference of the Association for Machine Translation in the Americas
October 6 – 9, 2020, Volume 2: MT User Track

Development Partnership

- HLT Development Organization designed as a "sister org" with common goals for success

- Previous Research successes built up model deployment infrastructure there
  - *Own and provide necessary hardware*
  - *Own the enterprise wrapper for machine translation; no separate User Interface needed*

Proceedings of the 14th Conference of the Association for Machine Translation in the Americas
October 6 – 9, 2020, Volume 2: MT User Track

Open Source Software

- Several well-designed platforms for building neural models

- Cost savings on initial push to Operations (though beware the maintenance tail)

- **Allows control of training data and model building**

Proceedings of the 14th Conference of the Association for Machine Translation in the Americas
October 6 – 9, 2020, Volume 2: MT User Track

Current Status

- Six languages deployed in beta status
- Very well received
- What's left?
  - Scaling! Throughput, architecture
  - More languages
  - Tradecraft: Feedback loop from translation at workstation to model retraining
  - Modernizing analyst translation interface *in tandem* with deploying to current portal

Proceedings of the 14th Conference of the Association for Machine Translation in the Americas
October 6 - 9, 2020, Volume 2: MT User Track

Plugging into Trados:
Augmenting Translation in the Enclave

Corey Miller, Chiara Higgins, Paige Havens, Steven Van Guilder,
Rodney Morris and Danielle Silverman

October 8, 2020

Proceedings of the 14th Conference of the Association for Machine Translation in the Americas
October 6 – 9, 2020, Volume 2: MT User Track

UNCLASSIFIED

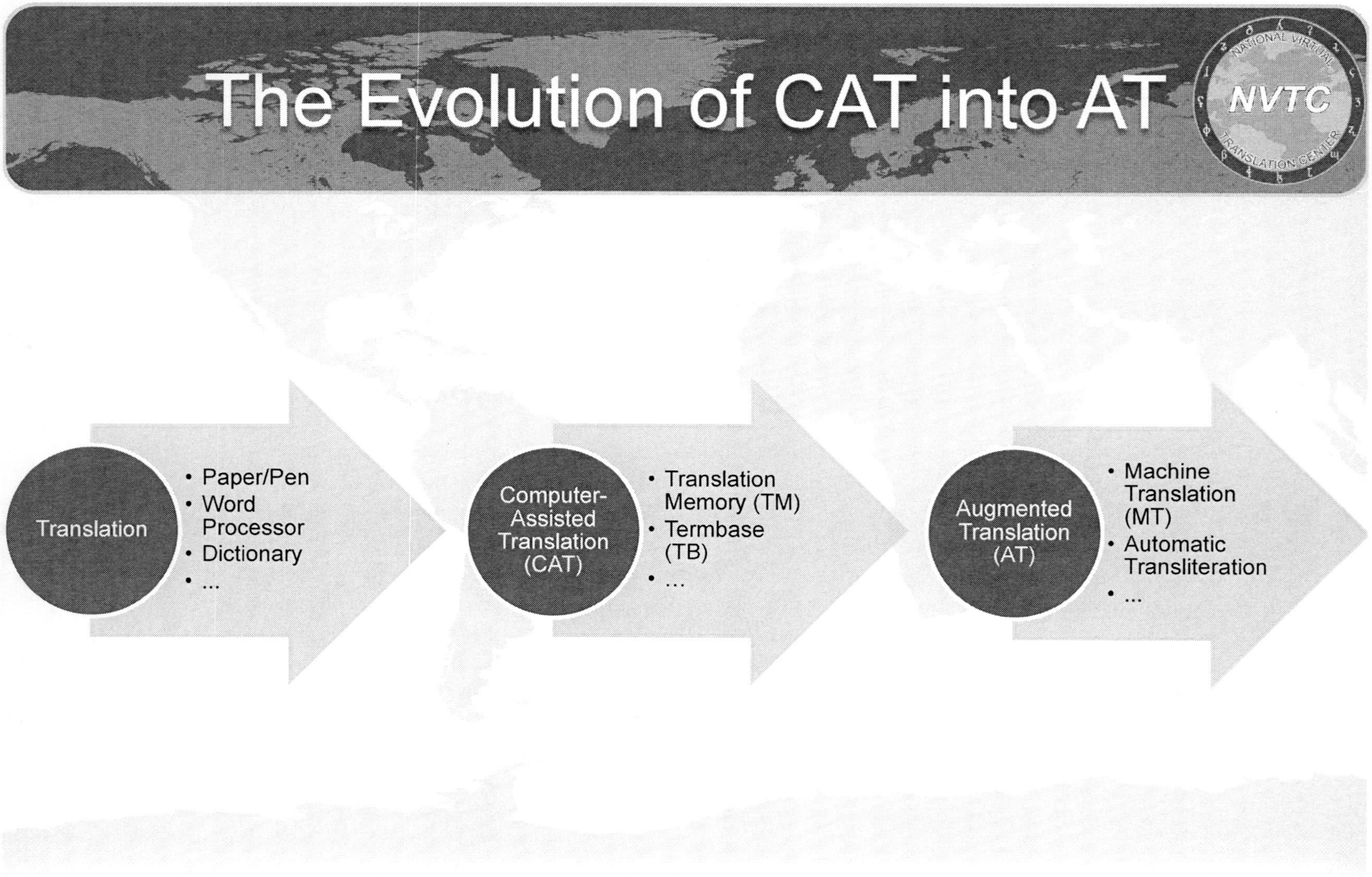
The Evolution of CAT into AT
NATIONAL VIRTUAL TRANSLATION CENTER
NVTC
Translation
• Paper/Pen
• Word Processor
• Dictionary
• …
Computer-Assisted Translation (CAT)
• Translation Memory (TM)
• Termbase (TB)
• …
Augmented Translation (AT)
• Machine Translation (MT)
• Automatic Transliteration
• …

UNCLASSIFIED

AT with MT on the Internet

- SDL Automated Translation
  - BeGlobal
    - Could be used in an enclave
  - Language Cloud
  - Google Cloud
- Lilt
  - On prem solution in development

AT in the Enclave

- NVTC uses Symphony
  - MT portal featuring several COTS and GOTS engines
  - Transliteration portal featuring Basis Rosette Name Translator (RNT)
- NVTC developed Trados plugin
  - Symphony MT when no sufficient TM match is found
  - Person & place name transliterations on demand

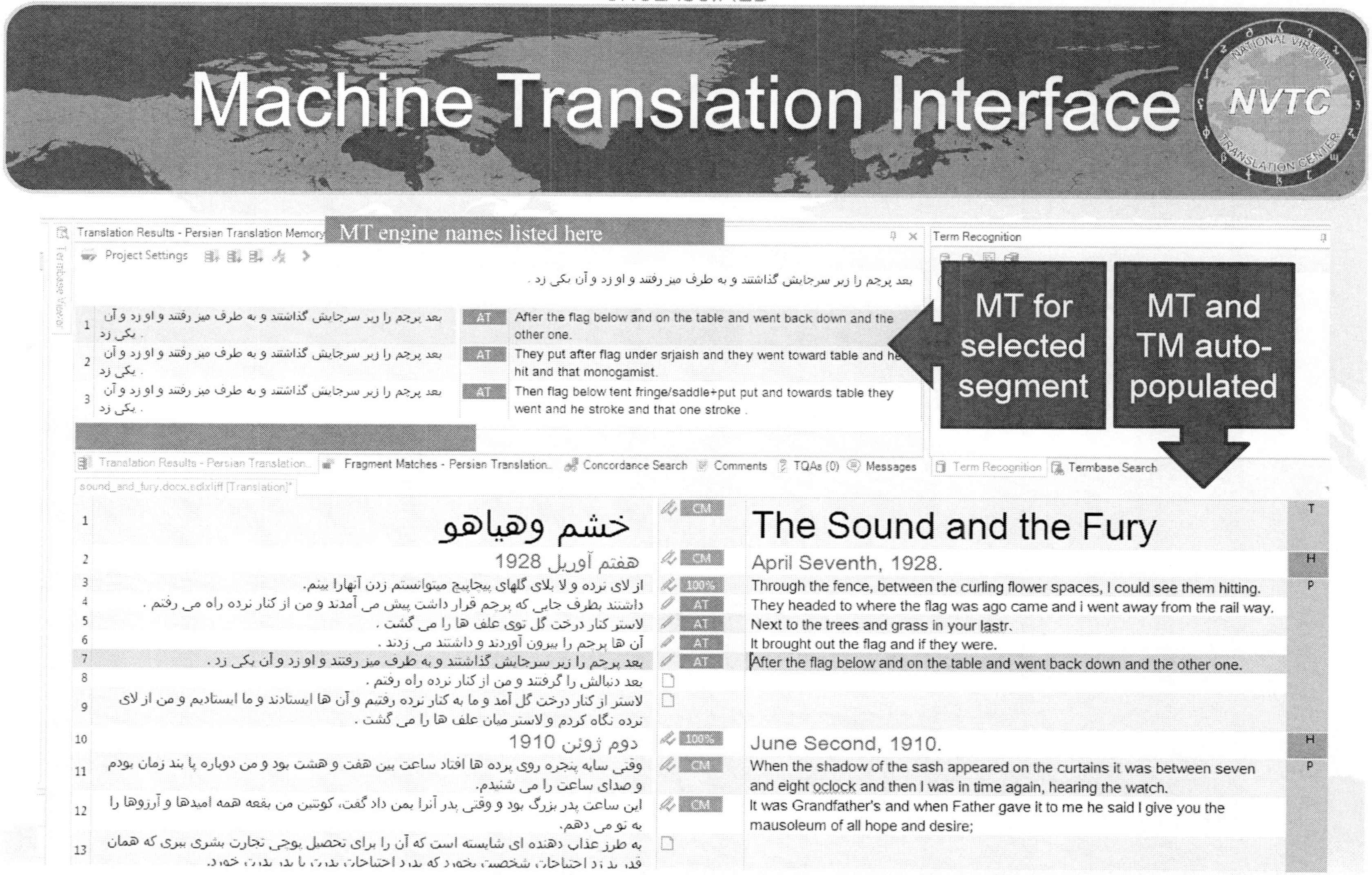

Machine Translation Interface

NVTC

MT engine names listed here

MT for selected segment

MT and TM auto-populated

Translation Results - Persian Translation Memory

Project Settings

بعد پرجم را زیر سرجایش گذاشتند و به طرف میز رفتند و او زد و آن یکی زد .

1	AT	After the flag below and on the table and went back down and the other one.
2	AT	They put after flag under srjaish and they went toward table and he hit and that monogamist.
3	AT	Then flag below tent fringe/saddle+put put and towards table they went and he stroke and that one stroke .

بعد پرجم را زیر سرجایش گذاشتند و به طرف میز رفتند و او زد و آن یکی زد .
بعد پرجم را زیر سرجایش گذاشتند و به طرف میز رفتند و او زد و آن یکی زد .
بعد پرجم را زیر سرجایش گذاشتند و به طرف میز رفتند و او زد و آن یکی زد .

Translation Results - Persian Translation... | Fragment Matches - Persian Translation... | Concordance Search | Comments | TQAs (0) | Messages | Term Recognition | Termbase Search

Term Recognition

Termbase Viewer

sound_and_fury.docx.sdlxliff [Translation]*

1	خشم وهیاهو	CM	The Sound and the Fury	T
2	هفتم آوریل 1928	CM	April Seventh, 1928.	H
3	از لای نرده و لا بلای گلهای پیچاپیچ میتوانستم زدن آنهارا بینم.	100%	Through the fence, between the curling flower spaces, I could see them hitting.	P
4	داشتند بطرف جایی که پرجم قرار داشت پیش می آمدند و من از کنار نرده راه می رفتم .	AT	They headed to where the flag was ago came and i went away from the rail way.	
5	لاستر کنار درخت گل توی علف ها را می گشت .	AT	Next to the trees and grass in your lastr.	
6	آن ها پرجم را بیرون آوردند و داشتند می زدند .	AT	It brought out the flag and if they were.	
7	بعد پرجم را زیر سرجایش گذاشتند و به طرف میز رفتند و او زد و آن یکی زد .	AT	After the flag below and on the table and went back down and the other one.	
8	بعد دنبالش را گرفتند و من از کنار نرده راه رفتم .			
9	لاستر از کنار درخت گل آمد و ما به کنار نرده رفتیم و آن ها ایستادند و ما ایستادیم و من از لای نرده نگاه کردم و لاستر میان علف ها را می گشت .			
10	دوم ژوئن 1910	100%	June Second, 1910.	H
11	وقتی سایه پنجره روی پرده ها افتاد ساعت بین هفت و هشت بود و من دوباره پا بند زمان بودم و صدای ساعت را می شنیدم.	CM	When the shadow of the sash appeared on the curtains it was between seven and eight oclock and then I was in time again, hearing the watch.	P
12	این ساعت پدر بزرگ بود و وقتی پدر آنرا بمن داد گفت، کوتین من بقعه همه امیدها و آرزوها را به تو می دهم.	CM	It was Grandfather's and when Father gave it to me he said I give you the mausoleum of all hope and desire;	
13	به طرز عذاب دهنده ای شایسته است که آن را برای تحصیل یوجی تجارت بشری بری که همان قدر پدر زد احتیاحات، شخصت بخورد که پدر احتیاحات پدرت، یا پدر پدرت، خورد.			

Transliteration Interface Examples

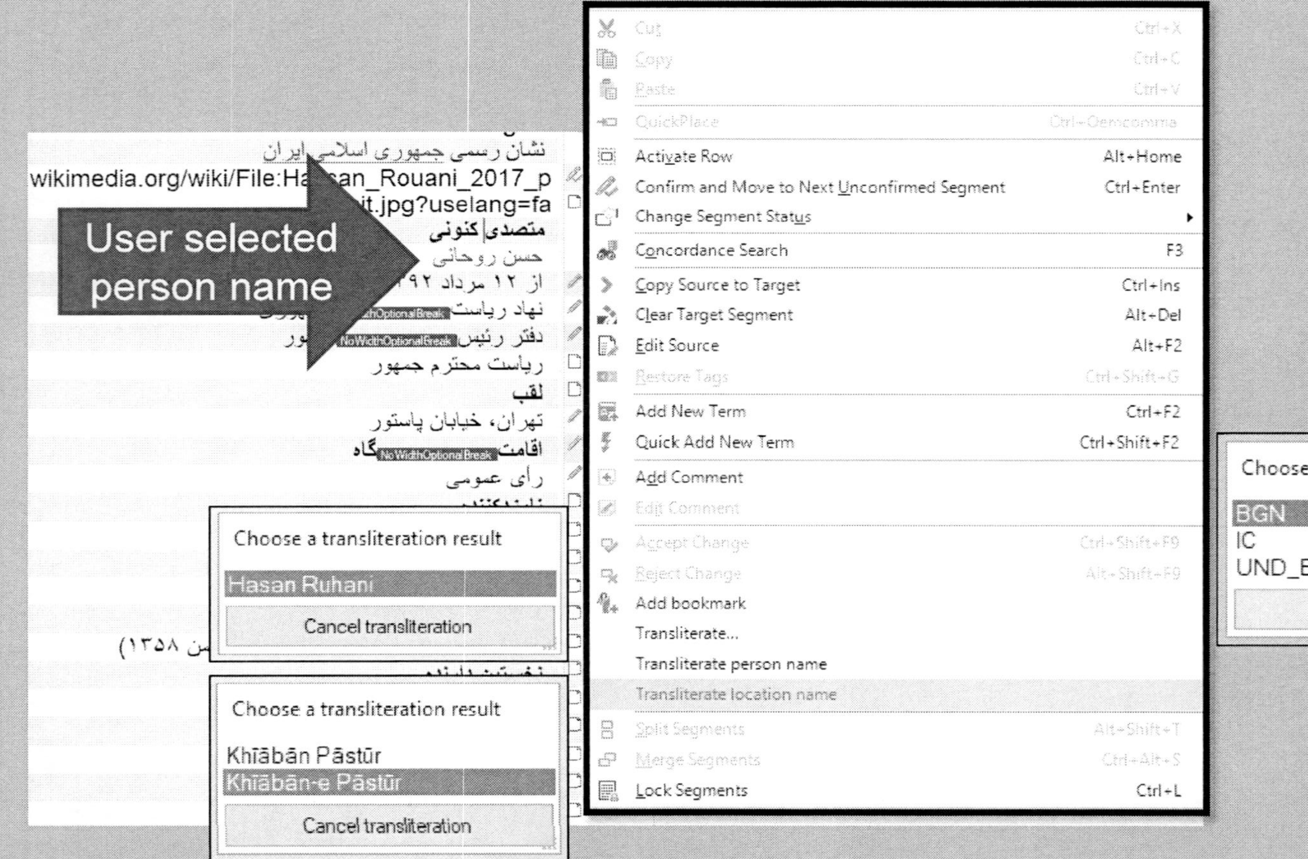

Proceedings of the 14th Conference of the Association for Machine Translation in the Americas
October 6 – 9, 2020, Volume 2: MT User Track

Operational Pilot

- October – February 2020
- Integrated with operational work – no staged tasks
- 11 linguists, 43 documents, 9 languages
- User survey
- BLEU scores calculated against pilot documents

Post-editing MT at NVTC

- Small 2016 NVTC study showed slight productivity declines with PEMT
  - MT quality issue
  - Linguists found MT results useful but not forced post-editing
- Why pilot?
  - Ensure plugin would achieve user acceptance and enhance NVTC translation workflow
  - Learn best practices to optimize the use of MT via the plugin
  - Better understand the quality of available MT
  - Better understand how the quality of MT provided by the plugin impacts NVTC translation outcomes

User Acceptance Results

- All pilot linguists reported that the MT plugin was helpful

- Specific reported benefits
  - The display of variant translations by different MT engines saved time in either word or grammar choices and sometimes provided better alternatives that linguist would not have considered
  - When MT quality was good it was a big time-saver especially combined with TM and terminology resources already in Trados

- Unhelpful aspects of MT reported
  - Most of these were about the scenarios where MT is poor
  - Sample of specific issues individual linguists reported
    - Lack of appropriate transliteration by MT (should be solved by version 2)
    - Source document still has post-OCR errors that propagate to MT

User Post-editing Results

- Is auto-population useful?
  - All available MT results are always displayed at the top of the CAT editor window and can be pasted into the target translation cell for post-editing
  - Auto-population inserts the results of the first listed MT engine in translation field forcing a post edit or delete decision

- Results
  - 8 of 11 linguists chose having MT auto-populated at least part of the time
  - Linguists deleted the auto-populated MT segments between 20% and 100% of the time depending on the document.
  - On average, pilot linguists who chose auto-populate MT chose to post edit 36% of the time and deleted 64% of the auto-populated segments
  - 3 linguists never chose auto-population but 2 of those 3 indicated that they sometimes pasted the MT segment into the target translation field and post-edited

Machine Translation Quality

- The linguists rated each MT engine available to them on a scale of 1 to 5 with 5 being the highest
- The number of raters varied due to the availability of MT per language and how many MT results linguists chose to display
- BLEU scores were calculated for 27 of 43 pilot translations using the finished translation as the single reference translation
- BLEU scores are averages across all languages
- BLEU results roughly map to linguist judgment

Solution Name	No. of Raters	Average User Rating	Average BLEU
COTS MT A (neural)	10	4.3	31.6
COTS MT B (neural)	8	3.38	26.7
COTS MT C (neural)	7	4.14	28.6
COTS MT D	7	2.86	19.6
COTS MT E	4	3.5	N/A*
GOTS MT F	5	2.4	10.68

 *Decommissioned before pilot ended

Proceedings of the 14th Conference of the Association for Machine Translation in the Americas
October 6 – 9, 2020, Volume 2: MT User Track

Looking Ahead

- Pilot demonstrated that MT plugin can be implemented without disruption to current NVTC workflows
- Actual PEMT will likely be around 35%, with all plugin-enabled jobs benefiting from multiple MT outputs for reference*
- Version 2 with transliteration to be operationalized in 2021
- NVTC is considering other efforts in the direction of AT including incorporation of named entity recognition (NER) into the plugin
  - Person and place names would be automatically identified and colored differently to alert the linguist that transliteration is needed
  - Would facilitate linguists' subsequent use of the transliteration plugin

*Only applies to jobs that can be done in Trados in languages for which MT engines exists.

Proceedings of the 14th Conference of the Association for Machine Translation in the Americas
October 6 - 9, 2020, Volume 2: MT User Track

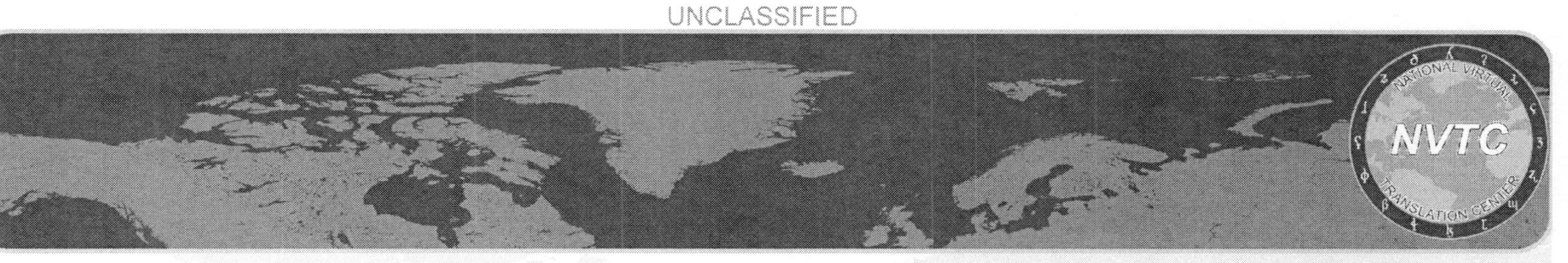

Backup Slides

Proceedings of the 14th Conference of the Association for Machine Translation in the Americas
October 6 – 9, 2020, Volume 2: MT User Track

Transliteration Challenges

- Mapping between Trados locales (flags) and language pair script information
  - Only a subset of languages have relevant script-based locales, like Serbian Cyrillic vs. Latin

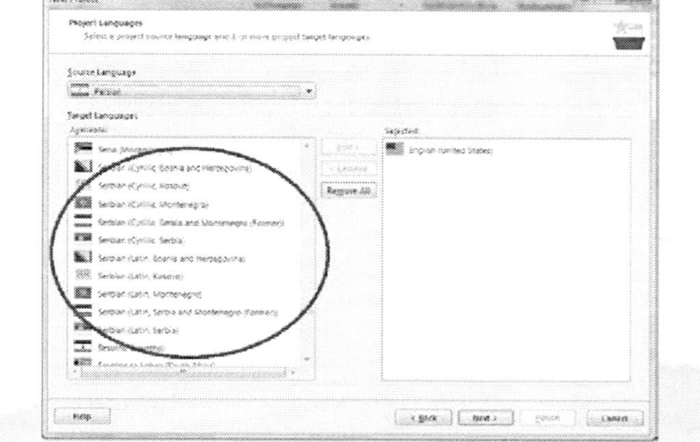

"Overloading" Locales

- We require some non-canonical scripts like Latinized Russian, Arabic and Persian that don't have such locales, so we repurpose locales like English (St. Vincent and the Grenadines)
  - We're already using arbitrary locales per language, e.g. English (United States)

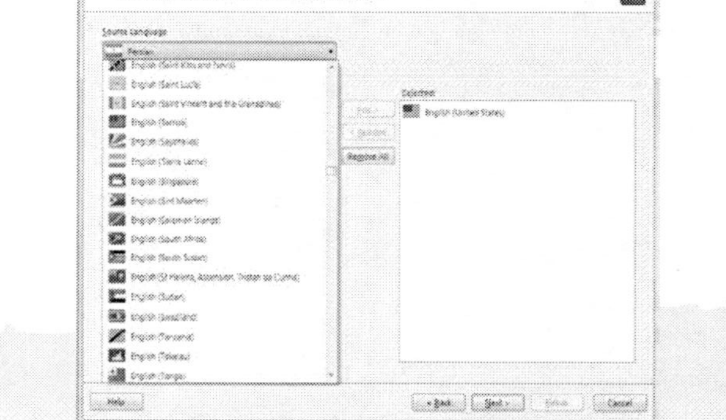

PEMT in the Public Sector: Discovery, Scoping, and Delivery

Konstantine Boukhvalov and Eileen Block

ManpowerGroup Public Sector, Inc

ManpowerGroup

Proceedings of the 14th Conference of the Association for Machine Translation in the Americas
October 6 – 9, 2020, Volume 2: MT User Track

ManpowerGroup Public Sector

- **25+** years supporting commercial and government clients in over 200 languages and dialects
  - Translation and l10n, transcription, interpretation, language technology support, linguist placements, multimedia analysis and reporting
- **Super user of Human Language Technology (HLT)**
  - 20 years customizing language automation/HLT tools in 60 languages to achieve efficiencies, process voluminous materials, and provide cost savings
  - Leverage and adapt commercial products and combined tools to optimize technology to best meet customers' needs
  - Translation Management System (TMS), Machine Translation (MT), CAT/Localization Tools, Authoring, eLearning, Desktop Publishing/Graphics Design, Audio/Video Production, Lexical Data Management, Optical Character Recognition

Proceedings of the 14th Conference of the Association for Machine Translation in the Americas
October 6 – 9, 2020, Volume 2: MT User Track

Presentation Objective

- Concerns about protecting data and challenges with implementation and measuring ROI have historically prevented public sector clients from using MT, CAT, and TMS

- We will show how our team successfully met client objectives while addressing data protection concerns to develop a practical, domain-specific Post-Edited Machine Translation (PEMT) solution to enable implementation by Public Sector clients.

Key Takeaways:
- How to develop a customized PEMT solution for Public Sector
- How to build and optimize TM corpora for statistical and neural MT training
- How to measure technological and procedural efficiencies for overall program success and scalability

Historical HLT Challenges for Public Sector (PS) Clients

- **Limited HLT use due to various contract constraints**
  - No co-mingling of data, no data in cloud
  - No data (TM/TB) retention
  - CONUS resources with citizenship, various clearance levels
    - HLT use was not widespread among PS linguist base (freelance)

- **No process automation**
  - Longer production timelines
  - Project-based translation

Early Steps

- Secure isolated **IT infrastructure**
- Dedicated **enterprise-level CAT** setup
- **Centralized TM/TB**
- Training for resources, e.g. **CAT-trained linguists/project managers**
- **TM/TB corpora** included as a **deliverable**

Case Study

- **Objective:** Translate multiple domain-specific content streams with more automation and increased speed
- Large-volume legacy material alignment
- Geographically dispersed workforce
  - ➢MGPS
  - ➢Client stakeholders
  - ➢Linguists

Program Requirements

- Centralized HLT Resources
  - Projects
  - Integrated Domain-Specific Machine Translation
  - Translation Memories/TermBases
  - Tech Support/Strict IT Infrastructure Requirements
- Integrated Project Management
- Data and Personnel Security
  - Dedicated HLT resource instance
  - Controlled human access
- Continuous MT improvement cycle
- Process automation
- Seamless integration of cloud and local-install HLT solutions

ANSWER?
Cloud-Based Post-Edited Machine Translation

- Post-Editing CAT/MT hybrid solution in an integrated TMS environment

- The Benefits of PEMT
  - Faster processing time than CAT alone
  - Greater consistency of terminology and style
  - Future leveraging and ROI
  - Workflow customization and efficiency

Define Stakeholders and Budget

- Dedicate a representative team of production experts – include the client!
  - Get early buy-in from the future production team
  - Start building the TMS operations culture
  - Let the production-side stakeholders define a business case and the best solution
- Align Budget and HLT options
  - Define Scope and Level of Effort - manage budget and expectations
  - Calculate HLT costs (CAT/TMS/MT)
  - Determine IT setup (local install vs. SaaS)

Challenge

There are a growing number of strong HLT solutions. How do you select the right one, and how do you implement effectively?

Choosing/Validating the Right Solution

- Perform preliminary research
  - *What do I need?*
  - *What are my options (commercial/custom/open source)?*
  - *What are my community peers saying?*
- Choose solution candidates
- Set up orientation calls with solution developers
  - *Identify dedicated contacts for technical and contractual questions*
  - *Explore data security options for data and support*

Choosing/Validating the Right Solution (cont.)

- Create an evaluation matrix
  - *Use the same criteria to evaluate all products*
  - *Standard criteria include:*
    - Key features
    - Benefits
    - Shortcomings
    - Technical and contract support
    - Deployment options
    - Costs

PUT THE DATA ASIDE –
TIME FOR WHITEBOARDING!

Whiteboard Your Workflows

- Define and document/update existing production processes
- Do *not* adjust workflows based on the solutions' limitations
  - If it doesn't fit, it's not right for you
- Generate a master workflow that addresses the variations
  - Define production steps as "required" or "optional"
- Whiteboard other business requirements/expectations
  - Manage expectations

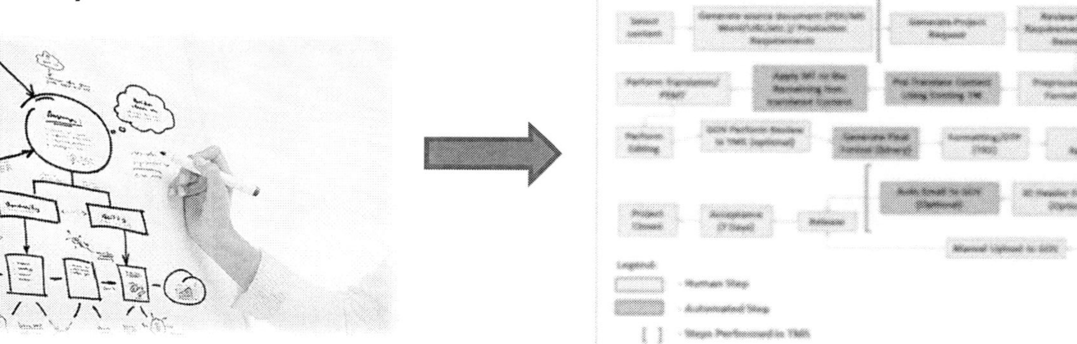

See What "Fits" – Select and Acquire

- Combine your research with your master workflow and business requirements
- Identify the solution that provides the most value
- Generate TMS/MT Selection Report:
  - Fund the acquisition and deployment
  - Maintain technology knowledgebase
  - Validate your decision
- Finalize the deployment plan
- Minimize the time between the acquisition and production deployment

Initial Configuration

- Master production workflow
- Sample business rules
- Sample linguistic resources (TMs, TBs, baseline MT)
- Optional/custom components and workflow steps (forms, fields, etc.)
- Production pilot
  - ➢ *Test the workflow, not just the filters*

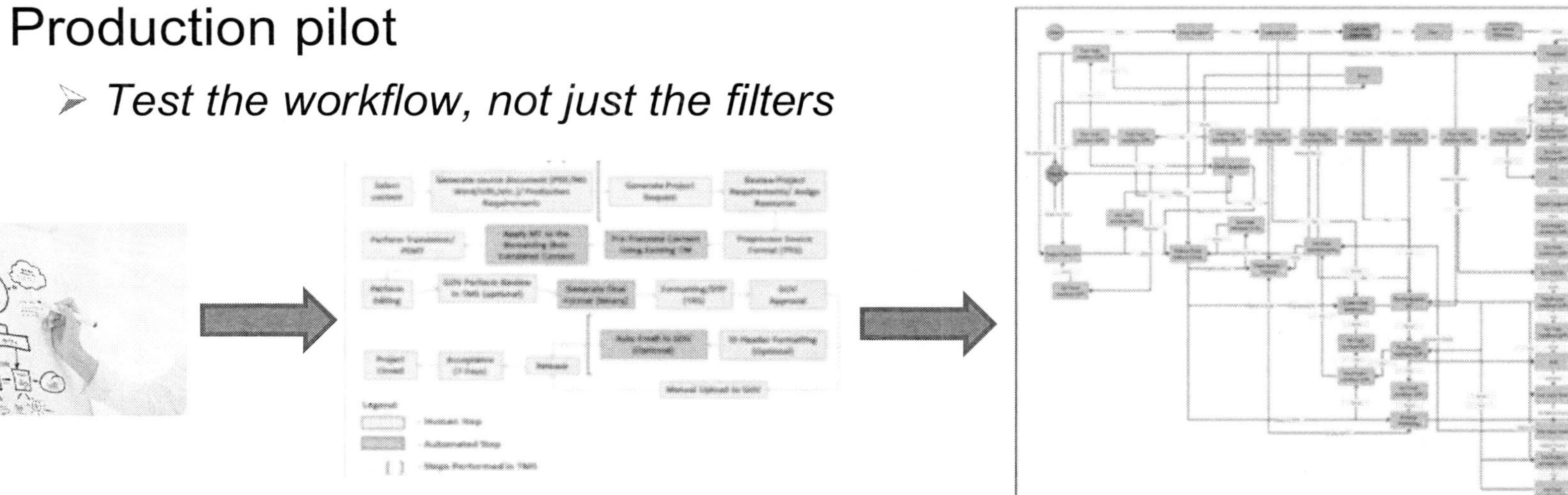

Document TMS/PEMT Production Procedures – Role-Specific Instructions

- Project Managers
  - *Production*
  - *Offline procedures*
- Linguist Users
  - *Production*
- Client Users
  - *Portal access/request*
  - *Production*
- Other Production Roles (as applicable)

Develop and Implement Training

Client stakeholder participation and buy-in is key to project success.

- Develop a reusable curriculum
- Provide a general system overview
- Provide role-specific training

Production Deployment

- Configure and deploy client portal and other auxiliary components
- Align legacy content
- Optimize TM corpora for MT training
  - Segmentation
  - Markup
- Perform initial training of Domain-Specific MT engines/language pairs
- Perform first automated and human evaluation of MT – start measuring

Start PEMT!!!

- Start production for the selected Task Orders/Programs

- Adjust configuration, procedures, and documentation, as applicable
  - *Deliver the updates to the appropriate parties*

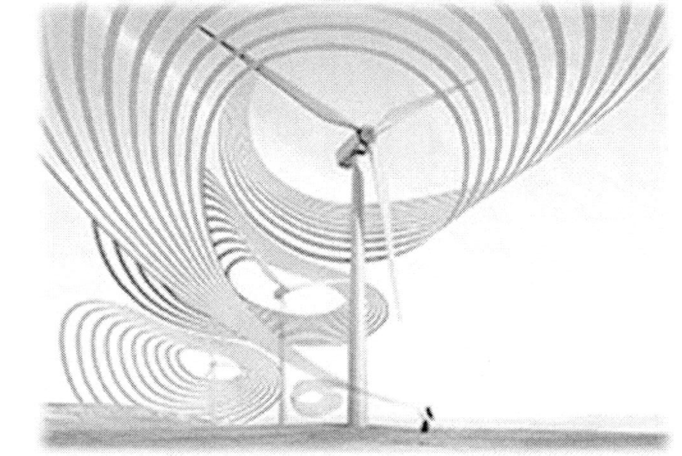

Continuous MT Improvement Cycle

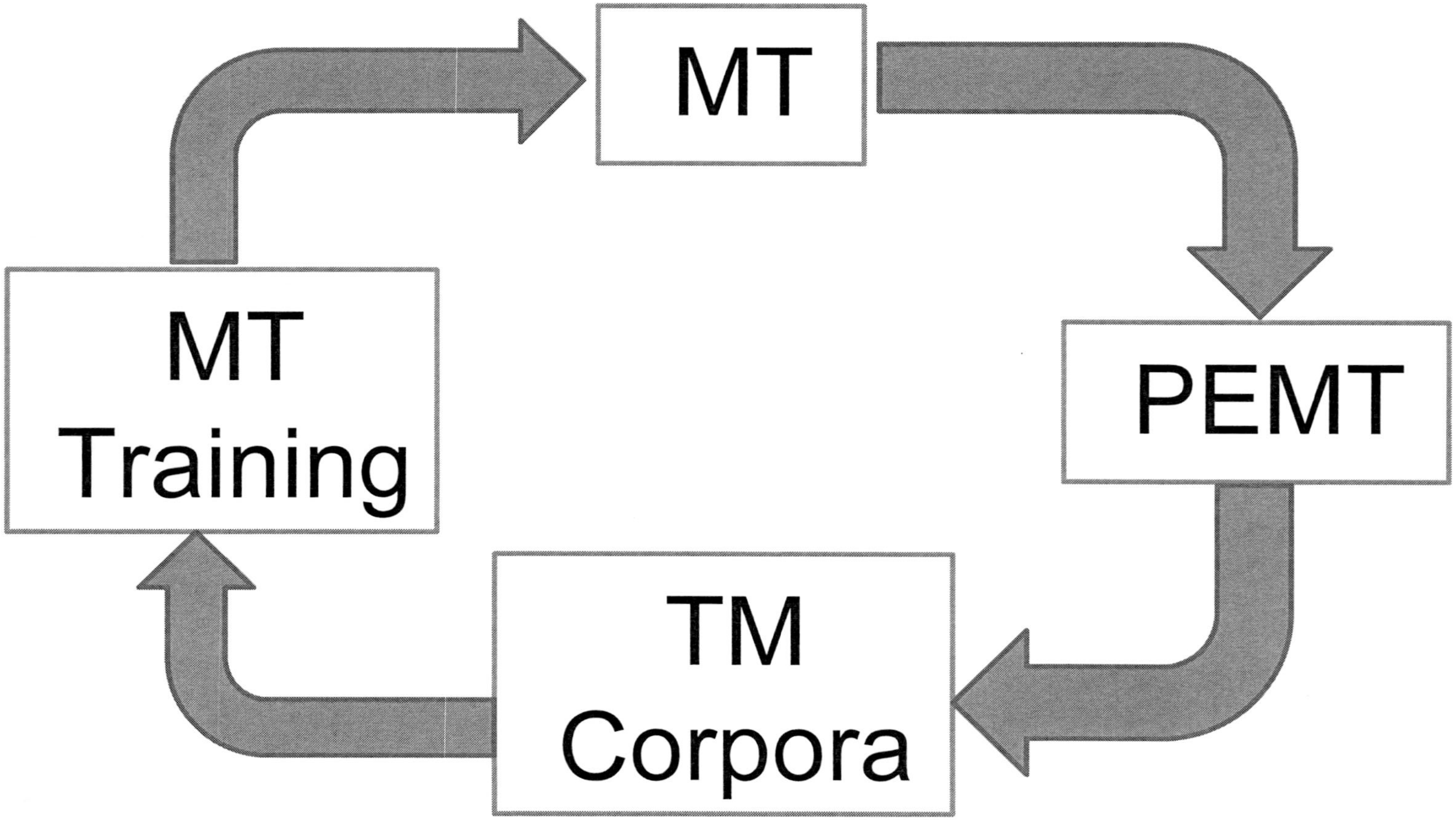

Proceedings of the 14th Conference of the Association for Machine Translation in the Americas
October 6 – 9, 2020, Volume 2: MT User Track

Additional Automated Workflow Options

TM-MT Only

TM-MT with Edit

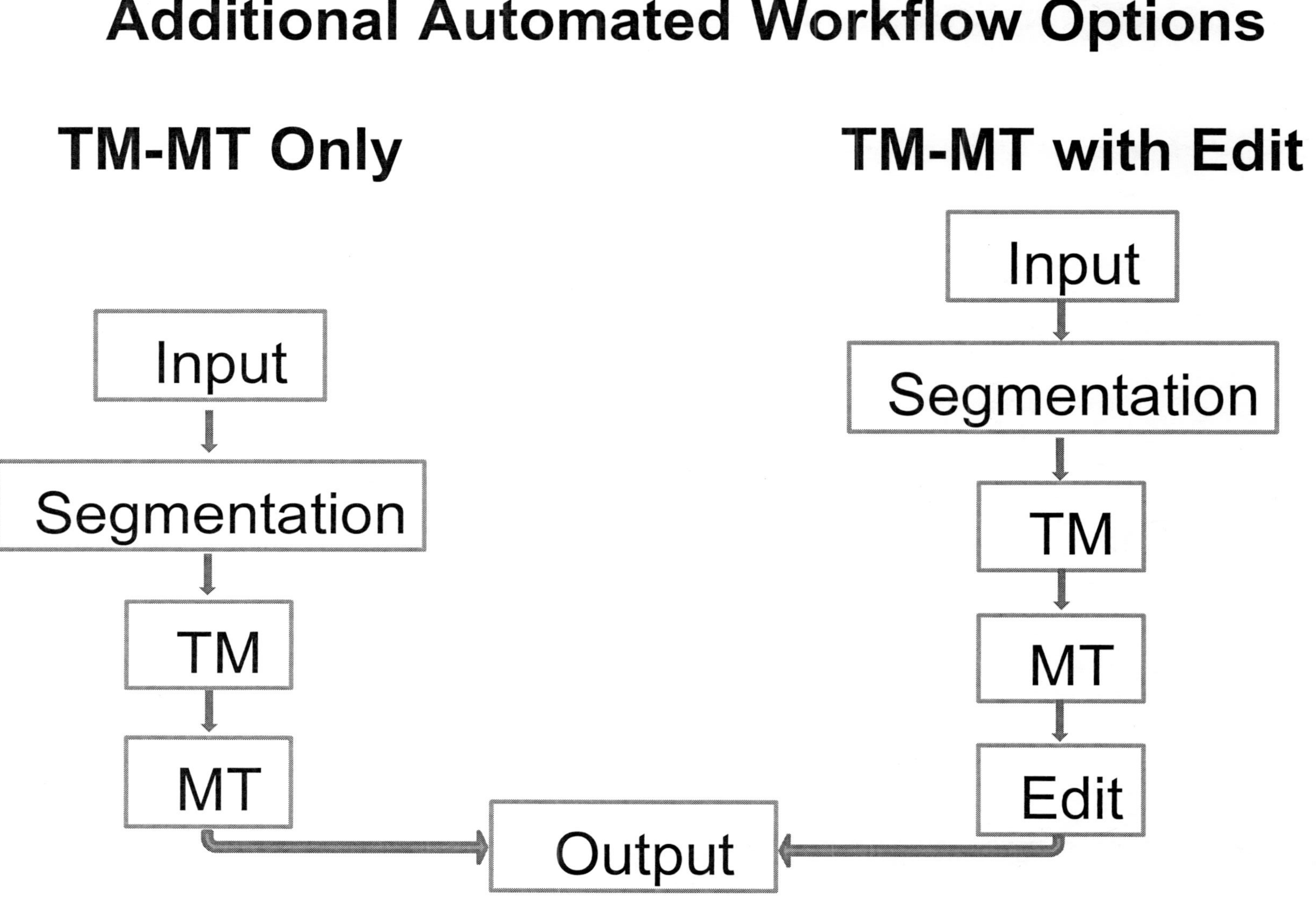

Program Launch

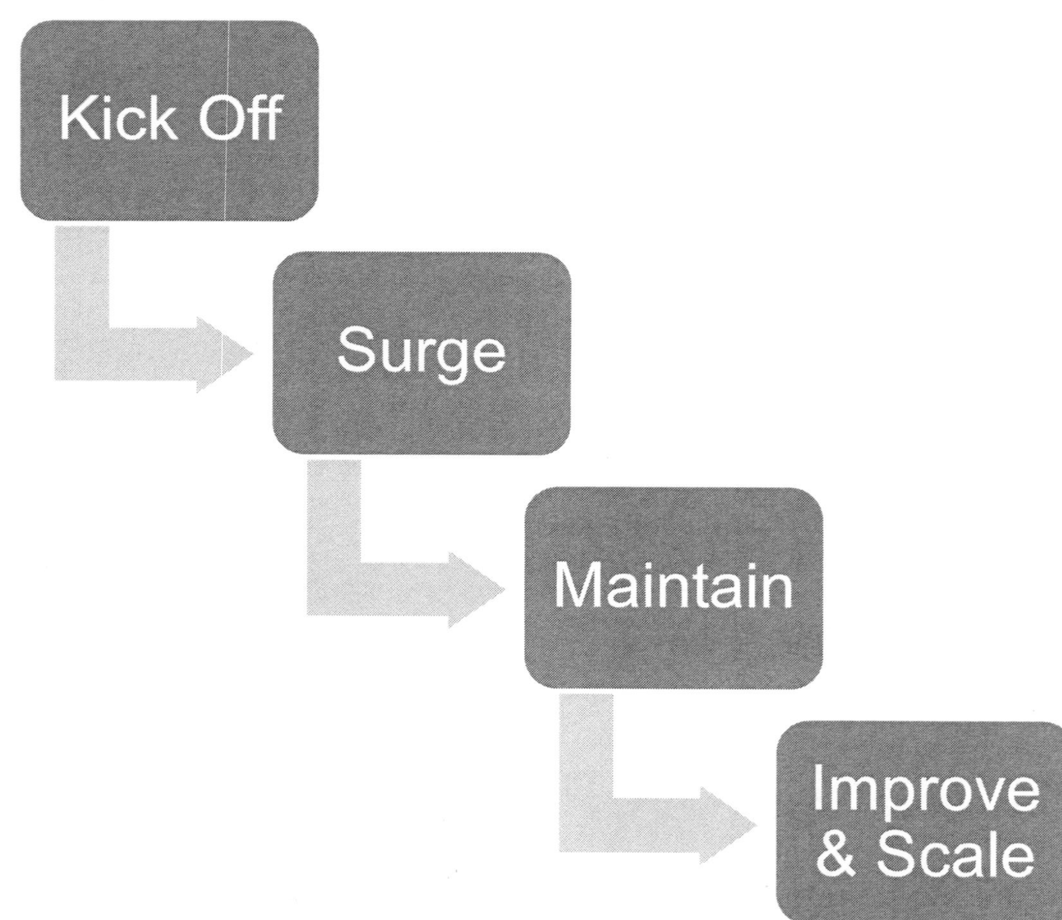

Kick Off

- **Review Statement of Work (SOW)**
  - ➤ Hold kick-off meeting to set expectations, and clarify parameters and assumptions with stakeholders

- **Inform Stakeholders – before, during, after kickoff!**
  - ➤ "Engineer for success" with source selection, MT training corpus
  - ➤ Manage expectations for productivity, timeline
  - ➤ Confirm client's priorities, preferences, and level of involvement

- **Set Goals and Key Performance Indicators (KPIs)**
  - ➤ Linguist productivity
  - ➤ Tool effectiveness

Surge

- **Build a Team**
  - Linguists, Engineers, PM
- **Train**
  - PEMT objectives and workflow
  - Client-specific tools and style guides
  - HLT tools/resources including CAT, TMS, TM/TB, MT
- **Baseline**
  - Translate sample set of material (larger = better) outside of PEMT environment to measure productivity sans HLT
- **Document / Track Everything!**
  - Client communications
  - Workflow adjustments
  - Technology data
  - Performance data

Maintain

- **Prioritize Knowledge Sharing**
  - Training materials, lessons learned, documentation
  - Meet regularly
- **Monitor, Report, Adjust**
  - Provide reports and recommendations monthly
  - Metrics
- **Evaluate Linguists' Performance**
  - Define and share performance and productivity metrics based on collected data
- **Review Client Level of Engagement**
  - Client involved too much or too little?
  - Client requests within contract scope?

Improve & Scale

- **Monitor technology developments and provide recommendations as necessary**
  - Escalate questions/issues to software developers as needed
  - Test and troubleshoot
  - Receive PM and linguist feedback on potential implementations
- **Evaluate MT output monthly; experiment and make adjustments as needed**
  - Capture qualitative and quantitative data
- **Communicate success stories and lessons learned**
  - Continually demonstrate ROI
- **Scale with additional domains and locales**
  - Ensure HLT solution can accommodate growth and address locale-specific criteria

Recap

- Review historical challenges
- Describe big picture and take incremental steps
- Receive client buy-in
- Customize the HLT solution -- one size does not fit all
- Document/track for reusability and scalability
- Develop talent through training
- Ask for client feedback and evaluate your success
- Continue to improve

Future Enhancements

- Neural MT Non-Formal Language Support
- Post-MT Automated Editing
- Dynamic Learning NMT
- Substring tokenization
- Integrated speech-to-text supported by TMS/CAT/MT

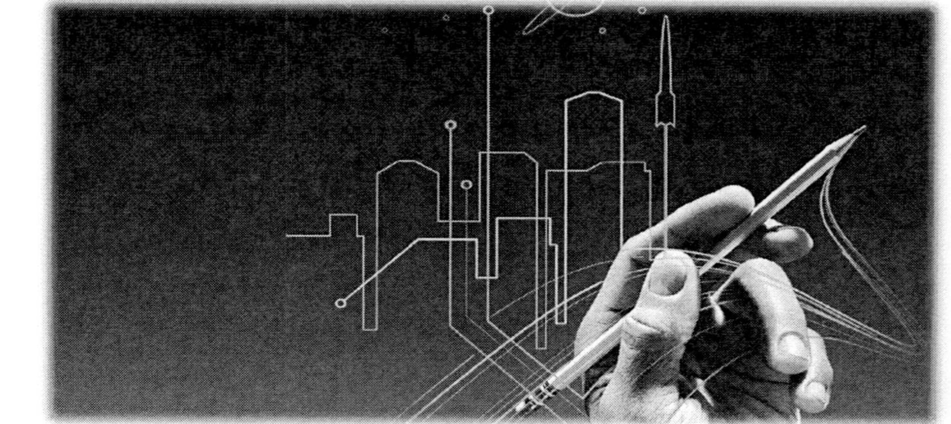

Thank you

Konstantine G. Boukhvalov
Operations Manager, Engineering
ManpowerGroup Public Sector
1-703-245-9372
Konstantine.Boukhvalov@Experis.com

Eileen Block
Engagement Manager
ManpowerGroup Public Sector
1-703-245-9363
Eileen.Block@manpowergroupsecure.com

U.S. ARMY COMBAT CAPABILITIES DEVELOPMENT COMMAND – ARMY RESEARCH LABORATORY

Shareable TTS Components

Dr. Steve LaRocca

Computer Scientist and Team Lead

Battlefield Information Systems Branch

20 AUG 2020

DISTRIBUTION STATEMENT GOES HERE

Proceedings of the 14th Conference of the Association for Machine Translation in the Americas
October 6 – 9, 2020, Volume 2: MT User Track

The Team

Institutions: U.S. Army Research Laboratory[1], United Tribes Technical College[2], Cornell University[3]

Individuals: Zakariya Al Sagheer[1], Katherine Blake[3], Vince Iglehart[2], Stephen LaRocca[1], John Morgan[1], Jerral Murray[2], Gerardo Cervantes[1], G. Hazrat Jahed[1]

Proceedings of the 14th Conference of the Association for Machine Translation in the Americas
October 6 – 9, 2020, Volume 2: MT User Track

TEXT-TO-SPEECH (TTS)

- **A system that converts written text to audible speech**

- **TTS is an important enabling language component**
  - For Speech-to-Speech systems (ASR → MT → TTS)
  - For information delivery tools such as 'talking books'
  - Ultimately, every language community needs a TTS capability

- **USG has relied on commercial TTS software**
  - Licensed commercial products are cumbersome
  - Recent growth in neural computing for TTS with open tools
  - New prospects for more and better shareable TTS components

- **Publicly available neural implementations of TTS, such as Ito's implementation of Google's Tacotron, make creating one's own shareable components easier**

MAKING A SHAREABLE TTS COMPONENT

- **Recent neural (deep learning) methods simplify data preparation**
  - Google's 2017 Tacotron project followed by Keith Ito's implementation

- **Keith Ito's "LJ English" model built with 24 hours of training data**
  - ARL has developed Android Arabic TTS capability using deep learning methods and only 10 hours of training data

- **Compute time and computer resource requirements are substantial**
  - Aging GPU equipment not up to the task, not compatible with current libraries

- **Shareable data and shareable software is an important aspect**
  - ARL is using single speaker data based on in-house translation materials and VOA-type newswire as prompts

- **Neural TTS computes a spectrogram, then renders that data as synthesized speech using a vocoder**

Proceedings of the 14th Conference of the Association for Machine Translation in the Americas
October 6 – 9, 2020, Volume 2: MT User Track

OUR WORK TO DATE

- **Zak Al Sagheer: created 10 hour Arabic dataset**
  Trained (K. Ito) Arabic Tacotron model
  Trained Arabic Tacotron2 model
  Trained more Arabic models: current success using FastSpeech 2
  Trained vocoders using Arabic data and neural methods.

- **Hazrat Jahed: created 10 hour Pashto dataset**

- **UTTC (Vince Iglehart and Jerral Murray):**
  Learned Python programming
  Trained (K. Ito) Tacotron English model
  Conducted experiments (formal vs. informal text; full vs. ablated dataset)
  Surveyed possibilities for Northern Ute and/or Lakota dataset → TTS model

- **Gerry Cervantes provided Android expertise, TensorFlow, tflite**

Proceedings of the 14th Conference of the Association for Machine Translation in the Americas
October 6 – 9, 2020, Volume 2: MT User Track

LET'S SYNTHESIZE SOME ARABIC!

- **Demonstration by Zakariya (Zak) Al Sagheer**

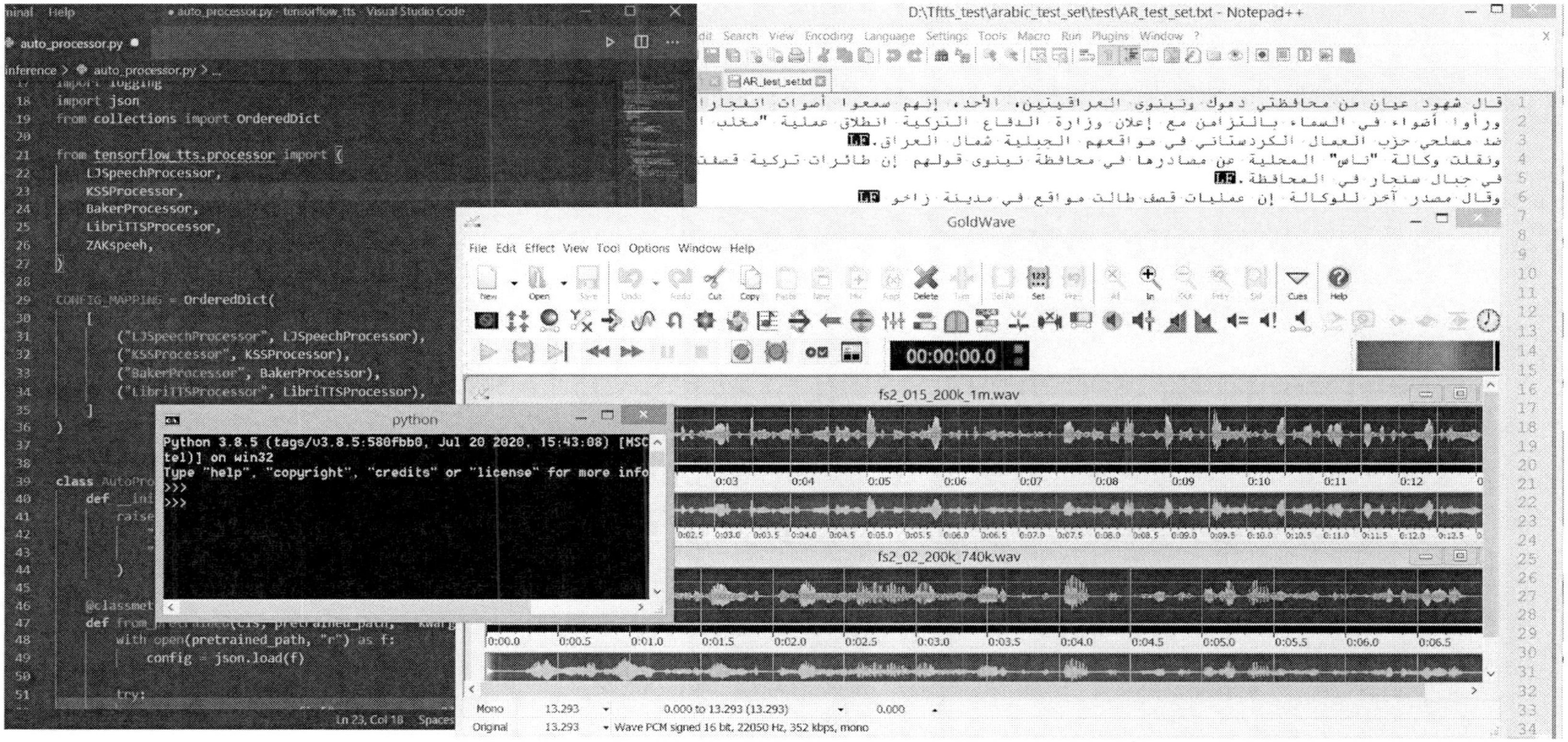

A UTTC PERSPECTIVE: GOALS/CHALLENGES

- Tacotron experiment this summer: small data results in a worse model

- Implications for building TTS models for under-resourced/under-documented languages

- Creating data resources for some of these languages: Northern Ute, Lakota

- Challenges for TTS models that are based on Native American language data

- TTS models offer new capabilities for communities

Proceedings of the 14th Conference of the Association for Machine Translation in the Americas
October 6 – 9, 2020, Volume 2: MT User Track

TTS FOR ACADEMICS

- Teaching materials: introduction to STEM, computational linguistics for linguists and language enthusiasts alike

- Second language acquisition: empowering students to practice pronunciation outside the classroom

- Experimental materials: a component of the experimental paradigm and a better way to administer instructions to bilingual participants/those with weaker literacy

- Language documentation/revitalization: bridging the gap between reading and speaking

- Accessibility: free/easy access to screen-readers in many languages for a diverse student body

Proceedings of the 14th Conference of the Association for Machine Translation in the Americas
October 6 - 9, 2020, Volume 2: MT User Track

GOALS

- Extend the Ito implementation of Tacotron to build models for additional languages: Pashto, Native American languages, which can be shared.   For free.

- Make these models transparent and well-documented so that they are easily modified to serve the needs of the military, the academy, and language communities

522

CONCLUSION

- Speech technology including TTS serves military interests because it aids in the communication between Soldiers and local nationals who may not have a language in common or an interpreter available

- Speech technology including TTS serves Native American communities because it can help to preserve and revitalize Native American languages

Proceedings of the 14th Conference of the Association for Machine Translation in the Americas
October 6 – 9, 2020, Volume 2: MT User Track

REFERENCES

[1] Ito. "Tacotron." (2020). Retreived June 2020, from https://github.com/keithito/tacotron.

[2] Littell, P., Kazantseva, A., Kuhn, R., Pine, A., Arppe, A., Cox, C., & Junker, M. O. (2018). Indigenous language technologies in Canada: Assessment, challenges, and successes. In *Proceedings of the 27th International Conference on Computational Linguistics* (pp. 2620-2632).

[3] Wang, Y., & Skerry-Ryan, R.J., (2020). Expressive Speech Synthesis with Tacotron. Retrieved 21 July 2020, from https://ai.googleblog.com/2018/03/expressive-speech-synthesis-with.html.

[4] Wang, Y., Skerry-Ryan, R.J., Stanton, D., Wu, Y., Weiss, R.J., Jaitly, N., ... & Le, Q. (2017). Tacotron: Towards end-to-end speech synthesis. *arXiv preprint arXiv:1703.10135.*

[5] Ren, Y., Hu, C., Qin, T., Zhao, S., Zhao, Z., & Liu, T.Y. (2020) FastSpeech 2: Fast and High-Quality End-to-End Text-to-Speech. *arXiv preprint arXiv:2006.04558.*

[6] Abadi, M., Barham, P., Chen, J., Chen, Z., Davis, A., Dean, J., ... & Kudlur, M. (2016). Tensorflow: A system for large-scale machine learning. In *12th {USENIX} symposium on operating systems design and implementation ({OSDI} 16)* (pp. 265-283).

Proceedings of the 14th Conference of the Association for Machine Translation in the Americas
October 6 – 9, 2020, Volume 2: MT User Track

A Tale of Eight Countries or the EU Council Presidency Translator in Retrospect

Kristine Metuzale
Client Relationship Manager
Tilde

Alexandra Soska
Language Services Division
Federal Ministry of the Interior, Building and Community, Germany

Mārcis Pinnis
Chief AI Officer
Tilde

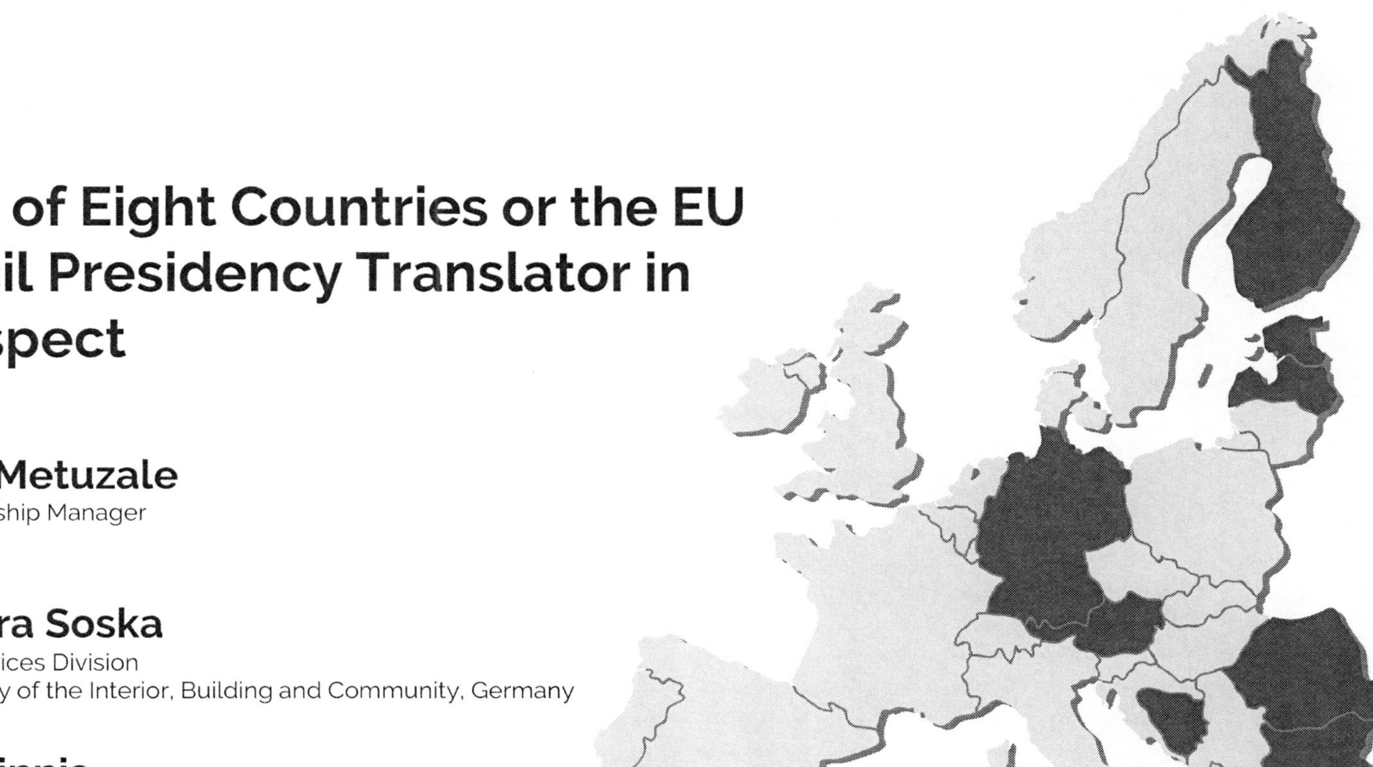

Proceedings of the 14th Conference of the Association for Machine Translation in the Americas
October 6 - 9, 2020, Volume 2: MT User Track

Proceedings of the 14th Conference of the Association for Machine Translation in the Americas
October 6 – 9, 2020, Volume 2: MT User Track

THE PRESIDENCY OF
THE COUNCIL OF THE EU

- The Council of the EU is the key decision maker in the EU

- Presidency rotation every 6 months

Proceedings of the 14th Conference of the Association for Machine Translation in the Americas
October 6 – 9, 2020, Volume 2: MT User Track

Challenges

- Massive amounts of official documentation & texts
- Fast communication of the Presidency work & activities
- Collaboration between delegates, journalists and Presidency staff
- Facilitation of multilingual communication in Europe
- Challenging languages

Proceedings of the 14th Conference of the Association for Machine Translation in the Americas
October 6 – 9, 2020, Volume 2: MT User Track

Solution
The EU Council
Presidency Translator

- Secure cloud-based pan-European MT infrastructure

- Customized NMT solution to the Presidency requirements

- Integration of relevant in-domain data & terminology

- Facilitation of multilingual communication in Europe

- Workspace integration of NMT systems

Proceedings of the 14th Conference of the Association for Machine Translation in the Americas
October 6 - 9, 2020, Volume 2: MT User Track

Powers communication across languages benefiting:

- Presidency staff & delegates
- Professional translators
- Journalists
- Presidency visitors
- All EU citizens

Proceedings of the 14th Conference of the Association for Machine Translation in the Americas
October 6 – 9, 2020, Volume 2: MT User Track

Functionality

- Online translation workspace
  - Text snippet, document and website translation
  - terminology lookup
- CAT tool plug-in for SDL Trados Studio
- Website translation widget
  - Integrated in https://eu2020.de
- Online CAT environment for non-professional translators
- Access to custom and third party MT systems

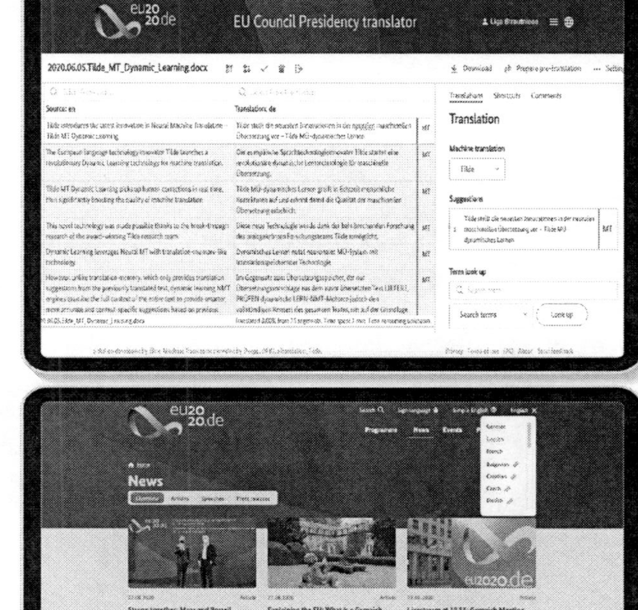

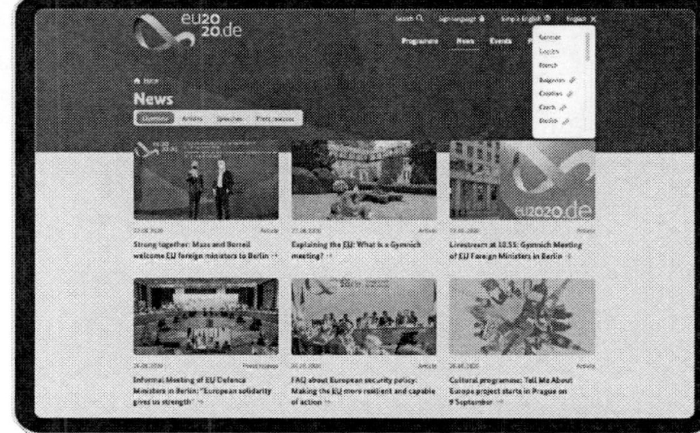

Architecture

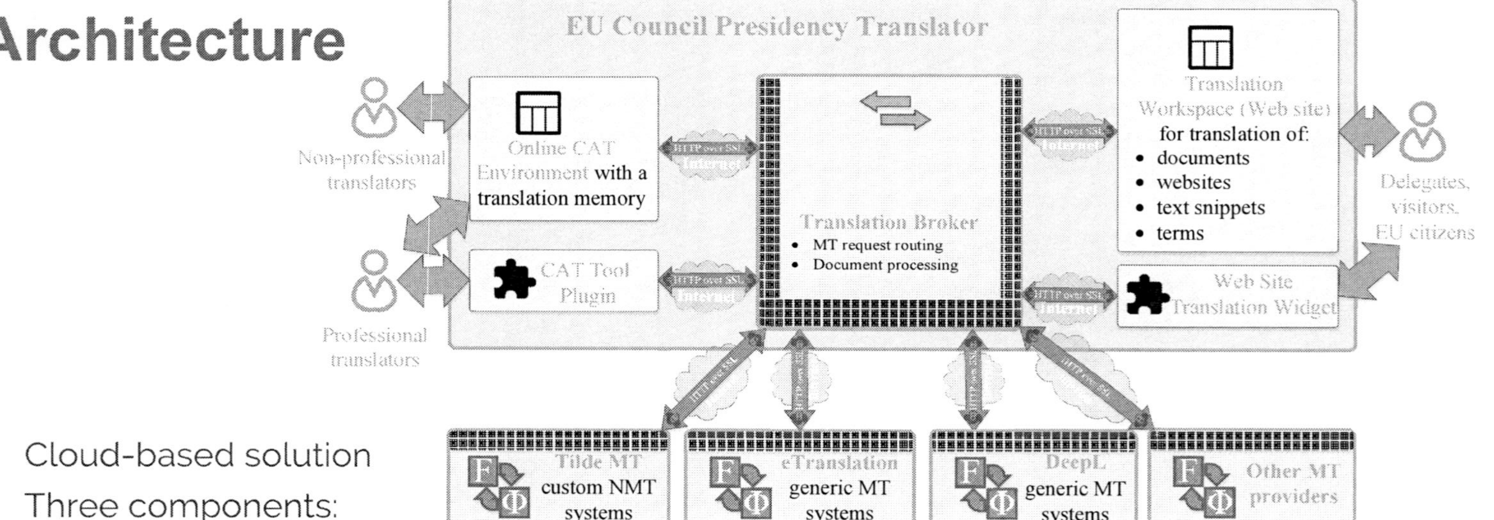

- Cloud-based solution
- Three components:
  - MT systems
    - Custom systems deployed on Tilde MT
    - Third party systems integrated through interfaces
  - Translation broker
  - Translation interfaces for users

Proceedings of the 14th Conference of the Association for Machine Translation in the Americas
October 6 - 9, 2020, Volume 2: MT User Track

Machine translation systems

NMT Toolkit	NMT Architecture	Language pairs
Nematus/AmuNMT	MLSTM	EN↔ET (till 2018), EN↔BG,EN↔DE (for Austrian Presidency)
Sockeye	Transformer	EN↔ET (since 2018)
Marian	Transformer	EN↔DE (since 2020), EN↔RO, EN↔FI,FI↔SV, ET↔FI, EN↔HR, DE↔IT, DE↔ES,DE↔PL, DE↔FR

- **Custom MT systems**
  - For main translation directions of each presidency
  - Keep up with latest NMT technology
  - Adapted using in-domain data
  - Address country-specific dialects
    - FI↔SV for the Finnish Presidency
    - DE↔EN for the Austrian Presidency
- **Generic MT systems**
  - Cover many language pairs
  - Provided by:
    - eTranslation (for all Presidencies)
    - DeepL (for the German Presidency)

Proceedings of the 14th Conference of the Association for Machine Translation in the Americas
October 6 - 9, 2020, Volume 2: MT User Track

Usage analysis – overall statistics

- Total amount* of translations:
  - **157.7 million words**
  - 14.9 million sentences
  - 4.9 million requests

~300-400 years of work for
a productive translator

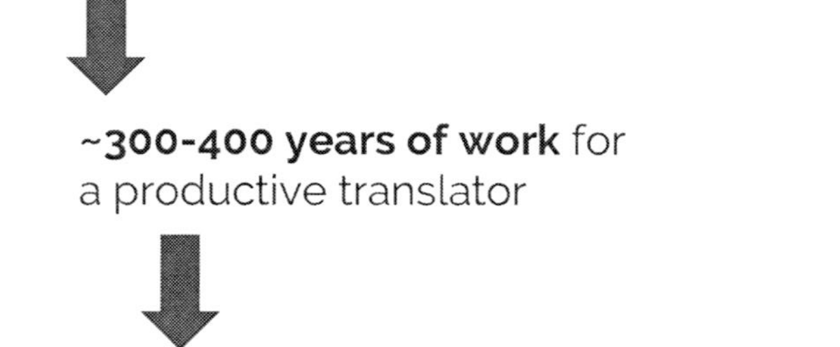

~1017 books of the size of an
average Harry Potter book

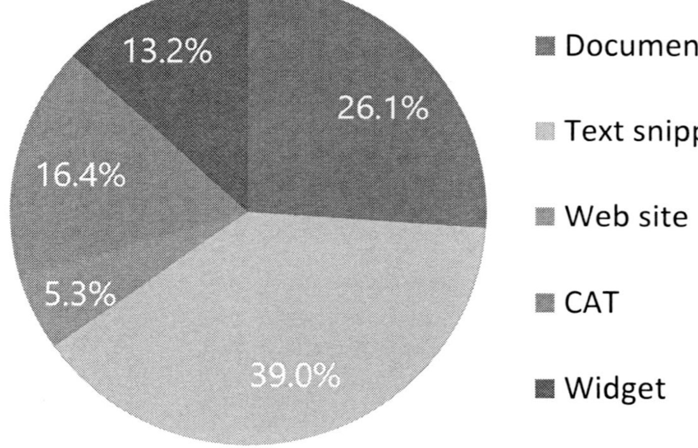

*Since the official launch of the EU Council Presidency Translator in 2017 till September 30, 2020

Usage analysis – growing trend

- Translation volume is increasing
- The eu2020.de widget contributes strongly

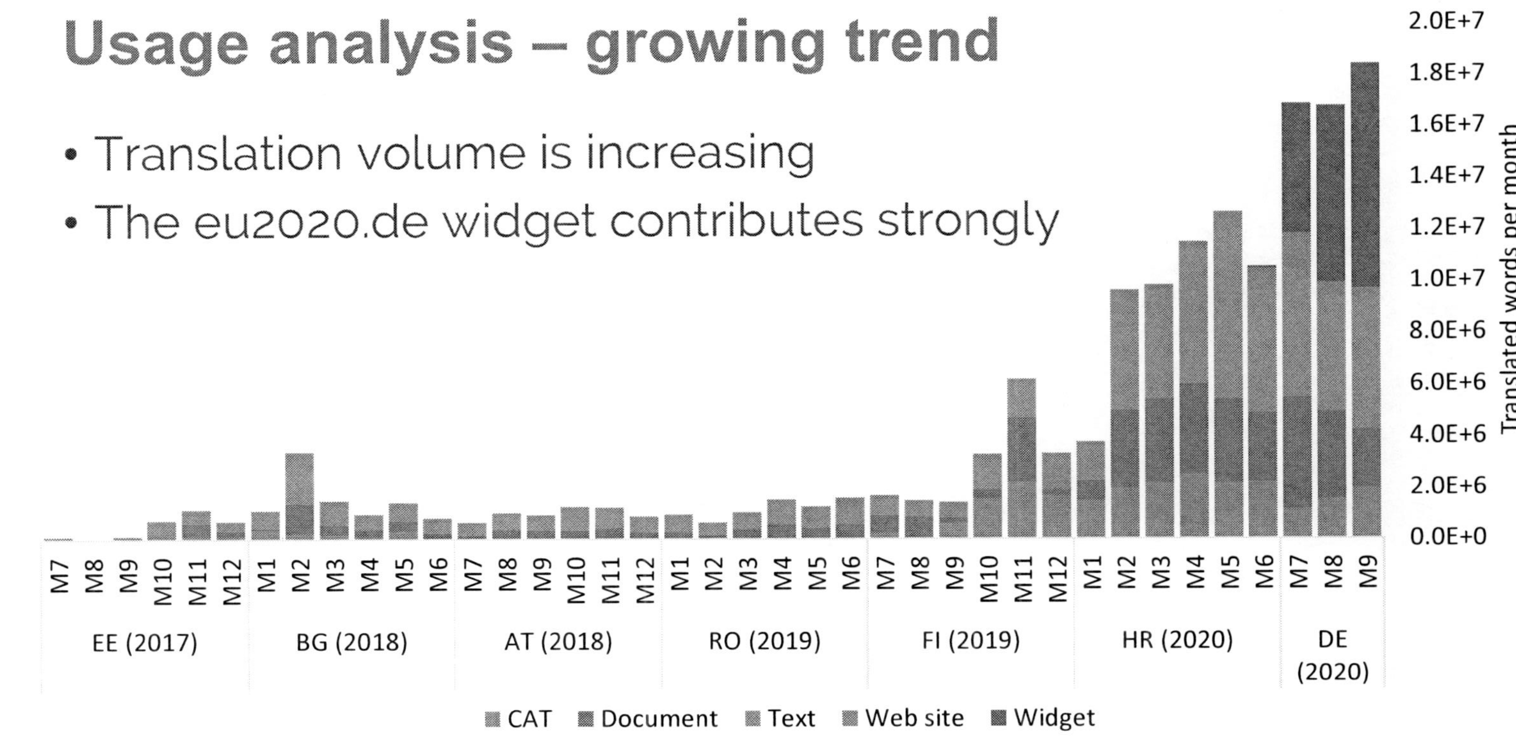

Proceedings of the 14th Conference of the Association for Machine Translation in the Americas
October 6 - 9, 2020, Volume 2: MT User Track

Usage analysis – custom vs. generic systems

- Custom systems process the majority of translations
- The eu2020.de widget has increased the use of generic engines

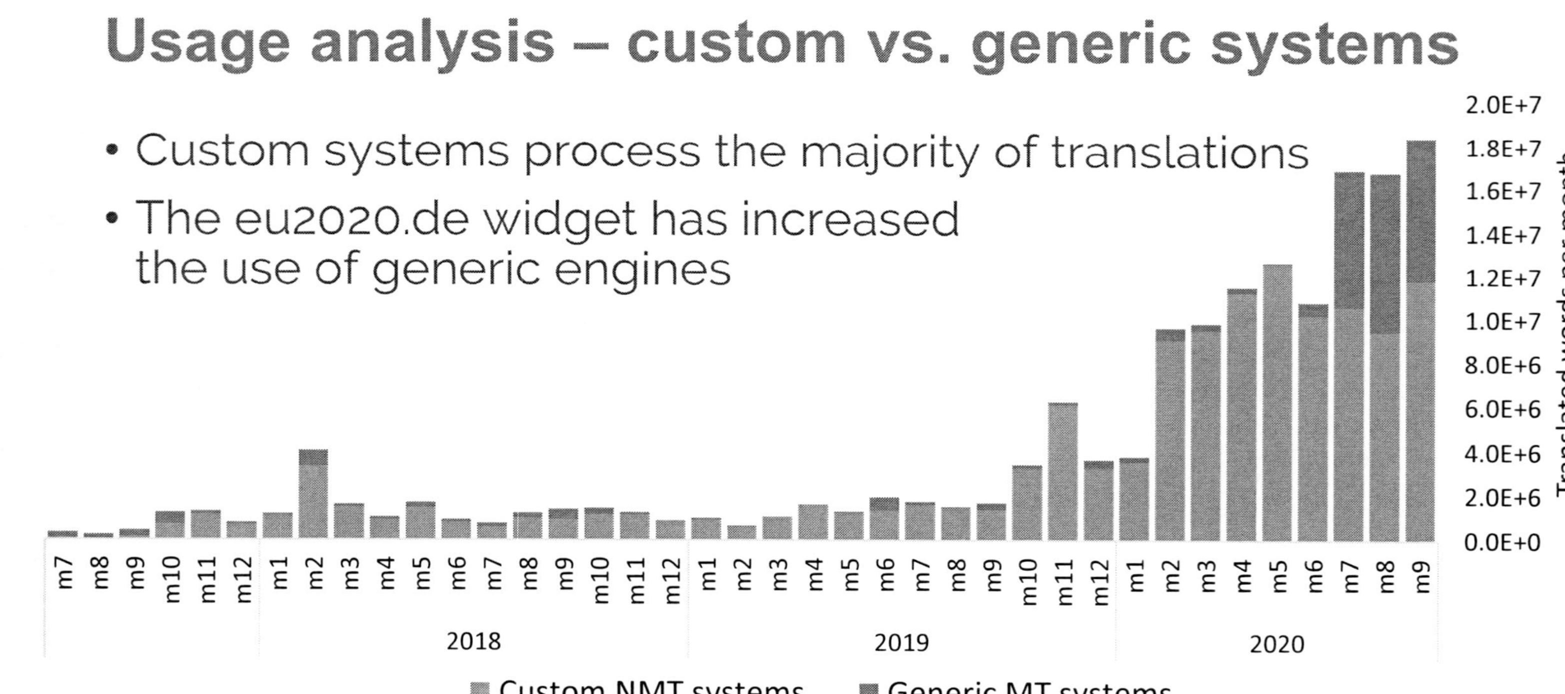

Proceedings of the 14th Conference of the Association for Machine Translation in the Americas
October 6 – 9, 2020, Volume 2: MT User Track

Usage analysis – custom NMT system use over time

- Users continue using the custom NMT systems long after presidencies conclude

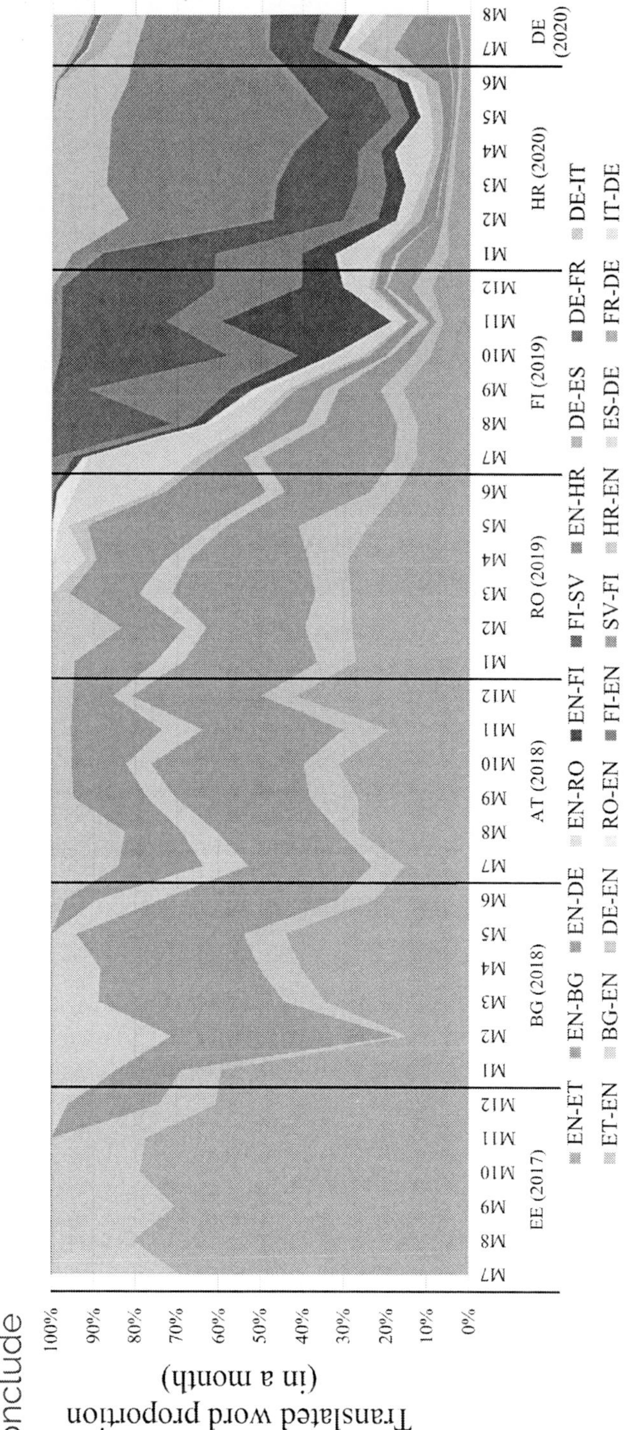

Proceedings of the 14th Conference of the Association for Machine Translation in the Americas
October 6 – 9, 2020, Volume 2: MT User Track

Usage analysis – primary systems of each Presidency

- Usage differs from country to country
- Higher use evident in countries that integrated the Translator in the official Web sites of the Presidency

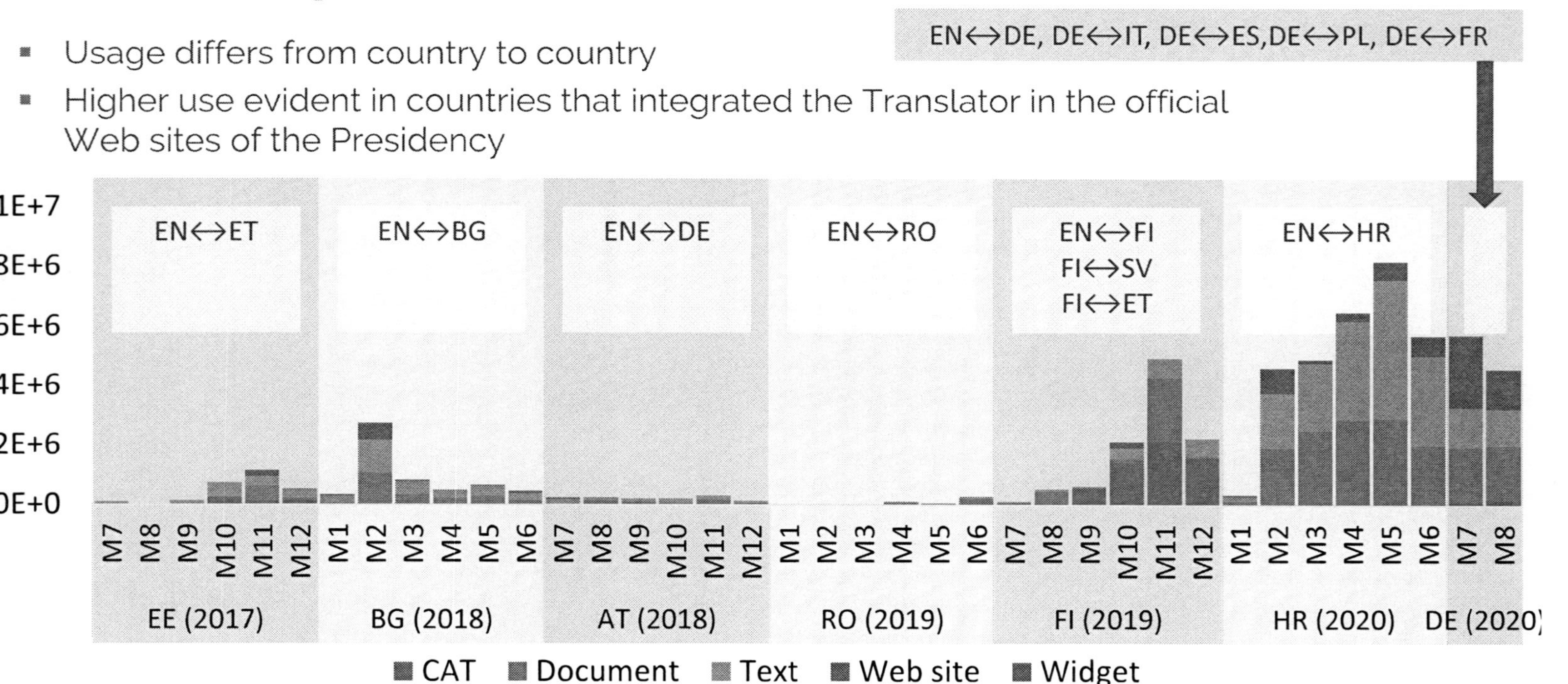

Proceedings of the 14th Conference of the Association for Machine Translation in the Americas
October 6 – 9, 2020, Volume 2: MT User Track

Usage analysis – primary systems of each Presidency

- Primary system usage during each Presidency allows us to analyse the adoption of different interfaces by each EU Council Presidency

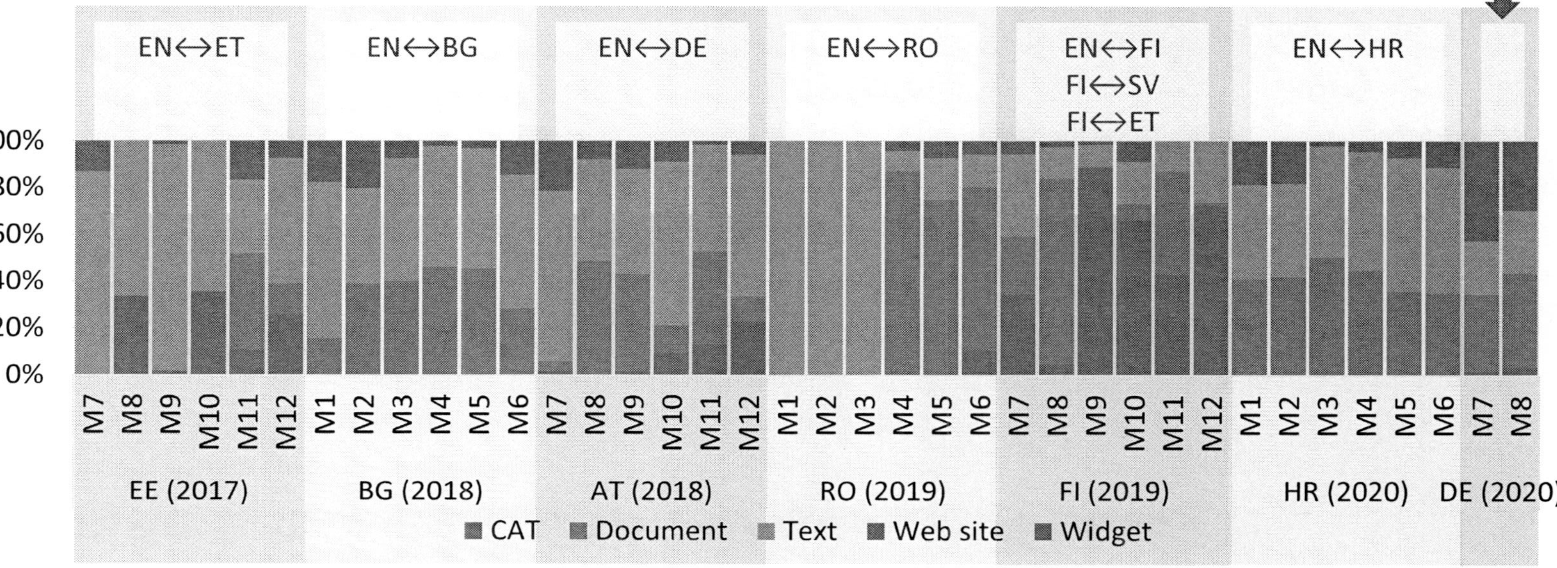

Proceedings of the 14th Conference of the Association for Machine Translation in the Americas
October 6 - 9, 2020, Volume 2: MT User Track

Usage analysis – primary systems of each Presidency

- The CAT tool interface was the most popular in Finland (960 thousand words per month translated on average during the presidency)

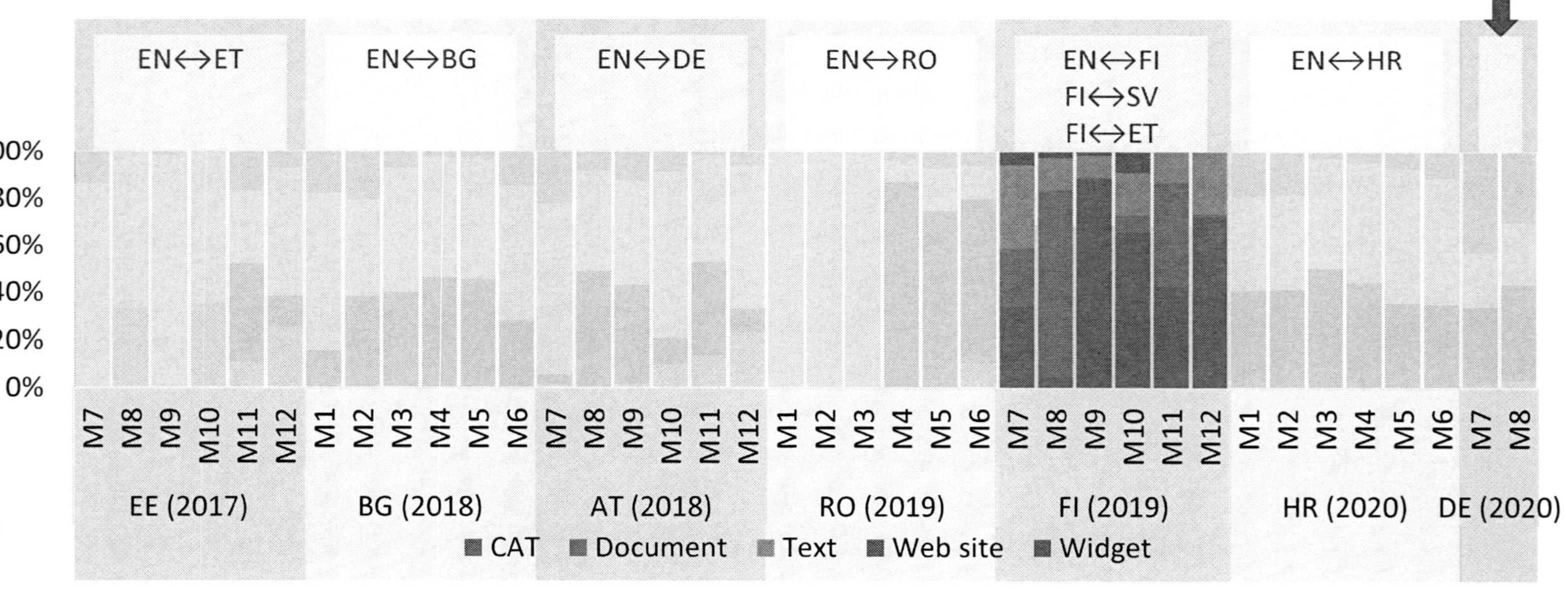

Proceedings of the 14th Conference of the Association for Machine Translation in the Americas
October 6 – 9, 2020, Volume 2: MT User Track

Usage analysis – primary systems of each Presidency

- The CAT tool interface was not used in Bulgaria, and Croatia
- In Romania, translators started using the CAT interface in the last month of the presidency

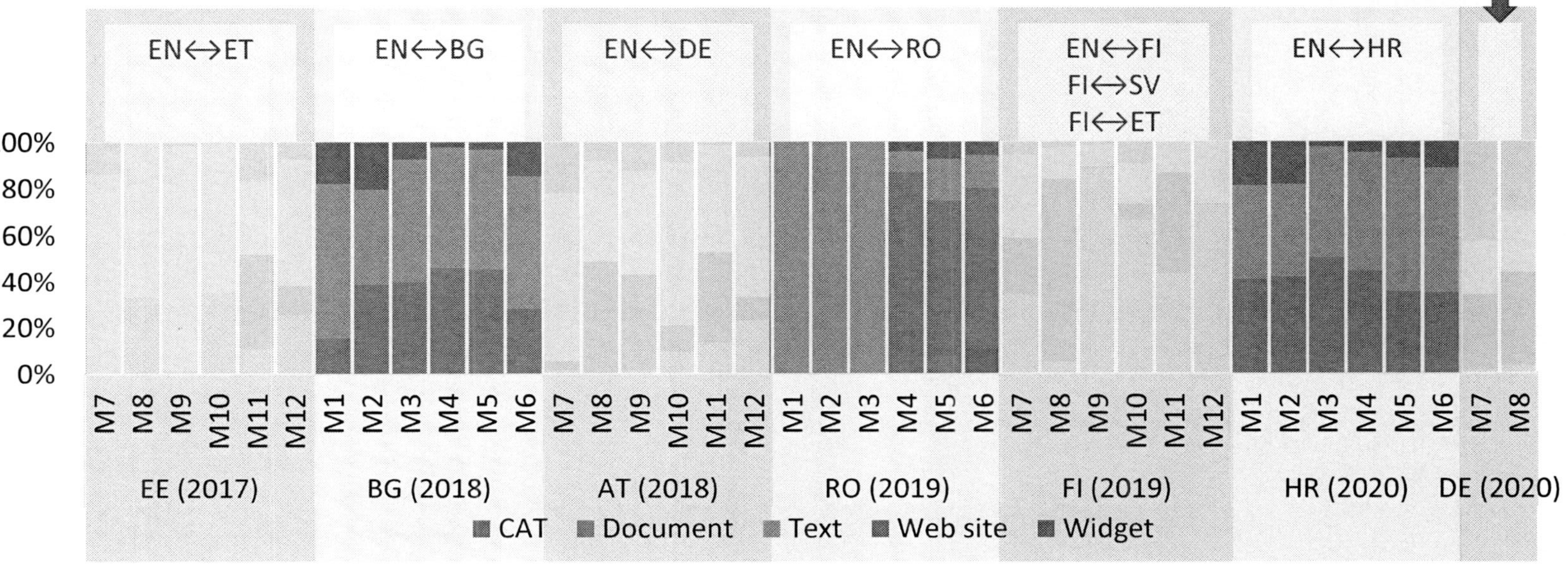

Proceedings of the 14th Conference of the Association for Machine Translation in the Americas
October 6 – 9, 2020, Volume 2: MT User Track

Usage analysis – primary systems of each Presidency

- Text translation was the most popular in Estonia, Bulgaria, Austria, and Croatia
- In Croatia, an average of 2.5 million words were translated this way each month

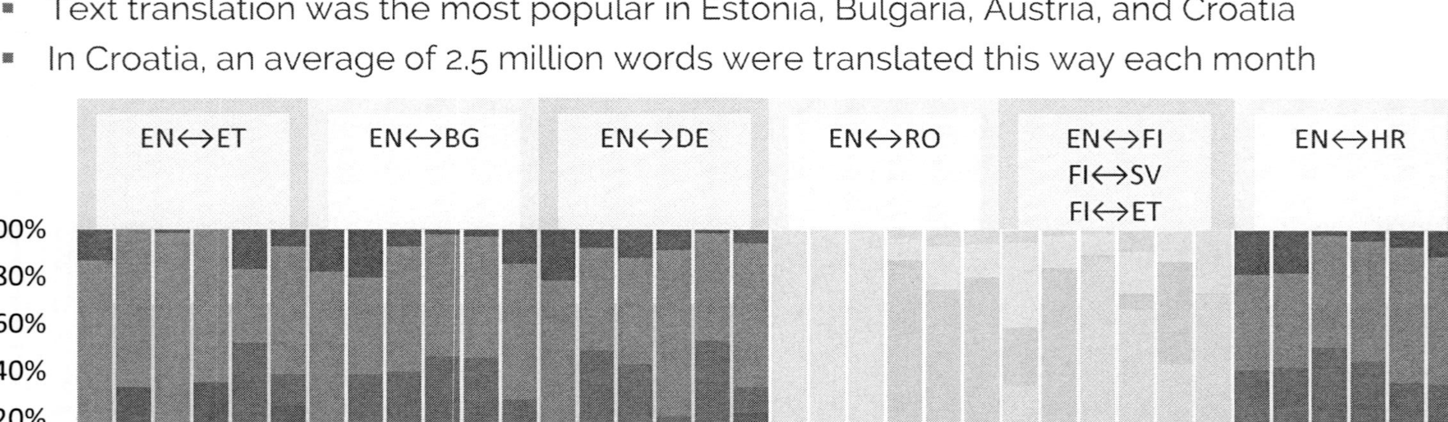

Proceedings of the 14th Conference of the Association for Machine Translation in the Americas
October 6 - 9, 2020, Volume 2: MT User Track

Usage analysis – primary systems of each Presidency

EN↔DE, DE↔IT, DE↔ES,DE↔PL, DE↔FR

- Document translation was the most popular in Romania, however the most words were translated during the Croatian Presidency (2.1 million words on average each month)

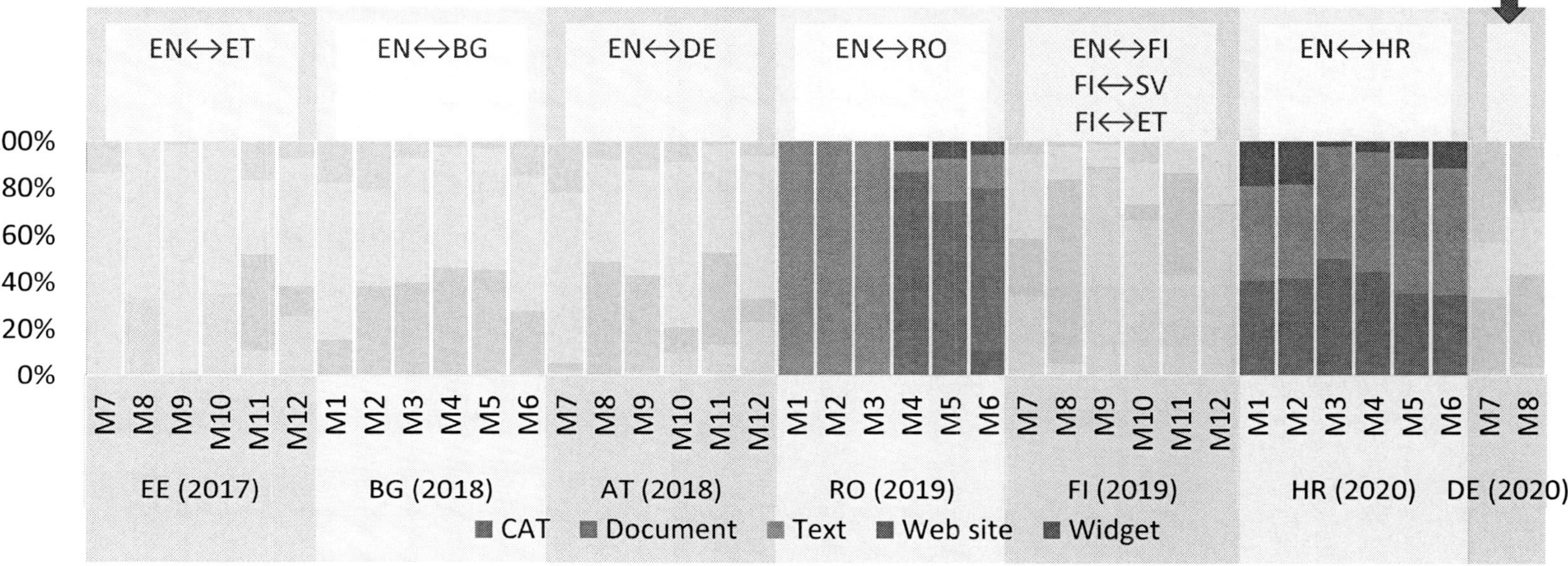

Translators' perspective

Contribution
- Collecting language resources
- Testing quality

Benefits
- Learning about MT
- Working more productively
- Feeling empowered

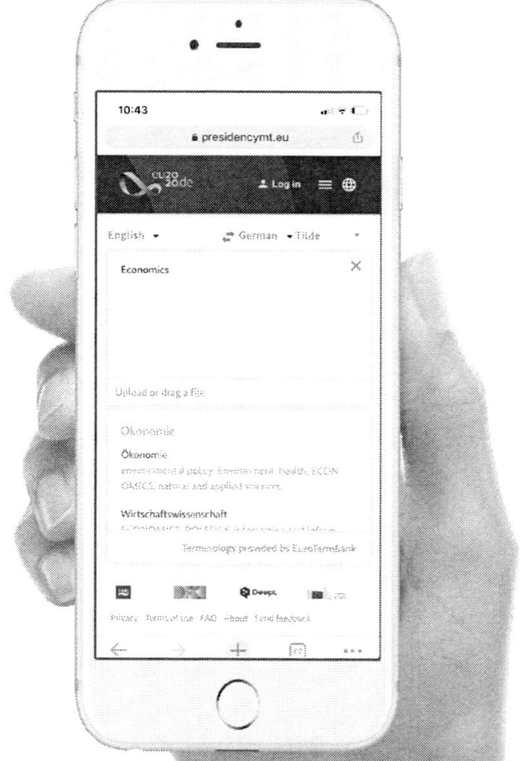

Conclusions

- We presented the EU Council Presidency Translator, a secure cloud-based solution that integrates MT systems from different MT providers and implements a wide spectrum of interfaces for end-users

- We presented its functionality and analysis of its adoption by users in seven EU Council Presidencies

- Although the use differs from country to country, we see that there is a need for all types of offered translation interfaces

- The use of the public interfaces depends on how well the EU Council Presidency Translator is exposed to users in the official web sites of the Presidencies

- The use of CAT tool interfaces depends on each country's translation practices

Proceedings of the 14th Conference of the Association for Machine Translation in the Americas
October 6 - 9, 2020, Volume 2: MT User Track

Kristine Mētuzāle
Client Relationship Manager
Tilde
kristine.metuzal@tilde.com

Alexandra Soska
Language Services Division,
Federal Ministry of the Interior,
Building and Community, Germany
alexandra.soska@bmi.bund.de

Mārcis Pinnis
Chief AI Officer
Tilde
marcis.pinnis@tilde.com

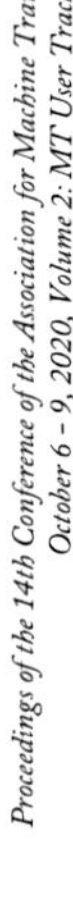

Proceedings of the 14th Conference of the Association for Machine Translation in the Americas
October 6 - 9, 2020, Volume 2: MT User Track

DragonFly

- Technology to enable the deaf and hearing to seamlessly communicate with one another without the assistance of an interpreter
  - Automated Machine Translation (MT) capabilities for enabling communication between speakers of American Sign Language (ASL) and English
  - Dragonfly will operate on the majority of IOS and ANDROID wearable devices including smart phones, tablets, and smart watches

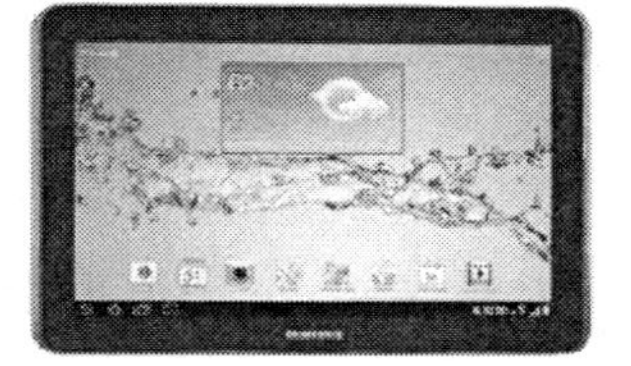

Face-to-Face… Naturally… Anytime… Anywhere…

Proceedings of the 14th Conference of the Association for Machine Translation in the Americas
October 6 – 9, 2020, Volume 2: MT User Track

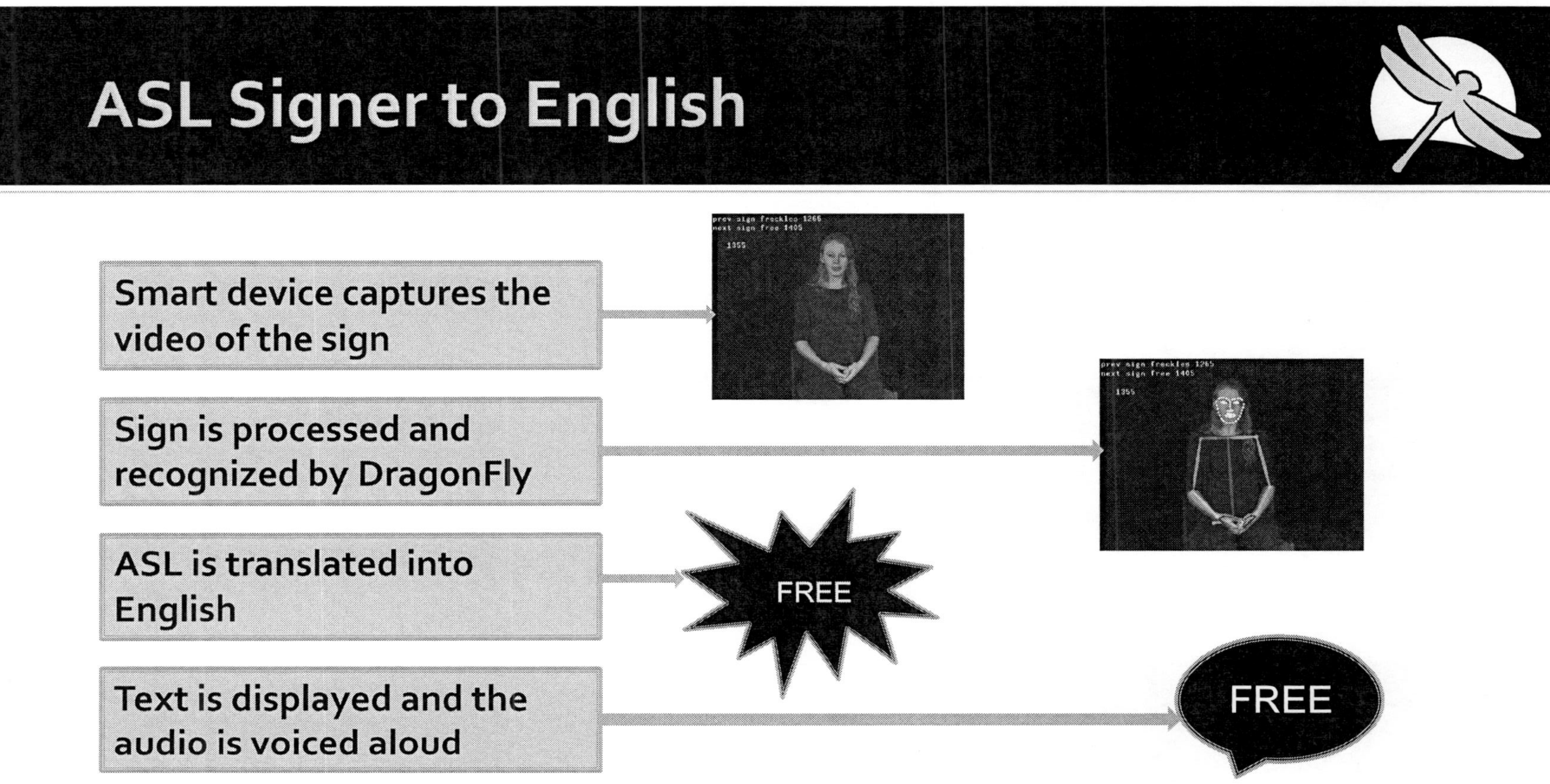

Proceedings of the 14th Conference of the Association for Machine Translation in the Americas
October 6 – 9, 2020, Volume 2: MT User Track

English Speaker to ASL

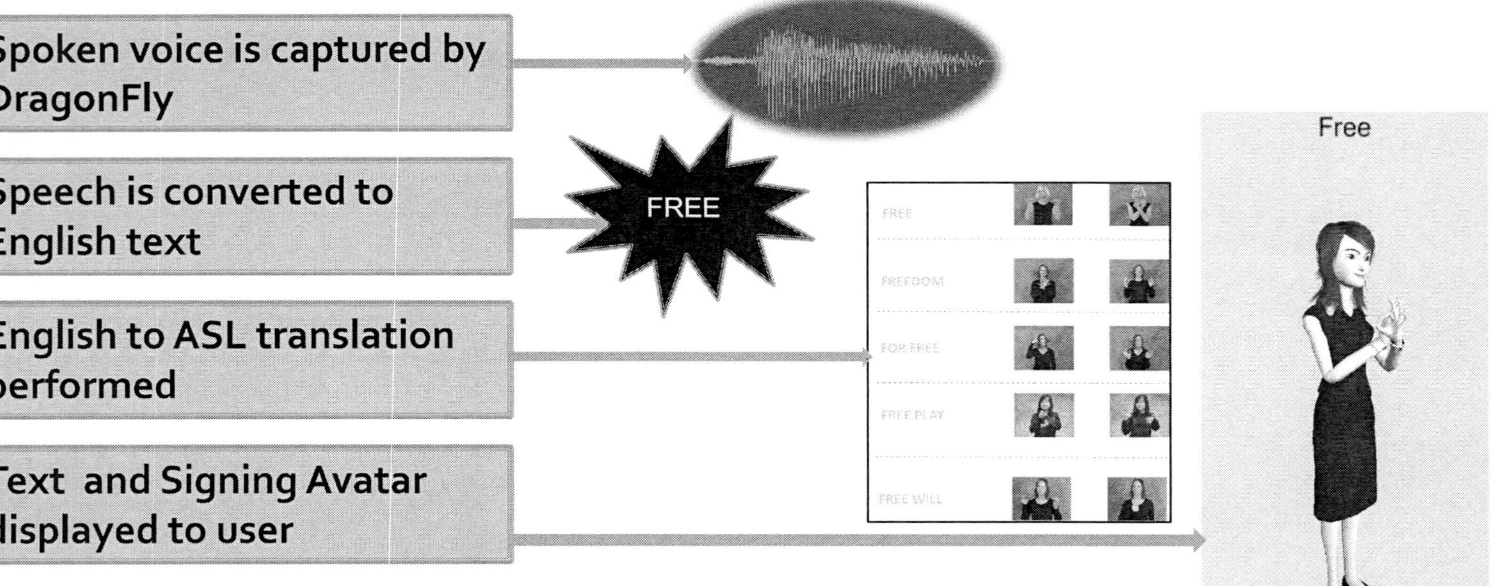

Proceedings of the 14th Conference of the Association for Machine Translation in the Americas
October 6 – 9, 2020, Volume 2: MT User Track

ASL Translation Challenges

Sign/Signer Variability

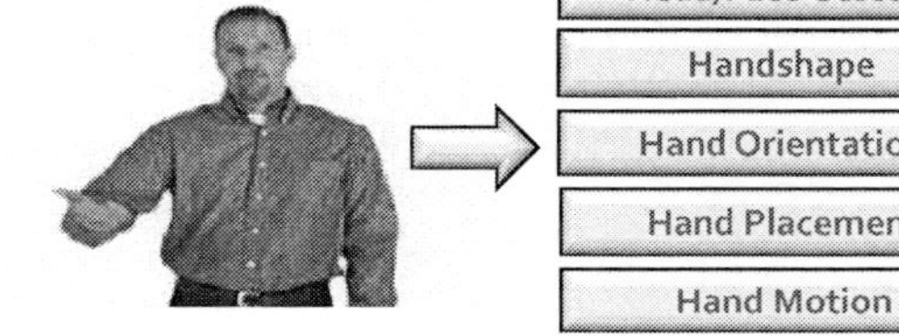

Distinct language with broad sign variation across signers

Sensor Variability

e.g. 2D/3D, fixed/mobile sensors

Session Variability

e.g. observation angle

Signal Complexity

Data Availability

- Limited availability of well annotated ASL<->English content

What we did

- Integrated the ASL Recognizer (ASLR) into an automated MT system that can be used in real time ad-hoc communications between signers and non-signers

- Implemented deep learning-based models (in OpenMT)
  - ASL video-to-ASL symbol sequence classifier
  - ASL symbol sequence-to-English sentence generator
  - ASL video-to-English sentence generator

Proceedings of the 14th Conference of the Association for Machine Translation in the Americas
October 6 – 9, 2020, Volume 2: MT User Track

What we did - Continued

- Leveraged sources in addition to BU and Purdue data (e.g. closed-captioned ASL from The Sign Language Channel)

- Created and incorporated the use of computer-generated Synthetic Data to augment training data

- Development and testing of a Handheld Prototype

Proceedings of the 14th Conference of the Association for Machine Translation in the Americas
October 6 - 9, 2020, Volume 2: MT User Track

Handheld Prototype 

- Web-based application

- ASL Video captured in real time on Smartphone or Tablet

- Seamlessly transmitted to Amazon Cloud for processing

- English MT text delivered and displayed in chat window

- Text-to-speech performed locally

Proceedings of the 14th Conference of the Association for Machine Translation in the Americas
October 6 - 9, 2020, Volume 2: MT User Track

Cafe DragonFly Demo

What we learned

- Computer generated Synthetic Data improved overall ASLR performance
  - Per sign raw recognition improved over 10% in initial testing
  - Key driver is using "valid" synthetic data to train the models

- Dramatically improved the speed and accuracy of ASLR

- However, we encountered both classic neural net and synthetic data validation challenges

Proceedings of the 14th Conference of the Association for Machine Translation in the Americas
October 6 - 9, 2020, Volume 2: MT User Track

Neural Net Challenges

- MT Output Errors
  - Error Types typical of neural net encoder-decoder architecture model for low resource languages (Vardaro et. al 17 September 2019:Informatics, Koponen et.al 2019: Machine Translation).
    - Substitution
      - Input: "I want hamburger without mayonnaise, please."
      - Output: "I will have a chicken sandwich without mayonnaise please."
    - Reordering /Addition
      - Input: "I want cheeseburger and soup, please."
      - Output: "I will have soup, cheeseburger and french fries please."
    - Omission
      - Input: "I want hotdog with ketchup and mustard, please ."
      - Output: "I want hotdog with ketchup and mustard, ___________."
    - Addition /Substitution
      - Input: "I want cheeseburger with extra spinach ."
      - Output: "I want cheese pizza with extra spinach and bacon ."

Sequence-to-Sequence Challenges

- Lack of scalability: inability to easily add new words
  - Multiple training sentences required for each flavor of ice cream
    - I want chocolate ice cream
    - I want vanilla ice cream
    - I want strawberry ice cream, etc.
    - Some words characterized as only nouns so unable to say "peach Ice cream"
  - Multiple permutations required for each sentence instead of for individual words (want, would, love, like chocolate, vanilla, milk, pudding)
    - I want chocolate ice cream; I would like chocolate milk, I love chocolate,
    - I want chocolate pudding, I like vanilla pudding, I like chocolate milk, etc.

Proceedings of the 14th Conference of the Association for Machine Translation in the Americas
October 6 – 9, 2020, Volume 2: MT User Track

Continuous Sign Recognition

Continuous Sign Recognition Approach with Explicit Sign Segmentation and Sign Classification Steps

Sign Segmentation Process

(Khan 2014; Farag & Brock 2019), and

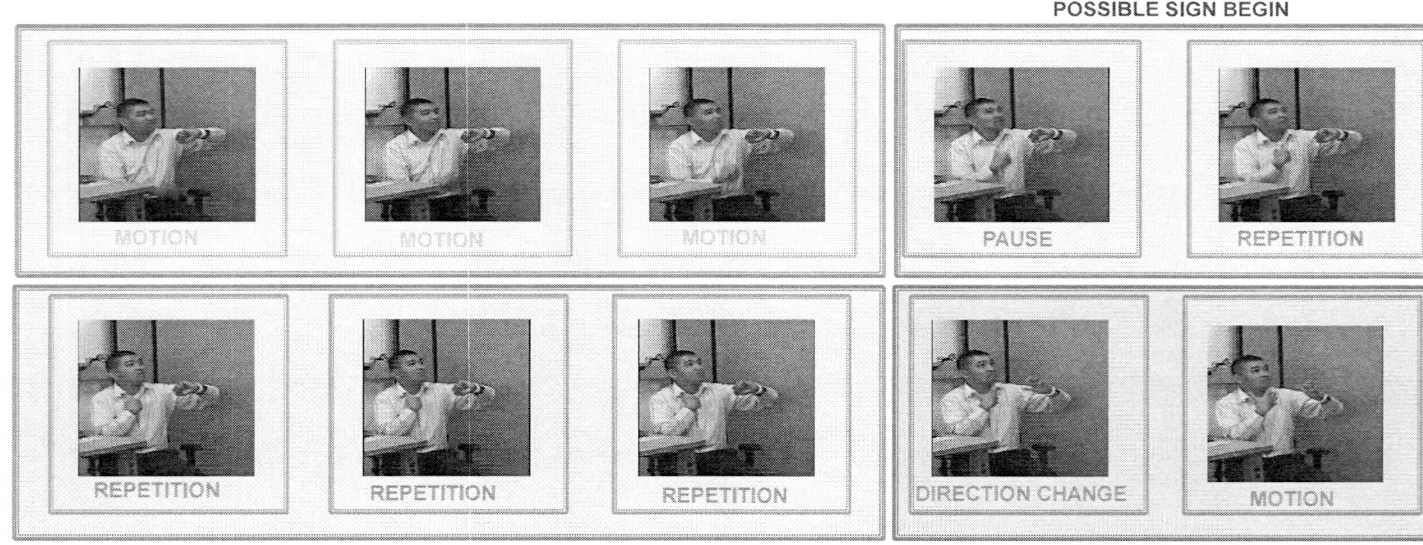

Future Plans

- Full scale development, test and evaluation of hand-held operational prototypes

- Platform (iOS, Android, and Windows) and browser (Chrome, Firefox, and Edge) compatibility and user field testing

- Incorporation of ASL avatar for signing synthesis

- Commercial partnerships for product delivery

Proceedings of the 14th Conference of the Association for Machine Translation in the Americas
October 6 – 9, 2020, Volume 2: MT User Track

Proceedings of the 14th Conference of the Association for Machine Translation in the Americas
October 6 - 9, 2020, Volume 2: MT User Track

Why is it So Hard to Compare Translation Evaluations
and How Can Standards Help?

AMTA 2020

9 October 2020

Jennifer DeCamp

jdecamp@mitre.org

Why is it so Hard to Develop Comparable Translation Evaluations and How Can Standards Help?

There are several standards and guidelines that may be relevant to MT and that are in use or anticipated to be ready for use this year, including *ASTM 2475 Translation Quality Requirements, ASTM WK46396 Analytic Evaluation of Translation Quality, ISO 17100 Translation services — Requirements for translation services*, and the Interagency Language Roundtable Skill Level Descriptions for Translation Performance.

This presentation reviews these standards and guidelines and discusses how they can be applied to evaluation of MT, whether HT, MT, or some combination. Such comparisons may include: a new version of MT with the previous version; one company's MT with that of another company, one product with another product; a language service provider's performance in one year vs. another, or one organization with another. The presentation also addresses gaps and provides recommendations, including to for become involved with improving these standards and thus improving MT evaluation.

Proceedings of the 14th Conference of the Association for Machine Translation in the Americas
October 6 - 9, 2020, Volume 2: MT User Track

Why Is It So Hard to Develop Comparable Translation Evaluations?

1. Variation in the translations
   - Languages, dialects, registers, domains
   - Genres
   - Cultural information
   - Processes
   - Tools
   - Purposes
   - Terminology
   - Need for reliability
   - Etc.

2. Variation in translation evaluations
   - Purposes
   - Requirements
   - Methods
   - Tools
   - Terminology
   - Need for reliability
   - Etc.

Proceedings of the 14th Conference of the Association for Machine Translation in the Americas
October 6 - 9, 2020, Volume 2: MT User Track

Purposes for Translation Evaluation

1. Development progress and direction
2. Acquisition
   - Write and administer contracts
     - *48 Code of Federal Regulations (CFR) § 15.101-2 - Lowest price technically acceptable source selection process*: The evaluation factors and significant subfactors that establish the requirements of acceptability shall be set forth in the solicitation.
   - Make decisions
     - Obtain
     - Upgrade
     - Replace
3. Management
   - Deploy resources
   - Determine performance
     - Track performance over time
     - Benchmark
4. Determine quality of deliverable
   - Send it for revision
   - Deliver it to the customer

Proceedings of the 14th Conference of the Association for Machine Translation in the Americas
October 6 - 9, 2020, Volume 2: MT User Track

Types of Evaluation

- Product
  - Reference
    - Human translation
  - No reference
    - Impact in workflow (e.g., impact to entity extraction)
    - Detailed error analysis
      - *ATA Certification Scoring*
      - *ASTM WK46396 Analytic Evaluation of Translation Quality*
- Process
  - *ISO 17100 Translation services — Requirements for translation services*
  - *ASTM 2575 Requirements for Translation Evaluation*
  - Skill descriptions by ILR, DLPT, ACTFL, etc.
- Outcome
  - Impact of the translation (e.g., in comparison with source text)

Proceedings of the 14th Conference of the Association for Machine Translation in the Americas
October 6 - 9, 2020, Volume 2: MT User Track

Methods and Tools

"Current approaches to Machine Translation (MT) or professional translation evaluation, both automatic and manual, are characterized by

- *A high degree of fragmentation, heterogeneity and a lack of interoperability between methods, tools and data sets.*
- *As a consequence, it is difficult to reproduce, interpret, and compare evaluation results"* (G. Rehm et al, 2016)

Standards

- *ASTM WK46396 Analytic Evaluation of Translation Quality*
- *ASTM 2575 Requirements for Translation Evaluation*
- ISO and ASTM efforts in terminology management

Meet Customer Requirements

Translator or Language Service Provider	"What the customer wants"
Customer	"100% accuracy, fast, cheap"
MT Developer	"As good as a human"

Proceedings of the 14th Conference of the Association for Machine Translation in the Americas
October 6 - 9, 2020, Volume 2: MT User Track

Quality/Target

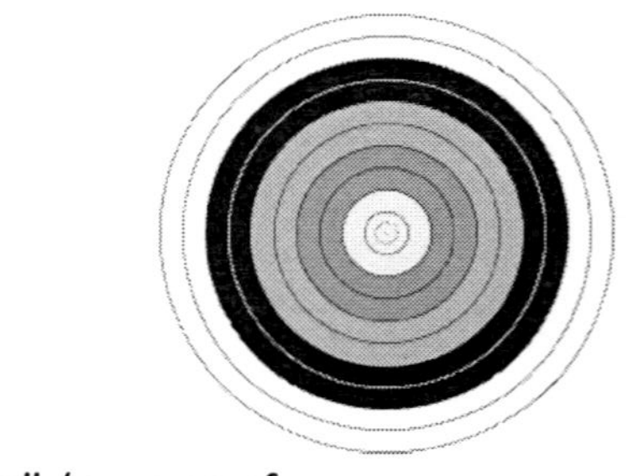

- Announcements of NMT equaling or exceeding human performance
  - As good as human translators (i.e., humans hired from a translation company)
  - "If they did that work at my company, they wouldn't be working for me for long" (owner of translation company at last AMTA meeting)
- But anyone can self-declare as a translator; any company can self-declare as a translation company
- And in the above methods, evaluators are not doing translator tasks
- Plus extensive issues with use of reference translations
  - Can't always use a reference translation (e.g., to determine whether a translation is ready to submit to a client)
  - Get different results with different reference translations or different number of reference translations or references from a different part of the translation pair
  - Numbers often not meaningful at quality levels needed for deliverables
  - Usually reviewed by people with no understanding of context
  - Provides little or no information on WHAT is wrong
  - May penalize for different terminology or word order
  - Etc.

A. Lommel (2016)

What Humans?

- American Translators Association (ATA) Certification
  - Focused on perhaps too high a level
  - Too time-consuming for most applications
  - Not available for many languages
  - Directory of translators with certification and resumes listed on ATA home page http://www.atanet.org

- *ISO 17100:2015 Translation Services – Requirements for Translation Services*
  - Human translation (no technology), with an amendment to cover requirements in the U.S., Canada, and several other countries
  - CHF 118 (=UDS 128.40)
  - Britain's Institute of Translation and Interpreting (ITI) has created a translator "qualification" for meeting requirements for translators
  - U.S. and others have proposed having a new standard to better meet the needs for certification

- Defense Foreign Language Proficiency Test (DLPT) and American Council on the Teaching of Foreign Languages (ACTFL) Scores

Interagency Language Roundtable
Skill Descriptions for Translation Performance

- **Level 2+ (Limited Performance)**

  Can render straightforward texts dealing with everyday matters that include statements of fact as well as some judgments, opinion, or other elements which entail more than direct exposition, but do not contain figurative language, complicated concepts, complex sentence structures, or instances of syntactic or semantic skewing.

- **Level 3 (Professional Performance)**

  Can translate texts that contain not only facts but also abstract language, showing an emerging ability to capture their intended implications and many nuances. Such texts usually contain situations and events which are subject to value judgments of a personal or institutional kind, as in some newspaper editorials, propaganda tracts, and evaluations of projects.

Interagency Language Roundtable
Skill Descriptions for Translation Performance

Level 4+ (Professional Performance Plus)

- Can successfully apply a translation methodology to translate texts that contain highly original and special purpose language (such as that contained in religious sermons, literary prose, and poetry). At this level, a successful performance requires not only conveying content and register but also capturing to the greatest extent all nuances intended in the source document. Expression is virtually flawless.

Level 5 (Professional Performance)

- Can successfully translate virtually all texts, including those where lack of linguistic and cultural parallelism between the source language and the target language requires precise congruity judgments and the ability to apply a translation methodology. Expression is flawless.

How can Standards Help in MT Evaluation?

1. Can provide a better understanding of the information needed by decision makers
   - Target level
   - Requirements
2. Can help provide a broader framework for structuring an evaluation
   - Broader information
   - Authority
3. Can improve communication through this framework and through standardized terminology

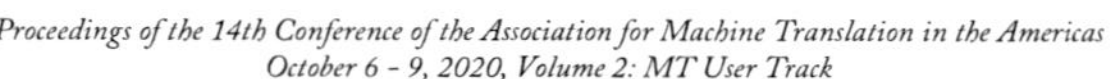

Proceedings of the 14th Conference of the Association for Machine Translation in the Americas
October 6 - 9, 2020, Volume 2: MT User Track

Recommendations

1. Work towards a common framework
   - Employ standardized terminology
   - Employ interoperability standards for exchange of data
   - Carefully test and document results

2. Become more specific
   - Look at customer requirements for translation and translation evaluation
   - Reduce ambiguity re "human"

3. Educate the customer on
   - Requirements and opportunities training
   - On the impact of evaluation methods on certain types of translation

4. Participate in developing standards
   - ASTM
   - ISO

Proceedings of the 14th Conference of the Association for Machine Translation in the Americas
October 6 - 9, 2020, Volume 2: MT User Track

References

48 Code of Federal Regulations (CFR) § 15.101-2 - Lowest price technically acceptable source selection process. Retrieved September 25, 2020 from: https://www.law.cornell.edu/cfr/text/48/15.101-2

M. Dilllinger (2016). *MT Escaped from the Lab: Now What?* AMTA 2016. Retrieved September 25, 2020 from: https://amtaweb.org/wp-content/uploads/2016/10/Dillinger_AMTA2016Keynote_dist.pdf

G. Rehm, A. Burchardt, O. Bojar, C. Dugast, M. Federico, J. van Genabith, B. Haddow, J. Hajic, K. Harris, P. Koehn, M. Negri, M. Popel, L. Specia, M. Turchi, and H. Uszkoreit (2016). *Translation Evaluation: From Fragmented Tools and Data Sets to an Integrated Ecosystem,* Language Resources Evaluation Conference (LREC) Workshop, 24 May 2016. Retrieved September 25, 2020 from: http://www.cracking-the-language-barrier.eu/mt-eval-workshop-2016/

A. Lommell (2016). *Blues for BLEU: Reconsidering the Validity of Reference-Based MT Evaluation*, LREC Workshop on *Translation Evaluation: From Fragmented Tools and Data Sets to an Integrated Ecosystem*, 24 May 2016. Retrieved September 25, 2020 from http://www.cracking-the-language-barrier.eu/mt-eval-workshop-2016/.

American Translators Association (2020). *Directory.* http://www.atanet.org

ASTM (2020). *ASTM WK46396 Analytic Evaluation of Translation Quality.* Draft Standard. Copies available from ASTM for review.

ISO (2015). *ISO 17100 Translation services — Requirements for translation services. ISO Standard.* Retrieved September 25, 2020 from: https://www.iso.org/standard/59149.html

ASTM (2020). *ASTM 2575 Requirements for Translation Evaluation: Standard Practice.* Draft standard anticipated for publication 2020. Copies available from ASTM for review.

ASTM (2014). *ASTM 2575 Requirements for Translation Evaluation.. Standard Guide.* Retrieved September 25, 2020 from: https://www.astm.org/Standards/F2575.htm

Interagency Language Roundtable (ILR), ILR Skill Descriptions for Translation Performance. Retrieved September 25, 2020 from https://www.govtilr.org/Skills/AdoptedILRTranslationGuidelines.htm

Images

Tower of Babel	Slide 3	This Photo by Unknown Author is licensed under CC BY-SA
Keyboard	Slide 4	This Photo by Unknown Author is licensed under CC BY-NC-SA
Stars	Slide 5	This Photo by Unknown Author is licensed under CC BY-SA-NC
Dog	Slide 7	This Photo by Unknown Author is licensed under CC BY-SA
Target	Slide 8	This Photo by Unknown Author is licensed under CC BY-SA
Quality Stamp	Slide 15	This Photo by Unknown Author is licensed under CC BY-NC-SA

Using Contemporary US Government Data to Train Custom MT for COVID-19

Achim Ruopp

Polyglot Technology LLC

achim@polyglot.technology

Proceedings of the 14th Conference of the Association for Machine Translation in the Americas
October 6 - 9, 2020, Volume 2: MT User Track

Translation's Role in the COVID-19 Crisis

- Gretchen McCulloch's article "Covid-19 Is History's Biggest Translation Challenge" in WIRED
  - Communicating health information is an essential factor in addressing this crisis
  - Familiar issue that MT currently only supports 100+ languages
    - Languages with millions of speakers are unsupported
    - Long tail of thousands of human languages are unsupported/endangered
  - Some issues with register in the high resource languages
    - Japanese translation of "Wash your hands" in tone of a parent instructing a child
  - People want to gist information in their languages – accurate MT can help to address disinformation
- Translators without Borders did great work in previous health crises like Ebola, but scope of COVID-19 is unprecedented

Proceedings of the 14th Conference of the Association for Machine Translation in the Americas
October 6 - 9, 2020, Volume 2: MT User Track

The Translation Community Coming Together

- TAUS Corona Virus Corpora
  - English↔French/German/Italian/Spanish/Chinese/Russian
  - Translation data (mainly) selected from existing parallel corpora with a COVID-19 specific English query corpus
    - ~ 200k-900k segments
    - Creative Commons Attribution-NonCommercial 4.0 license
  - SYSTRAN built custom COVID-19 MT systems using the data
  - The MT broker Intento
    - did an extensive human evaluation/post-editing study with a test subset of the data https://try.inten.to/mt-evaluation-covid-domain
    - is creating a custom routing for COVID-19 content in their platform
    - customized MT with the TAUS Corona Virus Corpora
      - For only 2 out of 7 language pairs did the custom MT systems outperform the stock engines
      - Possible explanation provided by Intento: medical domain is wide – data might require clustering
      - Alternative customization with just a bilingual glossary failed

Proceedings of the 14th Conference of the Association for Machine Translation in the Americas
October 6 - 9, 2020, Volume 2: MT User Track

The Translation Community Coming Together

- Translation Initiative for COVID-19 aka TICO-19
  - Partners
    - academia: Carnegie Mellon University, Johns Hopkins University
    - industry: Amazon, Appen, Facebook, Google, Microsoft, Translated
    - non-profit: Translators without Borders
      - Strong track record communicating in previous crises (e.g. Ebola, Rohinga refugee crisis) and working with the non-profit organizations
      - Also runs COVID-19 Community Translation Program
  - Data
    - TICO-19 Translation Benchmark
      - 30 English documents with 3071 segments/69.7k words translated to 36 languages
      - English→Amharic, Arabic (Modern Standard), Bengali, Chinese (Simplified), Dari, Dinka, Farsi, French (European), Hausa, Hindi, Indonesian, Kanuri, Khmer (Central), Kinyarwanda, Kurdish Kurmanji, Kurdish Sorani, Lingala, Luganda, Malay, Marathi, Myanmar, Nepali, Nigerian Fulfulde, Nuer, Oromo, Pashto, Portuguese (Brazilian), Russian, Somali, Spanish (Latin American), Swahili, Congolese Swahili, Tagalog, Tamil, Tigrinya, Urdu, Zulu
    - COVID-19 specific translated terminologies (from Facebook and Google)
    - Creative Commons CC0 licensed
  - See website for links to many other COVID-19 related data projects (language data and beyond)

Proceedings of the 14th Conference of the Association for Machine Translation in the Americas
October 6 - 9, 2020, Volume 2: MT User Track

TICO-19 Translation Benchmark Diversity

Data Source	Example
CMU	are you having any shortness of breath?
PubMed	The basic reproductive number (R0) was 3.77 (95% CI: 3.51-4.05), and the adjusted R0 was 2.23-4.82.
Wikinews	By yesterday, the World Health Organization reported 1,051,635 confirmed cases, including 79,332 cases in the twenty four hours preceding 10 a.m. Central European Time (0800 UTC) on April 4.
Wikivoyage	Due to the spread of the disease, you are advised not to travel unless necessary, to avoid being infected, quarantined, or stranded by changing restrictions and cancelled flights.
Wikipedia	Drug development is the process of bringing a new infectious disease vaccine or therapeutic drug to the market once a lead compound has been identified through the process of drug discovery.
Wikisource	The federal government has identified 16 critical infrastructure sectors whose assets, systems, and networks, whether physical or virtual, are considered so vital to the United States that their incapacitation or destruction would have a debilitating effect on security, economic security, public health or safety, or any combination thereof.

Table 2: Samples of the English source sentences for the TICO-19 benchmark.

Anastasopoulos, A., Cattelan, A., Dou, Z.-Y., Federico, M., Federmann, C., Genzel, D., . . . Tur, S. (2020). TICO-19: the Translation Initiative for COvid-19. arXiv, 2007.01788v2.

Opportunity: Centers For Disease Control and Prevention COVID-19 Website

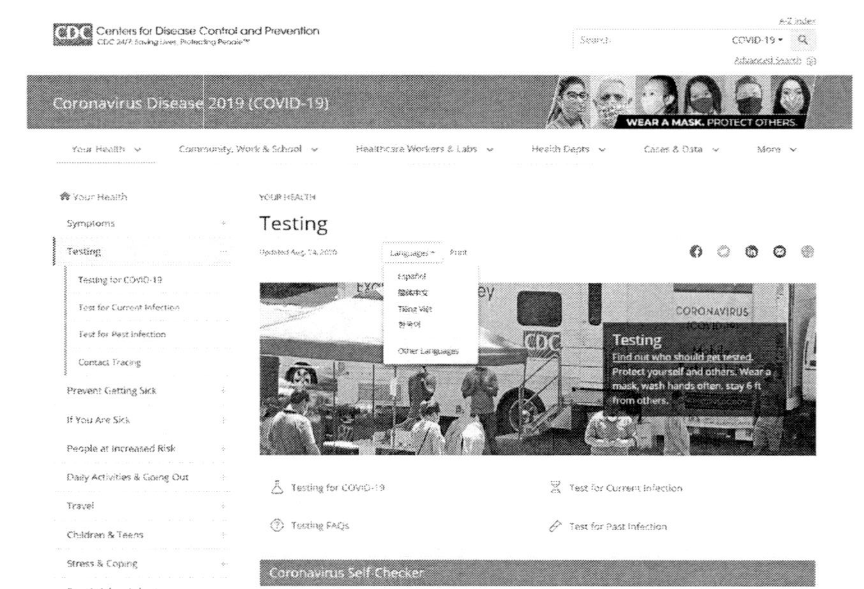

Proceedings of the 14th Conference of the Association for Machine Translation in the Americas
October 6 – 9, 2020, Volume 2: MT User Track

Information for Medical Professionals is not Translated

Proceedings of the 14th Conference of the Association for Machine Translation in the Americas
October 6 - 9, 2020, Volume 2: MT User Track

CDC COVID-19 Site Updates

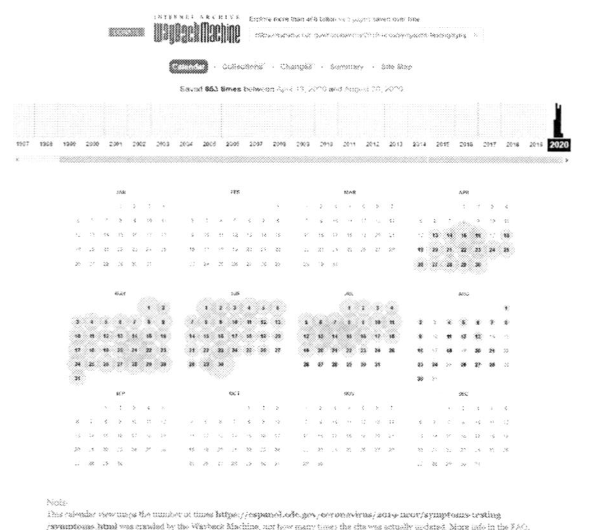

- Site frequently updated
- Crawled on June 24, 2020 and July 24, 2020
  - June 24 crawl yielded the most parallel data of the two
- Data represents translation practices of COVID-19 health info, but not ground truth about COVID-19 virus!

Proceedings of the 14th Conference of the Association for Machine Translation in the Americas
October 6 - 9, 2020, Volume 2: MT User Track

Data Statistics for CDC COVID-19 Parallel Data

- Non-deduplicated (in TMX with context)

English→	Segments	Source words	Target words	Target characters
Spanish (US)	79,106	538,842	696,471	
Vietnamese	79,757	550,066	895,573	
Korean	78,824	537,204	428,979	
Chinese	70,423	508,297		2,958,795

- Deduplicated & shuffled (TSV)

English→	Segments	Source words	Target words	Target characters
Spanish (US)	15,803	248,780	310,223	
Vietnamese	15,849	249,006	380,113	
Korean	16,532	262,393	197,402	
Chinese	11,911	254,876		1,413,993

- Volume in between TAUS Corona Virus Corpus and TICO-19
  - Test/validation/fine tuning data
  - Data with document context in TMX
    - Document context
      - original segment order
      - source-document property groups segments
      - Better: XLIFF (used in WMT)
    - Creation date
      - Better: webpage update date

- Custom crawling code based on Bitextor
  - Non-customized ParaCrawl/Bitextor contains only 5 English-Spanish segments from the CDC in the latest September 2020 release

- Additional medium resource languages/language variants covered
  - US-Spanish (≈ LatAm-Spanish?)
  - Vietnamese
  - Korean

Proceedings of the 14th Conference of the Association for Machine Translation in the Americas
October 6 – 9, 2020, Volume 2: MT User Track

CDC COVID-19 Parallel Data Licensing

- Content
  - Public domain
  - Disclaimer: Source: CDC; Reference to specific commercial products, manufacturers, companies, or trademarks does not constitute its endorsement or recommendation by the U.S. Government, Department of Health and Human Services, or Centers for Disease Control and Prevention; The public domain material is available on the agency website https://www.cdc.gov/ for no charge.
- Database/database structure, i.e. TMX/TSV
  - Made available under the Open Data Commons Attribution License: http://opendatacommons.org/licenses/by/1.0

Proceedings of the 14th Conference of the Association for Machine Translation in the Americas
October 6 – 9, 2020, Volume 2: MT User Track

Google AutoML Translation Customized with CDC COVID-19 Parallel Data

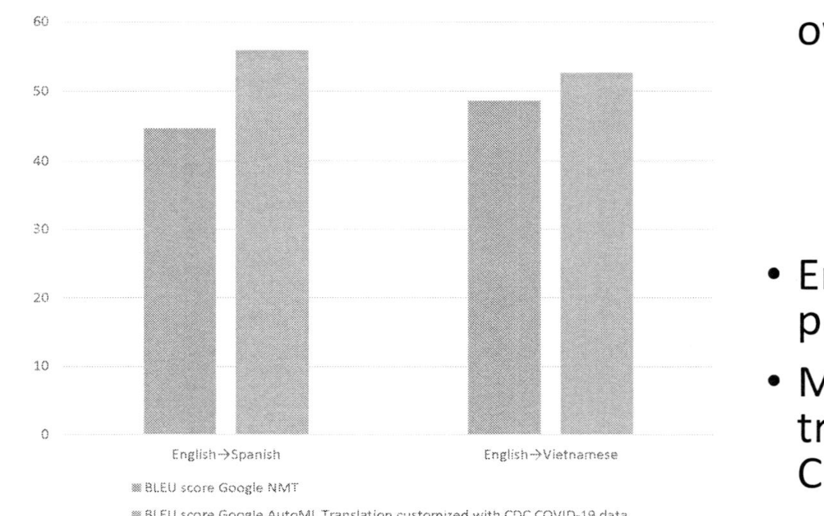

- Significant BLEU score increases over already high baselines
  - English→Spanish +11.27
  - English→Vietnamese +4.1
  - Confirmed results with TER and BERTScore
- Enables increased productivity in post-editing scenario
- More appropriate raw machine translations of new or revised CDC COVID-19 content

Proceedings of the 14th Conference of the Association for Machine Translation in the Americas
October 6 - 9, 2020, Volume 2: MT User Track

Google AutoML Translation Customized with CDC COVID-19 Parallel Data

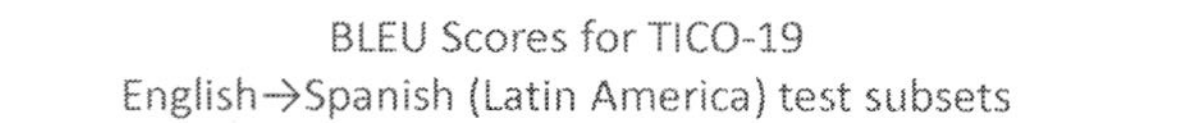

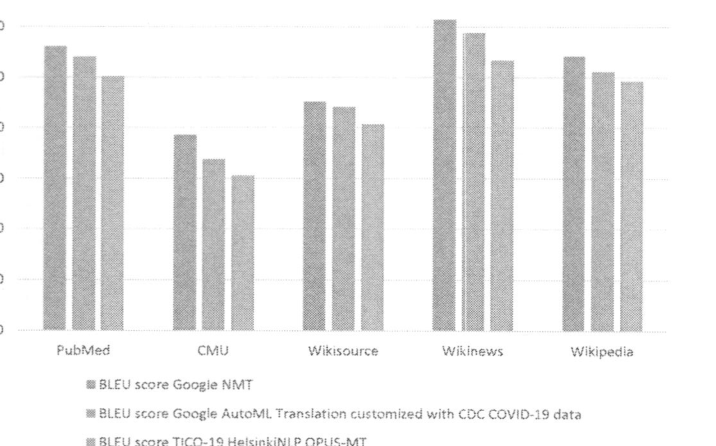

- Customized system performs worse with TICO-19 translation benchmark
- Hypotheses
  - Medical domain is wide
  - COVID-19 is not that "novel" from the health information translation perspective
  - Domain mismatch/overfitting to CDC data
    - Topic
    - **Modality** – TICO-19 corpora contain transcribed speech (CMU)
    - **Register**: Level of politeness – translator/project dependent
    - Intent – consistent
    - Style – translator/project dependent
    - **Language variant**

Proceedings of the 14th Conference of the Association for Machine Translation in the Americas
October 6 - 9, 2020, Volume 2: MT User Track

Larger Lessons – Future Research

- For high/medium resource languages
  - MT suppliers have now optimized Transformer-based NMT
    - Many ambiguities already resolved (especially intra-sentence ambiguities)
    - MT systems robust to variations in domain
  - Additional improvements for medium resource languages from transfer learning from other languages/massively multilingual systems
  - Research on using document-level context

$\Rightarrow$ It becomes harder and harder to beat the baseline models with custom MT!

Proceedings of the 14th Conference of the Association for Machine Translation in the Americas
October 6 – 9, 2020, Volume 2: MT User Track

Larger Lessons – Future Research

- Test/development data becomes ever more important - we can't detect if we beat the baseline if we don't specify what we expect!
  - Evaluation data is as crucial as evaluation measures
  - Development sets, e.g. for training data selection, cannot be source-only anymore
  - Opens a great opportunity to include linguists – human-in-the-loop MT
    - For the post-editing use case some MT suppliers already build this into their workflow: Lilt, ModernMT, Unbabel
  - MT suppliers need to improve guidance which data sets are sufficient/good – manual experimentation is tedious/expensive

Proceedings of the 14th Conference of the Association for Machine Translation in the Americas
October 6 - 9, 2020, Volume 2: MT User Track

Larger Lessons – Future Research

- Low resource languages still suffer from lack of language resources
  - Again coming into clear focus in the COVID-19 crisis – resource light approaches unlikely to help
  - Investment needed – public/private?

Proceedings of the 14th Conference of the Association for Machine Translation in the Americas
October 6 – 9, 2020, Volume 2: MT User Track

Other Parallel Corpora from Polyglot Technology LLC

- Healthcare.gov
  - Healthcare/health insurance content
  - English→Spanish
  - Blog article from May 2019
- US Department of State news releases/announcements
  - English→Arabic, Spanish, Farsi, French, Hindi, Indonesian, Portuguese, Russian, Urdu, Vietnamese, Chinese
- Custom Crawling

Proceedings of the 14th Conference of the Association for Machine Translation in the Americas
October 6 - 9, 2020, Volume 2: MT User Track